NJINGA OF ANGOLA

NJINGA OF ANGOLA

Africa's Warrior Queen

LINDA M. HEYWOOD

HARVARD UNIVERSITY PRESS

Cambridge, Massachusetts • London, England

2017

Library of Congress Cataloging-in-Publication Data
Names: Heywood, Linda M. (Linda Marinda), 1945– author.
Title: Njinga of Angola : Africa's warrior queen / Linda M. Heywood.
Description: Cambridge, Massachusetts : Harvard University Press, 2017. |
Includes bibliographical references and index.
Identifiers: LCCN 2016044098 | ISBN 9780674971820 (alk. paper)
Subjects: LCSH: Nzinga, Queen of Matamba, 1582–1663. | Angola—
Kings and rulers—Biography. | Angola—History—1482–1648. |
Angola—History—1648–1885.
Classification: LCC DT1365.N95 H49 2017 | DDC 967.3/01—dc23
LC record available at https://lccn.loc.gov/2016044098

Contents

NJINGA OF ANGOLA

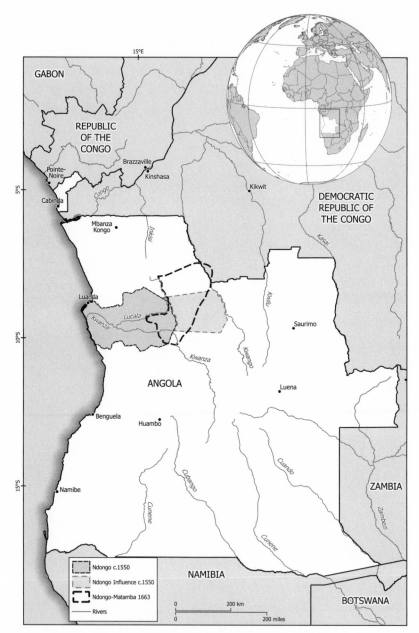

Ndongo (ca. 1550) and Ndongo-Matamba (ca. 1663)
situated in present-day Angola

Introduction

Queen Njinga, the seventeenth-century ruler of Ndongo, a kingdom in central Africa that was located in what is now a portion of northern Angola, came to power in Africa through her military prowess, skillful manipulation of religion, successful diplomacy, and remarkable understanding of politics. Despite her outstanding accomplishments and her decades-long reign, comparable to that of Elizabeth I of England, she was vilified by European contemporaries and later writers as an uncivilized savage who embodied the worst of womankind.[1] Europeans at the time portrayed her as a bloodthirsty cannibal who thought nothing of murdering babies and slaughtering her enemies. They also charged her with defying gender norms by dressing as a man, leading armies, keeping harems of male and female consorts, and rejecting the female virtues of caring and nurturing. Much later, eighteenth- and nineteenth-century writers who composed fictional accounts about Njinga depicted her as a degenerate woman driven by unorthodox sexual desires who reveled in barbaric rituals.

Njinga's life has continued to be viewed mostly as a curiosity. But the historical record reveals something different: it was this same Njinga who conquered the kingdom of Matamba and ruled it together with the remainder of the powerful Ndongo kingdom for three decades; defied thirteen Portuguese governors who ruled Angola between 1622 and 1663, keeping her kingdom independent in the face of relentless attacks; and made important political alliances not only with several neighboring polities but with the Dutch West India Company. It was this same Njinga

ANNE ZINGHA,

Reine de Matamba.

Traditional European depiction of Queen Njinga

whose religious diplomacy enabled her to make direct contact with the pope, who accepted her as a Christian ruler, and to establish Christianity within her kingdom.

Njinga's story is important on many different levels. On one level, it is a significant chapter in the history of resistance to colonialism. Throughout the four hundred years of Portuguese occupation of Angola (1575–1975), resistance never stopped. Njinga's place as the most successful of the African rulers in resisting the Portuguese influenced not only Portuguese colonialism in Angola but also the politics of liberation and independence in modern Angola. Njinga's life and history also had implications for the Americas. Africans captured by the Portuguese or purchased in the region where Njinga lived and ruled were sent as slaves to Brazil and Spanish America and were the first Africans to arrive in the North American colonies. These slaves brought Njinga's story and memory with them.

But Njinga's life and actions transcend African history and the history of slavery in Africa and the Americas. Her story reveals larger themes of gender, power, religion, leadership, colonialism, and resistance. Books on notable and sometimes notorious female European rulers, such as Queen Elizabeth I of England, who ruled two decades earlier than Njinga, and Catherine the Great of Russia, who ruled nearly a century afterward, number in the hundreds. Despite the many parallels Njinga shares with these women, no serious biography of her has existed until now in English, or in any other language. This book reveals the full and complex life that was Njinga's, focusing on themes of power, leadership, gender, and spirituality.

Setting the Scene

Before meeting Njinga, we need to make the acquaintance of the world she was born into in 1582—geographically, politically, and socially. Prior to Njinga's rule, Kongo, which formed the northern boundary of Ndongo, was the only central African kingdom known to Europeans. It is there we turn first, to understand the region Njinga would transform in ways that continue to inform not only the history of Angola but the place of women in politics in Africa and the world.

In 1483, almost exactly a century before Njinga's birth, the first Europeans arrived in central Africa. At the time, the largest kingdom in the region was Kongo, covering some 33,000 square miles and stretching nearly

300 miles from the Soyo and Dande regions on the Atlantic coast eastward to the Kwango River. Kongo's northern borders included lands just north of the Congo River, as well as some areas in the southern region of today's Democratic Republic of the Congo. The kingdom's southern frontier included lands between the Bengo and Dande Rivers. A colony of Kongo's citizens also lived farther south, on the island of Luanda, where they harvested the nzimbu shells that were the main currency in the kingdom. Despite its size, the kingdom was sparsely populated, containing only about 350,000 people, largely because its arid and flat western zone was inhospitable. Most of the population was concentrated in and around the capital, Mbanza Kongo (now in northern Angola and also known as São Salvador), as well as in the southwestern provinces.

The geographical reach of the kingdom was not the only factor that made it the dominant power in the region. Kongo's political organization set it apart from its smaller neighbors as well. The kingdom of Kongo was a centralized polity governed by an elected king chosen from several eligible royal lineages. Once elected, the king had absolute power. He selected close relatives from his own lineage to serve as his courtiers and as heads of the provinces. Mbanza Kongo, where the king's court was located, was the administrative and military center of the kingdom. It was from here that the king sent his courtiers or his standing army to relay his orders or enforce his will in the provinces. Provincial rulers, despite having sizable military forces themselves, had no security of office, and during the early years of the kingdom, kings concentrated enough military force in the capital that they were able to remove upstart provincial representatives from office and confiscate their goods.

The first rulers of the kingdom selected Mbanza Kongo as the capital for both strategic and defensive reasons. Situated on a high plateau above a river, the city was well protected and had a good water supply as well as fertile land for farming in the river valley. Paths connected Mbanza Kongo with the capitals in each province and were busy with provincial representatives, advisers, armies, religious personnel, and ordinary people traveling to the capital to attend religious and political ceremonies and pay taxes. These same paths provided access for invading armies.

Kongo gained additional power as a result of the relationship its kings developed with the Portuguese, who first arrived in Kongo's coastal province of Soyo in 1483. By 1491, King Nzinga a Nkuwu and the entire lead-

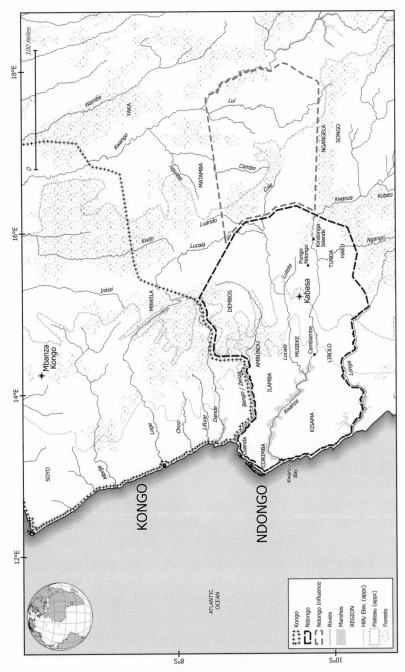

The kingdoms of Kongo and Ndongo, ca. 1550

ership of the kingdom had converted to Catholicism and implemented policies to transform the kingdom into the chief Catholic power in the region. The Kongo ruler who did the most to bring about this transformation was King Afonso (reigned 1509–1543), the son of Nzinga a Nkuwu. During his long reign he engineered the physical alteration of the city and oversaw a religious and cultural revolution that marked Kongo as a Christian state. Afonso sent the children of the elite to be educated in Portugal and other Catholic countries, and welcomed Portuguese cultural missions that brought skilled craftsmen who worked alongside the Kongolese to build the stone churches that dominated Kongo's capital. Afonso also ordered the construction of schools where elite children studied Latin and Portuguese.

Afonso's plans to transform the kingdom into a Christian state went beyond personal piety, religious scholarship, and the building of churches and schools. A cultural transformation of Kongo took root during his long rule as well. In Afonso's Kongo, members of the elite adopted titles such as duke, marquis, and count, and before long, Portuguese legal processes mixed with Kongolese precedents to govern court procedures. Moreover, the religious calendar of the Catholic church governed Kongolese life, and Kongolese children from both high and low families learned the catechism from local Kongo teachers, received both Christian and Kongolese names, and were baptized. There was always a shortage of priests in the kingdom, but the ubiquitous crosses found in villages throughout Kongo and the visits of Kongo priests served to remind villagers of their status as Christians.

The cultural transformation of the country and the Christian character of the kingdom were evident to European visitors to Kongo long after Afonso's death. Europeans who met Kongolese ambassador António Manuel, marquis of Ne Vundu, during his travels to Portugal, Spain, and the Vatican from 1604 to 1608, were astonished at his sophistication. They noted that although he had been educated only in Kongo, he knew how to read and correspond in Latin and Portuguese, and he spoke these languages as well as he did his native Kikongo.

But there was a tragic cost to Afonso's cultural engineering. Afonso had to engage both in wars of conquest and in slave trading to fund and sustain the project (as would the kings who followed him). During Afonso's rule, the number of people who were captured and brought into the kingdom as slaves or who were condemned to slavery as a punishment for their crimes increased exponentially. The trade in slaves led to the expansion of wars to capture slaves, as well as to increased slave trading and slave owning by the Kongo elite and their Portuguese partners. Kongo kings allowed the Portuguese to engage in slave trading in the kingdom, sent slaves as gifts to the Portuguese kings, and at times called on Portuguese military assistance either to deal with threats from inside the kingdom or to aid in the expansionist and slave-raiding wars that Kongo rulers made against neighboring states, including Ndongo.

It was during Afonso's rule that three distinct social groups with different life prospects emerged in the kingdom. At the top of Kongo society were the king and the members of the various royal lineages, identified by their Portuguese title as *fidalgos* (nobles). Members of this group had residences in the capital and made up the council of electors who chose the king and held court positions. The next group was made up of free villagers, called *gente*. Below the free villagers were the slaves, or *escravos*, captives from wars who were held mostly by the elite, but were also found in the households of ordinary villagers.

Subsequent kings followed the pattern Afonso had set. For example, Álvaro I (reigned 1568–1587), the king who was ruling Kongo when Njinga was born, expanded the diplomatic and political reach of Kongo. He cultivated relations not only with the Portuguese and Spanish courts, but also with the Vatican.

Kongo also had connections with other central African states, such as Matamba, a kingdom that would figure prominently in Njinga's life. Matamba was located east of Kongo and Ndongo and extended eastward to the Kwango River in the region known today as Baixa de Cassanje. Very little is known about the early history of the kingdom. Reference to a place called "Matamba" first appears in a letter from Afonso to the king of Portugal in 1530. In the letter, Afonso noted that he was sending two silver ingots (*manillas*) that he had received from a nobleman who lived in one of his lands called "Matamba."[2] From that time on, in the letters they sent to Portugal, Kongo kings always included Matamba as one of the areas they ruled. Other records, however, indicate that Matamba declared itself independent sometime between 1530 and 1561. In 1561, the "great queen" who ruled Matamba sent one of her sons to Kongo, where he met a Portuguese priest stationed there and told the priest that the queen was sympathetic to

Christianity and wanted to open communication with Portugal and become friends with the Portuguese.[3] We do not know what came of this overture, but, as we shall see, Matamba later became an important base for Njinga.

The Kingdom of Ndongo

At the time of the Portuguese arrival in Kongo, Ndongo was the second-largest state in central Africa, having an area about one-third that of Kongo. It encompassed what are today the provinces of Cuanza Norte, Cuanza Sul, Malange, and Bengo in modern Angola. (Angola derives its name from the word *ngola,* the title of the ruler of Ndongo.) Ndongo bordered the Atlantic Ocean and extended from the frontier with Kongo at the outlet of the Bengo River south to the bay where the mighty Kwanza River empties into the ocean. Ndongo's northern boundary wound its way eastward from the Atlantic through the Dembos region and the lands bordering Kongo's southern provinces, such as Mbwila, until it reached the Lucala River. The southern boundary followed the Kwanza River some 170 miles inland, including lands on both sides of the river, until it reached a series of large rock formations at Pungo Ndongo, located a few miles north of the river. Ndongo's eastern boundary began some miles beyond Pungo Ndongo, and included lands to the south as far as the Kutato River. The eastern boundary continued in a northeasterly direction, following the Lucala River to the border of Kongo.

Unlike Kongo, Ndongo had a few rivers that were navigable over many miles, but many also had treacherous falls and whirlpools. The Kwanza River, the main waterway that led to the center of the kingdom, was navigable by small boats for some 125 miles inland, but at that point the Cambambe waterfall, seventy feet high, made such navigation impossible. An even larger waterfall farther upstream imposed an additional barrier. The Lucala River, the other main watercourse in the kingdom and a tributary of the Kwanza, though navigable in some parts, has even more spectacular waterfalls that also prevented its full use for river transport. The most impressive of these waterfalls towered from a spectacular height of three hundred feet in an area studded with tall trees and dense underbrush.

While waterfalls proved hazardous to navigation, the shallowness of the rivers in other parts also placed limits on river travel. Parts of the Kwanza flowed through swamps containing crocodiles, hippopotamuses, and other dangers. Such conditions meant that even land transport near the banks of rivers was treacherous, and travelers were forced to disassemble bigger canoes and hire or commandeer humans to transport the boats and military hardware away from the river to settled areas, often miles away.

But the rivers were not as challenging to the local Mbundu population as they would be to the Portuguese, who arrived in the area in 1575. People used canoes that were easy to navigate over rapids or in the shallows. The upper reaches of the Kwanza River also contained a collection of large islands, the Kindonga Islands, that were economically and strategically significant. They provided excellent fishing grounds, and some were large enough to support villages and agriculture. A few were for the exclusive use of the ruler: one was used as a royal capital, while another was the site for the tombs of Ndongo rulers and members of the ruling lineages. The islands were also strategically located: they were close enough together that soldiers—or spies—could easily move between them, and during combat, soldiers posted on the low-lying hills could launch arrows against opposing armies approaching in canoes while still protecting themselves. In addition, since the islands were not far from the bank, a ruler who feared being attacked at the capital could easily relocate the court to the islands and continue to conduct war, send out diplomatic missions, and manage other state affairs, as Njinga would do on several occasions. Finally, if all else failed, leaders and soldiers could escape by using canoes to move from island to island undetected until they reached safety on the opposite side of the river.

Just as they found ways to make use of the rivers, the Mbundu people had been able to exploit the land resources and to connect all parts of the country. The people had adapted to a climate that ranged from semi-arid conditions on the coast, to cool and even frosty conditions in the plateau region, to humid and tropical conditions in the valleys and savanna areas. In the low-lying coastal areas south of Luanda, including parts of Kisama, the climate was semi-arid and inhospitable. Here, however, the majestic and imposing *imbondeiro*, the baobab tree, was the lifeline of the local population, providing water, food, shelter, and medicine. The Kisama region was famous for large slabs of rock salt, which were mined and distributed to all parts of the country.

The climate and resources of the plateau regions in the interior of Ndongo differed drastically from the dry coastal areas. The many rivers that flowed down from high mountains into meadows and valleys provided abundant water for fertile fields where people grew a range of tropical crops, and for pastures where they raised domestic animals, including cattle, goats, pigs, and fowl. The highlands offered natural protection, and it was here that the *ngola* (the ruler of Ndongo) located his capital. From here the Ndongo rulers and their officials supervised the slave and other dependent populations who also formed part of the military force and provided the various kinds of tribute and farm labor necessary for their upkeep.

Travel between the population centers could be treacherous. Uncultivated regions were covered by thick forests and harbored a wide variety of wild animals, including large pythons capable of swallowing a grown man, elephants, rhinoceroses, lions, leopards, and hyenas. The highlands also featured massive rocky outcrops, steep precipices, and ravines that presented challenges to even the most experienced travelers going from one community to the other.

The distribution of resources in Ndongo informed its political structure. The kingdom was divided into seventeen provinces that incorporated 736 territorial divisions called *murindas*. Some provinces, especially the four between the coast and the capital at Kabasa, had higher population densities and therefore more *murindas*. The *ngola* had more direct administrative and fiscal control over these four provinces.[4]

Kabasa, some 160 miles from the coast, was the official residence of the *ngola*, along with his wives, children, and relatives connected by descent and marriage. The first Portuguese delegation to visit the capital in 1560 described the ruler at the time as having more than seventy children and as many as four hundred wives and concubines. The chief wife ran the household and ensured that the slaves, serfs, and free people living within the walls of the household carried the goods they produced to the daily market and bought the supplies the household members needed.[5] Competition in court between different factions was intense, because relatives of the several different lineages related to past *ngolas* also lived in the capital or in the communities surrounding it.

Several important court officials who assisted the *ngola* also lived in the capital. The most important were the *tendala*, the *ngola*'s main adviser, who was in charge when the *ngola* was away from the capital, and the head of the military. In addition to these officials, the leading men of Ndongo, called *makotas*—perhaps related to the heads of the seventeen provinces—

also lived in the capital or maintained official residences there. Among this group were the *mwene lumbo,* who managed the *ngola's* household, the *mwene kudya,* who was in charge of tribute and taxes, and the *mwene misete,* who maintained the reliquaries of past rulers. The *mwene misete* was the most important ritual officer in Ndongo and supervised a large number of priests who performed the essential ritual functions the Mbundu believed were required for the protection of the *ngola* and of Ndongo itself.[6]

Besides the political power the *ngola* had in Kabasa and the smaller provincial capitals, he also controlled some state lands (*murindas*) and the residents who lived on them. The people who lived on these lands occupied three different legal categories: free people, serfs (*kijikos*), and slaves (*mubikas*). The free people comprised the bulk of the population and formed the peasantry. The status of the serfs was similar to that of their counterparts in Europe: they worked the lands of the *ngola,* and he could not force them off the land or sell them, since the land was held by the royal lineage. The slaves were either war captives or foreigners, and the *ngola* had the right to sell or remove slaves from the *murindas* in the capital and surrounding areas because he owned them directly.

Outside the capital, the *makotas* had political, economic, and spiritual authority that was similar to that of the *ngola.* Thus, *makotas* had their own system of hierarchy in their territories, and some of them were quite autonomous. Their status as heads of the *murindas* derived not from being sent from the capital to be the *ngola's* representative in the area but from the fact that they could claim descent from the oldest lineages that occupied the area. The *sobas* made up another group of important officials. The *makotas* were the electors and advisers, while the *sobas* carried out the day-to-day duties of running the villages. Just as the people accepted the *makotas'* right to rule because of descent from former *makotas,* so they expected the person who ruled as *ngola* to be a legitimate descendant of former *ngolas.*[7]

The *ngola* exercised a great deal of military, political, and fiscal authority over the provinces and the *murindas.* For example, the *ngola* had his own army stationed in Kabasa, but it was often greatly expanded when the call went out for forces to participate in Ndongo's frequent campaigns against its neighbors. The *ngola* led his own forces in combat, while the experienced captains he selected led other battalions. The army included large contingents of women who provided food, carried supplies, and performed the rituals considered crucial to the army's success. Women connected to the *ngola*'s household (his mother or wives, and their children) did not participate in the battle; a trusted general would protect the secret location where they were housed. Local priests also performed rituals, such as placing skulls and other sacred items on the landscape to intimidate the enemies. But the main military tools of the Ndongo soldiers were the spears, poison arrows, and battle axes they were known for. The soldiers, both men and women, used the battle axes in close combat. From early childhood, they practiced a rhythmic dance that bolstered speed and agility and allowed them to dodge the poison arrows of their enemies. They also owed their military successes to their familiarity with the natural defenses provided by the tall trees and heavy underbrush in the region, which provided excellent cover for surprise attacks.[8]

Apart from the *ngola*'s military strength, he also wielded legal authority in Ndongo through agents who traveled throughout the kingdom to make sure that people obeyed the laws. The *ngola* enforced strict regulations especially in the commercial transactions that took place in the large provincial markets. The agents paid special attention to transactions regarding the sale of captives (slaves) to make sure the exchange rate of the various items people used as money (including cloth, shells, and salt) was regulated and remained stable. The *ngola* also dispatched judicial officials to ensure that the *sobas* and the *makotas* complied with their obligation to send regular tribute in kind and in persons to the *ngola* and to offer food and lodging to his agents. In addition, the *ngola*'s military agents made regular visits to the provinces to ensure that local rulers fulfilled their obligation to send soldiers to join the *ngola*'s army. The *ngola*'s armies were active throughout the kingdom, whether for the purpose of enforcing these policies or invading neighboring territories and bringing new lands and people under Ndongo's control.

The economic system that undergirded Ndongo society was based on an extensive system of local, regional, and central markets. Apart from the markets that each *murinda* held regularly, the provincial and central markets brought natural and manufactured products from all over the country together into one place. Items for sale included a wide collection of tropical fruits, agricultural products, and domestic animals, axes and spears made by local blacksmiths, and fish and meat from domestic or wild animals. These markets also had on display a wide selection of birds, civet cats, and other small animals, as well as rare woods and myriad cloths made from tree bark or locally produced cotton. On market days people could also purchase the highly valued slabs of rock salt imported from Kisama.

Slaveholding and slave trading were vital parts of the economy of Ndongo. Slaves were often acquired during successful military excursions. They also came from the ranks of free villagers who were condemned by judges for religious infractions or civil disobedience such as treason and adultery, especially if the latter included any of the *ngola*'s numerous wives. In such adultery cases, all members of the lineage in that particular generation might be condemned to slavery. The more common means of acquiring slaves, however, was from captives taken in wars against provincial rulers or neighboring kingdoms. The captives were available for purchase at the provincial and central markets. The trade was highly regulated, and purchasing slaves was a protracted operation. In the markets in Kabasa, the *ngola*'s agents were required to oversee each slave transaction to make sure the sale was a legitimate one, in an effort to prevent unscrupulous trade in *kijikos*. Ndongo law regarded the *kijikos* as serfs, individuals who were tied to the land and were not slaves.[9] In addition to the slave trade, the *ngola* gained resources through a system of tribute contributed by the provinces and the *murindas*. The *ngola*'s agents, with their armed escorts, were able to exact tribute not only because they had the necessary military might, but also because people regarded the *ngola* as their supreme leader, despite the fact that their own local leaders also held a great deal of power.

Although some of the *ngola*'s legitimacy was based on his being a member of a ruling lineage, as well as on his ability to command military forces to victory and to accumulate economic resources, much rested on the spiritual position he occupied in Mbundu society. Ndongo tradition attributed the founding of the state to a skilled blacksmith from Kongo who was believed to be able to speak to a god named Zampungu or Zumbu.[10] People greatly respected the kings and religious authorities because they believed they possessed special powers. These mighty men and women had influence both worldly and otherworldly, controlling the rain and the fertility of the soil, wielding authority over life and death, and possessing omniscient knowledge.[11] Similar to the medieval idea of sacred kingship, once a person became the *ngola*, the people considered his body to be invested with special spiritual powers over the physical environment. Kings were imbued with a far more formidable power as well: they held divine authority to have people sacrificed.[12] Close members of the *ngola*'s household, as well as children who had unusual births or who survived devastating illness, were also believed to possess spiritual gifts.

The official religious authority at the court in Kabasa was a very important figure. One of the Portuguese Jesuits who visited the court of the Ndongo king in 1560 recalled that the *ngola* had sent his *feiticeira mor* (court religious official), accompanied by many people, to greet the visitors and look after their welfare as the embassy neared the court.[13] This official consistently refused to listen to the attempts of one of the priests, Father Gouveia, to tell him about Christianity. He adamantly insisted that "God was his Master" and that he was the best religious practitioner in the whole of Ndongo.[14] The Portuguese also reported that the *ngola* was venerated and that the founding ruler had instituted new rituals, including creating a religious group called *xingulas*, who could become possessed by spirits and were supposed to be able to create rain.[15]

To the Mbundus of the mid-1500s, Ndongo's sometimes perilous natural environment was an awesome spiritual force that needed to be appeased. The people performed rituals (sometimes involving human sacrifice) on the tops of mountains and at their bases, and passed down legends to explain the origins of some of the more impressive peaks. Priests made sure to carry out the appropriate religious rituals before entering the kingdom's uninhabited spaces.

These priests, called *ngangas*, were essential to the spiritual life of the *ngola*. They provided advice and carried out missions in the provinces and neighboring regions. Their core duty was to consult the royal ancestors and perform rituals involving those ancestors' bones, which, together with other ritual objects, were carefully guarded in a reliquary, or *misete*. The *ngangas* were healers, diviners, and restorers of order in times of crises and natural disasters. Their most important public role was to serve as emissaries of the *ngola* in wartime. *Ngolas* believed in the spiritual power of the *ngangas* and consulted them before any major decision, political, military, or otherwise.

The *ngola*'s role as chief judge was also part of his spiritual power. Plaintiffs came to Kabasa from throughout Ndongo to plead their cases in front of the *ngola* and his councilors. These public hearings were held in an open area at the first of the ten circular enclosures every visitor had to go through before reaching the *ngola*'s personal quarters. Here the *ngola* and his legal advisers were expected to repeat traditions so that precedents could be up-held, all aspects of the case discussed, and justice finally meted out.[16] In 1560, two decades before Njinga's birth, the first outsider provided a description of the *ngola* in his role as chief lawgiver. The report noted that throughout Ndongo, the people feared the ruler (not without reason: he had just ordered the execution of eleven *ngangas* who failed to make it rain during a drought), but they nevertheless preferred to make their way to his capital when seeking justice, because "he does great justice on them, and there is no day that he does not order justice."[17]

Women in Ndongo Political Life

From sometime before 1518 until 1582, when Njinga was born, the four *ngolas* who ruled Ndongo were all men. In 1624, when Njinga became ruler of Ndongo at age forty-two, she was the first woman to rule. Women, however, played a powerful role at court, and Njinga would have heard many stories about them as a child growing up in the court of her father, Mbande a Ngola. Women of the elite class were often in the inner circle, privy to the world of men. (Njinga herself claimed to have sat in on her father's councils when she was just a child.) One woman who figured prominently in these stories was Hohoria Ngola, one of two daughters of the earliest founder of Ndongo. Zundu, the other daughter, murdered Hohoria's son and then used guile to secure the throne. She herself was murdered at the instigation of Hohoria, who was seeking to avenge the killing of her son. The story captivated European missionaries decades later, when Njinga's elderly contemporaries shared it with them. It spoke to a still-emerging Mbundu system of governance that from its inception included women but also supported a political ideology that tolerated usur-pation and murder, fratricide, infanticide, militaristic expansion, and com-plicated political alliances.[18]

Women were important players in Ndongo's founding traditions, and they figured prominently in the written accounts of European eyewit-nesses in contact with Ndongo rulers from the 1560s on. It is significant that Hohoria was identified by name as the legal wife of Ngola Kiluanje kia Samba, the first historical king of Ndongo, and that it was their son who inherited the kingdom after his father's death. Although Ngola Kil-uanje kia Samba had several concubines whose children founded the numerous royal lineages that competed with the descendants of Hohoria for leadership of Ndongo, these women remained nameless.[19]

In later years, as the kingdom expanded and as Ndongo faced Portuguese military incursions, elite women were often privy to state information. This is evident in a story about a daughter of Ngola Kiluanje kia Ndambi, who learned that her father planned to kill the members of the first Portuguese mission in Ndongo. This news was far more than mere political intrigue for the young woman: the head of the mission, Paulo Dias de Novais, was reputed to be her lover. Although this story may not be true, it does reveal much about women's role at the time. The young woman supposedly revealed her father's plot immediately to Dias de Novais and spirited him and his party out of the country, sparing them her father's wrath and certain death.[20] The *ngola*'s daughter would never have been able to orchestrate her lover's escape without unfettered access to the goings-on in her father's court.

Other accounts also detail the crucial, yet more traditional part that women played in the religious life of Ndongo society. In 1585, Ngola Kilombo kia Kasenda is said to have paused just before launching an attack across the Lucala River, ordering "his mother and many male and female religious practitioners" to perform rituals that would give his army protection.[21] Apart from religious roles, women attached to high-status men often accompanied their husbands to major public events, as was the case recorded that same year when a lord of Ndongo took with him "500 and more women, all dressed in rich headdresses (*ferraguelos*) of Portugal" as he ventured out in public.[22]

Despite what it might look like to our modern eyes, the presence of large numbers of women attached to a single man did not mean that women occupied a subordinate position. One of the earliest eyewitness reports regarding the status of ordinary women in Ndongo society noted that a woman kept her independence even when she lived in a household with hundreds of other women. Both the chief wife and the concubines were free to leave the arrangement any time they wished. A woman who left her husband was not ostracized or even reprimanded but was instead welcomed back into her father's lineage, where she was free to stay until she chose another husband or partner.[23]

Interestingly, such a woman might have spent her entire childhood in the household of her future husband. At first the relationship would have resembled that of a playmate or a sibling. Under Ndongo custom, families could send their daughters to the household of the king or another prominent man "while still being carried in their mothers' arms" to be reared alongside the chosen son. When the son reached marrying age, he would set up his own household, selecting one of his favorite female childhood companions as his chief wife. Positions of women were changeable, and a chief wife could be replaced at her husband's whim, either from the pool of concubines already in the house or from another noble household—young girls were sent to the king's household all the time.[24] Njinga's own mother, Kengela ka Nkombe, was sent as a gift to the man who would father Njinga, Mbande a Ngola, the king of Ndongo. Mbande a Ngola was already married when he made Kengela his principal concubine, a status just below that of his chief wife. He would father Njinga and three other children by her.[25] We will hear much more about all of these children. But first, we turn to Njinga's predecessors and the events that occurred in the decades before her birth.

1

THE NDONGO KINGDOM AND
THE PORTUGUESE INVASION

Njinga, born in 1582, was the descendant of a royal line reaching back to the founding of the kingdom of Ndongo. Her predecessors consolidated Ndongo as a powerful force in central Africa and contended with the arrival of a Portuguese mission in 1560 and a subsequent military force in 1575. They would establish strong ruling traditions that she would later maintain, while at the same time facing a daunting challenge from abroad that she would struggle with in turn.

Ndongo's Early History

The founder and first historical king of Ndongo, Ngola Kiluanje kia Samba (reigned ca. 1515–1556), took power only a few decades before Njinga's birth.[1] Ngola Kiluanje kia Samba was a peaceful consensus maker, but a complex mix of political intrigues and wars had precipitated his rise as ruler. He set the stage for the dynasty's dominance by restoring a fractured kingdom, one that had witnessed the murder of his son by a jealous uncle, against whom he and his wife had wreaked vengeance.

According to tradition, Ngola Kiluanje kia Samba began his rule sometime before 1515. He consolidated power in Ndongo by maintaining internal peace, while significantly expanding the country's borders by conquering many neighboring states. In 1518, seeking to enhance his power and compete with the more powerful Kongo kingdom, Ngola Kiluanje kia Samba sent two ambassadors to Portugal seeking trade and broader cultural relations, but a return mission from Portugal in 1520 had no lasting impact. His successors maintained the model he established, subjecting small, independent provinces to Ndongo's overlordship while continuing to form diplomatic alliances with neighboring states as well as with the Portuguese.

The kings who followed Ngola Kiluanje kia Samba were expert military leaders and state builders, although, according to oral history, political cohesion was undermined during the short, brutal reign of his successor, Ndambi a Ngola (reigned 1556–1561). Ndambi a Ngola is said to have ascended to the throne after murdering all but two of his siblings; the surviving pair only narrowly escaped the same fate by fleeing to neighboring kingdoms.[2] Ndambi a Ngola held onto the throne through terror and intimidation and, according to the Capuchin missionary Giovanni Antonio Cavazzi, when he died, he was honored with the sacrifice of "innumerable human victims."[3] Later rulers, including Njinga, considered this custom of human sacrifice an essential part of the burial rituals honoring Ndongo rulers and other members of the elite.

Detailed historical accounts and oral traditions of Ndongo begin with the rule of Ngola Kiluanje kia Ndambi (reigned 1561–1575), who took power after Ndambi a Ngola's death. A century after his death, elderly members of the Mbundu elite and their Portuguese contemporaries still regaled Capuchin missionaries with tales of his impressive military feats, which resulted in all the provinces along the Dande, Zenza, and Lucala Rivers, all the way up to Luanda, being brought under Ndongo's control. His legacy was long-lasting. During the 1650s, the Portuguese fort of Muxima, on the lower Kwanza River, was called Isandeira in honor of the "isanda tree" (*imbondeiro*, or baobab) that Ngola Kiluanje was said to have planted there to mark his military conquests in the region.[4]

Ngola Kiluanje kia Ndambi began his reign in 1561, after his father's death and shortly after the arrival of the first official mission from Portugal in spring 1560. This mission was headed by Captain Paulo Dias de Novais, who would play an important role in the later military conquest of Ndongo. Reports by members of this delegation provide us with a vivid picture of the kingdom just before the conquest began, during the transition from Ndambi a Ngola's rule to that of Ngola Kiluanje.

King of Congo and King of Angola, frontispiece of a work by
António de Oliveira de Cadornega, ca. 1680

Knowledge that the kings of their powerful neighbor Kongo had opened their lands to strangers from across the waters had motivated the rulers of Ndongo to send their own emissaries to Portugal to request missionaries, starting in 1518 and continuing through 1556, when Ngola Kiluanje kia Samba sent representatives to Lisbon.[5] A mission was finally dispatched to Ndongo on December 22, 1559. The Portuguese who left Lisbon on that day had instructions from regent Dona Catarina, who was reigning on behalf of her grandson Sebastião, to travel to Ndongo to begin missionary work there. The delegation, which included four Jesuit missionaries, stopped at São Tomé to pick up Portuguese experts with local knowledge of Ndongo and arrived at the outlet of the Kwanza River on May 3, 1560. Two Mbundu members of the party, who had traveled to Portugal with the original emissaries, were immediately sent to the interior to alert the Ndongo king of the party's arrival. According to António Mendes, one of the Jesuits in the group, they waited for four months moored in the bay before officials arrived to grant them permission to make the long trip to the capital.[6] The wait was grueling. Ndongo was in the grip of a severe drought, the heat was intense, and disease-carrying mosquitoes abounded; food and water supplies were also low. Ten members of the group, including one of the priests, died. The survivors were saved only when the local ruler of the region supplied the group with cattle, goats, and local produce.

With the arrival of the king's emissary, at the head of a military party, Dias de Novais and the remainder of the party could begin the journey that would take them up the Kwanza River and then overland to Kabasa, Ndongo's capital. Leaving their large caravel, they transferred their supplies onto longboats and canoes. They traveled a hundred miles up the Kwanza River, until they reached the point where rapids and islands prevented further travel upstream. The local official in charge of the port at this point in the river attended to their needs. For the next month, they traveled on land to Kabasa. During the trip, the group moved from one territory to another, and each territorial leader made sure the travelers were fed, housed, and protected, as was his duty. When the party finally reached Kabasa, the king had three cottages prepared for the visitors in his own compound.[7]

Some five days after arriving in Kabasa, the Portuguese were allowed to enter the king's headquarters, situated in a well-watered area of the city and protected by large palm trees. One of the first things that stood out to the Portuguese was the intricate security they had to go through before reaching the king's residence, which sported a large patio and was surrounded by massive painted columns.

One of the Jesuit priests, Father Mendes, was impressed by the imposing physical appearance of the king, Ndambi a Ngola, who was in the final year of his reign. He was, the priest wrote, "one of the tallest in the land, like a giant and very strong."[8] Ndambi a Ngola was most likely dressed in the attire and adornments that would become the official regalia of Ndongo royalty in the years to come: a red feather (most likely from a peacock)[9] in his hair, a red cloth covering his chest and shoulder, and a cloth made of sheepskin with black and white spots covering him from the waist down.[10] His body would have been splashed with powder, signifying the spiritual and military esteem that he had attained as a result of his prowess on the battlefield.[11] His impressive physical appearance reflected his tremendous power. At the time of his meeting with the Portuguese, Ndambi a Ngola was said to have controlled five hundred "principalities" whose leaders paid him tribute and led squadrons of their own subordinates in the many wars that he fought. Nearly one thousand dependents attended him in the capital city, a number that skyrocketed to nearly thirty thousand during public festivals.[12] According to the Portuguese missionaries, Ndambi a Ngola was regarded as divine by his subjects; he "had himself worshipped as a God" and openly boasted that he was "the lord of the rain."[13]

From his majestic seat made of palms, Ndambi a Ngola listened to the Portuguese missionaries' explanations of the tenets of the Christian faith that they hoped he and his people would adopt. Although suspicious of their motives, he ultimately gave the group permission to begin their mission work in Kabasa and selected fifteen to twenty of his own children and those of his leading advisers to be the foreigners' first students.

The arrival of the Portuguese, with their religious and political plans, created a dilemma for the rulers of Ndongo. The Jesuit missionaries practiced a religion that had the potential to undermine the spiritual and legal power of the king and his advisers. Furthermore, the political relations that Dias de Novais indicated his monarch in Portugal sought with Ndongo could potentially diminish the powerful political position the king held in relation to provincial and territorial leaders as well as the rulers of surrounding states, such as Kongo and Matamba. Added to this was the threat the newcomers posed to the entire social fabric of Ndongo. Before the Portuguese arrived, the *ngola* was unquestionably the most powerful person in a state held together by the payment of tribute from less powerful but autonomous political entities. These payments were enforced by the *ngola*'s army. The Portuguese brought not only guns but also different cultural values regarding spirituality, justice, notions of social status and inherited status with rights to rule, freedom and slavery, serfdom and captivity, hospitality, trade, and the like.

Thus, although Ndambi a Ngola allowed the Portuguese visitors to remain in Kabasa, and even permitted the Jesuits to open a school, this welcome did not last. When he died sometime in 1561 and his son, Ngola Kiluanje kia Ndambi (Ngola Kiluanje), took power in Ndongo, the situation changed. Ngola Kiluanje turned against the Portuguese, convinced that the real motives of the group were to "spy on his land."[14] He imprisoned Dias de Novais and several other members of the delegation, along with some local Mbundus who had assisted the Portuguese, and expelled the rest of the delegation, sending them back to the coast under a military escort. Ngola Kiluanje eventually released one of the priests and later, in 1565, Dias de Novais was released. Only one of the priests, Father Francisco de Gouveia, stayed behind in Kabasa, where he died ten years later.[15]

Although Ngola Kiluanje had let Dias de Novais go, he held some members of the Portuguese delegation hostage in the capital for nearly five years, a decision that had as much to do with statecraft as with his suspicions about Portuguese motives.[16] A captain in Dias de Novais's second expedition later contended that Ngola Kiluanje and Dias de Novais had worked out an arrangement whereby Dias de Novais would return to Lisbon to use the alleged hostage situation as a ploy for raising arms for the *ngola*, who was threatened by an uprising of a powerful provincial noble. In return for Dias de Novais's military help, Ngola Kiluanje may have promised to sign a commercial treaty with the Portuguese.[17]

Ngola Kiluanje made strategic use of power in internal affairs as well as external affairs. He maintained his subordinates' allegiance, for example, by keeping young women of the leading families as hostages in the districts where his principal wife, secondary wives, and concubines lived. In 1564, he moved his headquarters to the city of Angoleme, not far from the capital of Kabasa. Here he lived with his principal wife, Quilundonanboa, more than four hundred concubines, and at least seventy children.[18] He wielded his power deftly, yet he was also remembered as a kind and just king; according to the Jesuits, even his enemies submitted to him without resistance.[19] Father Gouveia noted that court proceedings were orderly and open to the public. Although he admired the king's transparency, the Catholic priest was appalled by some of his "heathen customs," such as dispensing justice in court by means of death sentences.[20] These acts did not diminish Ngola Kiluanje's reputation among his subjects, however; in their eyes, he was akin to a god.[21] By the end of Ngola Kiluanje's reign, the country's borders had expanded significantly. Ndongo had developed from a small province located more than two hundred miles from the port of Luanda to one that encompassed all the Kimbundu-speaking peoples living between the southern borders of the Kongo kingdom and the lands south of the Kwanza River.

The next ruler of this powerful kingdom was Njinga's grandfather, Ngola Kilombo kia Kasenda (reigned 1575–1592), or Kasenda. Kasenda began his rule with several political disadvantages, not the least of which was a relatively weak claim to the kingdom. He was not a direct descendant of Ngola Kiluanje kia Samba, the founder of Ndongo, but rather a descendant from a different lineage.[22] Kasenda and his partisans in Kabasa had triumphed in a bloody coup but were not interested in changing the direction of the country. During his reign, Kasenda took up arms against his enemies; some were intimidated and forced back into the fold, while others were alienated and never forgave him or his descendants their ascent to the throne.[23] He also conquered additional provinces, such that the number of territorial rulers subject to Ndongo (most of whom were obliged to pay tribute to Kasenda) reached two thousand by 1586.[24] Ndongo covered so much territory that one European observer at the time mistook the three largest provinces for a "kingdom in their own right."[25]

The Portuguese Invasion of Ndongo

Although Kasenda expanded the boundaries of Ndongo and gained power over several regions, the start of his reign coincided with the return of the Portuguese and a protracted military, economic, and spiritual crisis that would culminate decades later in the defiant campaigns of Queen Njinga in the early 1600s.

The Portuguese had been strengthening their relationship with Kongo between 1565 and 1575, and by 1574, the king of Kongo had given them permission to build a small settlement on the island of Luanda, which Kongo claimed. The first thing the Portuguese did was build a temporary church on the island. In 1575, the small group of Portuguese in Luanda welcomed back Paulo Dias de Novais, who had headed the first Portuguese mission to Ndongo in 1560. This time he brought with him a significant military and civilian force. Thus began the Portuguese military conquest of lands that Ndongo had long claimed. As Ngola Kiluanje had suspected, the real intent of the Portuguese was to conquer Ndongo and integrate it into the Portuguese empire. Jesuit missionaries sustained the conquest by giving their blessing to the Portuguese military and civilian actions.

Dias de Novais had left Lisbon on October 23, 1574, bearing the weighty title of first governor and *capitão-mor da conquista do reino de Angola* (captain-general of the conquered kingdom of Angola) and commanding an armada of nine ships, seven hundred men, "much artillery," and four priests. His directions from the king of Portugal were to "subjugate and conquer the kingdom of Angola."[26] The fleet arrived in the port of Luanda on February 20, 1575.[27] After he was alerted to the arrival of the Portuguese, Kasenda wasted no time in contacting them. On June 29, one of his officials arrived in Luanda with a delegation and delivered a message from the king in a church the Portuguese had constructed.[28] Kasenda offered the Portuguese slaves, provisions, livestock, and other goods. In return, Dias de Novais offered Kasenda presents from King Sebastião of Portugal. Kasenda and Dias de Novais subsequently joined forces on campaigns against recalcitrant provincial leaders, and Dias de Novais's men were given free access to Ndongo's markets.[29] Following a short period of cooperation, however, relations deteriorated after Kasenda, convinced that the Portuguese were intent on conquering his kingdom, arrested and killed forty Portuguese in Kabasa, confiscating their merchandise and many slaves. Kasenda's suspicions were well founded. Dias de Novais had been conducting his own military campaigns in the region, conquering more than seventy leagues (about two hundred miles) of Ndongo territory and subordinating many of Kasenda's tribute-paying vassals.[30] By March 1582, the year of Njinga's birth, Dias de Novais had informed King Sebastião of his conquest of "seventy knights" so powerful that "each one of them can resist all the power of the king of Angola."[31] Throughout the 1580s, the Portuguese and their African allies made significant gains in many parts of the kingdom.

The first interior fort was established at Massangano, at the confluence of the Lucala and Kwanza Rivers, in 1582. Father Baltasar Afonso, one of the four priests in Dias de Novais's delegation, boasted to the king of Portuguese successes. Writing to King Sebastião in October 1582 to request additional materiel and men for Dias de Novais's campaigns, he noted that with just one hundred men, the governor had taken "half the kingdom of Angola, subordinating many grand lords . . . [and] in three months he has won three wars against the king of Angola, killing and capturing infinite numbers of people."[32] Although we do not have independent confirmation of casualties from Ndongo sources, Portuguese records are replete with descriptions of the devastating human and physical cost of these early campaigns against Kasenda. In one 1583 campaign alone, Kasenda was supposed to have lost forty thousand men, while Portuguese losses numbered a mere seven. In another battle, the Portuguese forces were said to have come so close to the capital that, after they fired only two shots, the king "without waiting took off and fled with his people." The infant Njinga would have been among that group.[33]

The continuing advance of the Portuguese and the loss of some of his vassals forced Kasenda and members of the court to flee from Kabasa again, two years later. During the flight, Kasenda made several temporary forts, each one a day's journey from the one before it, to avoid capture by the Portuguese and their African allies in pursuit.[34] In 1585, at the battle at Talandongo in the province of Museke, just a four-day journey from Kabasa, Kasenda sent a large army, "the flower of Angola" to face the Portuguese, but it proved no match for the enemy. At the end of the fighting, Portuguese forces admired a battlefield where only severed heads were visible, as "men fled to save their lives!" Among the dead were many of Kasenda's high-ranking military officials. Other high officials and relatives of Kasenda were captured alive.[35] Kasenda faced an even more disastrous loss in 1586 when all but twenty of seven hundred Ndongo troops drowned as they attempted to cross the Lucala River.[36]

Many of Ndongo's neighboring regions and subordinate territories experienced destruction, brutality, and humiliation at the hands of the Portuguese. In 1581, in an operation near the salt-rich province of Kisama, one hundred and fifty Portuguese soldiers stormed the lands of a local lord to avenge the death of their comrades. They seized one hundred slaves and burned the villages. A missionary witness observed that the provisions they took or destroyed—among them livestock, oil, honey, and also "houses full of salt," the main export of the province—were so abundant that "one can fill two slave ships [*navios da India*]" with them.[37] In another campaign, a provincial lord who had been captured offered the Portuguese one hundred slaves as ransom. The Portuguese accepted the slaves—and went ahead and decapitated the lord in the public square anyway.[38]

During these operations, the Portuguese began the gruesome practice of cutting off the noses of people they killed in the wars and sending them back to the Portuguese camps as trophies. In one engagement, 619 noses were cut off from fallen Ndongo soldiers; in another, so many Ndongo soldiers were killed that the Portuguese employed twenty porters to carry all the severed noses to their headquarters.[39] On another occasion, the Portuguese forces killed so many people that soldiers were reported to have nowhere to walk but "on top of them."[40]

The campaigns against Ndongo were not only wars of conquest but also slave-raiding operations. Thousands of noncombatant Mbundus were enslaved and sent to work on plantations being developed outside Luanda, or, as had been happening elsewhere in Africa for some seventy years by this time, they were sold across the Atlantic to the Americas. Between 1575 and the 1590s, the Portuguese exported as many as fifty thousand Mbundus to Brazil as a result of their wars and slave-trading operations against Ndongo.[41]

Despite all the setbacks Kasenda faced, the formidable armies he fielded fought bravely against the Portuguese, and they did have some successes. In 1581, he confronted an army composed of a small, 120-man Portuguese force fighting alongside large numbers of Kongolese soldiers.[42] Kasenda's army prevailed, and the retreating Kongo army reportedly left "thousands of their wounded and dead on the field."[43]

Kasenda and his partisans regularly attacked provincial lords who had allied themselves with the Portuguese. In 1582, for example, Kasenda's army invaded the lands of Popo Ngola, who had become a vassal of the Portuguese.[44] The next year, Kasenda assembled a major army that Portuguese eyewitnesses at the time estimated to be in the hundreds of thousands. The Ndongo forces, organized into three large squadrons and commanded by leading nobles, were so large that they spread over many miles.[45] Provincial lords who had turned against Kasenda sometimes reversed course when they calculated that their own security rested more with Ndongo than with the foreigners. This happened during the 1581 battle against the combined Portuguese-Kongo forces when "some lords" who had already joined the Portuguese side "grew so suspicious" of the Portuguese that they declined to help them.[46] A few years later, "a great number of lords" rose up against Dias de Novais's forces, and on other occasions provincial lords and their people went so far as to pretend to surrender but then turn on the Portuguese forces when the opportunity arose.[47] In 1588, a few of Kasenda's closest allies convinced Dias de Novais that they would help him capture Kabasa, but they then led his troops into an ambush.[48] The following year, the Portuguese executed some Ndongo allies after discovering a plot they had hatched to betray them.[49]

Kasenda's military skills and diplomatic expertise allowed him to assemble a pan–central African military confederation that handed the Portuguese a major defeat at the battle of Lucala in 1589–1590. In this campaign, which included troops from the kingdoms of Matamba and Kongo, the alliance first assaulted the Portuguese fort at Massangano and then moved the fighting up to the port of Luanda.[50] Luis Serrão, who had taken control of the Portuguese forces after Dias de Novais's death, saw his forces defeated when twenty or thirty provincial lords who had formerly been allies turned against him. He had to make a quick escape.[51] A new governor, Francisco de Almeida, arrived in Luanda in 1592 with 400 white soldiers and "50 African horsemen" with the order to "expand the conquest and bring the mines under our complete dominion." He raised additional forces and started on a campaign, but the outbreak of an epidemic forced him to return to the city. Almeida abandoned the colony in 1593, leaving his brother in charge.[52]

But Kasenda was not able to maintain Ndongo's integrity, despite some impressive victories. By the time of his death in 1592, he had already lost control of many *makotas* and *sobas*. In the view of these local leaders, Dias de Novais and the Portuguese were no worse than the Ndongo rulers in Kabasa, since both required them to send tribute and provide men for military service. Some of these leaders claimed descent from royal lineages and questioned Kasenda's legitimacy. Others seized the opportunity of the chaos of war to cease sending tribute or military support, thus depriving

Kasenda of valuable resources. The case of the *soba* Muxima Kitangombe illustrates particularly well the situation Kasenda found himself in. In 1581, Muxima offered aid to the Portuguese if they would assist him in subjugating "one of his enemies," promising that "he in the company of all his vassals would help [Dias de Novais] against the king of Angola [Kasenda]." He became a vassal of the Portuguese and sent the army "a lot of provisions, pigs and cattle."[53] The *soba* of Bansan likewise switched his allegiance from Kasenda to the Portuguese, bringing with him other members of his lineage, including his brother, his son, and his son-in-law.[54] Notable among those who became allies of the Portuguese were individuals of the Hari lineage, who laid claim to the throne because they were descendants of one of the concubines of Ngola Kiluanje kia Samba, the founder of Ndongo.[55]

The tributary state system that Kasenda had inherited from his predecessors began its slow demise during his reign. In the past, provincial leaders had faced the threat of conquest from within. After defeat by the Ndongo king, the *sobas* would not be removed from their land, but instead would be forced to send tribute to Kabasa, as well as contingents of soldiers when needed. Even when the Ndongo kings chose to remove the vanquished *sobas* from their lands, installing their "sons" in their place, these new rulers were expected to send regular tribute. Failure to do so would result in the disobedient leader's removal by the army.[56]

The enemy was now an external one. The system that the Portuguese established, both in conquered lands and in the lands of *sobas* who voluntarily pledged their loyalty to the colonial power, rested on ownership of lands, goods, and people by the Jesuits and the Portuguese soldiers and merchants. In 1581, for example, Dias de Novais gave Father Baltasar Barreira, head of the Jesuit community, lands that included the "freed slaves, rents, and lands [*pensãos*]" that had belonged to eight powerful lords in the region of the Lucala, Zenza, and Kwanza Rivers as well as "as much of the lands and lakes that the kings of Angola gave to Francisco de Gouveia . . . and anything else that he might possess and which belongs to him."[57] Other distributions followed as the conquests advanced. In 1587, Dias de Novais gave the lands of a powerful *soba* of the Museke province to a Portuguese colonist.[58] At this point the Portuguese goals were clear: conquer Ndongo and give the land to Portuguese religious orders and settlers.

Religious Conquests

The religious penetration and spiritual advances of the Portuguese were as influential in undermining Kasenda's authority as were the military conquests. When Dias de Novais arrived in Luanda in 1575, he was fully prepared to deploy the religious weapons the king of Portugal had armed him with. His group disembarked in Luanda with pomp and pageantry. Alongside the hundreds of Portuguese soldiers were four Jesuits who carried reliquaries dedicated to the legendary eleven thousand martyred virgins of St. Ursula. One of the priests carried the reliquaries below an ornamented canopy, while the rest of the party sang hymns accompanied by a corps of trumpeters.[59] By the end of Kasenda's reign, twenty-six Jesuit missionaries had arrived to join Portuguese forces.[60]

Dias de Novais made no decision without first consulting the Jesuits. In 1575, for instance, he delayed meeting with Kasenda's ambassador until he had time to pray in the small church his soldiers had built. During the meeting two priests stood guard on either side of his velvet-covered seat.[61] Dias de Novais believed that to win on the battlefield, soldiers had to be "armed with the sacrament of confession and communion" and had to perform religious exhortations. Soldiers were encouraged to "come to the church five times to do devotions" before going on a campaign, and the priests who accompanied the army "said mass for them and litanies."[62] Icons held tremendous importance as well. When a small portable altarpiece adorned with the image of the Virgin Mary disappeared, all regular activity ceased until it was found. After it was located, the men reportedly performed litany after litany in front of it to show their reverence.[63] Dias de Novais and his followers attributed their military successes to the guidance of "the Virgin our Lady."[64]

Although they clearly carried their Catholic faith in their hearts, Dias de Novais and his men had other goals in mind, as well. Determined to complete not only the military conquest of Ndongo but also the religious conversion to Catholic Christianity, Dias de Novais made sure that all religious rituals were performed in public as a way to attract the local population. His first targets would be the Ndongo elite, followed by the Ndongo wizards (*feiticeiros*), priests (*ngangas*), and children.[65]

Early on in their campaign, Dias de Novais and the missionaries made significant headway among crucial elements of the regional leadership. In an elaborate ceremony in Luanda in early 1581, Father Barreira baptized one of Kasenda's sons-in-law, a powerful nobleman, and Dias de Novais served as his godfather. The nobleman, dressed in opulent Portuguese regalia, adopted Dias de Novais's first name as his own, calling himself Dom Paulo.[66] The process of conversion was akin to that of courtship. In the case of Dom Paulo, Dias de Novais had showered him with gifts, attention, and privileges, perhaps most significantly, bestowing upon him the right to carry the "royal bow," a signature of royalty among the Ndongo that signified his status as a military leader and indicated his legitimacy as a descendant of the royal line.[67] Dias de Novais accorded him yet another honor, allowing him to sit "on a chair covered with a rug" whenever they met.[68] There is no question that Dom Paulo was won over. Six months after his conversion, Dom Paulo, now allied with the Portuguese, headed an army of five to six thousand of his own troops to put down an uprising in Cambambe.[69] One year later, he once again went into battle against Ndongo forces. He and his men attributed their victory against Kasenda to the apocalyptic appearance of a cross in the sky during the battle. The Portuguese referred to the battle as "the war of the sky and of God" and called it Our Lady of Victory (*Nossa Senhora da Victoria*) in honor of the Virgin Mary.[70]

Dom Paulo was far from the only success story in the Portuguese campaign to gain converts and allies. Many other Ndongo provincial leaders and their followers were baptized in rituals similar to those used in Dom Paulo's ceremony. The *soba* Songa, for example, along with his son and a brother, was baptized in a lavish ceremony in Luanda in the presence of 216 witnesses, and Dias de Novais ordered them home to their lands to serve as examples to their people.[71] Accompanied by a Jesuit on their return, Songa and his son, renamed, respectively, Dom Constantinho and Dom Thomas, gave the Jesuits permission to baptize hundreds of villagers and to erect crosses in place of the idols. They scourged the countryside, publicly burning the shrines and the huts where the *ngangas* and villagers kept their paraphernalia. They also recruited young boys to collect the idols and burn them in great bonfires. In return for his collaboration, Dias de Novais appointed Songa captain-general (*capitão-mor*) of the African troops and, as he had done with Dom Paulo, gave him the "royal bow" and a seat "before the governors on a carpet."[72] One Ndongo nobleman was so eager for baptism that he threw out his "idols" and presented himself for baptism with his "wives, his children and his friends." After the baptism

ceremony, he legally married one of his wives and gave up the others, adhering to the church's prohibition against polygamy. In 1586, the Jesuit
priest Diogo da Costa calculated that he had baptized no fewer than one
hundred provincial nobles at their own request. He speculated that these
nobles were eager to secure an alliance with the Portuguese because of
the "cruelty of the king [of Ndongo]."[73] The number of Mbundus who
were baptized grew steadily, increasing from a little more than one thousand in 1584 to twenty thousand by 1590.[74]

This religious dimension of Portuguese strategy was devastating to
Kasenda's prestige. His spiritual role had always been a central element of
his statecraft, and religious professionals played an important role in the
kingdom. In 1585, Kasenda boasted that he knew that there were only
three kings in the world—himself, the king of Portugal, and the king
of Kongo—but that he, "the king of the land, the sea and the sky" was
primary.[75]

The Jesuits concentrated much of their effort on weakening the people's
faith in the *ngangas,* the Ndongo priests, who were easily identified by
their distinctive dress and physical appearance. The Jesuits regarded them
as sorcerers who spoke with the devil. The detailed descriptions the Jesuits
left of their conversations with these "sorcerers" and of their physical appearance, religious paraphernalia, and public shrines leaves no doubt that
they were a powerful force in Ndongo.[76] Many of them were public figures
who presided over major religious ceremonies during droughts or warfare,
while the *ngangas* in the villages officiated at births, naming rituals, illnesses, and deaths. *Ngangas* in regions conquered by the Portuguese faced
forced conversion. The Jesuits arrested those who were still in their shrines
and forced them to learn "the things of God."[77] In 1582, Father Barreira
interviewed a very old, important religious official who was the spiritual
authority in a province allied with the Portuguese. This official was believed to have the power to control the weather, ensure the health of the
population, and provide other important services. Barreira was alarmed at
the *nganga's* appearance, noting that he was apparently living as a woman,
at least outwardly—his hair was long and flowing, and he was dressed in a
long robe "made from his hair" that was wrapped with many layers of cloth
(*panos*) normally worn only by women. When Barreira confronted the
nganga, he revealed that he had been born a man but the "demon" had told
his mother that he would die immediately unless he "became a woman."[78]

Barreira publicly shamed the local *nganga* by cutting off his hair and taking away his "superstitious" religious paraphernalia. He went even further, planting a cross where the *nganga* had been operating and immediately setting to work to build a church on the very spot where the *nganga*'s shrine had stood.[79]

Despite the many attempts the Jesuits made to undermine the *ngangas*, their numbers may actually have increased during Kasenda's reign. Certainly, there is much evidence that traditional religious beliefs continued to have a strong hold on the population. As they had done since long before the arrival of the Portuguese, for example, people continued to follow the teachings of the *ngangas* by wearing ritually cleansed copper and iron rings on their arms and legs (as Njinga would later do) in the belief that these protected them from illnesses.[80] Major religious practitioners who served in the courts and provincial capitals were believed to have the ability to contact deceased rulers, who would reputedly possess the priests and speak through them during times of political crises. In 1586, a captured Ndongo noble excused his people's loss of the important province of Ilamba with tales of such a vision. He claimed that the troops had fled the Portuguese in terror because of "a woman of much authority that they saw in the sky, accompanied by an old man with a sword of fire in his hand."[81] Veneration of dead warriors was also a core element of Ndongo religious practice. Victorious soldiers made tombs from the skeletons and skulls of fallen comrades at the site of battles.[82] Human sacrifice may also have increased during Kasenda's reign, for when he died in 1592 a number of people were killed and buried with him.[83]

Throughout his reign, Kasenda promoted Ndongo religious traditions and rituals, perhaps as a counterweight to the factions at the court who had become attached to Christianity and the Portuguese. This might explain why he sent his chief religious representative rather than his *tendala* (the chief administrative officer of the court) to oversee the visit of Dias de Novais and the Jesuits in 1575. As his suspicions about the motives of the Portuguese grew, Kasenda did not hesitate to move against both African and European Christians in his court. In 1580, when he gave the order to kill forty Portuguese in Kabasa, he also gave approval for the murder of a thousand Christian Ndongo slaves who were in Kabasa trading on behalf of the Portuguese.[84]

The situation of the *ngangas* and other religious practitioners was paradoxical. Despite the assault on them, the Ndongo leadership—even members who had become allies of the Portuguese—placed great faith in the efficacy of these traditional priests and in the rituals they oversaw and the advice they gave. In one case in 1581, a provincial lord who had become an ally of the Portuguese and who had planned to assassinate Kasenda called on his religious practitioners for protection before crossing the river for a meeting with Dias de Novais.[85] In 1588, Kafuxi ka Mbari, another Ndongo lord who initially was an ally of the Portuguese, blamed his military losses on the fact that it had not rained.[86] To improve his chances, he called on "his priests called *Gangas* throughout his lands" to conduct the necessary ceremonies.[87]

Rituals that the *ngangas* and other spiritual leaders performed were considered vital to success in wars and other important events. No king or provincial ruler undertook any major public event without including religious practitioners in their entourage. Religious practitioners were also present at religious ceremonies held every five days following the death of a provincial ruler, where personal attendants might be buried with their masters.[88]

From the beginning of his rule, Kasenda took the advice of his religious practitioners. In 1585, for example, he sent his mother and "many male and female *ngangas*" to protect his army.[89] But his rule did not end happily. Years later, he was praised for strengthening Ndongo and prevailing against provincial rulers and members of rival lineages who had allied with the Portuguese.[90] But Kasenda realized that his wars and his priests had failed to dislodge the Portuguese. Unable to accept the reality that the Portuguese conquests had left him with only a fraction of the kingdom he had inherited, Kasenda abandoned fighting and retreated to Kabasa. For the last years of his life, he lived with the ignominy of an expanding Portuguese city on the coast and permanent Portuguese forts that controlled most of the people and lands that had previously been subject to his power.[91] Kasenda died in 1592, as Njinga was approaching her tenth birthday. Although the son and grandson who followed him would continue the tradition of wars and resistance, it was his granddaughter Njinga who would ultimately succeed in resisting the Portuguese.

2

CRISIS AND THE RISE OF NJINGA

After Kasenda died in 1592, two more of Njinga's relatives held power before she became queen in 1624. The first was Kasenda's son Mbande a Ngola (reigned 1592–1617), and the second was his grandson, and Njinga's brother, Ngola Mbande (reigned 1617–1624). During this period, the kingdom was in crisis. Battles with the Portuguese continued, more and more people became ensnared by the growing slave trade, and the kingdom was internally fractured. Repeated attempts at diplomacy failed, but Christianity had begun to gain a foothold.

Mbande a Ngola's Troubled Reign

Mbande a Ngola was already a mature man and the head of a large household when he was elected to be the next ruler after Kasenda. His family consisted of a chief wife, who was the daughter of a powerful provincial ruler, and numerous concubines and children. His oldest son was the child of his chief wife, and he had four children by his favorite concubine, Kengela ka Nkombe. The eldest of these children was Ngola Mbande, and there were three younger daughters: Njinga (ten years old when her father took power), Kambu, and Funji.

Mbande a Ngola faced formidable obstacles when he became Ndongo's ruler, challenged on nearly every front by his own people and by the

Portuguese. Two of his half brothers challenged the legitimacy of his election, as did many people living in regions that had been conquered by the Portuguese. To become an effective ruler, Mbande a Ngola had the daunting double task of demonstrating that he was capable of regaining control over the economy, which was now dominated by the slave trade, while simultaneously continuing to resist the Portuguese.

There was no question that the Portuguese had gained the upper hand militarily, and resistance proved extremely difficult. During his twenty-five years as king, Mbande a Ngola or his allies fought wars against the Portuguese every year. His first test came in 1593, when a combined force made up of Portuguese soldiers and their Ndongo allies, consisting of twenty-six *sobas* along with their armies, invaded and temporarily controlled the salt-producing district of Kisama, which also housed the king's treasury. In another campaign shortly thereafter, the united Portuguese-Ndongo forces encircled Mbande a Ngola's army and within fifteen days advanced across some 276 miles of territory under his control, decimating much of the population.[1]

Portuguese forces did suffer one major defeat in 1594, at the hands of Kafuxi ka Mbari, a powerful *soba* who controlled a region south of Kisama, near Cambambe. Here, hundreds of Portuguese and as many as forty thousand of their African allies lost their lives.[2] The joint forces soon counterattacked, however, and the onslaught on *sobas* loyal to Mbande a Ngola was relentless throughout 1595 and 1596.[3]

Mbande a Ngola's failure to mount successful military assaults against the Portuguese was partly a result of the opposition he faced from members of the court who did not support his election. Alliances were not always easy to follow or predict, and Kafuxi was one of several *sobas* who opposed both the Portuguese and Mbande a Ngola. Kafuxi's military prowess elevated his popularity among his fellow *sobas* and confirmed his status as a direct threat to the *ngola*. Mbande a Ngola feared that the people might depose him if they believed that Kafuxi could better defend them against the Portuguese.

The Portuguese advances continued, however, resulting in the defeat of Kafuxi and other powerful *sobas* and the construction of a new fort at Cambambe, on the Kwanza River. Sometime in 1603, the Portuguese, under the command of Governor Manuel Cerveira Pereira, invaded Cambambe, about fifty miles from Kabasa, in search of supposed silver mines.[4]

Although Mbande a Ngola "went into the field with all his power," he could not stop the Portuguese onslaught. Cambambe was a core province, whose *soba* had refused to recognize Portuguese overlordship. Unable to weather the barrage of Portuguese might, the *soba* fled. Governor Pereira beheaded the *soba* that Mbande a Ngola sent as a replacement; he then put in place a more compliant *soba* and built a fort, which he garrisoned with 250 soldiers.[5]

The political crisis that Mbande a Ngola faced in Cambambe was compounded by the Portuguese conquest that same year of Museke, a nearby province that was ruled by his father-in-law. These consecutive losses led to a stampede, as one after another of the independent *sobas* publicly transferred their allegiance from Mbande a Ngola to the Portuguese.[6] Continued defeat also prompted Mbande a Ngola to seek to improve relations with Governor Pereira, but, as we shall see later in this chapter, this attempt at diplomacy did not bear fruit.[7]

Another threat to Mbande a Ngola was posed by the Imbangala—mercenary bands of young men known for their violent and cultlike behavior (including cannibalism), who had allied themselves with the Portuguese. Imbangala bands had already invaded territories south of Ndongo and destroyed the lands of Mbande a Ngola's uncle in the province of Tunda.[8] The Imbangala invasion of Kafuxi's lands in 1607 effectively dashed any hopes Mbande a Ngola may have harbored of recovering the territories conquered by the Portuguese. The alliance proved a godsend for the Portuguese, who could allow the Imbangalas to destroy Ndongo and reap the benefits, including slaves from the large numbers of refugees, land, and *sobas* willing to switch allegiance from Ndongo to Portugal.[9] Although Mbande a Ngola and his remaining independent provincial allies would continue to have sporadic brushes with the Portuguese, Ndongo had all but collapsed.[10]

The long downward spiral that would eventually culminate in Mbande a Ngola's death began in 1611, when the Portuguese army, backed by local Mbundu allies and Imbangala bands, undertook campaign after campaign in the areas east of Cambambe and demolished Mbande a Ngola's former allies in both the northern and southern regions. Pockets of resistance did persist, however. A 1612 report to the king of Portugal identified several provinces in which "powerful enemies" controlled "large territories." Furthermore, the same report noted, provincial rulers south of the Longa River and around the Portuguese fort of Muxima disrupted the commercial and

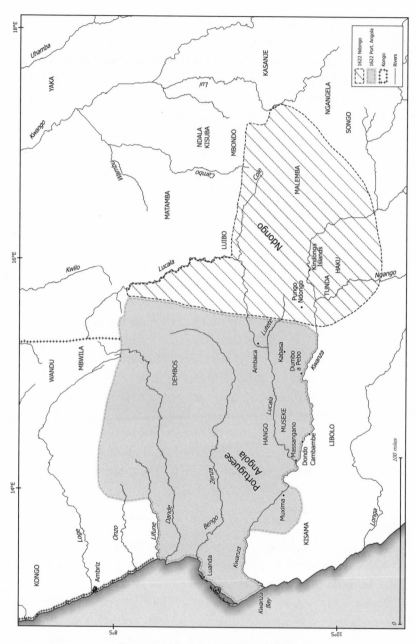

Portuguese Angola and Ndongo, 1622

political alliances that had developed between the Portuguese and the province of Hari, formerly a core region of Ndongo, and prevented easy access to trade from regions beyond Ndongo, such as Matamba and Tunda. Mbande a Ngola still commanded some respect, even among those *sobas* who had been forcibly integrated into the Portuguese colony of Angola. Burdened both by the Portuguese freebooters who robbed them of their populace and their provisions and by the excessive demands for slaves and soldiers for the Portuguese army and forts, some of the *sobas* began to rebel, preferring to ally with the Ndongo king, who only demanded tribute once a year.[11]

Nevertheless, the clock could not be turned back; the Ndongo state that Mbande a Ngola had inherited was a thing of the past. The battles that he and his few supporters continued to wage against the Portuguese never attained the scale—or the success—of earlier encounters. In the last years of his reign, he was unable to raise the fighting forces of thousands necessary to defend the kingdom. Support for Mbande a Ngola continued to dwindle as the Portuguese built additional forts in the lands of the remaining provincial rulers. In 1614, a report from the Portuguese governor, Bento Banha Cardoso, noted that the colony of Angola was at peace and that he had built a fortress in Hango, where the two most powerful *sobas* and some lesser ones "have made obedience."[12] In another report dated a year later, Cardoso said that a large number of *sobas* had been forced to submit to the Portuguese as a result of the wars with the Imbangala. In these conquered territories, each *soba* was now required to send tribute to a designated Portuguese overlord. This was tribute, of course, that had previously been sent to Mbande a Ngola.[13]

Growth of the Slave Trade

The expansion of the slave trade, which was initiated and controlled by the Portuguese, presented a major obstacle to Mbande a Ngola's recovering power over the tributary provinces he had lost.[14] The complex social structure that characterized Ndongo society offers insight into how the slave trade undermined Ndongo's independence. We need to step back in time for a moment to understand how the trade had evolved in previous decades. As elsewhere in Africa, Ndongo society was made up of both free and unfree individuals. Unfree individuals fell into two categories: *kijikos*, who occupied a position similar to that of European serfs and were inherited with the land and considered state patrimony, and *mubikas,* who were slaves in the traditional sense, either descended from war captives, purchased in the local markets, or somehow brought into the possession of the king or a provincial or territorial leader.[15] The status of the *kijikos* was somewhat ambiguous; during some periods they could be sold as slaves, and during other periods they could not. As early as 1565, Father de Gouveia listed slaves among the items that Ngola Kiluanje kia Ndambi was sending to the king of Portugal.[16] In the early years of Kasenda's rule, the category of the enslaved expanded to include those "slaves who were raised from others whom their ancestors took in wars [*kijikos*]," recent captives, and criminals condemned to death. All were available for purchase at markets in Kabasa and in the provinces.[17] After observing the inner workings of the slave trade in Ndongo in the early 1580s, the Jesuit priest Baltasar Barreira concluded that nowhere else in Africa was it possible "to buy them [slaves] more securely" than in Angola.[18] It was illegal, however, to sell a free person (or at times a *kijiko*). Slave markets were tightly monitored to verify the legality of any sale, and no effort was spared to rescue a free person illegally sold into bondage.

The slave trade expanded significantly after Paulo Dias de Novais returned to Ndongo in 1575, the first year of Kasenda's reign. Large numbers of Portuguese and their African assistants came to Kabasa to sell merchandise in exchange for slaves during the wars following Dias de Novais's return, according to the Capuchin priest Father Gaeta, based on information gathered from interviews done nearly a century later.[19] Indeed, the estimated fifty thousand slaves who were sent to Brazil from Angola between 1575 and 1578 must have come largely from the Ndongo slave trade.[20] With every victorious battle, hundreds of thousands of *kijikos* and *mubikas* were transferred to Jesuits, Portuguese captains, and other favorites, along with control of the conquered territories. Many of Dias de Novais's military campaigns against Kasenda were effectively slave-raiding expeditions. Moreover, as the Portuguese gained control over an increasing number of territories, the settlers formed private armies and organized their own pillaging expeditions, enslaving villagers, destroying fields, and leaving large swaths of land depopulated.[21] In 1587, the Jesuits themselves had control over nine *sobas* and their people in the lands that Dias de Novais had given to them as private property. This yielded around three hundred slaves per year, whom they sold to the traders bound for the

Americas.[22] Between 1579 and 1592, when Kasenda died, an additional fifty-two thousand slaves had been exported from Ndongo.[23]

The slave trade proliferated during the twenty-five-year rule of Mbande a Ngola, as the Portuguese captured additional provinces. By 1606, Portuguese merchants were exporting between ten thousand and thirteen thousand slaves annually from Angola, a figure that would only increase after the Portuguese army joined forces with the Imbangala in 1607.[24] Portuguese merchants headquartered in Luanda also sent an increasing number of their slaves (*pumbeiros*) out to the provinces to serve as merchants on their behalf.[25]

The conflicts between Ndongo and the Portuguese often centered on the latter's use of *kijikos* as slaves on their plantations or for export to the Americas.[26] By 1616, many of these battles could be classified as trade wars; a judicial investigation from that year pointed out that "the king of Angola and other powerful *sobas*" descended on the markets to "rob, kill, and capture the people of the Portuguese [i.e., Africans] who serve there."[27] Sometimes Mbande a Ngola and his loyal *sobas* targeted Africans who traded on behalf of the Portuguese. Following the attacks, the Portuguese merchants complained that the forts they had established were at risk of being attacked and destroyed. In truth, Mbande a Ngola's primary goal was not to destroy these Portuguese holdings but to regain control over the *kijikos* whom the Portuguese had captured.[28]

By the end of Mbande a Ngola's reign, his campaigns against Portuguese positions amounted to little more than raids against the markets that the Portuguese had set up throughout Ndongo; giving up his claim on the *kijikos* and *murindas* would have signaled the demise of the kingdom. The resistance to Portuguese claims over the land and the dependents would loom large in the relationship between Mbande a Ngola's son and heir, Ngola Mbande, and his sister Njinga. In the meantime, Mbande a Ngola tried a different tack in his resistance to the Portuguese: diplomacy.

Diplomacy, Christianity, and the Fall of Mbande a Ngola

Having lost most of his kingdom and the support of many *sobas*, as well as access to the tribute he was due, Mbande a Ngola decided to pursue diplomacy with the Portuguese. Part of this strategy involved assuring them of his readiness to accept baptism and to allow Jesuits into his remaining lands. Diplomacy was his only hope once he recognized that he could not beat his adversary on military or economic grounds.

Yet he would fail even here. This failure is apparent when we look at the spread of Christianity during his reign. Portuguese Angola at the time did include thousands of Mbundu Christians, but they were found mostly in the Portuguese-occupied provinces, especially in Luanda and around the Portuguese forts of Massangano and Cambambe. Jesuits were joined by Franciscans, many of them familiar with the Kimbundu language and culture, in converting a growing number of Mbundus. One Jesuit priest alone was credited with converting twenty thousand Mbundus on the island of Luanda.[29]

In spite of the number of conversions, however, the missionaries were not satisfied with the version of Christianity practiced by the Mbundus. A 1606 report by a Jesuit priest noted that regional lords still had many wives (supposedly numbering in the hundreds at times), and the *ngangas* (Mbundu priests) still wielded significant power. In a region that was home to two thousand Christians, for example, there still stood "a house of many idols" replete with statues of men and women, animal bones, and the like. The missionaries had to burn these shrines themselves because the Mbundu believed that anyone who touched the idols would die.[30] Mbande a Ngola himself came to rely on the *ngangas* even more than Kasenda had. Christianity would continue to meld with Mbundu ideas of spirituality through the end of Mbande a Ngola's reign.[31]

In the realm of formal diplomacy, Mbande a Ngola's attempts also failed. His first attempt came in 1599. Exhausted by the wars, he sent his ambassadors to Luanda to negotiate a peace treaty and announce his desire to embrace Christianity. To show his commitment, he made an offering of some noble children to the Portuguese. The Jesuits taught these hostages about Christianity while waiting for a response from European authorities.[32] (There is no record of a response.) Mbande a Ngola turned to diplomacy again in 1603, after Portuguese forces had routed the powerful *soba* Kafuxi ka Mbari and forced him to flee. Mbande a Ngola sent an embassy of about fifteen people, among them his own relatives, to Luanda with a message of peace. His ambassadors made it clear that Mbande a Ngola's greatest pleasure would be for the Portuguese to restore his lands to him, but short of that, he hoped that they would be satisfied with their territorial conquests to date. At the very least, he wished to keep "his royal city [Kabasa] up to our fort at Cambambe." Lastly, the ambassadors reiterated Mbande a Ngola's statement that he had always desired and "still desires to be a Christian."[33]

This approach also went nowhere; the several governors who ruled Portuguese Angola continued to make war against Mbande a Ngola, ignoring the directives from royal officials in Lisbon and Spain to make peace with Ndongo, to call off war in favor of converting the *ngola* and the *sobas*.[34] Instead, the Portuguese, in alliance with the mercenary Imbangalas, captured hundreds of thousands of Mbundus who were either exported to the Americas or relocated to plantations controlled by Portuguese soldiers and the church.

In 1607, Mbande a Ngola became so frustrated by the relentless attacks that he arrested a Portuguese diplomat who had been sent to Ndongo, giving as his reason the fact that the former governor, Manuel Cerveira Pereira, had made "war on him without cause."[35] The attacks continued, even though Francisco Correia da Silva, who was appointed governor in 1611 (but did not serve) was told to do all in his power "to make peace with the king of Angola to get him to agree to convert to our holy faith."[36]

By 1612, the situation in Ndongo had descended into chaos. Provinces that the Portuguese had previously conquered were in open rebellion. The constant pillaging, murder, and robbery undermined any possibility of peaceful relations between Mbande a Ngola and the Portuguese.[37] Few vassals remained from whom the king could exact tribute, and he had lost thousands of *kijikos*, who were working as slaves on Portuguese plantations along the Kwanza River and elsewhere.[38] Bento Banha Cardoso, the governor from 1611 to 1615, erected yet another fort near the Ndongo capital, an unmistakable show of Portuguese might. Most of all, Mbande a Ngola had lost so much goodwill among many of the remaining powerful *sobas* that by the time King Philip III issued new directives in 1616 to Governor Manuel Cerveira Pereira (serving his second term), Mbande a Ngola was desperate.[39]

The official orders from the king to the governor were clear. He was tasked with negotiating a peace that would force Mbande a Ngola to submit to the Portuguese king and sway those *sobas* still loyal to Mbande a Ngola to "agree to have our faith in his kingdom." The situation on the ground, however, allowed no room for diplomacy.[40] Mbande a Ngola never met with the governor. He had already lost considerable tribute-paying lands and supporters.[41] Several provincial lords had been publicly executed or imprisoned, with an additional eighty *sobas* forcibly integrated into the Portuguese kingdom of Angola.

Mbande a Ngola's status had already declined when Kakulu ka Hango, the important *soba* of Hango (the site of the new Portuguese fort), became the most powerful opponent of the Portuguese. Many discontented *kijikos* and *sobas* fled Portuguese-controlled areas to join him in his revolt. Governor Pereira quickly crushed the uprising, however, restoring Portuguese authority and turning over to Portuguese soldiers and functionaries all the *kijikos* and other Mbundus who had joined in the resistance.[42]

It was another embarrassing loss for Mbande a Ngola. His prestige among the remaining independent lords all but disappeared, and his enemies began to plot their revenge. These enemies consisted of nobles who had contested his father Kasenda's nomination as king. Early in 1617, they convinced Mbande a Ngola to send reinforcements to relieve forces battling a provincial lord who had risen up against him. Mbande a Ngola seized this chance to rebuild his tarnished reputation and accompanied the relief column to the Lucala River, where the forces were reported to have been pinned down. But the report was fake. As he approached the river, he was ambushed by his own men and murdered.[43] Despite this betrayal, his royal burial was on a par with those of his more illustrious forebears, replete with "mourning and the appropriate sacrifice."[44]

Mbande a Ngola's sudden death left a much reduced Ndongo, a divided nobility, and no designated successor. The months following his burial saw unrivaled bloodletting and political intrigues as the various factions sparred for control of the kingdom.

Ngola Mbande's Losing Battles

As had been the case during Kasenda's ascension to the throne some forty-five years earlier, the disputes over succession after the death of Mbande a Ngola were a messy business, involving court officials responsible for electing the next king, the children and relatives of Mbande a Ngola's principal wife and concubine, and aspirants from eligible lineages who still held important positions in core provinces. This chaos at court allowed anyone who could mobilize sufficient support—whether it be one of Mbande a Ngola's children or a member of an eligible lineage—to take control of the capital. Ngola Mbande, Mbande a Ngola's son by his favorite concubine and full brother of Njinga, Funji, and Kambu, was the ultimate victor. After his father's death, he immediately mobilized his own partisans in Kabasa, who supported his contention that his older half brother, the eldest son of his father's principal wife and therefore the legitimate heir according to Mbundu rules of descent, was ineligible to inherit the kingdom because his mother had been convicted of adultery and imprisoned.[45] Ngola Mbande had his partisans proclaim him king before many of the electors traditionally involved in the selection of the king arrived at Kabasa.

To consolidate his position, Ngola Mbande unleashed a bloodbath against potential rivals. His half brother, his half brother's imprisoned mother, and all of her siblings were murdered in short order. He then went on to kill prominent members of the court, including the *tendala* (the chief administrative officer) and other court officials along with their families.[46]

Ngola Mbande's own sisters did not escape his wrath, although he did spare their lives. He had a longstanding rivalry with Njinga, now thirty-five years old. During their childhood and young adulthood, she was their father's favorite, reportedly outdoing her brother with both her mental aptitude and her military prowess.[47] In an attempt to secure his succession, Ngola Mbande first killed Njinga's newborn son, the offspring of one of her many male concubines. Then, according to reports of her partisans, collected years later, he ordered the sterilization of Njinga and her two younger sisters: oils combined with herbs were thrown "while boiling onto the bellies of his sisters, so that, from the shock, fear & pain, they should forever be unable to give birth."[48] No eyewitness records verify this account, but it is known that neither Njinga nor her sisters gave birth to any children after 1617. Ngola Mbande, however, married and had a son who he believed would rule after him. In addition, he had many children with his numerous concubines as a means of increasing the population under his direct control. As was customary, the concubines came from regions outside of Kabasa, thus ensuring that their lineages would provide tribute during peacetime and military units during war.[49]

In committing fratricide and various other crimes to secure the leadership of Ndongo, Ngola Mbande followed in the footsteps of his immediate forebears. However, he disdained their military and domestic strategies, according to stories collected by the Capuchin missionary Giovanni Antonio Cavazzi, who later lived in Njinga's court.[50] Ngola Mbande sought inspiration from earlier Ndongo leaders in his efforts to restore the kingdom to its former glory. One of his first steps was to reach beyond the partisans in Kabasa who had engineered his election and to try to increase the number of *kijikos* on state lands away from the capital. In dealing with the Portuguese, he rejected diplomacy; instead, he gathered a large army and moved against Portuguese positions shortly after he took power.[51]

Unfortunately for Ngola Mbande, the Portuguese were also revisiting their strategy for dealing with Ndongo. A new governor, Luis Mendes de Vasconcelos, was now in place who, during his four years in office, would carry out massive military campaigns that would culminate in the sacking of the capital city of Kabasa and the capture of thousands of slaves. When Mendes de Vasconcelos arrived in Luanda in the summer of 1617, shortly after Ngola Mbande took power, he had grandiose plans to conquer not only Ndongo but all the kingdoms up to Mozambique, around the Cape of Good Hope at Africa's southern tip. He planned to finance this enormous military venture by capturing and selling Africans for the slave trade. Just as Ngola Mbande looked to the founders of Ndongo for inspiration, Mendes de Vasconcelos revered his predecessors, the early conquerors such as Dias de Novais who had precipitated Ndongo's decline.[52]

It wasn't long before Mendes de Vasconcelos put his plans of amassing a vast fighting force into action, and he brooked no dissent from his own countrymen; he imprisoned, killed, or sidelined any Portuguese officials in Luanda and at the forts who opposed him. He also reached out to disaffected Mbundu local officials, many of whom submitted themselves voluntarily to his authority.[53] Within a few months, Mendes de Vasconcelos had put together a large army comprising Portuguese settlers and their slaves, soldiers, Imbangala bands, Mbundu *sobas*, and free Mbundus. Under the guise of attacking one of the few powerful *sobas* still allied with Ngola Mbande, the army instead marched to the fort at Massangano, a stopping point on the way to Kabasa, Mendes de Vasconcelos's ultimate destination. Mendes de Vasconcelos had the support of a *soba* from a competing lineage to that of Ngola Mbande, who not only promised to bring along his own soldiers but also allowed the Portuguese troops to pass through his lands.[54]

Mendes de Vasconcelos's army did encounter resistance along the way to Kabasa. Many powerful *sobas* in Museke, where Ngola Mbande and his sister Njinga still enjoyed strong support, engaged in bloody battles against the Portuguese troops. Mendes de Vasconcelos retaliated brutally by carrying out mass beheadings. Despite, or, more likely, because of this brutality, the survivors of these massacres maintained their support for Ngola Mbande and later for Njinga, when she became queen.[55]

The resistance of these *sobas* was not adequate to turn aside Mendes de Vasconcelos's army, and sometime in late 1617 or early 1618, with the support of large contingents of Imbangala forces, he reached Kabasa, the traditional capital of the Ndongo rulers, in the heart of the kingdom, having destroyed every village on the road from Massangano to Kabasa. When this large army arrived in the capital, Ngola Mbande's forces were overpowered; the king narrowly escaped with some members of his household, fleeing to his lands to the east. The army found well-maintained houses built with local materials and intricately decorated with images of local flora and fauna. They wreaked wholesale havoc on the city. A Portuguese official described the Imbangala as "capturing, eating and killing thousands of people, cutting down palm trees and destroying everything in their wake."[56] In addition, hundreds of *sobas* who had avoided Portuguese overrule thus far were forced into submission.[57] The troops also captured thousands of people who had not had time to escape, including *kijikos* whom Ngola Mbande had been using to farm state lands. Word was sent to Ngola Mbande that he had to appear before Mendes de Vasconcelos to discuss conditions of peace. He refused, and the governor responded by relocating the fort that Bento Banha Cardoso had built in 1611 in Hango to Ambaca, a site within one day's travel of Kabasa.[58] Three Portuguese forts now encircled the core areas of Ndongo: in addition to Ambaca, Massangano and Cambambe were located in the province of Museke between forty-eight and sixty miles from Kabasa.[59]

The violence was far from over. Forced to return to Luanda to recuperate from an illness, Governor Mendes de Vasconcelos handed control of the army to his nineteen-year-old son, João, who continued the rampage, invading the lands of Ngola Mbande's main ally, Kaita ka Kabala, and executing him and ninety-four other *sobas*.[60] Over the next two years, 1618–1619, João Mendes de Vasconcelos pummeled the neighboring regions, including Matamba, relentlessly, his forces strengthened by the participation of the Imbangala and a group of four thousand Christian Mbundus who had been "made Jagas [Imbangalas]."[61]

The shock of the attacks on Kabasa only energized Ngola Mbande. Between 1619 and 1621, he reoccupied Kabasa following João Mendes de Vasconcelos's retreat, sent emissaries to Luis Mendes de Vasconcelos to negotiate a peace treaty, and again assembled an army. His troops besieged the fort at Ambaca and attacked the *sobas* loyal to the Portuguese.[62]

Ngola Mbande harassed the Portuguese forts and loyal *sobas* ceaselessly, but he was fighting a losing battle. In one instance, his forces moved on Ambaca but were beaten back by Imbangala allies of the Portuguese. Following the siege, Luis Mendes de Vasconcelos called a public gathering of all the rebellious *sobas*, purportedly to provide them with a forum in which to air their grievances. Instead, he "cut the throats" of those he deemed guilty of disloyalty.[63]

In 1621, João Mendes de Vasconcelos's forces attacked Kabasa for a second time.[64] Although Ngola Mbande was able to escape, his circle was not so lucky. Many of his core supporters were killed, and the Portuguese struck very close to home, capturing Ngola Mbande's principal wife, his mother, his two younger sisters, Funji and Kambu, and several members of the court.[65]

Ngola Mbande took refuge in the Kindonga Islands, a group of islands far upstream in the Kwanza River that had belonged to the Ndongo kings from the time of the kingdom's foundation. He then reappeared in the neighboring region of Haku, where he reconstituted his forces as a guerrilla army. His guerrillas attacked Portuguese strongholds even as his emissaries continued attempts to negotiate a peace treaty with Luis Mendes de Vasconcelos.[66] Ngola Mbande said that he would agree to the terms of the treaty after the Portuguese released members of his family who had been imprisoned. In exchange, he promised to remain on friendly terms with the Portuguese, to return the Mbundus who had joined him, and to redeem other slaves.[67]

In four years of fighting, Luis Mendes de Vasconcelos had brought a total of 190 *sobas* directly under Portuguese control.[68] More than half of these men—109, to be precise—were subjugated during the campaigns led by Mendes de Vasconcelos's sons, and each of them was required to pay four slaves to the Portuguese king.[69] In addition, the governor imposed a tribute of one hundred slaves annually on Ngola Mbande and ordered the provincial lords and their *kijikos* to pay tribute and taxes as well.[70] Finally, Mendes de Vasconcelos attempted to install a new king in Ngola Mbande's place, a man by the name of Samba Atumba, who had taken the Christian name of Antonio Carreira.[71] The population refused to recognize Atumba, however.

Even as Ngola Mbande was negotiating the release of his wife, mother, sisters, and the other prisoners in 1621, he was making an alliance with the Imbangala leader Kasanje, who himself had forged an alliance with another Imbangala leader, Donga.[72] Both leaders had formerly been on the Portuguese side but had become disaffected. Kasanje had crossed Mendes de Vasconcelos before; once an ally of the governor, he had taken off with Portuguese booty as well as a large number of *kijikos* and thousands of free Mbundus.[73] These new Imbangala alliances enhanced Ngola Mbande's status as an increasing number of Mbundus joined the resistance movement. Ngola Mbande further deepened his connection with the Imbangalas by turning over his son and heir to the Imbangala leader Kasa for military training. Ngola Mbande continued to present a major stumbling block to further Portuguese military and economic penetration of Ndongo.[74]

Although Ngola Mbande remained a threat, the Portuguese had made major gains. The campaigns carried out by Luis Mendes de Vasconcelos and his sons had brought a Portuguese military and administrative presence into the core regions of Ndongo for the first time. In December 1620, as part of the Jesuits' beatification ceremony of Saint Francis Xavier in Luanda, Governor Mendes de Vasconcelos put on a spectacle to remind everyone of his military victory over Ngola Mbande and the Mbundu. The ceremony included songs, poems, and skits, including one that featured a dwarf who had been captured in the wars against Ndongo. The dwarf, dressed in "a tunic of scarlet velvet, white shoes and rainbow beret," played the buffoon to the delight of the Portuguese onlookers.[75] It is not difficult to imagine how humiliating this and other such spectacles of African subservience must have been to the thousands of Mbundus who witnessed or heard about them.

Portugal's booming slave trade, which depended on the conquest, kidnapping, and commodification of the Mbundu population, must have been an even more potent source of shame and humiliation for Ngola Mbande's people. During the four years of Mendes de Vasconcelos's governorship, more than fifty-five thousand Mbundus had been captured and sent as slaves to the Americas. In addition, Portuguese authorities had transferred hundreds of thousands of *kijikos* to Portuguese settlers to use as slaves on their expanding plantations in the fertile regions along the

Lucala and Bengo Rivers near Luanda and in the villages around their forts. Thousands of other Mbundus had been captured by the Imbangalas, who had laid waste to large swaths of territory. Refugees from these wars sometimes joined the Imbangala raiders, creating even greater chaos.[76]

Seeing no military option for restoring his kingdom, Ngola Mbande turned again to diplomacy, as many of his predecessors had done. The hurdles he had to overcome were formidable. He not only had to persuade the Portuguese to end their campaigns against him and remove the fort at Ambaca, but he also had to reassert control over the parts of Ndongo that were still independent and regain access to the lands and *kijikos* that the Portuguese had taken.

Njinga Spreads Her Wings

The moment for negotiations came when a new governor, João Correia de Sousa, replaced Luis Mendes de Vasconcelos in October 1621. As soon as Ngola Mbande learned of the new governor's arrival in Luanda, he decided to nominate his estranged sister Njinga to head a delegation to negotiate the peace. For several years, Njinga had been living in the kingdom of Matamba, east of Ndongo. Although he was aware that Njinga had never forgiven him for murdering her son and ordering the sterilization of herself and her sisters, Ngola Mbande knew that she harbored political ambitions, had a loyal following among some important factions in Ndongo, and, like him, was intent on rebuilding Ndongo and limiting further Portuguese advance. Njinga, too, was playing a political game with her brother, knowing that acceptance of this assignment would enhance her own status among the Ndongo leadership.[77]

Ngola Mbande spared no expense in putting together an impressive delegation. Njinga and her party left Kabasa with a large military escort, musicians, slaves as gifts for the governor, and "a good many pages and waiting women" to look after Njinga's welfare. More important than even the "various privileges and kindnesses" with which Ngola Mbande showered Njinga before she left, he honored her with a new title, Ginga Bande Gambole: Njinga Mbande, official envoy.[78] She was now authorized to negotiate on Ngola Mbande's behalf. In addition, Ngola Mbande gave Njinga permission to undertake a public baptism—a crucial element of negotiations for the Portuguese—if she believed it would be to the advantage of Ndongo.[79]

Ngola Mbande could not have selected a better envoy. Njinga, the first member of the Ndongo royal family to visit Luanda, left for the city as head of what must have been the largest official central African delegation ever to travel through the regions of Ndongo conquered by the Portuguese. Indeed, her party's arrival at the entrance to the city became the primary topic of conversation among both the Mbundu population and the Portuguese. Portuguese records contain numerous accounts of her arrival, but Njinga left her own account as well, which survived in folk memory centuries after many official records were lost.

The grand treatment accorded to Njinga and her party by Governor Correia de Sousa indicates that the Portuguese regarded Ngola Mbande as the major African power in the region. A Portuguese military escort accompanied the delegation into the main square of Luanda, where they were welcomed by the entire administrative, business, and religious elite of city. The delegation received an elaborate military salute that included volleys of artillery and musket fire, and they were serenaded with music played on both European and Mbundu instruments.[80] Perhaps most significantly, the Portuguese government housed the group and paid all of their expenses.[81]

In her first official audience with the governor and his council, Njinga promised that Ngola Mbande would live in peace with the colonists, return slaves the Portuguese claimed were theirs but who had fled to his ranks, and cease military attacks. She explained her brother's aggressive actions against the Portuguese as youthful indiscretions. Finally, Njinga pledged that her brother would embrace any ally of the Portuguese. Both powers, she insisted, would support each other in the fight against common enemies.[82]

Njinga held out against one of the Portuguese demands, adamantly refusing to allow her brother to pay annual tribute in slaves to the Portuguese king. Other conquered provincial rulers had done so, but Ngola Mbande would not. Tribute, she argued, could only be imposed on someone who had been conquered. Njinga reminded her audience that Ngola Mbande had not been conquered; he was a sovereign king who had voluntarily sought friendship with another sovereign, and agreeing to pay tribute was tantamount to becoming a slave. "He who is born free," Njinga was reported as saying, "should maintain himself in freedom, and not submit to others. . . . [B]y paying tribute her king . . . would become [a] slave instead of free."[83] When the governor and his council continued to question Ngola Mbande's commitment to peace, Njinga deployed the last weapon she had in her arsenal:

Njinga's baptism in 1622, by Antonio Cavazzi, ca. 1668

she offered to study the catechism and other elements of Christianity and to become baptized. At forty years old, Njinga participated in a lavish public baptism in the mother church in Luanda (an event that we will hear about in more detail in Chapter 3).[84] By the time Njinga left Luanda, she had secured the governor's assurances of a treaty between the Portuguese and Ndongo.

Njinga made her triumphant return to Kabasa in the fall of 1622. Ngola Mbande publicly celebrated his sister's accomplishments, but this jubilation wouldn't last long. At the same time that negotiations with the Portuguese were entering a new phase, thanks to Njinga, the Ndongo alliance with the Imbangala Kasanje, which had elevated Ngola Mbande's standing among his people, broke down, and the king and his relatives, Njinga among them, were forced to flee the capital. Once again they found themselves in the royal hideout on the Kindonga Islands in the Kwanza River. The Portuguese were eager to continue negotiations, however, and did not let location stand in their way; sometime before December 1623, a priest, Dionisio de Faria Baretto, traveled to the islands to work out the terms Njinga had negotiated. Peace now hinged on Ngola Mbande's conversion to Christianity and subsequent return to Kabasa. The Portuguese promised that once these conditions were met, they would expel Kasanje and his guerrillas from the region, restore the *kijikos* and *sobas* that Mendes de Vasconcelos had taken, and relocate the fort at Ambaca farther east.[85]

Ngola Mbande agreed to the terms and began the process for baptism, learning the catechism from Father de Faria Baretto and even agreeing to give up his many concubines and some Mbundu religious customs. He also returned to Kabasa and appeared to be ready to cement the new relationship with the Portuguese.[86] Security returned to Ndongo for a time, and one optimistic official report stated that "the king of Angola has once again been *reducido* [reduced] to our friendship and already the slave markets [*feiras*] are functioning well."[87]

The word *reduced* is telling. Apparently Njinga, for her own political motives, capitalized on the dismissive attitude of the Portuguese that such language reveals and began to pressure her brother not to undergo the Christian baptism he had agreed to. It would be an affront to Mbundu tradition, she said, which prohibited the king from bowing his head in front of an inferior. And because Father de Faria Baretto was not a white Portuguese but rather a mulatto with Mbundu roots, Njinga and Ngola Mbande not only considered him an inferior; they considered him their slave. While continuing to assert that he was prepared to be baptized, Ngola Mbande, under pressure from Njinga, came to believe that the political costs of baptism outweighed the benefits.[88] By accepting baptism in the requisite public ceremony, Ngola Mbande would risk the disaffection of many of his Mbundu supporters, who admired him precisely for his willingness to resist the Portuguese.

In addition, Ngola Mbande harbored an unshakable distrust of the Portuguese, whom he blamed for depriving his father and himself of their lands and people. Considering what was going on in the region around Ndongo, his distrust was well founded. In 1623, the governor had tricked a number of *sobas* from a nearby region into appearing in Luanda to formally submit to the Portuguese king. When they did so, he kidnapped them along with additional commoners—1,211 people in all—and sent them as slaves to Brazil. He distributed the prime lands the group had occupied to Portuguese soldiers.[89] It is likely that news of this deception had reached Ngola Mbande.

For Ngola Mbande, the crisis was both personal and political. He came to rely more and more heavily on Njinga and would make no decision without her input. Still vacillating about whether to undergo baptism, the king sent Njinga and their two sisters to Luanda to obtain a commitment from the governor to honor the terms of the earlier treaty. Of critical importance to Ngola Mbande was that his sisters press the governor to follow through on the promise to send troops to dislodge Kasanje and his guerrillas, who continued to brutalize Ndongo.[90] Kambu and Funji were baptized during that visit, but the Portuguese delayed confirming the terms of the treaty. Terribly suspicious, Ngola Mbande sent yet another group of emissaries to make his case before Bishop Simão de Mascarenhas, a new governor who took office in August 1623.

Ngola Mbande realized that the Portuguese governors and officials in Luanda had no intention of keeping their side of the agreement. The government did indeed send troops against Kasanje, but instead of traveling by way of the Lucala River, as Ngola Mbande had requested, the commander led his troops overland to the fort in Ambaca—the very fort the Portuguese had agreed to relocate as one of the terms of the treaty.[91]

Ngola Mbande's response was decisive: he adamantly refused to be baptized. He then entered into a deep depression, similar to the one his father, Mbande a Ngola, had experienced following the Portuguese victories in Museke.[92] Proud and defiant to the end, Ngola Mbande rejected the ministrations of Father de Faria Baretto, turning on him and forcing him to flee. Instead, he relied on the treatment of Mbundu religious practitioners, who called on the Mbundu high god to heal him.[93]

The treatment was not successful. In the spring of 1624, Ngola Mbande died shortly after ingesting poison that he either voluntarily consumed or, as some believed, his sister administered. António de Cadornega, the Portuguese soldier-turned-chronicler, wrote that Njinga "helped him to die with the aid of a poisoned drink."[94]

Ngola Mbande's death left a void that Njinga stepped in to fill immediately. Her ascension to power would initiate a new chapter in Mbundu history. Battling Portuguese aggression had devastated her father and brother, who had been unable to bring back Ndongo's former glory. Njinga, who inherited a kingdom that was just a shadow of what she had known in her youth, fearlessly picked up where her brother left off, energized by the prospect of rebuilding her ancestral land. Her love and respect for her predecessors and her hatred of the Portuguese became consuming passions, driving her for the rest of her life. For her entire reign, from 1624 to 1663, Njinga would work to reassert Ndongo hegemony and limit Portuguese power in the region, the goal she had expressed so eloquently for the first time in 1622 when she was dispatched to present her brother's case to Governor Correia de Sousa.

3

A DEFIANT QUEEN

Even before the death of her brother, Ngola Mbande, in the spring of 1624, Njinga had positioned herself to take over the leadership of Ndongo and govern it in a way that recalled the country of her youth. Her grandfather and father—Kasenda and Mbande a Ngola, respectively—had controlled a vast territory that covered a large portion of modern-day northern Angola, garnering respect from and instilling fear in their enemies and followers alike during the majority of their reigns. Their armies were powerful and massive. The two kings fielded hundreds of thousands of troops, but they also sought diplomatic relations with the Portuguese and neighboring allies when warranted. Their personal wealth came in part from the tribute sent to the court by numerous subordinate rulers across Ndongo, as well as from income earned through the labor of hundreds of thousands of serfs and slaves who farmed state lands. Kasenda and Mbande a Ngola supplemented this income with taxes they imposed on local markets in which their agents operated, trading for slaves and other goods. In addition, they controlled access to the routes to markets in regions east of Ndongo, beyond their territorial borders. Riches aside, much of Kasenda and Mbande a Ngola's position derived from the unique spiritual status Ndongo leaders were believed to possess. Njinga's grandfather and father held fast to Mbundu traditions despite the inroads Christianity had made in pockets of Ndongo's population. The *ngangas* conducted ritual services throughout the kingdom, reinforcing the leadership's status. That Njinga aspired to re-create the Ndongo of her childhood should come as no surprise. But after Ngola Mbande's death, she seemed to dream of surpassing the political and spiritual achievements of her predecessors.

Njinga's Youth and Military Education

Njinga stood out from the moment of her birth in 1582, according to stories that she and others furnished in later years to her biographers Giovanni Antonio Cavazzi and Antonio Gaeta, both of whom lived in her court. Surrounded by Ndongo priests and other attendants, she was born in the position we today call breech, her "face upturned" and, further, her umbilical cord was wrapped firmly around her neck. Mbundu beliefs held that a baby born in this so-called unnatural manner would not live a normal life, and that the manner of a person's birth predicted the character of the adult. Her father, alluding to her unusual birth, named his daughter Njinga, from the Kimbundu root *kujinga*, which means "to twist, to turn, to wrap."[1] Those present at her birth dutifully performed the many designated rituals pertaining to childbirth, among them washing the baby in the herbal solutions they believed were necessary to protect her. As the story goes, the onlookers stared at the newborn in "amazement and wonder" and, contemplating the life she was destined to lead, sighed, "mà mà, o aoè aoè" (Oh! My mother). Cavazzi explained that this was the usual expression of astonishment when remarkable events occurred. He interpreted its meaning as, "What an example of ferocity this child would be!" In any event, even when Njinga was in her seventies, her people still sang many songs in her honor, one of which had the refrain, "Oh! My mother, Oh! Oh!"[2]

During her childhood, say her chroniclers, Njinga exhibited an intellectual and physical prowess that distinguished her from other young people at court, including her own brother, and she forged a unique relationship with her father that continued into young adulthood. Her close relationship with her father seems to have been unusual for a girl—or, for that matter, for any child of a ruler. Rulers ran the risk of alienating relatives of their principal wife or concubines if they favored a particular offspring. Mbande a Ngola, however, flouted convention, openly preferring this daughter of his favorite concubine over his other children. It was widely believed that Njinga had received a special blessing, and this enhanced her standing at court.[3] Traditions passed all the way down to the present portray Njinga as doubly privileged because she had inherited royal status through her mother, member of a Mbundu royal lineage—the Mbundus are matrilineal—and she was also the daughter of a reigning king.[4]

What was Njinga's early life in court like? We know that Njinga's childhood was marked by repeated attacks from both external and internal enemies and by constant disruptions caused by the campaigns that were fought around Kabasa. No family, royal or otherwise, was unaffected: all men were expected to serve as soldiers, and all women were expected to contribute food and labor to the war effort. In fact, in the year of Njinga's birth, her grandfather, Kasenda, faced three successive devastating campaigns by Portuguese forces. In January of the following year, before Njinga's first birthday, her grandfather and the rest of the court were forced to flee Kabasa after hearing the sounds of Portuguese guns fired in the direction of the capital.

We know much about the many battles that went on during Njinga's first decade of life, but we can only imagine the impact this unrelenting violence and tremendous loss of life would have had on the young girl. Whether or not she hoped to prove that she warranted special attention from her father, throughout her childhood and into young adulthood Njinga eagerly learned the political, military, and ritual activities generally reserved for the sons of rulers. She was allowed to attend the numerous judicial, military, and other councils over which her father presided. She also became a serious student of the practices and customs of the court, which she learned from the venerable older women who served as her nurses and caretakers. Her contemporaries noted that throughout her life she was fastidious about respecting and observing the "laws, rites and customs of her ancestors."[5] Njinga was also renowned for outshining her brother Ngola Mbande and other children in the *ngola*'s household in her skill with the battle ax, the royal symbol of the Ndongo people. She boasted about her expertise even in her seventies, and her biographer Gaeta wrote that he was impressed with her knowledge of the art of military dancing and her ability to wield the ax.[6] Despite her military expertise, as a young woman Njinga did not neglect her appearance and her place as a privileged young woman in the court. A painting by Cavazzi, depicting her as a woman of forty in audience with Portuguese governor João Correia de Sousa in 1622, provides the only evidence we have of what she might have looked like (see illustration on p. 63).

While it is likely that Njinga's gender influenced her decision to become such a diligent student of ritual, she made clear through her actions that her gender did not preclude her from enjoying the same liberties as her male counterparts. In addition to having in her service a coterie of female attendants and slaves, she kept a large number of young male consorts (concubines), and she is reported to have had multiple lovers throughout her long life. Although none of them became her principal husband, when she was younger she led an active sexual life. Cavazzi reported that even as a septuagenarian, Njinga, like other Mbundus who followed the traditions, had "nine or ten cuts on her arm" that were still visible and had been made by her many lovers. The son that her brother murdered (or had murdered) only a few days after his birth was likely fathered by one of these lovers.[7]

Some members of the court apparently did not think that it was appropriate for Njinga to carry on in the same way as a man, however. According to Cavazzi, a male functionary who was scandalized by Njinga's many amorous affairs pointed out to her that her behavior brought disrespect upon her father's court. He paid dearly for the "crime" of offering unsolicited advice to a superior: Njinga had the outspoken man's son murdered before his eyes. Then she had him murdered as well.[8] Like her royal ancestors, Njinga followed the tradition of demanding absolute deference from subordinates.

At some point as a young adult, Njinga became a leader in the war effort. Unlike other women who accompanied the army into action, Njinga seems to have played some role in mobilizing resistance against the Portuguese.[9] It is difficult to reconstruct Njinga's military career before 1624, when she became the ruler of Ndongo. The first reference to her participation in military action comes from António de Cadornega's history of Angola. In his discussion of the campaigns of 1602–3, in which the Portuguese sent troops to suppress rebellious *sobas* in the province of Ilamba, he noted that the rebels had responded to "the voice of Queen Njinga their Lady, who always worked to build up in those whom we had conquered hatred encouraging them to make movements and alterations."[10] Njinga would have been nineteen or twenty years old at the time, and although there are no details recounting her battlefield experience, she could only have been effective if she herself had been actively engaged in the fighting.

She appears for the second time in the military record of a battle in the province of Museke, in which Cadornega describes a confederation of

Njinga's supporters joining her in the struggle against the Portuguese after they had succeeded in conquering much of Ndongo.[11] Cadornega also pointed out that during the last two years of her father's reign, in several Portuguese campaigns carried out from Kisama to Massangano, the people found ways to resist the colonial power, "induced and ordered by that cunning Queen our capital enemy who never tires of looking for ways to ruin us."[12]

Njinga probably gained her most extensive military experience during the disastrous wars her brother Ngola Mbande fought against João Mendes de Vasconcelos, the son of Governor Luis Mendes de Vasconcelos. Perhaps lacking faith in Ngola Mbande's ability to win the war against the Portuguese, Njinga had left the court to live in another part of the kingdom, most likely in eastern Ndongo, near Matamba.[13] From her remote headquarters, she seems to have led her own troops against the young Mendes de Vasconcelos in his campaigns against eastern Ndongo and Matamba. For many months, Cadornega wrote, João was unable to share any news of his progress with his father in Luanda because the "Queen of Angola Ginga" had blocked the route, preventing all communication. She also appears to have fought alongside two Imbangala leaders in 1620 after they broke with the Portuguese, for Cadornega tells us that João's troops fought "great battles" against Njinga and the Imbangalas.[14]

According to Cavazzi, she referred later in life to military experiences she had had before she became queen. She recalled that while she was in Luanda as her brother's envoy, even though she was "accustomed to battles," she had been both dazzled and intimidated by the display of military gunfire and the disciplined exercises the Portuguese army performed as part of her welcome.[15] After returning to Kabasa, she went back to the battlefield immediately. In fact, increasingly disappointed with her brother's running of the war, Njinga began to consolidate her own base of support among the Ndongo troops. It was around this time that she also encouraged some *sobas* to join her. Njinga's role in the resistance against the Portuguese, as well as the popularity she gained among important segments of Ndongo's population, proved invaluable after her brother's death.[16]

In addition to honing her skills as a military leader, Njinga capitalized on other opportunities during the disastrous years of Ngola Mbande's short reign to promote herself as a viable alternative to her brother. In an arrogant letter that Ngola Mbande received from Governor Correia de Sousa sometime after Njinga's return to Kabasa, he was ordered to convert, among other demands. It's impossible to know whether Njinga took greater umbrage at the request itself or at the fact that the letter's format defied etiquette, but one thing she made clear: had she been ruler, she would have handled the situation much differently. She insulted her brother's masculinity. If he could act neither as a king nor as a man, Njinga needled, he should retire to a small farm, and work it himself. She hurled these and "other injurious words [at which] the king her brother became very emotional and thought of ways of protecting his diminished sovereignty and fearing the audacity of a woman who was still his sister."[17]

As Ngola Mbande contemplated his decision to make peace with the Portuguese by agreeing to a public baptism, his sister's merciless taunting took its toll. It was widely believed that Ngola Mbande's depression at the end of his life was brought on by Njinga's actions and her constant undermining of his authority.[18]

Early Diplomacy

Njinga's gender, her regal bearing, and her pride in Mbundu traditions all coalesced to make her a political force even before she took over the kingdom. Heading the delegation to Luanda in 1622 to negotiate with Governor João Correia de Sousa presented her with one such opportunity to do so. Let us now look in more depth at that event than we did in the previous chapter, using the detailed reports left by a number of eyewitnesses and chroniclers to paint a picture of Njinga on the threshold of her reign.

From the moment she received her assignment from Ngola Mbande, Njinga seized the opportunity to contrast herself with him. The king, at her request, provided her with a large entourage to accompany her on the two-hundred-mile journey from Kabasa to Luanda. Mbundus living in the regions of Ndongo that Njinga's entourage passed through would have seen or heard of an arresting scene: a large number of attendants of both sexes catering to Njinga; strong male slaves carrying the "Lady of Angola" on their shoulders; other slaves transporting the numerous gifts Njinga had insisted on bringing for the officials she would be meeting. Her consummate performance, however, was in the negotiating room with the governor and his advisers, where her royal demeanor and legal arguments would become legendary.

While in Luanda, Njinga refused to wear Portuguese clothing, instead strategically choosing to highlight Mbundu fashion. She knew that the Portuguese would defer to royal deportment and etiquette, and she made a vivid impression on the officials when she appeared majestically in the doorway. During the meeting Njinga wore "numerous cloths," and her arms and legs were covered with "priceless jewels." Moreover, Njinga wore in her hair "colored feathers." Njinga's ladies-in-waiting and female slaves dressed in a similar manner.[19] Later in life when she had access to European imports, Njinga expanded her wardrobe to include "silk drapes, velvets, brocades," and a variety of "scents and perfumes" that she used to enhance her appearance even into her sixties and seventies.[20] Njinga's dramatic entrance trained the spotlight entirely on her; although she was Ngola Mbande's official envoy, she had placed herself at center stage in the negotiations of weighty political and economic issues she had come to undertake with the Portuguese.

But her performance did not end there. Njinga knew that Portuguese officials had a way to humiliate defeated Mbundu leaders: while the governor sat on "a chair covered with velvet embroidered with gold," servants would arrange seating for the Mbundu visitors by spreading velvet covers on a carpet on the floor. The arrangement forced those having an audience with the governor to display their subordinate status—a status the Portuguese reserved for conquered Africans. Njinga, however, refused to lower herself. Without pause, she signaled haughtily to a female attendant, who immediately dropped to all fours and assumed the position of a human chair. She remained that way throughout the long hours of the discussion.[21] Upon escorting Njinga from the negotiation room, Governor Correia de Sousa pointed out that the young attendant was still on her hands and knees on the floor. Njinga dismissed the governor's concerns: she had not forgotten the attendant at all, she explained; she had left her there deliberately. An envoy of her status who represented a kingdom such as hers should never have to sit on the same chair twice—after all, she remarked, she had many others just like it.[22] Indeed, Njinga not only achieved the political ends that her brother expected but also gained some political leverage for herself. At her departure, the governor promised privately that the Portuguese would maintain mutual friendship with the region of Matamba, where Njinga had consolidated her own power.[23]

LIBRO QVINTO. 605

che quefta pretenfione poteuafi efigere da gente foggiogata, mà non
già proporre à coloro, i quali volontariamente efibifcono fcambieuole
amicizia, fi contentarono di non aftringerla à quefto punto, affodando
folamente la reftituzione de' Schiaui Portoghefi, e la vicendeuole affi-
ftenza contro i nemici dell'vna, e dell'altra Nazione. Terminati i dif-
corfi, mentre il Gouernatore le ftaua del pari, accompagnandola (come à Principeffa fi conueniua) gentilmente auuifolla, che l'accennata
Damigella non per anche moueuafi dal fuo pofto, che perciò le piacef-
fe di permetterle il leuarfi da quella ftrauagante foggezione: mà ella,
che con arte haueua vfato quel tiro, rifpofe à quefta vfficiofa iftanza,
con dire, che lafciaua colà quella fua Seruente, non già per inauerten-
za, mà perche all'Ambafciatrice del fuo Rè farebbe ftato difdiceuole
affettarfi la feconda volta, doue fedette la prima; e che non effendo per
mancarle in altre occorrenze fomiglieuoli Sedie, perciò non ne teneua
conto, nè voleua più riconofcerla per fua. Frà tanto, conuenendo à
Zingha trattenerfi in Loanda, il Sofa, che verfo di lei haueua concepu-
ta molta ftima, e la rauuifaua per vn Soggetto capace di apprendere gli
argomenti della Cattolica Religione, più volte gli ne toccò i punti
principali, e quando la vide inclinata, ò curiofa di afcoltarne le Dot-
trine, procurò, che da graui Perfone le fofero efattamente dichiarate.
Laonde fentendofi, mediante lo fuelamento de' profondi Mifteri tocca-
to il Cuore dalla mano di Dio mifericordiofo, abbracciò la noftra Santa
Fede: e lo fteffo Anno 1622. quarantefimo di fua età, effendo con
solen-

Il Sofa' le manda Perfone, che le parlino del la Cattolica Fede.

Njinga using a servant as a chair during her meeting with Governor João Correia de
Sousa in 1622, from Giovanni Antonio Cavazzi da Montecuccolo, *Istorica Descrizione
de' tre' regni Congo, Matamba et Angola* (Bologna: Giacomo Monti, 1687)

Njinga later expressed appreciation for the gracious way the Portuguese treated her during her time in Luanda. She recalled the banquet the governor held in her honor as an occasion of "festivity and gaiety . . . and splendor." She made herself available to all the high-status officials in Luanda who called on her and exchanged gifts with her visitors. She exhibited profound interest and engagement with her hostess, Ana da Silva, wife of the judge with whom she and her delegation were staying. Later, Njinga confessed that during those months in Luanda, she experienced "a profound happiness and an extraordinary peace."[24]

Njinga's skillful negotiations ensured the delegation's success; however, it was the combination of her defiant display of pride in the traditions and culture of Ndongo, her adroit use of her gender, and her political sagacity that laid the foundation for her later career as a Mbundu nationalist. If she had dreamed of the day when she could avenge herself and her sisters for their brother's cruel mistreatment, she had now been able to do so on the very public stage where she represented him. Her success in Luanda contrasted dramatically with her brother's ineffective leadership. Njinga had made clear to the Portuguese and Mbundus alike that she would use both her gender and the power that came with her royal status to take charge of Ndongo politics and lead the kingdom back to the greatness her brother had so far failed to achieve.

The Consolidation of Power

Following her return from Luanda, Njinga had essentially become the de facto leader of Ndongo. Indeed, Ngola Mbande had already indicated that she should rule after his death, leaving "the little that he had" to her.[25] Njinga had to consolidate her position as ruler, however, and soon after her brother died, she had partisans at her court in the Kindonga Islands, in the Kwanza River, confirm her as ruler by the customary election. At that time she also took possession of all the ritual objects and symbols associated with Ndongo royalty, an essential act that validated her power. Some of the details of this transition period are uncertain. Njinga may have traveled from one of the islands, called Danji, to the court at Kabasa. What is known is that by 1625, she had enlarged her court at Danji and brought more people from Kabasa and other regions to occupy several of the islands, some of which she fortified. As one chronicler noted, the islands had become "the pride of the Kwanza [River]" within a very short time.[26] It is unclear whether Njinga received the title Queen of Angola (Ngola Kiluanje) at this time—as Cavazzi wrote, based on interviews with Njinga and her courtiers several decades later—or whether the electors only addressed her as "Lady of Angola"—as the newly appointed Portuguese governor Fernão de Sousa reported in his official letter of August 15, 1624, a few months after her nomination.[27] Whatever her official title at the time, Njinga may also have had her chief male concubine, Kia Ituxi, given the title of king.[28]

Once elected, Njinga had to consolidate her control.[29] She led her partisans in a campaign to eliminate anyone in the court (including members of her own family) who refused to accept her as ruler. Her brother had earlier turned over her seven-year-old nephew—his son, the legitimate inheritor to the throne—to the Imbangala Kasa for safekeeping and training as a soldier, and a major goal of Njinga's campaign was to get the child back. At that time, Kasa's *kilombo* (war camp) was in the region of Kina, not far from Njinga's base. By September 1625, Njinga had gotten rid of her concubine and approached Kasa. She reportedly used her wiles and wealth to persuade him that she was passionately in love with him, displaying her affection publicly and showering him with gifts. At first Kasa resisted, disturbed that Njinga was older than he was, and convinced that she wanted to marry him only to get her hands on the boy. Eventually, however, he agreed to a union and to surrender the boy.[30] The wedding was held somewhere not in the Kindonga Islands but farther inland in the vicinity of Matamba, where Njinga had one of her headquarters. Her young nephew accompanied Kasa to the site. The ceremony wasn't even over before Njinga seized the little boy, murdered him, and "threw his body in the Kwanza River and declared that she had revenged her son." Njinga also killed many of her other relatives who were in attendance. Although her actions led some of her supporters to flee, many of the Mbundu people stayed loyal. They regarded Njinga as the legitimate ruler of Ndongo, and her murderous acts did not change their view.[31]

The next step in Njinga's plan was to return to Kabasa to reoccupy the traditional capital and reassert royal rule over the parts of Ndongo that the Portuguese, under Luis Mendes de Vasconcelos, had taken over during her brother's reign. Throughout this period of consolidating her position, Njinga sent frequent emissaries with letters to Governor Fernão de Sousa, seeking a resolution to the situation with the Portuguese authorities. In August 1624 she reminded him of an agreement his predecessors had made with Ngola Mbande that once the Portuguese removed the fort from Ambaca and returned the *kijikos* and *sobas* taken from Ndongo by Mendes de Vasconcelos, she would immediately leave the islands and return to Kabasa. Under the terms of the agreement, she would then reopen the markets in Kisala, where they had been traditionally located; her own people would go to the markets with slaves—a condition to which she and her councilors had already agreed—and the people would begin to farm again. Njinga also spelled out details concerning the role the Jesuit missionaries would play in Ndongo.[32]

Njinga's version of events jibed with the official documentation that Fernão de Sousa examined. His predecessors had concluded that the wars waged by Mendes de Vasconcelos against Ndongo had been unjust; they had recommended that the fort at Ambaca be moved and the *kijikos* returned. Fernão de Sousa advised the Portuguese king that finalizing the resolution with Njinga would be beneficial not only to Angola but to the coffers of the king: having the roads and markets reopened, de Sousa wrote, would be "very important to the treasury of your majesty as well as to this kingdom which lacks slaves."[33]

The governor himself, in his first official report to the king on the status of the colony, had described Angola as being in a "miserable state." But de Sousa had no intention of allowing Ndongo to be rebuilt under the leadership of this ambitious Mbundu woman—and, like his predecessors, he refused to honor the terms of the agreement to the letter. He demanded that Njinga return to the Portuguese the *kimbares* (Mbundu soldiers serving under Portuguese officers) and slaves who had fled to join her before he could make any decision about the *kijikos'* return. He also demanded that she become a vassal of the Portuguese king "in her own name and in the name of all her successors to the Ndongo kingdom" and "pay a small tribute."[34]

By early fall 1624, when Njinga received de Sousa's response, the economic and political situation around Luanda had deteriorated, and at least some of the terms of the agreement had been violated already. Njinga knew that the governor had sent Portuguese officials to Ndongo and neighboring areas to reopen the slave markets and provision centers and that new officials had been appointed to oversee them, something she had intended to do herself, with her own people. Furthermore, these officials were attempting to recruit *sobas* to the Portuguese cause by offering to remain on peaceful terms with them and encouraging them to become allies.[35] By July 1626, de Sousa recorded that in addition to the 109 *sobas* who were already vassals of the Portuguese king, he had added 83 more.[36]

Each of these *sobas* participated—either willingly or by force—in the degrading ceremony of vassalage called *undamento*. Every aspect of *undamento* was designed to strip the *soba* of his dignity. The *soba* would appear at the fort to stand humbly before the governor or another official, who explained to him his duties and obligations as a vassal of the king: payment of tribute in slaves and provisions not only from him and his descendants, but from his councilors as well.[37] Immediately thereafter, the official threw flour over the *soba*'s hands and shoulders. Then, to signify his new status, the *soba* fell to the ground in front of the official and agreed to the obligations that would pass from him to his descendants. The *soba*'s name was inscribed in a book, and at the end of the ceremony, he placed his mark next to it. From beginning to end, it was a humiliating spectacle, and many of the *sobas* who underwent the ceremony never understood that they had agreed to pay tribute in perpetuity.[38]

By pressuring provincial leaders to become vassals, the Portuguese unwittingly bolstered Njinga's support. She became emboldened as an increasing number of Mbundus refused to pay tribute and looked to her for leadership. She refused to comply with Fernão de Sousa's demand that she herself pay tribute; she did not consider herself a vassal of the Portuguese king. By December 1624, a large number of slaves owned by the Portuguese, as well as many *sobas* who had become vassals, had fled the Portuguese area and joined Njinga's ranks.

Through her many officials who traveled between the Kindonga Islands and Luanda, Njinga kept in direct contact with both Portuguese officials and the Mbundu people. In Luanda, for example, one of her spokesmen informed the governor that she could not return the slaves who had fled to her—because she had none, she claimed. Fernão de Sousa dispatched his representatives to send messages to Njinga as well, warning her that if she failed to return the *kimbares* and slaves now aligned with her army, he would "end all contact with her and . . . she should not send any more messages."[39] To reach the larger Mbundu population living in the Portuguese-controlled area, Njinga employed her messengers (*makunzes*) to deliver a message at odds with the Portuguese demands. In the vicinity of Portuguese farms and forts, these *makunzes* relayed Njinga's instructions to the slaves and *kimbares* who were still fighting on the side of the Portuguese, urging them to abandon the Portuguese and join Njinga's cause. Her network was extremely effective and instigated many large-scale slave flights during the early months of 1625: whole villages fled Portuguese farms, and contingents of Mbundu *kimbares* absconded from their ranks. In a letter dated March 19, 1625, de Sousa expressed concern over the state of affairs and advised the king of Portugal that Njinga was persuading more and more Mbundus to leave the Portuguese and join her cause with promises that "she would give them land where they could till and live" and that they "were better off being masters of their native land than our captives."[40] Njinga had impressed the Mbundu people in ways that Ngola Mbande never had; her 1622 performance in Luanda was no doubt still alive in their minds, whether they had seen her themselves or merely heard tell about it. The Mbundu masses rallied around Njinga's cause, which she had expressed so passionately in her negotiations three years earlier. By the beginning of the summer of 1625, Njinga had recruited so many Mbundus that none of de Sousa's emissaries could persuade her to hand over the slaves who had joined her. Instead, Njinga simply continued to claim that she had been misunderstood and that she had no such slaves.[41]

Njinga's position in 1625 represented a turning point in the Ndongo-Portuguese relationship. From 1575 to 1624, the Portuguese had maintained the upper hand in their relations with Ndongo. During the fifty years since Paulo Dias de Novais began the conquest of Ndongo, the Portuguese, with the help of their Imbangala allies, had conquered or claimed lands whose rulers had formerly sent tribute to Ndongo kings. Additionally, Portuguese-led armies had killed or co-opted thousands of local officials and turned hundreds of thousands of free villagers and other dependent groups into outright slaves, either forced to work on Portuguese-owned plantations or sold into the Atlantic slave trade. The Portuguese had also turned tens of thousands of Ndongo subjects into *kimbares* who were forced to serve as soldiers fighting against Ndongo itself.

Njinga seems to have created the conditions for the first popular Mbundu uprising against Portuguese exploitation. She attracted to her cause Mbundu *sobas* who had become part of Portuguese Angola, including 109 *sobas* in the province of Hari who had become allies of the Portuguese during Luis Mendes de Vasconcelos's governorship but now refused to send tribute to Fernão de Sousa.[42] Many Mbundus supported Njinga because they wanted to see their land led by a ruler who was a descendant of the ancient kings rather than a puppet of the Portuguese. The uprising had been successful. De Sousa wrote in 1626 that he couldn't collect the tribute he had counted on because "of the war and the uprising of Dona Ana [Njinga] and because many of the *sobas* of his majesty have gone over to her side."[43]

Njinga had thus created a political and military climate among the Mbundu that for the first time threatened the very foundations on which Portuguese economic and political strength in Angola rested. De Sousa summed up the situation succinctly in a letter of August 1625 to the king, noting that he was particularly concerned about the "armed slaves" who were joining Njinga's ranks. The organized slaves, he feared, would "empower her and weaken this kingdom" and inspire the "*sobas* who are enemies conquered by force" to join her as well. The uprising, he warned, would ruin Luanda because "entire villages were fleeing"; in fact, some Portuguese had already lost "one hundred and fifty slaves" who fled together.[44]

Rivalries for Power

Faced with continued resistance from Njinga, Fernão de Sousa and his cabinet decided to install their own, hand-picked candidate as the successor to the Ndongo throne, while at the same time branding Njinga a usurper and sending troops to oust her and her relatives and supporters from their base in the Kindonga Islands. De Sousa informed the Portuguese king that he had deliberately selected a *soba* named Hari a Kiluanje, whom he knew to be both an enemy of Njinga and a close relative, to place on the throne. Hari a Kiluanje was a descendant of Ngola Kiluanje kia Samba, whose lineage had lost out to Njinga's grandfather Kasenda. The two lineages had never resolved their differences, and during Ngola Mbande's reign, members of this competing lineage had become close allies of the Portuguese. Njinga's election as ruler had been an affront to the members of this lineage, who believed that they were rightful heirs to the throne, and tensions resurfaced, especially as her popularity and audacity grew. Her assertion of authority over the *sobas* whom Luis Mendes de Vasconcelos had conquered was particularly vexing. Several members of this lineage would figure prominently in the war against Njinga.[45] Sometime in the summer of 1625, Njinga moved against one of the older relatives from this rival lineage, who, although her uncle, had refused to accept Njinga's election. While he was making his way to the fort at Massangano with many of his people to have his eldest son baptized, Njinga tracked him down, beheaded him, and captured most of his people. His son managed to escape with a few followers and ended up in Luanda, where he was brought up by the Jesuits.[46]

Njinga's greatest rival within this competing lineage would be Ngola Hari, a half brother of Hari a Kiluanje. Rulers of lands called Hari, located in the naturally fortified region of Pungo Ndongo, both Hari a Kiluanje and Ngola Hari had under their authority many *sobas* who had become allied with Mendes de Vasconcelos.[47] During João Correia de Sousa's governorship, Hari a Kiluanje had become a "vassal of the king our Lord," and Governor Fernão de Sousa considered him the legitimate inheritor of the Ndongo kingdom. Sometime in mid-1625, the Portuguese identified Hari a Kiluanje as the king of Ndongo.[48] What Fernão de Sousa did not acknowledge, however, was that Ndongo court advisers and the population at large questioned the status of Hari a Kiluanje and Ngola Hari, since both were descended from lineages that were not considered eligible to rule.[49] Perhaps because of his murky background, Hari a Kiluanje was fearful of Njinga, and in August 1625 he left Pungo Ndongo and traveled to the fort at Ambaca to request a military bodyguard and troops. Although Fernão de Sousa was in negotiations with Njinga at the time, he promised to honor Hari a Kiluanje's requests and to launch a military campaign against Njinga. This campaign involved forcing *sobas* who supported Njinga to comply with their obligations to send tribute in slaves and provisions and to allow Portuguese troops to pass through their territories. He also wanted these *sobas* to move against others who supported Njinga.[50] In December 1625, Hari a Kiluanje went to the fort at Ambaca and was given a small military contingent to lead him back to his lands.[51]

Once Njinga discovered that the Portuguese had provided Hari a Kiluanje with troops, she commanded her own forces to attack his lands. At the same time, she dispatched officials to Luanda to meet with de Sousa to press her claims against Hari a Kiluanje. She complained that Hari a Kiluanje had stopped her people from traveling to a slave market near his lands and had confiscated the forty-eight slaves she had sent to the market.

The governor dismissed the complaint and instead sent thirty-four Portuguese soldiers, along with several African archers and *kimbares,* to defend Hari a Kiluanje. When the reinforcements arrived, they fought Njinga's forces. In spite of suffering numerous casualties and having some of their officials captured, her forces managed to kill three Portuguese, including the captain, and capture six soldiers, whom they took to Njinga.[52] The captured officials from Njinga's forces were sent to Luanda, where they confessed that Hari a Kiluanje had not taken Njinga's slaves after all, but that Njinga had waged war against him for "[going] to the fort without asking her permission and she considered this treason and a rebellion against her." Having gotten the information he wanted out of them, the governor put the captives on a slave ship and sent them off to Brazil to be sold into the slave trade.[53]

Stalling for Time

The rebellion that Njinga had stirred up among the Mbundu was still so widespread and successful in early 1626 that de Sousa and other Portuguese officials had to find a way to justify the full-scale war they were planning against her. They decided to focus on Njinga's gender as grounds for disqualification to the throne. Writing to the Portuguese king in February 1626, de Sousa declared Njinga an illegitimate ruler and argued that Hari a Kiluanje was the rightful ruler of Ndongo because "a woman had never governed this kingdom."[54] In a subsequent letter written two weeks later, de Sousa said that Njinga's war against the Portuguese threatened the colonial power's entire conquest because so many *sobas* were joining Njinga and taking Portuguese slaves with them to wage war "against us." Hari a Kiluanje was the legitimate ruler, claimed de Sousa, because he was an ally of the Portuguese.[55] Njinga dismissed such claims outright and proceeded to demonstrate to the Portuguese that her gender did not in any way hinder her from leading Ndongo. Her refusal to allow the Portuguese to delegitimize her right to rule would spur her on in her resistance.

Once Njinga learned that de Sousa and other officials in Luanda had voted to mount a "just war" against her, capture her, and proclaim Hari a Kiluanje as king of Ndongo, she sharpened her leadership style and surrounded herself with a group of devoted officials who protected her from capture. The two years she spent on the Kindonga Islands allowed her to orchestrate the general uprising from her base there, to communicate directly with her officials and the *sobas,* and to participate in military operations. And had she found herself in danger of being captured, the islands themselves provided her with a route to safety. Linked to Luanda by a road that passed through Pungo Ndongo, the islands were also connected to the nearby region of Dumbo a Pebo, home of Njinga's maternal relatives.[56] Indeed, Njinga was assured of safe passage through many regions because so many *sobas* resented de Sousa's policy of opening up markets and installing Portuguese overseers—a situation that forcibly integrated the *sobas* into the Portuguese commercial network, threatening their income and prestige while enhancing that of the Portuguese.[57]

Despite her rising popularity and successes against the Portuguese, Njinga realized that she was not yet prepared for all-out war. She turned to diplomacy as a delay tactic. Her emissaries promised de Sousa that peace would return to Ndongo under Njinga's leadership, and the slave markets would once again be teeming with slaves. When Portuguese forces arrived at the fort of Ambaca in February 1626, Njinga sent her top envoys to Luanda to lay out her position; they indicated that she was ready to accept missionaries and make peace. They also presented several questions to de Sousa: Why had the captain at Ambaca provided military assistance to Hari a Kiluanje, when he knew that Hari a Kiluanje was Njinga's *soba* and subject? And why had the captain at the fort treated her so poorly? The envoy made clear that he was speaking on behalf of Njinga by concluding that he had come to the city to "do for his lady as she had ordered him."[58]

Fernão de Sousa's response was not encouraging. He told the envoy that the choice was now up to Njinga: she could either "choose war or peace as she wished."[59] A few days later, Njinga made a second attempt at negotiations, sending her private spokesman (*moenho*) to Ambaca with a letter from the captured Portuguese soldiers to the military commander. The letter noted that although the prisoners had suffered the indignity of being taken to Njinga nude, she had immediately ordered them dressed, and from that point on they had been well treated and supplied with ample food every three days. The prisoners praised Njinga's officials for their humane treatment and fairness, speculating that if not for this special protection, they certainly would have been murdered. There would be a small price for ransoming them, the letter concluded: the governor would need to turn over to Njinga one of her *sobas* whom the Portuguese had captured, and deport

Hari a Kiluanje to the Americas or Portugal.[60] After the commander read the letter, the *moenho* verbally repeated each detail contained in it; this sort of oral communication was an integral part of Ndongo diplomacy. He dismissed Njinga's attempt at negotiations, telling the *moenho* that he had no time to seriously consider Njinga or her offer, and if she did not hand over the Portuguese captives, "he would send [his men] to look for them."[61]

Governor de Sousa recognized Njinga's move as a delaying tactic, meant to buy time either to secure reinforcements to defend the islands or to plan her escape. Captain Bento Banha Cardoso, the former governor who had forged an alliance with the Imbangalas against Njinga's father, Mbande a Ngola, was at the time on his way from the fort at Massangano to Ambaca, and de Sousa urged him to gather up all the neutral *sobas* among the military contingents and to make their way quickly to the islands. Cardoso complied, forcing many *sobas* to join the war against Njinga and beheading those who resisted.[62]

But this aggression did not deter Njinga from continuing her efforts for a negotiated settlement. On March 8, 1626, as Cardoso's troops were preparing to leave Cambambe, where they had stopped on the way to Ambaca after the roundups, Njinga's *makunzes* arrived with a long letter, written a few days earlier and addressed to the captain-general of the fort. Once again, she laid out her reasons for attacking Hari a Kiluanje: he had attacked her army and confiscated the slaves she had sent to comply with her duties as a vassal according to the agreement her brother had made with the Portuguese. In truth, she asserted, she had the right to attack Hari a Kiluanje because he was *her* vassal, and, indeed, Portuguese forces that she had welcomed in her lands had attacked her army. Although the presence of the Portuguese army in her lands concerned her, she had welcomed them nonetheless, since she regarded herself as a Christian and thus as a vassal of the king of Spain, whom she "recognize[d] and obey[ed] as a Christian that I am." Njinga did admit that her forces had captured six Portuguese soldiers. She also noted that she had received news of a large number of Portuguese troops gathered in Ambaca who were awaiting word to move against her and free the six captives, but she warned that nothing would be resolved by force, and such a move would be harmful to both herself and the prisoners. The letter ended on a threatening note: if there were settlers who had convinced the governor and the captain to launch a war so they could get out of debt—a reference to the slave trade—they were welcome to do so, but she herself wished Captain Bento Banha Cardoso no harm.[63]

As she would do in several other missives to Portuguese officials in the coming years, Njinga included a paragraph requesting a variety of personal items, among them a hammock, some wool, a cover for her horse, wine, wax for candles, muslin, lace tablecloths, a broad-brimmed hat made of blue velvet, and one hundred folios of paper (for official correspondence).[64] Njinga signed her baptismal name, Ana, but for the first time in writing she presented herself with the title "Queen of Dongo [Ndongo]." With this letter, and with the dueling signatures, she signaled both her willingness to be a Christian and her determination to assert her authority in Ndongo as the legitimate ruler.

Cardoso's response of March 15 dismissed Njinga's claim to be the legitimate ruler of Ndongo. The captain rebutted every assertion Njinga put forth about her rights and every accusation against the Portuguese, underscoring her own failure to comply with the promises she had made—particularly her baptismal vows—as the cause of the conflicts between herself and the Portuguese. He maintained that Njinga had refused to hand over the Portuguese *kimbares* and slaves who had fled to her ranks and that she had treated the Portuguese captured by her troops shabbily by not releasing them. Finally, he denied her the items she had requested. He could not deliver them to her, he wrote, because he was already on his way to bringing the war to her. Cardoso ended his letter with the dire warning, "God protect you if he can."[65]

Leadership and Spirituality

In Njinga's efforts to find a peaceful solution to her conflicts with the Portuguese during her first two years as ruler of Ndongo, she often underscored her willingness to live as a Christian, to give her officials permission to be baptized, and to allow missionaries to work in Ndongo. Although de Sousa and other officials never took these statements seriously, Njinga seems to have regarded spirituality as a vital part of her leadership style, and it informed her entire life. She expanded the role of indigenous beliefs and customs beyond what they had occupied during her grandfather's and father's reigns, and added to them a dedication to Christianity.

The first glimpse we have of Njinga's emphasis on spirituality comes after her successful negotiations on behalf of Ngola Mbande in Luanda, in 1622, when she agreed to prolong her stay for months so that she could be officially prepared for baptism. Given her commitment to Ndongo traditions, why did Njinga agree to be baptized? Many provincial lords and *sobas* in Ndongo, including members of her own lineage, had undergone elaborate public baptisms, and Njinga was well aware that religion was a core component of Portuguese politics. Although Ngola Mbande had allowed Njinga to decide for herself whether to be baptized, her agreement to do so probably had more to do with the role she envisioned spirituality playing in her own efforts to take over the leadership of Ndongo than it did with advancing her brother's political agenda. Njinga may also have calculated that by undergoing baptism, she would gain respect from the Portuguese and garner the support of the large numbers of Christian Mbundus who were either slaves in the city and plantations or had fled the wars and become refugees.[66]

Maybe this explains why Njinga threw herself so enthusiastically into her preparations for the ceremony, listening attentively to the governor explain the benefits of conversion and what she stood to gain by forsaking Mbundu rites and rituals. She readily complied when the church appointed a priest knowledgeable in Kimbundu to teach her the catechism; and on the appointed day, in the presence of "the nobility and people," she solemnly underwent the ceremony in the official church the Jesuits had built in Luanda. Governor João Correia de Sousa himself was her godfather, and Ana da Silva, her hostess, served as godmother. Njinga received the baptismal name Ana de Sousa in honor of both godparents.[67] Government and church officials showered her with gifts, among them religious icons suggestive of their hope that Njinga's baptism and return to Ndongo would ultimately lead to the conversion of Ngola Mbande and other members of the Ndongo ruling elite, who had so far thwarted the Jesuits' attempts to bring Christianity to the region.

Despite her baptism and her acceptance of the church's gifts, Njinga never rejected her own Mbundu religious beliefs, or the rituals that were so essential to Ndongo's ruling elite and ordinary villagers alike. Indeed, during her stay in Luanda, Njinga never once removed the several iron rings and relics that adorned her arms and legs.[68] But she also embraced her new religion, at least on the surface. On the first leg of her return journey to Kabasa, surrounded by the official entourage provided by the governor, Njinga proudly displayed the Christian icons she had been given, reassuring her escorts of her deep piety. The Portuguese detail remained with Njinga only as far as the outskirts of Luanda, and so did her pose. Soon after the Portuguese departed, Njinga removed the Christian symbols from her person and placed them for safe keeping in their reliquaries. According to a later account by the missionary Cavazzi, she performed various "heathen ceremonies" to safeguard her journey back to Kabasa and "put on her satanic relics used by those Ethiopians [Africans] and sold by their priests."[69] From 1622 to 1624, as Njinga maneuvered to present herself as a viable alternative to Ngola Mbande, she used her insider knowledge of Christianity to try to make inroads with Portuguese officials and also to frustrate her brother's efforts to use Christian conversion to advance his own political aims. In fact, decades later, Njinga would admit to Cavazzi that on several occasions during those two years, she had deliberately counseled Ngola Mbande against baptism. Njinga may have feared that Ngola Mbande's own baptism would jeopardize her hard-won special status.[70]

While advising Ngola Mbande to shun baptism, Njinga also promoted Mbundu spiritual beliefs, taking charge of the public ceremonies where local religious practitioners called on the ancestors, burned incense, performed human sacrifices, and participated in dances and other rituals.[71] Njinga's attempt to demonstrate her familiarity with Mbundu traditions began in earnest with her brother's death in 1624, when she organized an elaborate funeral for him in the Kindonga Islands that included the ritual sacrifice of a number of servants, who would accompany him to the land of the ancestors. Njinga also preserved some of her brother's remains; respectfully removing several bones from Mbande's corpse, she arranged them on handmade silver plates, covered them with rich carpet, and placed them in a portable reliquary chest (*misete*) similar to the ones that Ndongo religious practitioners carried. With this act Njinga made the *misete* the focal point of veneration that in time would be associated with rituals involving human sacrifice, lighted vessels, incense, and the like.[72] Njinga's practice of human sacrifice and the keeping and consulting of the bones of her ancestors would scandalize the European missionaries when they learned of it. Although the missionaries condemned both practices, the veneration of her brother's relics was not unlike the medieval Roman Catholic tradition of enshrining the remains of saints in monasteries, convents, and churches.

Njinga's letters to Governor de Sousa and other Portuguese officials during the two years of negotiations that preceded her ascension to the throne provide significant insight into the role religion would play during her reign. In her first letter to Governor de Sousa soon after he took up his post in Luanda in June 1624, Njinga noted that she wanted Jesuit missionaries to come to her lands to baptize those people who wished to become Christians.[73] In doing so, Njinga was presenting a vision for a Christian presence in Ndongo where she and her officials—and not the missionaries—would oversee its spread. Aware that members of her own lineage, allied with the Portuguese, were seeking baptism, Njinga did not wish to stop priests from coming to Ndongo, but instead she wanted to be the one who determined how those priests reached the population.

De Sousa ignored Njinga's request, however; the Portuguese had their own plans for setting up a formal religious presence in Ndongo. In fact, by June 1624, church correspondence had listed Ndongo as one of the locations where "the king of Angola resides" and which needed to have at least one residence that could accommodate six missionaries.[74]

Whether Njinga was aware of these plans or not, she did remember what had happened in Ambaca during her brother's reign. The governor at the time, Luis Mendes de Vasconcelos, had established a Portuguese brotherhood to oversee construction of a church called Our Lady of the Assumption in Ambaca, a short distance from the Ndongo capital of Kabasa. To fund the construction, he had forced several *sobas* in the region, including one of Njinga's relatives, Ngola Kanini, to send their tribute payments to the brotherhood instead of to Kabasa.[75] As the new ruler of Ndongo, Njinga wanted such initiatives to be under her control. Portuguese priests who accompanied the army, Njinga knew, had full authority over the religious life of the conquered population. The situation was complicated, however, by the fact that Njinga did not consider Ndongo a conquered area. Governor de Sousa made clear Njinga's concern in a letter he sent to the king of Spain in December 1624: "Dona Ana Lady of Angola is very much pressing me to keep the pledge that governor João Correia de

Sousa gave her to change the fortress of Ambaca, and [. . . that] soon she will move to the mainland, and will have priests from the Companhia [Jesuits] brought in, and will build churches."[76]

Every letter Njinga sent to Fernão de Sousa and Bento Banha Cardoso between 1625 and August 1626 made reference to the place she was making for Christianity and missionaries in Ndongo, as did the verbal messages her officials relayed.[77] Indeed, during that time, the *sobas* against whom she carried out attacks were often relatives of hers who had been baptized and who had become (or intended to become) Portuguese allies without her permission.

It is impossible to know whether Njinga would have collaborated with the missionaries (as she did several years later) if de Sousa had responded positively to her requests for a meeting with officials from the church. The fact was that Christian conversion was an integral part of Portuguese policy in Angola, and governors and other officials, including the Jesuits, continued to view the spread of Catholic Christianity under Portuguese control as a core element of their colonial project. Thus, from the beginning, every Portuguese governor in Angola had his doubts about Njinga's sincerity, whether in her own writings or when her messengers carried reports that she was ready to come back to the church. De Sousa himself brought this up in several letters to the king. In an extensive missive written in August 1625, he warned the king of Spain that he was skeptical about Njinga's request for missionaries and said that he believed she was acting more "out of fear than devotion." He proposed a safeguard: if the king were to send two missionaries to the fort at Ambaca, Njinga should first be required to give them some slaves, and only then would the missionaries proceed to Ndongo. If they went to Ndongo before Njinga handed over the slaves, de Sousa wrote, this "would be the reason to make war against her," and the missionaries should be held back.[78] Authorities in Lisbon, in receipt of many similarly dubious accounts, remained suspicious of Njinga as well.[79]

Members of the religious hierarchy in Luanda were no different from their predecessors, who had fully supported the Portuguese conquest of Ndongo's lands and the enslavement of the population during the reigns of Njinga's grandfather and father. When the governor and other officials presented the case for war against Njinga, the religious authorities were in full agreement. Writing in February 1626, Governor de Sousa noted that theologians with the College of Jesuits in Luanda agreed that the war was "necessary and just." As they had done in previous campaigns, the Jesuits covered the cost of two priests to accompany the army.[80] Religion and military might continued to be inextricably linked.

The Road to Guerrilla Warfare

The army that Fernão de Sousa assembled to fight Njinga and her troops consisted of the usual mix of Portuguese soldiers and Mbundu archers and *kimbares*. The troops left Luanda on February 7, 1626, under the leadership of former governor Bento Banha Cardoso, a seasoned commander in the wars against Ndongo. The Portuguese were seen off with the usual celebratory martial music and words of encouragement from de Sousa, who reminded them that their purpose was to fight "in the service of God, the king [of Spain] and the good of the Kingdom."[81] After the group arrived in Massangano, Cardoso received word from Governor de Sousa to head directly to Pungo Ndongo, and he arrived there on March 30. Pungo Ndongo became the base for Portuguese operations against Njinga because of its natural fortifications and its easy accessibility to the Kindonga Islands, where her forces were based. Throughout April, the two Portuguese commanders leading the military operations against Njinga, Cardoso and Sebastião Dias, attacked the powerful *sobas* in Museke, around the fort of Cambambe, and in Ndongo itself, and forced their submission. The conquered *sobas* were crucial to Portuguese success because they supplied them with much-needed provisions and led their troops into battle in the war against Njinga.[82]

Once the war began in the core regions of Ndongo, where Njinga enjoyed her greatest support, her primary tactical problem was to keep the lines of communication open with the *sobas* who still supported her. She knew that the Portuguese had posted spies who reported on movements along the route between the islands and the mainland. This hindrance to good communication was extremely detrimental and dangerous to Njinga, because Ndongo had become even more politically fragmented during her brother's reign, and Njinga knew she could not rely on the *sobas*' loyalty, even those who had been her core supporters. When the *soba* Ngola Ndala Xosa, for example, saw Cardoso bombard his stronghold and kill many of his people, he requested a pardon from the governor and explained that although during João Correia de Sousa's governorship he had obeyed Njinga, now his loyalty was to Hari a Kiluanje and the king of Portugal. In the future, he promised, he would do whatever the governor wanted him to do.[83]

The successful military campaigns of Sebastião Dias against the *sobas* along the Kwanza River spurred many of them to switch their allegiance from Njinga to the Portuguese.[84] The *sobas* of Museke and Kisama, in the past strong supporters of Njinga who had laid siege to the fortress at Ambaca, were among those defeated by the Portuguese before Njinga had implemented her overall military strategy.[85]

The tide had turned against Njinga, and she could no longer even rely on the unmitigated support of the people of Dumbo a Pebo, her mother's birthplace. The *soba* here, who had close relations with his now-defeated counterpart in Museke, had been among Njinga's most loyal supporters and had refused Cardoso's demand for military assistance. This *soba* had even captured some of the *kimbares* who were passing through his lands on their way to the Portuguese camp in Pungo Ndongo. In retaliation, Cardoso arrested the *soba* and some of the *makotas*, eventually sending a number of the captives to Luanda to be exported and sold into slavery in the Americas.[86]

Time was certainly not on Njinga's side. De Sousa pressed Cardoso during the last week of May of 1626 to get his troops to the island and "take it before she became stronger."[87] To prepare for the Portuguese attack, Njinga gathered many soldiers to protect herself and the supporters who had joined her. One such soldier, whom the Portuguese captured after he left the island, provided the only eyewitness account of Njinga's military preparations. He reported that she protected the islands by heavily fortifying them with trenches. On Danji, she had carved out an entrance in a great rock and dug well-camouflaged caves that served as natural hiding places. Around that island she had stationed the Mbundu soldiers, who were armed with the arquebuses and rifles they had brought with them when they fled the Portuguese army. She had also constructed defenses on other islands, where she stationed additional troops. Because Njinga did not have enough arms to face Cardoso's army and had not been able to mobilize forces on the mainland, she had stocked the islands with provisions, livestock, and people in preparation for a prolonged siege.[88] Despite some weaknesses, Njinga remained a dangerous enemy: she was popular with the Mbundus in Cardoso's army and might still persuade many of them to abandon him and join her. Cardoso had little means of maintaining the loyalty of the Mbundu fighters and others who had been forced to accompany the army; in purely practical terms, he was short on supplies, and Njinga had ample food and drink to win them over.

Her provisions might ensure her a large measure of popularity, but Njinga knew this wasn't enough; even if Cardoso's Mbundu fighters joined her, she still needed other allies. As she faced imminent invasion, she retained some indirect support from nearby rulers, who sent her supplies, but she lacked critical support from the Imbangala.[89] Although her estranged husband, Kasa, who had fought alongside her brother Ngola Mbande and whose base was still nearby, was now an enemy of the Portuguese, he failed to send aid to Njinga.

The military operations against Njinga began in the last week of May 1626 and ended in the last week of July. Cardoso and Dias's troops camped at the western edge of the region today called Baixa de Cassanje, and crossed over to the islands using canoes, fishing boats, and two vessels specially built for the campaign. Njinga had set up a coordinated system of defense. As the Portuguese boats approached the islands, soldiers (many of them *kimbares* who had deserted the Portuguese army) fired volleys from muskets and shot arrows from their positions on the islands. Njinga's troops were not taken by surprise because Njinga had devised an intricate system of communications among sentries stationed in guardhouses and naturally protected lookouts on each island who rang bells to warn of approaching troops.[90]

Njinga stationed most of her best troops on Mapolo Island, which Cardoso and Dias chose to capture first, since it served as the entryway to the others. Njinga's soldiers fought valiantly, using a range of Portuguese and African arms and techniques, including arquebuses, flintlocks, bows and arrows, spears, and fire-hardened logs. Because Njinga's soldiers were embedded inside trenches, the Portuguese had to capture each trench individually. Many of those Portuguese soldiers who were fortunate enough to escape death by drowning, gunshot wounds, or arrows met their demise or succumbed to injury instead from wounds received in the fighting to take over the trenches. Nevertheless, the Portuguese emerged victorious, having killed many of Njinga's bravest men, and were rewarded with provisions, cattle, and "all that was necessary for our famished troops."[91] The

Portuguese managed to capture many of the people on the island, but a good number fled.

Leaving a garrison on Mapolo, Cardoso then captured a second island, which was the headquarters of Njinga's *tendala* (chief administrative officer). This island was even better fortified than the first, and most of Njinga's best fighters were stationed here. As was the case in Mapolo, Njinga's troops suffered great losses and had to abandon the island when they were overwhelmed by Portuguese firepower. This island, too, offered ample provisions and a large population, even accounting for the many who drowned while trying to escape to the other islands. Despite the Portuguese victory, Cardoso ultimately enslaved only 150 captives because so many people had escaped. He took over the *tendala*'s island for his headquarters, from which troops fanned out and conquered other islands, including one on which the commander of Ndongo's forces had been stationed with his troops as well as a few Imbangala allies. In addition, Cardoso secured the island on which the *mwene lumbo*, another high official, had his headquarters. In effect, Cardoso formed a sort of naval blockade around the island of Danji, where Njinga had set up her court.[92]

On June 7, Njinga emerged onto the lookout in full view of Cardoso, surrounded by *kimbares* armed with arquebuses and flintlocks. She seemed to be contemplating whether to engage Cardoso's troops. Although she might have been able to defend the island, she apparently thought it best not to attack outright. By the end of June, she decided to seek a negotiated peace. The timing was right: Portuguese ammunition was low, a smallpox epidemic had left four thousand Portuguese *kimbares* dead, and the rest were starving thanks to inadequate supplies. The smallpox outbreak had begun to affect Njinga's forces as well and might explain at least in part why she was reluctant to fight.[93]

The Portuguese still had the upper hand. Njinga was isolated on her island fortress without the ability to order new supplies of either ammunition or people, but Cardoso was able to receive reinforcements, and his troops landed on Danji on July 12 without encountering any resistance. Njinga did hold a trump card, however—the six Portuguese hostages whom she had captured at the beginning of the year and were being held at her headquarters. She decided to try to use the hostages as a tactic to delay a Portuguese military attack against her long enough that her remaining supporters could escape safely to Tunda. From her fortified base she dispatched a messenger (*makunze*) to meet with Cardoso. Knowing that he had Njinga cornered, Cardoso was dismissive of the *makunze*'s declaration that Njinga was an "obedient daughter of the captain," that she wished to know "why he was making war against her, and that she was willing to travel to where his camp was located in Tabi and surrender with her court in three days." Expressing impatience with Njinga, Cardoso told the *makunze* that his lady "had no shame"; she should know that the Portuguese had taken up arms against her because she had failed to comply with the judgments that had been made against her. After receiving Cardoso's response, Njinga sent another representative, this time her *mwene lumbo,* whose message was no different from the *makunze*'s. Although he realized that Njinga was stalling, Cardoso wanted to make sure that she would hand over the six Portuguese hostages alive, and he listened to the secretary—who was, after all, a high official—and gave Njinga a twenty-four-hour deadline for surrender of the hostages. Njinga complied, and before the deadline had expired, the *mwene lumbo* had returned with the six healthy-looking Portuguese captives—as well as an additional message for Cardoso: Njinga wanted no more damage done to the islands, and she wanted to become a Portuguese vassal. The *mwene lumbo* reported that she would appear in his camp in person, with members of her court, within three days to sign a peace treaty. In discussing her offer, Cardoso and some other veterans of earlier campaigns referred to Njinga as "warlike," even though she was a "woman and queen or king as she called herself because she did not like to admit that she was a woman." Following the discussion, Cardoso ordered the *mwene lumbo* to tell Njinga that she had two days (or three, according to Cadornega) to hand over the *kimbares* who had deserted the Portuguese army.[94]

Cardoso then returned to his base at Tabi, where he waited for Njinga to appear.[95] But surrendering the *kimbares* would have been tantamount to admitting defeat. So while Cardoso waited, Njinga ordered her best fighters to retreat under cover of night in canoes, braving the guns and arrows that the Portuguese sentries fired. She also instructed her people to burn the boats that Cardoso planned to use against her fortifications the following night, and to set fire to the food supplies she had hoarded. She herself escaped to Tunda, right under the noses of Cardoso's troops. Although they pursued her, they may have been too exhausted to thoroughly search the many large caves in the region of Kina where she and her people hid on the way to Tunda. Whatever the reason, by the time Cardoso sent out his scouts in hot pursuit, they had no idea which route Njinga had taken during her escape from the island.[96] The *sobas* and other Mbundus who had remained on the island killed many Portuguese with their arrows. But many of them died from bullet wounds or drowned while trying to escape.[97]

There is no question that skillful diplomatic ploys were at least partly responsible for Njinga's escape, but her manipulation of Mbundu spirituality may also have helped. Sometime before she escaped, she had made an ideological shift as momentous as the one she made in 1622, when she decided to be baptized in Luanda. As Cardoso's troops pressed in on her hideout, Njinga realized that the Portuguese would never accept her as ruler of Ndongo. By then she also knew that they were intent on replacing her with their own candidate. Aware that she could never survive as the leader of Ndongo without a firm commitment to Mbundu spirituality, she deployed the relics she had made from the bones of Ngola Mbande. Njinga knew that according to Mbundu spiritual beliefs, Ngola Mbande was a stronger spiritual force as a deceased king than he had been as a living one, and she took advantage of this belief so that her supporters would have full faith in her decisions. If she abandoned the island without paying proper deference to her dead brother, she would risk his vengeance and jeopardize the support of her followers. Thus, at some point before evacuating, she called on her priests to perform the rituals that would allow them to commune with the spirit of Ngola Mbande. During the ceremony, Ngola Mbande's spirit possessed a priest, who communicated his desires and warned Njinga that becoming "a vassal of the Portuguese was to lose freedom and become a slave" and that "it was better to retain one's liberty by flight." Njinga took this advice and honored her brother by sacrificing fourteen young women on his grave.[98]

By carefully following Ngola Mbande's counsel, Njinga illustrated to her followers that she had the blessings of the ancestors to continue the resistance against the Portuguese. From the time she made the decision to venerate her brother's relics until her death in 1663, Njinga would manipulate spirituality and make it a central element in her statecraft. She added new elements to it when necessary, but always ensured that she ultimately controlled it.

4

TREACHEROUS POLITICS

A fter having fled from the Kindonga Islands, Njinga faced daunting
odds in her attempts to reinsert herself back into Ndongo politics. Governor Fernão de Sousa wanted to ensure that she remained out of commission; the Portuguese had not yet conquered eastern
Ndongo, and de Sousa feared that she would use the region as a base for
attracting supporters and undermining the gains he had made, possibly
even threatening the survival of the colony. De Sousa's plans to install Hari
a Kiluanje as king and have Njinga either captured or imprisoned had been
derailed as a result of Hari a Kiluanje's death from smallpox sometime
before October 1626, before he could be crowned king of Ndongo. Another of de Sousa's plans, to persuade Njinga to become a Portuguese agent
and convince the *sobas* in the lands beyond Ndongo to agree to be vassals
of the Portuguese, was also thwarted.[1] But de Sousa had other options. He
immediately selected Hari a Kiluanje's half brother, Ngola Hari, who controlled the area of Pungo Ndongo, as king of Ndongo.

Ngola Hari had not been at the top of de Sousa's list of replacements
for Njinga; he was descended from another branch of the royal lineage of
Ndongo, but was considered ineligible to rule because he was the son of a
slave woman in Ngola Mbande's court. Both Njinga and her sister Kambu
regarded him as their dependent; although his birth at court protected
him from being treated as a slave, his mother's lack of royal lineage made

his status uncertain.[2] Mbundu notions of kinship held that the *sobas* should not obey him. De Sousa's choice of Hari a Kiluanje as king had been based on the premise that he was a more respected and eligible candidate. To avoid any rumors about the legality of Ngola Hari's nomination, de Sousa demanded that Captain Bento Banha Cardoso bring together all the *sobas* loyal to Ngola Hari along with the *makotas* and other electors of the kingdom and have them go through the traditional procedures for electing a new king.[3]

It was at this point that de Sousa introduced the argument that Njinga's gender disqualified her from ruling. He urged Cardoso to persuade the *sobas* and electors that "Njinga was not a queen, neither could she be, as a woman" and that she had been "tyrannically" placed as the head of Ndongo. Moreover, he demanded that Cardoso impress upon the electors that they had to choose Ngola Hari as the legitimate successor of the Ndongo throne according to Mbundu custom and "place him on a chair and obey him as a natural king."[4] Ngola Hari's election took place on October 12, 1626, at the fort in Ambaca in the presence of Portuguese officials and his "*sobas, quizicos [kijikos]* and the *macotas* who were the electors." The new king took the oath of vassalage (*vassalagem*) to the Portuguese king and agreed to pay an annual tribute of one hundred prime slaves (*peças da Índias*) along with other obligations. Although the terms of the vassalage contract that Ngola Hara signed at his inauguration are not extant, the document would have included language similar to that in the contract that Hari a Kiluanje had signed, including paying tribute in slaves, converting to Christianity, sending soldiers to fight on the side of the Portuguese, and fulfilling other onerous and humiliating obligations.[5]

To guarantee that the people would accept Ngola Hari as their legitimate king, the Portuguese ordered him to leave Pungo Ndongo and build a new residence either in Kabasa or Vungo, where Ndongo kings had traditionally located their courts. De Sousa posted two companies of infantry along with additional troops in Pungo Ndongo to protect Ngola Hari from any attacks that Njinga and her supporters might launch.[6] The conditions de Sousa imposed on Ngola Hari were the same ones that Njinga had rejected when she negotiated on Ngola Mbande's behalf in 1622. Her refusal to accept these conditions would continue to haunt her and remain a central problem during her many attempts over the years to arrive at a peaceful settlement with the Portuguese. She would never forgive Ngola Hari for accepting to become a vassal of the Portuguese.

Njinga's Flight

In the months before Ngola Hari's election, the Portuguese, under Cardoso, made valiant but ultimately unsuccessful efforts to pursue and capture Njinga. She managed to evade capture through a combination of resourcefulness and political connections. The first four days after she escaped from the Kindonga Islands were harrowing. Cardoso had sent eighty cavalry and foot soldiers in hot pursuit of Njinga and her entourage, which included her relatives, closest officials, supporters, and slaves who had escaped the islands. They narrowly avoided capture by hiding in several large, naturally fortified caves. The ragtag group, many of whom were now suffering the effects of smallpox, had to claw their way through the eastern part of Ndongo.

During the trek, Njinga abandoned many of the slaves who had escaped with her. This was a brilliant tactical maneuver. Because the Portuguese prioritized rounding up the slaves over following Njinga, she gained time.[7] Putting some distance between herself and the Portuguese allowed her and her followers the opportunity to fight against *sobas* who refused to assist them and to pick up a number of new followers as well. Which supporters remained faithful to her may have depended on whether they had taken a specific oath that bound them to her. Once Mbundus took this oath, they preferred death to breaking it.[8] Despite her harrowing retreat and the loss to smallpox of many of her followers and close relatives, Njinga survived. By the time Cardoso's cavalry and spies reached the border of Ndongo, Njinga was nowhere to be found. Some reports blamed the Imbangala Kasa for allowing her to pass safely through his camp, while others noted that he had refused to help her.[9] Whichever version was true, Njinga eventually ended up in the small region of Kina, where the *soba* Catamuito took pity on her and her desperate party.

Njinga's popularity grew during her extraordinary flight. She was able to persuade many reluctant *sobas* in eastern Ndongo and the neighboring kingdoms to join her cause and keep her whereabouts secret. This was no small request. Cardoso's troops attacked the *sobas'* lands and tortured them in the hopes that they would reveal her whereabouts. They stayed mum.

During the search for Njinga, Cardoso set in place a major propaganda machine, sending out messengers and spies to eastern Ndongo to praise Ngola Hari. They pointed out to the *sobas* and their people that his election would be legitimate and that he would bring many material benefits to them after he was crowned king. They would have security and free access to the markets, among other things. Cardoso's agents crossed into the neighboring regions of Malemba and Matamba, where large numbers of Mbundus from Ndongo had taken refuge, and attempted to bribe their rulers, offering alliance with the Portuguese and other incentives to anyone who agreed not to help Njinga. Cardoso's deputies warned people that if Njinga appeared, they should either expel her from their lands or turn her in. If they did not comply, they should expect retaliation.[10]

While de Sousa had Cardoso and his agents searching for Njinga and planning Ngola Hari's election, Njinga was fighting her way through Malemba. If she did find temporary refuge at Kasa's base, she would not have stayed long in the vicinity of his *kilombo;* she did not trust her safety to Kasa, whom she had betrayed in the past. Njinga's instincts about Kasa were not misguided: a few months later, one of Ngola Hari's spies reported that the Imbangala leader was willing to hand over Njinga or kill her if he could be assured of a reward.[11] Nor could Njinga be certain of a safe haven in Malemba, since de Sousa had put a contract on her head; indeed, some of her own *sobas* had pursued her with their armies as she fled through the region. Njinga managed to evade them and took refuge in some dense woods beyond Malemba.[12] Even here she was not safe, for Ngola Hari had singled out some of her supporters, among them Njinga's relative the *soba* Zunge a Moke, and declared war against them because they refused to obey him. The Portuguese captain Sebastião Dias invaded Zunge a Moke's lands with an army of seventy-eight Portuguese and many Mbundu *kimbares.*[13]

Ngola Hari was actively encouraging the thousands of Ndongo residents who had become refugees in Malemba and Matamba to return to Ndongo. If Njinga had considered trying to recruit them to follow her, she thought better of it. Some of them would not have hesitated to reveal her hideout if it meant securing permission to return to their homes. Any hope of garnering the support of those who had remained on the islands was dashed when they proclaimed their allegiance to Ngola Hari and recognized him as the legitimate king.[14]

Despite these setbacks, Njinga remained a formidable obstacle in Ngola Hari's path to legitimacy. In early 1627, he pleaded with de Sousa to authorize another campaign against her upon learning that Njinga was near Pungo Ndongo and that Imbangala Kasa, Zunge a Moke, Ndala Kisuba, and Ndongo refugees were assisting her.[15]

Ngola Hari was right to be concerned about Njinga. She had not only made alliances with nearby rulers but also had the support of King Ambrósio of Kongo, the most powerful independent African kingdom in the region. Kongo kings had supported Ndongo from the time of Dias de Novais's arrival, especially after 1622, when João Correia de Sousa's troops invaded Kongo and captured many Kongo Christians, shipping them across the ocean to be sold into slavery in Brazil. Kongo had so far resisted the Portuguese, and the kingdom had made several diplomatic attempts to restore peace, but Kongo rulers remained alarmed over continued Portuguese military expansion. At the same time that Fernão de Sousa was sending troops against Ndongo, he had also ordered troops into the Dembos region; in these lands, which lay between Kongo and Ndongo, local rulers had maintained their autonomy and avoided paying tribute by continually shifting their allegiance between the two kingdoms. Fernão de Sousa, however, insisted that because they had formerly owed obedience to the king of Ndongo, they now therefore owed tribute to the king of Portugal, who had conquered Ndongo. In 1627 he discussed ordering troops into the region to force the ruler of Mbwila (in the Dembos region) to recognize Portuguese sovereignty and pay tribute.[16] When Njinga fled Ndongo in 1624, the new Kongo king, Pedro II, was sympathetic; he sent one of his officials to her, who brought with him "a chair and a carpet"—symbols of royalty.[17]

Although the *sobas* of Ndongo were not always willing to back her publicly, Njinga's popularity continued to rise. Most Mbundus regarded her as having a more legitimate claim to the Ndongo throne than did Ngola Hari. In addition, Ngola Hari's increasing reliance on the Portuguese damaged whatever support he might have gained. During the early months of Ngola Hari's reign, de Sousa's many attempts to make the Mbundu population accept him as the legitimate ruler were largely unsuccessful. One of Ngola Hari's first mistakes was allowing missionaries to operate in Ndongo. The first missionary he welcomed was the Jesuit priest Francisco Pacconio, whom de Sousa had nominated as the incoming ruler's spiritual adviser. By December 1626, Ngola Hari had built a church in Pungo Ndongo and allowed the priest to begin instructing his household as well as his followers in the Catholic doctrine. But Ngola Hari found himself in a Catch-22. He realized that before he could take up residence in Kabasa, as Cardoso and de Sousa had demanded, he would have to participate in the Mbundu rituals that would enable the people to regard him as a legitimate ruler. Thus he tried to delay his baptism, explaining to a frustrated Father Pacconio that he was obligated to "do certain customary ceremonies"; neglecting them would lead to a lack of legitimacy in the eyes of his people.[18]

Although Mbundu religious authorities were supposed to play a central role in some of these ceremonies, Father Pacconio was attempting to reduce their influence, and they could not participate openly. In fact, Ngola Hari kept two Mbundu priests who advised him not to give up his traditional beliefs, leading Father Pacconio to plead with de Sousa to have them expelled. Their continued influence over the king and people, the Jesuit said, was detrimental to missionary work.[19] In February 1627, Father Pacconio complained to the governor that Ngola Hari, his councilors, and the population were too attached to their *feitiços* (priests, ritual objects). The people went to the king to obtain rain, he said, and they refused to listen to Father Pacconio's protestations, "for this was the power and custom of their ancestors." They were especially dismissive of his ideas about the afterlife, scoffing at his teachings and responding that "they wanted to send someone there to verify whether paradise and hell truly existed."[20]

The Portuguese were fighting an uphill battle in their efforts to sway public opinion toward Ngola Hari. In addition to the difficulty in convincing him to reject Mbundu beliefs and ritual practices, they were not successful in their military campaigns against the *sobas* and *makotas* whom they suspected of helping Njinga. Many Mbundus had become convinced that Sousa had replaced Njinga with Ngola Hari simply because he was more pliable. Indeed, in a letter to the secretary of state in Portugal, de Sousa admitted as much. He explained that he had attacked Njinga because the Portuguese living in Angola feared her more than they did Ngola Hari: her "continuous persuasions led the *sobas* to revolt and the Portuguese slaves to flee to her, and in effect created a general rebellion, and a great loss of revenue."[21] De Sousa was optimistic that replacing Njinga with Ngola Hari would improve the economic situation of the colony.

Fernão de Sousa made many onerous demands on Ngola Hari. First, he was supposed to centralize the slave trade in specific markets that were under the control of one of his officials rather than leaving it up to village officials, as was the custom. Second, he was to make sure that all Portuguese merchants could travel safely to the markets and would not have to pay taxes. Third, he had to agree to participate in joint propaganda campaigns with Portuguese officials throughout the area to convince the people that Njinga had fled and that he was the legitimate king. Finally, he was required to respect Father Pacconio and listen to his advice as "the kings and lords of Portugal do."[22] De Sousa also warned Ngola Hari that he did not have the authority to send his officials to collect tribute from the *sobas* or other regional lords without representatives of the fort accompanying them, since the *sobas* were allies of the Portuguese king and not his vassals; and the *sobas* would now be required to pay only a certain traditional tax to him. Finally, Ngola Hari had to turn over to the Portuguese within two weeks any slave belonging to the Portuguese who had fled to the lands of a *soba;* otherwise, he would have to pay the cost of the slave.[23] In short, de Sousa expected Ngola Hari to behave not as an independent king who had become a Portuguese ally, but instead as a conquered *soba* who was integrated into the Portuguese colony of Angola.

The relationship that Ngola Hari formalized with de Sousa made him wholly dependent on the Portuguese, and his power was irrevocably diminished. Unlike earlier kings of Ndongo, he could not exact tribute from the *sobas* under his control, and during his early years as ruler, his requests to de Sousa for military assistance to move against *sobas* who refused his demands were all denied. Ngola Hari was also not allowed to tax either Portuguese or African merchants without first getting approval from the forts.

His weak position was evident from the very beginning of his rule, when he requested de Sousa's help in repopulating Ndongo. The area had become a wasteland, much of its population lost after nearly a decade of wars. Ngola Hari's several requests to repatriate the *kijikos* and free Mbundus who were in Luanda and elsewhere in the Portuguese areas were futile. Nothing panned out, despite several schemes that de Sousa suggested, one of which involved an exchange of free Mbundus living in Luanda and on various Portuguese-owned plantations for the *kijikos* who had fled to Ndongo. De Sousa went so far as to propose that a decree be publicized in Luanda and near the forts that would encourage free Mbundus to return to Ndongo. However, officials in the Camara (the advisory body to the governor) refused to sign it, fearing that such a step would encourage mass flights by *kijikos* and other enslaved Mbundus and would destroy the economic livelihood of the Portuguese owners.[24] Even if the scheme to repopulate Ndongo had worked, Ngola Hari would not have been able to exact tribute from the Mbundus who returned to Ndongo, because he was not considered ruler of these lands. As a relative of Njinga, he had natural rights over the *kijikos* in his provinces of Pungo Ndongo and Hari, but he could not claim the same rights over those from Ndongo, who belonged to Njinga's direct lineage.

This conundrum was just one of many examples of de Sousa's failure to create the conditions that would make Ngola Hari into a dependable ally and the legitimate ruler in place of Njinga. It was not enough for de Sousa to install him on the throne. Ngola Hari still feared Njinga, and he was not alone; many of the leading members of his lineage also considered her their enemy. They believed that if she were to reconquer Ndongo, she would enslave them all, since, as the popular saying went, "whoever is king has no relatives."[25] At the same time, many Mbundus were determined to follow Njinga if she returned.

Although Ngola Hari did not have the traditional power associated with Ndongo kings, he realized that to retain his position, he would have to go along with de Sousa's demands, chief among them the requirement to become a Christian. Putting aside his former resistance, he was baptized in 1627 by Father Pacconio, along with his wife and other relatives. He also sent his young son to Luanda to be baptized in a lavish ceremony in the main church. In a dramatic step, Ngola Hari also abandoned the notion of plural marriage that had been so central to the leadership of the rulers of Ndongo and remarried his wife in a Christian wedding.[26]

Njinga Resurfaces

The fears of Ngola Hari and the Portuguese about Njinga's resurgence were realized in 1627, when Njinga started reaching out to some of her old allies in an attempt to reform her base of support. De Sousa first heard of her activity in March, when news reached him that Njinga had sent two low-level representatives (*makunzes*) from Tunda, where she was temporarily based, to Kisama, a salt-producing province that had formerly been a major source of revenue for Ndongo but had resisted Portuguese rule. The *makunzes* met with several *makotas* (elders) and *sobas* who had earned the opprobrium of the Portuguese for harboring Imbangalas and refusing to allow Portuguese to settle in their lands.[27]

A few months later, in September, Njinga decided to make her way to the frontier of Ndongo to test the waters. Arriving with the Imbangala Kasa, with whom she was temporarily on better terms, she attempted to reconstitute her base. She soon discovered, however, that the political environment had shifted dramatically in favor of the Portuguese, albeit not toward Ngola Hari. As a result of Cardoso and Sebastião Dias's successful military operations, many *sobas* and nominally independent regional powers in a large area stretching from the southern border of Kongo to the eastern frontier of Ndongo and the lands on both sides of the Kwanza River had either accepted terms of vassalage or agreed to be allies of the Portuguese, despite the fact that they had previously been sympathetic to Njinga and had joined in her earlier rebellion. Even the *sobas* in Tunda and Songo who had formerly resisted the Portuguese now had slave markets and allowed Portuguese and African merchants to trade in their territories.[28] Another factor making it difficult for Njinga to find support was Ngola Hari's role in de Sousa's strategy for controlling Ndongo. As a result of Ngola Hari's baptism and apparent willingness to call on Portuguese military assistance, many *sobas* were intimidated; they were reluctant to welcome Njinga's return, fearing repercussions from the Portuguese.

Njinga realized that she had to be careful about revealing her whereabouts and kept as her confidants only those *sobas* who were members of her lineage and had lands located in Ndongo.[29] As a result, she enjoyed the support of only two *sobas*. After having been abandoned by Kasa again, Njinga was alone in the new war camp she had built in eastern Ndongo.[30] She knew she had only two options: return to the bush and continue fighting to regain her throne, or attempt to reopen negotiations with de Sousa. Njinga chose the latter.

In November 1627, Njinga sent her highest official (her *mwene lumbo*) and some attendants to the fort at Ambaca to present her case. Most of what the *mwene lumbo* had to say was not new. He reiterated Njinga's decision to become de Sousa's subordinate and dependent (*filha*). Njinga, however, did not concede her right to rule Ndongo, and the *mwene lumbo* stressed that the queen had returned because she was the rightful ruler and, quite frankly, she was tired of wandering through the woods. Njinga, he reported, blamed her councilors for advising her to flee and was now ready to take part in the vassalage ceremony and pay tribute to the king of Portugal. He went on to discuss the origins of the conflict. He stressed that Njinga believed that when Hari a Kiluanje had become a vassal of the Portuguese in 1624, he did so solely because he wanted to inherit her kingdom. He also noted that Ngola Hari, whom the Portuguese had elected, was lying when he said that she had returned to begin a war. How could this be, since she did not have any enemies in Ndongo? They were all her dependents. In conclusion, the *mwene lumbo* indicated that Njinga was ready to reopen the slave market. On her behalf, he presented the captain-general of the fort with a number of slaves: six for the governor and four for Cardoso. In addition, the *mwene lumbo* handed over 400 slaves and 150 head of cattle as tribute to the Portuguese king from Njinga and Kasa.[31]

Learning of Njinga's reappearance, Ngola Hari sent his own *mwene lumbo* with a letter to de Sousa, complaining that he had been advised about Njinga's messengers at the fort and noting that he heard that she had a great number of slaves chained together waiting in Ambaca to send to de Sousa. He accused Njinga of having paid bribes to enable her return to Ndongo. Furthermore, he stressed that the *sobas* living along the Kwanza River still preferred Njinga over him, and, he noted that she might have gone to the island where her brother Ngola Mbande was buried, presumably to begin strengthening her forces again. Ngola Hari pleaded with de Sousa to help him, as his father.[32]

De Sousa, with appeals from both Njinga and Ngola Hari, preferred to support the latter. Njinga's manipulation of Cardoso and her escape from the islands had embarrassed him, and he was now firmly committed to supporting the more pliable and weak-willed Ngola Hari. De Sousa knew that Ngola Hari would not be able to carry out his duties if Njinga remained a threat, and so he quickly moved to embolden him. While sternly rebuking him for accusing the Portuguese of taking bribes from Njinga, he promised to send reinforcements. But he ordered him to keep the people away from the islands—to prevent them from joining Njinga—and to send soldiers out to gather information on Njinga. De Sousa demanded that Ngola Hari prepare his soldiers for battle and encourage his people to farm so that the soldiers would have food. In the meantime, he urged the

Queen Njinga giving judgment, by Antonio Cavazzi, ca. 1668

captain-general at Ambaca and Father Pacconio to encourage Ngola Hari: under no circumstances should they desert him at this time.[33]

With Njinga, de Sousa took no chances. Not only did he refuse her appeal; he accused her *mwene lumbo* of being a spy and ordered the captain-general to arrest him. The *mwene lumbo* was placed in chains along with those who accompanied him, and the slaves he had brought were confiscated.

De Sousa ordered the captain-general to gather troops, pursue and kill Njinga, and cut off the heads of any *sobas* who joined her.[34]

Concerned when she did not hear back from the *mwene lumbo*, Njinga sent two of her favorite *makunzes* to Ambaca, with additional slaves. They arrived at the fort on December 5, 1627, the very day of her *mwene lumbo*'s arrest. In short order the captain-general arrested them, too, along with some of Njinga's other supporters.

Njinga, of course, knew nothing at this point of the fate of her emissaries. While awaiting news, she tried to illustrate to the Portuguese her willingness to live in peace. She relocated to the island of Zongo, in the Kindonga Islands, about a two-day journey from Ambaca, to avoid fighting the *soba* Andala Gonga Cangombe of the Lucala region, who had attacked her after she asked him to turn over to the fort all the *kimbares* (slave soldiers) of the Portuguese who had fled to his lands during the earlier uprising.[35] She even ordered her *makunzes* to ask for Cardoso's permission to remain on the island. In addition, Njinga sent one of her supporters on a mission to the *soba* Candele of Kisos, one of her main bases of support east of Pungo Ndongo, to ask him to treat well those Portuguese *kimbares* and *pumbeiros* (African traders working for Portuguese merchants) who were in his lands with their trade goods. Candele dismissed Njinga's plea and instead turned against the merchants, robbing and attacking them, and in the process killing three Africans belonging to the Portuguese, one freeman and two slaves. The remaining Portuguese traders and slaves fled to the lands of the *soba* Ndala Kisuba, a vassal of the Portuguese who vowed to protect them with his life.[36]

This incident exposed Njinga's main weakness. She now had to confront the reality that she had lost the support she had previously had among the major *sobas* in the region. Stung by this realization, Njinga went into a severe depression, locking herself in a room and refusing to speak to anyone. It was in this state, from her new location on a different island in the Kwanza River, that she dispatched two more envoys to Ambaca to tell de Sousa that she was not responsible for what Candele had done in Kisos. To convince de Sousa of her sincerity, she requested that when the envoys arrive they were to undergo a brutal trial, called *kilumbo*, in which a hot knife was placed on the skin of the oath taker; if no wound was detected, the person was considered to have spoken truthfully.[37] When no word came from her messengers, Njinga, not knowing that their fate had been sealed, became desperate and sent her personal secretary to the fort on January 4, 1628. He was not allowed to cross the Kwanza River, however; he was blocked by a *soba* who had declared support for Ngola Hari. Njinga was effectively isolated on the island. Most of the *sobas* in the region around the Kwanza River who had formerly supported her were now camped at Pungo Ndongo, waiting for reinforcements that would allow them to move against her under the leadership of Ngola Hari.[38]

In the meantime, Njinga's two envoys underwent the ordeal at the fort. They defended their queen and protested her innocence, denying that she had ordered the murder and capture of the *kimbares* and *pumbeiros* in Kisos or confiscated the merchants' goods.[39] But these legal procedures were just for show; de Sousa had already made up his mind that Njinga's officials were spying on him, and he discounted the results of the ordeal. De Sousa ordered a military tribunal to gather in Luanda to begin formal proceedings against the *mwene lumbo*. The tribunal convicted him of spying, of carrying false messages from Njinga, and, indeed, of responsibility for almost all of Njinga's actions, including joining forces with the Imbangala Kasa and encouraging the *sobas* to rebel. The tribunal condemned him to death by beheading in the presence of the *sobas*. The two *makunzes'* lives were spared, but they were condemned to be transported overseas and sold into slavery. Before carrying out the sentences, the captain-general and other Portuguese military brass at Ambaca tortured the *mwene lumbo* and the two *makunzes*. Under duress, the *mwene lumbo* provided details of how Njinga had succeeded in returning to Ndongo. He continued to insist, however, that Njinga was genuinely interested in making peace with the Portuguese and was prepared to become a Portuguese vassal.[40] The *makunzes* also revealed details regarding Njinga's movements since her return to Ndongo, but, like the *mwene lumbo*, affirmed separately that Njinga was ready to make peace and become a subordinate of the Portuguese. Their confessions, however, did not save them. The *mwene lumbo* was beheaded on December 23, 1627.

Three weeks after the execution, on January 15, 1628, the captain-general at Ambaca sent eleven of Njinga's envoys and supporters to Luanda. The group included the two *makunzes* and other officials who had either been arrested upon their arrival at the fort or had been picked up elsewhere in Ndongo. Among the group were a *soba* of Lucala and three companions who supported Njinga. All of them gave sworn testimony that revealed Njinga's whereabouts and actions. They all, however, unanimously swore that Njinga had returned because she wanted to make peace with the Portuguese.[41]

While the two condemned *makunzes* were kept prisoner in Luanda, awaiting embarkation to Brazil, de Sousa returned the rest of the party to the fort at Ambaca. Accompanied by a Portuguese official, they carried a message to Njinga from the governor. In it, he informed Njinga that if she was earnest about wanting to be his dependent, she needed to go to the fort at Cambambe. He reassured her that he would guarantee her safety and clear the roads, whether she came by way of Ambaca or across open country. She should know, he assured her, that as a Christian and a person of high status, she would be treated with dignity, and he pleaded with her not to risk her life by going back to the woods. For added incentive, de Sousa would allow her to bring Kasa. He asked her to have confidence in him, as he considered her a dependent. However, de Sousa made it clear that this was Njinga's last chance. If she failed to take up his offer, the Portuguese would "come and look for you," and she would not enjoy the guarantees that the message promised. In fact, de Sousa stated that if Njinga sent more envoys to the fort, they would be beheaded. In conclusion, he cautioned Njinga to consider seriously what she would lose if she failed to obey and to recall the risks that she had already faced during her escape. Surely it would be better for her to spend the remainder of her life resting, without having to worry about her survival and upkeep.[42]

Mobilizing Popular Support

Through her various emissaries, Njinga had indicated to Fernão de Sousa that she was willing to become a vassal of the Portuguese king. His response shows how differently the two leaders envisioned the role of a woman in a royal family. De Sousa's view was based on the early modern European model. He expected Njinga to give up any claim to the lands and throne of Ndongo and accept Ngola Hari as the legitimate king. He also wanted her to accept the lower-status title of "sister of the king" and agree to retire from the public sphere and live quietly off the generosity of her guardian, the governor himself.[43]

In many respects, what he was offering her was a better option than the ones that most women from royal families in Europe faced if they challenged their exclusion from political leadership. A similarly defiant woman in Europe might have been married off to a prince in some distant land, banished to a nunnery or dungeon, or even murdered.[44] In this context, it is not difficult to see why de Sousa might have expected Njinga to find his offer attractive. He was not aware of the political reality in Ndongo, where women were major players in governance.[45]

De Sousa attempted to solve the political crisis in Ndongo, which was caused by decades of wars and a commercial policy based on the extraction of slaves, by casting Njinga's gender as the overriding cause of the conflict. When he laid out Njinga's two options—submit and become a powerless woman, or face Portuguese troops—de Sousa miscalculated. He had taken Njinga's appeals to him as a sign of weakness and clearly did not understand either the depth of Njinga's perception of herself as a leader or the political and cultural traditions that motivated her. Had he understood those factors, he would not have been surprised by Njinga's response: she would fight until death for her kingdom. She was willing to become a vassal under conditions that would allow her to retain power, but not under the conditions that de Sousa was offering.

In the meantime, between December 1627 and March 1628, Njinga had begun an intensive campaign to recruit *sobas* to her cause, even as the envoys that de Sousa had sent were making their way to her with his message. De Sousa, not waiting for a response from her, was already preparing for a new campaign. His first priority was to make sure that Njinga would not consolidate her position in the Kindonga Islands or in the region between Ndongo and Matamba. He faced the recurring problem that *sobas* were still refusing to accept Ngola Hari as their legitimate leader. Even those who had reluctantly supported him at first were simply ignoring his orders to bring men and supplies for the new campaign against Njinga.

Once again, Ngola Hari's demands on the *sobas* had the effect of undermining their support for him. When Njinga arrived in the lands of Ndala Kisuba and Matamba, where many of the Ndongo *sobas* and their people had taken refuge, they welcomed her, and she was soon able to establish a war camp in the region. Njinga's growing popularity stood in stark contrast to the contempt with which both the Portuguese and the Mbundus regarded Ngola Hari.

Ngola Hari was in a pitiable situation. He had no soldiers of his own, and the *sobas* in Ndongo were in open rebellion against him. By the end of

March 1629, Ngola Hari and the Portuguese had already planned to move against these *sobas*. Before doing so, they sent out messages ordering the *sobas* to appear before Ngola Hari. Not a single *soba* showed up because, as Ngola Hari and his *makotas* acknowledged, they all obeyed "Njinga Ambande." Ngola Hari flew into a tantrum when Paio de Araújo de Azevedo, the captain-general who had replaced Bento Banha Cardoso, demanded that he force the *sobas* to comply with his orders.[46] He and Njinga were both dependents (*filhos*) of Azevedo, he exclaimed, and he could well allow her return to Ndongo; he himself would leave Ndongo and move back to Andongo or to Lembo, near the fort at Massangano, where the Portuguese could "cut off his head." During the outburst Ngola Hari took a straw, handed it to his interpreter, and walked away. With this gesture Ngola Hari was indicating that he was giving up his rights to the kingdom.[47]

The Portuguese knew that the *sobas* preferred to follow their orders rather than those of Ngola Hari, despised as he was for his poverty and his inability to maintain the kingdom on his own. Nevertheless, the alliance with Ngola Hari was important, and de Sousa was committed to shoring up the king's control by trying to force the *sobas* to obey Ngola Hari. Ngola Hari urged de Sousa to go farther and to behead several of Njinga's *makotas* or *sobas* as an incentive to her supporters to turn themselves in to the fort. He also wanted the Portuguese to capture Njinga, warning that if she were to remain free and continue her alliance with Ndala Kisuba, she would become more powerful or even destroy the kingdom.[48] De Sousa essentially followed Ngola Hari's advice.

Beginning in June 1629, the captain-general at the fort in Ambaca arrested and imprisoned many Ndongo *sobas,* who were released only after they agreed to become vassals of the king of Portugal. Others were arrested and branded with the king's mark. These actions did nothing to improve Ngola Hari's situation, and indeed only exacerbated the *sobas'* ill feelings toward him. Mbundu *sobas* had high expectations for their kings. All previous rulers of Ndongo, as well as Njinga, had gained the respect of the *sobas* and other regional lords by leading large armies and winning battles. Ngola Hari had been stripped of the ability to do any such thing. By preventing him from undertaking military campaigns independent of them, the Portuguese had deprived him of one of the main functions that set Ndongo kings apart from *sobas*. As a Portuguese vassal, Ngola Hari could never achieve this status. Ngola Hari had admitted as much on a previous occasion, when he made an unexpected visit to Ambaca. He wanted to know why he could not go to war, since "his life and liberty [*quietação*] consisted in making war in order to sustain the kingdom." The only advice that the sergeant-major could offer him was to suggest that he return to Pungo Ndongo instead of going to Lembo to farm; relocating to Lembo would indicate to the people that "he did not want to be king."[49]

Ngola Hari's situation had become so pathetic that he complained of having only "his advisers (*makotas*) and women" around him, and that he was unable to initiate a campaign against even the discontented *sobas*.[50] In fact, the *sobas* were so disrespectful of Ngola Hari that the captain-general of Ambaca arrested and imprisoned many of them, forcing them to return to Pungo Ndongo and to declare again that they were his vassals. Such attempts of Portuguese military officials only made the situation worse, and Ngola Hari's status continued to decline.[51] The situation was especially explosive in the province of Hari, where many *sobas* had stopped paying tribute altogether. Ngola Hari himself could not raise the one hundred slaves he was obligated to provide as tribute.[52]

In the meantime, Njinga was continuing her efforts to mobilize popular support. She accepted the fact that de Sousa refused the various offers she had made (beginning in 1625) to become a Portuguese vassal under certain conditions, and now believed that he distrusted her entirely; that, in a word, he was her enemy.[53] She was also aware of the many obstacles that faced her in continuing to oppose him. She had learned that he had ordered reinforcements of Portuguese soldiers and cavalry from Luanda for all the forts, as well as numerous African free and slave soldiers from many regions.

Njinga's strategy was to move fast to prevent Portuguese reinforcements from reaching Ambaca and Pungo Ndongo to shore up Ngola Hari. By July 1628 she had already succeeded in regaining the support of the *sobas* near the Kwanza River, who had come out in strength at a public meeting where she appeared with Imbangala Kasa at her side. At this meeting, Njinga proclaimed herself the "Lady [of Ndongo]." She didn't stop there: she announced that Ngola Hari was her slave and that she was prepared to become a vassal of the king of Portugal and pay tribute "from the lands that her father gave her."[54] Shortly thereafter, de Sousa received word that Imbangala Kasa was leading a large force toward Ambaca. Meanwhile, Njinga had received another message from de Sousa ordering her to appear in Luanda to negotiate conditions of her vassalage; of course she dismissed it.

She sent an envoy to let de Sousa know that she considered him "her enemy who wanted to send her to Spanish America [presumably as a slave]."[55]

Continuing her fight against Ngola Hari, Njinga waged psychological war against him as well as confronting him on the battlefield. When she heard that Cardoso had left Pungo Ndongo, where he had been protecting Ngola Hari, Njinga sent a threatening message to Ngola Hari along with some fetishes that, according to de Sousa, "these heathens fear more than arms." Ngola Hari was terrified and could neither confront Njinga nor muster the courage to lead his forces across Ndongo to show that he was in charge. Instead he remained in Pungo Ndongo and sent messages urging the Portuguese for reinforcements to "protect him from the black woman."[56]

Njinga had by then gone back to the Kindonga Islands, and her stature among the *sobas* was improving daily. Despite de Sousa's efforts to force them to accept Ngola Hari as king, they believed that Njinga was the legitimate ruler of Ndongo and that, according to Mbundu notions of lineage, Ngola Hari was Njinga's dependent.[57] It was not only his own people who undermined his authority. The Portuguese soldiers who lived in Pungo Ndongo who were supposed to protect him were extremely disrespectful and exploited him mercilessly.[58]

The knowledge that Njinga was on the islands, had traveled to Matamba and the lands of Ndala Kisuba, and had the support of Imbangala Kasa encouraged more *sobas* to support her. Many of them expressed this support simply by resisting demands from Ngola Hari or the Portuguese— either by sending in very little tribute or ignoring the requests altogether. In some cases, it was not even possible for them to come up with the requisite tribute: many *sobas* had become destitute since the first campaign against Njinga, during which thousands of their people had been captured and enslaved or had died in the smallpox epidemic. More important, however, was the fact that a number of slave trading routes had been disrupted. Renewed ties between Njinga and Kasa had blocked the roads to the lands of Ndala Kisuba, and the wars had closed routes through Ndongo. In addition, Njinga's presence in the islands had led to the closure of some routes to the fort at Ambaca.[59]

While Njinga was working to gain support, de Sousa was sending envoys to Ndala Kisuba to negotiate the reopening of the routes. He considered Ndala Kisuba a "very powerful lord" and believed that if he could reopen the slave market in his lands, Ngola Hari and the Ndongo *sobas* would once again participate in the slave trade and be able to pay their tribute.[60] De Sousa had built the market in Ndala Kisuba's lands during the first campaign against Njinga. Ndala Kisuba had gained tremendously as a result of these campaigns. The frontier for slaving was much farther east than it had been when the kings of Ndongo had been powerful enough to prevent direct contact between the Portuguese and the eastern lands. By 1628, the region had become a major source of slaves.[61] De Sousa's primary concern now was to secure Ndala Kisuba, who at one point had given Njinga refuge, as a Portuguese ally; his envoy had many points to cover, and he had to be exceptionally persuasive. The Portuguese wanted Ndala Kisuba to relocate the slave market to military camps, where their security would be assured. To sweeten the deal, they brought him a variety of gifts and conveyed verbal assurances of long-term peace and security against his enemies, Njinga being high on the list. In addition to bribing Ndala Kisuba with gifts, de Sousa built a new fort between Pungo Ndongo and the Kindonga Islands so that Portuguese and African troops could patrol the region and force neighboring *sobas* to contribute to the war effort.[62]

De Sousa realized that in order to open the slave route and enable Ngola Hari to rule, he had to began a new campaign against Njinga. The campaign would be led by Paio de Araújo de Azevedo, the new captain who had arrived in the fall of 1628 to replace Cardoso, who had died during the summer. In September 1628, Azevedo led an attack against Njinga. The army was made up of the same Portuguese and African veterans from Luanda who had fought in previous campaigns, together with additional slave troops led by captains such as Sebastião Dias, who joined in from the forts of Massangano and Ambaca. Azevedo hoped to add local troops that were to be supplied by Ngola Hari and the *sobas*. Governor de Sousa had gathered a great deal of information about Njinga's whereabouts, and his aim now was to defend Ngola Hari, to "prevent that black woman from getting stronger in the island where she was," and to pursue her wherever she was so that she would be unable to rebuild her base.[63]

Azevedo did not attack Njinga immediately upon his arrival in the area near the Kindonga Islands. The rainy season made travel difficult, but he also recognized that he needed to collect intelligence about Njinga's military strength and movements. Moreover, he had to build up Ngola Hari's confidence. De Sousa's intelligence had suggested that Njinga and Kasa's troops were all over Ndongo and that she continued to attract *sobas* who refused to pay the tribute to Ngola Hari and who, because of the earlier losses of their people, had been fleeing. When Azevedo's troops from Luanda (including 150 European soldiers and cavalry) arrived with their slaves, they joined thousands of African troops under Dias and moved against the *sobas* in the province of Hari who were supporting Njinga through passive resistance.[64]

In addition, before taking the war to Njinga, the combined troops intimidated some of the more powerful *sobas* and occupied strategic locations where Njinga's support was strong. *Sobas* in many different regions, including those around the Lucala River, in the border areas near the frontier, were targeted, and those who ruled certain strategic areas, such as Ndala Kisuba, were threatened with war if they refused to report Njinga's presence or if they allowed her to escape through their lands.[65]

Finally, Azevedo and his troops advanced on the Kindonga Islands. But when they arrived, Njinga was nowhere to be found.

A Game of Cat and Mouse

Despite the fact that the campaign had to be halted for nearly eight months because of the rains, Azevedo never stopped looking for Njinga, and he continued to harass those *sobas* suspected of aiding her. By February 1629, Njinga had still not been located. The little support that Ngola Hari had gained among the *sobas* had eroded, and he was confronting open rebellion. In a petition his officials brought to Azevedo, Ngola Hari complained that a large part of the population of Ndongo had fled to Matamba, and he questioned the Portuguese strategy. Because the army was so intent on capturing and destroying Njinga and her people, and Ngola Hari himself had been ordered to join in on raiding Ndongo villages, the petition noted, they were destroying what remained of Ndongo. Ngola Hari estimated that Portuguese soldiers had seized four thousand prime slaves along with many *sobas*.[66]

Through his envoys' words, Ngola Hari's despondence was evident. He was disrespected from all corners and could no longer control the troops he was leading. The letter described an incident in which his porters suddenly abandoned their responsibilities, brazenly stating that they were no longer interested in searching for or joining the battle against Njinga.

Adding tremendous insult to injury, they had called him a dog.[67] As he had done before, Ngola Hari threatened to leave Ndongo and move to Luanda or to Lembo.

In response, Azevedo sent troops into battle against the *sobas* in Matamba who were known to be harboring those rulers who had fled Ndongo to avoid both paying tribute to Ngola Hari and fighting Njinga. Although Njinga's supporters had organized themselves and fought bravely, the Portuguese side was largely successful, routing several camps, capturing three powerful *sobas*, and forcing several other *sobas* to swear vassalage to Azevedo.[68]

The Portuguese operations in Matamba did much to unravel Njinga's strategy. In the first place, it further thwarted her hopes to join forces with the most powerful of the Imbangala leaders, Kasanje. Kasanje had attracted large numbers of refugee Mbundus, and his following of bowmen was estimated at more than eighty thousand. He had rebuffed her initial advances, killing more than nine of the envoys that she sent to him.[69] And then, he was uprooted by the Portuguese incursions. When Kasanje learned of the Portuguese plans to invade his *kilombo*, he fled to the nearby Kongo province of Wandu, recently vacated by its own ruler. From Wandu, Kasanje boasted that he was ready to send to the Portuguese the cattle and slaves he had brought to the Kongo capital—in exchange for trade goods, powder, arms, and munitions.[70] Had Kasanje succeeded, he would have become the dominant African political force in the region, presenting a challenge to the Portuguese and possibly overpowering Njinga as well.

While these events were taking place, Njinga maintained her relationship with many of the *sobas* who refused to obey Ngola Hari. These alliances ensured that the slave trade route between Ambaca and points east to Kisos, located in the frontier with Ndala Kisuba's lands, remained blocked. The Portuguese incursions into Matamba had weakened the resolve of many *sobas* in Ndongo, who had fled and attached themselves to *sobas* in the interior of Matamba and in Ndala Kisuba's lands. Njinga continued her attempts to put together a broader coalition, sometimes going so far as to threaten to cut off a *soba*'s head if he refused to join her. She sent messengers to the three Imbangala leaders whose camps were located around Ndongo, but these attempts faltered.[71] Her hopes of an alliance with the Imbangala Kasanje had gone nowhere, and Kasa had turned against her again; he killed the two *makunzes* she sent and fled to Tunda. Kalunga, another Imbangala leader who was in Haku—an area in which Njinga had some support—also refused to join her and relocated to Libolo.

By early May 1629, Njinga had built some secure sites for her war camps in the borders of the lands of the *soba* Ndala Kisuba near Matamba, where three of his brothers backed her and where many of her supporters were located. Njinga's survival depended on the food, livestock, and other supplies provided to her by several powerful *soba*s in Ndongo.[72] She also had support from another brother of Ndala Kisuba, whose lands were on the border with Ngangela, southeast of Matamba.[73] Njinga knew that the Portuguese army had recruited many *makotas* from Ndongo to force Ndala Kisuba to send his army to find her or face an invasion by the Portuguese forces. The Portuguese also threatened the Ndongo *sobas* with the loss of their positions if they did not provide information on her whereabouts. Loyalty to Njinga remained strong, however; many of the *sobas* had sworn an oath to her and feared that they would die immediately if they revealed her location.[74] Thus, although some faced punishment from the Portuguese, others braved capture and traveled from Ndongo to the large camp that Njinga had built in Ngangela to bring her supplies.[75] As the Portuguese army, consisting of one hundred musketeers, some cavalry, and an army of African soldiers, tracked Njinga day and night, they left a path of destruction in their wake.

The Great Escape

Faced with grim reality, Njinga was forced back into guerrilla mode. During the last week of May 1629, she moved her war camp from Ndala Kisuba's lands to an area far beyond Malemba, to the Ngangela region. She hadn't been able to shake off her pursuers, but the rugged landscape in this remote region presented a major obstacle to them. According to Fernão de Sousa's account of these events, when the Portuguese army first came upon her camp on May 25, 1629, the lookouts, Njinga's bowmen, escaped with their queen by running to a rocky precipice that offered them protection. A small entrance to the precipice was only big enough for one person at a time to crawl through. It was reached by traversing a deep gully so treacherous that many Portuguese soldiers fell and died trying to get to the other side.

Njinga's fearlessness, military skill, and knowledge of her environment were on full display during this harrowing escape. As members of the Portuguese army pursued her for about three miles, they were unable to catch up—the narrow passageway allowed her to stay one step ahead of them. She succeeded in crossing dangerous ravines and rivers that stymied the soldiers pursuing her, and she was protected by skilled marksmen in the rearguard.[76]

Njinga knew she was not safe, however. On May 26, fresh forces, including sixty musketeers, arrived in the area, having crossed four rivers and seven ravines to find her. They almost caught up with her; they spent the night of May 27 at the very campsite Njinga had occupied the night before. By this time, she did not dare stay in any one location for long.

As she was crossing a narrow precipice, she was spotted by some Mbundu soldiers in the Portuguese army. In their haste to corner her, five of them rushed to the ledge. They lost their balance and tumbled down the precipice, their bodies cut into pieces as they fell. To protect Njinga, several hundred of her soldiers surrounded her, making a wall. As the soldiers pursuing her stood deciding on their best method of apprehending Njinga, they witnessed an awesome spectacle. Njinga, at this point a seasoned warrior nearing fifty years old, grabbed what appeared to be a rope (perhaps it was one of the strong vines that grew out of the rocky surfaces) from the top of the precipice and maneuvered her way down to a ravine where some of her people were waiting. The precipice Njinga descended was supposedly so high that if one stood at its top, the voices of people at the bottom were inaudible. How she planned this we can't know, but Njinga landed in the midst of a throng of people, ensuring her own survival and that of the two hundred (out of an estimated five hundred) soldiers who had made a cordon around her.[77] Njinga walked away without an injury.

Any respite from her Portuguese pursuers after this accomplishment was short-lived. The Portuguese captain immediately ordered the Mbundu soldiers to take off their shoes and climb down on ropes after her. They captured three hundred of Njinga's remaining troops who had managed to escape during the first battle at the *kilombo*. The revelations from some of the captured *sobas* and *kimbares* provide some insight into the state of mind of Njinga and her small group of supporters. After intense questioning, they reported that Njinga was at first inclined to surrender, when she recognized the severity of her situation. It was the *kimbares,* who had fled the Portuguese in order to join her, who encouraged her, pledging that "where she died they will die also."[78]

Their unflagging support must have buoyed Njinga's confidence. The Portuguese had no such boosters. Realizing that his troops could not mimic Njinga's feats, the Portuguese captain sent some soldiers to look for an alternate route. By the time they finally came upon a less intimidating hill, Njinga had put more than a day between herself and her pursuers.

After a few days spent combing the villages through which Njinga had passed, the captain concluded that it was useless to continue pursuing her, and he called off the search. Besides, she only had one hundred soldiers defending her. He was convinced that she would not be able to survive for long in a place where she was not known and where the residents were reputed to be cannibals. In their mop-up operations on the way back to Ndongo, the Portuguese soldiers found guns, gunpowder, ammunition, and clothing that Njinga's troops and porters had shed along the way.[79] Njinga obviously had encountered little difficulty in purchasing weapons, which led de Sousa to undertake an investigation about the management of military supplies in the forts, and to implement a ban on selling arms to Africans.[80]

Although Njinga had slipped through their hands, her pursuers had been able to find the camp in Malemba to which her sisters, other relatives, and advisers had relocated. Also in the camp were several Portuguese prisoners she had captured, as well as large numbers of *sobas* and *makotas.* The Portuguese army staged a surprise attack on the camp at daybreak. With Njinga's parting order to fight until the end echoing in their heads, the defenders put up a valiant, bloody resistance, but they were outgunned. The Portuguese soldiers captured several of the most important individuals, including Njinga's sisters, Kambu and Funji.[81]

With Njinga on the run and at least temporarily out of the picture, Fernão de Sousa set about to regularize Ngola Hari's rule in a way that he had not done before. He sent word to Ngola Hari to immediately begin building settlements in two locations in Matamba where Ndongo kings had formerly built their courts and where he had so far not been able to enforce his rule. De Sousa also advised him to build a settlement in Ndala Kisuba's lands, where Njinga had found a warm welcome, and to demand that the region's *soba* send home the refugees from Ndongo who had fled there. To establish himself as their overlord and their guarantor of security, de Sousa instructed, Ngola Hari must send gifts to the leaders of the neighboring regions in which Ndongo kings had formerly had vassals. Lastly, the governor commanded Ngola Hari to open the slave trade routes and markets.

Even before he heard from Ngola Hari, Ndala Kisuba sent his officials with gifts for Ngola Hari and swore obedience to him and to the Portuguese. He was not the only *soba* to do so, once it became known that Njinga's supporters would not be punished for having sided with her. The *sobas* were urged to pay the hundred slaves in tribute that they had failed to pay the previous year and were reminded of their obligations to provide Ngola Hari with men and supplies to maintain the security of the kingdom. By June 1629, with Njinga out of the way, Ngola Hari was sufficiently confident in his position as king that he promised to open up the slave markets and to collect tribute from the *sobas*.[82]

Although Njinga's whereabouts were unknown, her sisters were now captives who could be used for political purposes. Decisions the Portuguese took about these captives would inform many of the choices Njinga would make in subsequent decades. After their capture, Kambu and Funji, Njinga's aunt Kiloge, and eleven *sobas* and *makotas* were taken to Luanda through Ndongo and were paraded naked along the way. Ngola Hari sent a message confessing that he was Kambu's "slave" and noting that although he would not visit them, he wanted them to have the clothing and presents he sent. Kambu and Funji were as adamant as Njinga about their claims to the kingdom and remained dedicated to her cause. They refused his gifts, telling the messengers they would never obey him; as long as they were alive, they proclaimed, the kingdom was rightly theirs.[83]

De Sousa, however, viewed the captives' march into Luanda as the perfect public showcase in which to dramatize his military success over Njinga. When the prisoners arrived in July 1629, he made the sisters undergo a variation of the vassalage ceremony that was typically forced upon conquered *sobas*, but which Njinga had never undergone. In preparing to meet them, he staged a ceremony similar to the ones that earlier governors had held for African royalty. He arranged with the captain of the guard at the governor's residence to have the naked prisoners brought before him for a public audience. "I received them sitting on a chair whose arms were covered with crimson velvet set against a wall where the weapons were; which was in the antechamber," de Sousa wrote, "with my military staff, a gold chain and a gold sword, dressed in brown with a small belt, and leaning against the wall were more people and captains of the city."[84] When the party arrived, de Sousa rose slightly from his chair and opened his arms as if to embrace them. He then ordered a carpet to be put down for them to sit on, and through an interpreter, who was kneeling, he told them that he was pleased to receive them and that he wished they had come under different circumstances, with their sister. He attempted to soothe them. They should not be sad, he said; rather, they were lucky because God had shown them good fortune, and the king of Portugal would show them mercy. At the end of his speech, the governor ordered them to get dressed and sent them to the house of Dona Ana da Silva, the same woman who had hosted Njinga and had become her godmother when she was baptized in 1622. The spectacle became even more humiliating when de Sousa rose from his chair, leaving all the prisoners "lying on the floor naked [*em pee descubertos*]" and turned to congratulate their guard, Captain Domingues Lopes de Sequeira, praising him for acting "with valor."[85]

After months of intense brainwashing, Kambu and Funji finally agreed to be baptized. The baptism, which took place at the official church, recalled Njinga's own ceremony years earlier, as all "nobility of the land" turned out to witness the ceremony. De Sousa stood as their godfather, and two prominent "ladies of Luanda" served as their godmothers. Funji, the older of the two sisters, was given the Christian name of Graça, and Kambu received the name Barbara. After the ceremony, de Sousa held the two sisters hostage in Luanda while he waited for advice from officials in Portugal about what to do with them.[86]

Fernão de Sousa was also waiting for definitive word about Njinga's whereabouts. Reports had recently come in that she had not been eaten by cannibals or killed by wild beasts, but instead, had crossed the Kwango River and joined the Imbangala Kasanje. Two Mbundus, Alexandre Ladino and Manuel de Nobrega, were sent out from the fort at Ambaca to visit a *soba* whose lands bordered the Kwango. Their orders were to go directly to Kasanje's *kilombo* and verify whether Njinga had actually teamed up with the powerful Imbangala. The party must have arrived soon after Njinga crossed the river, for they were able to collect details about her movements from some of the local *sobas*. The details they obtained alarmed them as they realized that Njinga had temporarily joined up with Kasanje and had sworn to continue the resistance.

After her spectacular escape down the precipice, Njinga had concluded that the small band of followers who were still with her could not shield her from the local people whom the Portuguese had bribed to chase her out of their lands. She continued her trek farther east, but when she learned that de Sousa had withdrawn his soldiers, she quickly made her way back to Malemba again, where she began to build a new camp in the same place where she had had one before—it was this camp, in fact, from which the Portuguese had captured her sisters.[87] From here, she sent a desperate message to the Imbangala Kasanje, whose camp was on the other side of the Kwango River, and asked him for refuge from the Portuguese. Kasanje, who had earlier refused to collaborate with Njinga and had even killed the messengers she sent to him, decided this time to help her.

Help was one thing, however, and trust another. Kasanje did not trust Njinga, but he believed that subordinating Njinga would not only get rid of a fierce rival but would add to his prestige. Additionally, Njinga would bring along her many Mbundu supporters, which would increase the number of people Kasanje controlled.

But Kasanje was not interested in giving away his help for free. He told Njinga that he would only accept her into his camp on the condition that she would agree to become his wife and dispose of her *lunga* (the large military bell carried to war by Mbundu military captains). Kasanje made it clear to Njinga that he would be in charge of his *kilombo:* he did not want two masters in his camp.[88]

Kasanje may have had little expectation that Njinga would accept his proposal, since she had a reputation as being a powerful and dominant woman—an alpha female, in modern terms. She kept several male concubines and valued her status as a formidable warrior, as represented by the *lunga* itself. This great bell was the treasured symbol of military authority. Surely Njinga would not agree to take on the role of an Imbangala captain's wife, unable to participate herself in wars and obliged to refrain from all sexual contact until her husband returned from battle. A lady-in-waiting who had been with Njinga since she fled Ndongo was present when Njinga first received Kasanje's affirmative response and conditions. She later told Alexandre Ladino, one of the Mbundus dispatched by the Portuguese to gather information about Njinga's whereabouts, that Njinga did not hesitate when she received Kasanje's response. She accepted his terms without question, and when he came to meet her in his canoe, she bade

A priest performing a ritual (*second from left*) and an attendant carrying a *misete* (*third from right*), by Antonio Cavazzi, ca. 1668

farewell to her remaining followers, threw the *lunga* into the bush, and crossed the river with Kasanje and her female attendants.[89] As Njinga crossed the Kwango River, another attendant notified Njinga of her sisters' capture.[90]

Those of her followers who had remained with her up to the time she left with Kasanje reluctantly headed to Matamba or to the lands of Ndala Kisuba or other *sobas*, armed with the remaining war materiel and waiting to see what would become of Njinga's sisters. Many of Njinga's dispirited followers, including a number of *sobas* from eastern Ndongo, refused to return to Ndongo to live under Ngola Hari. Even Ngola Hari's *tendala* (chief administrative officer) refused to obey him, settling with his people in an area near the Kindonga Islands.[91]

Ngola Hari's Continuing Struggle

Despite Njinga's remote location, she was never far from de Sousa's mind. The governor realized that the Mbundus were becoming more and more connected to Njinga as well as to her captive sisters. Although Ngola Hari allowed himself for a time to believe that he was secure in his position as king thanks to de Sousa's strategic planning, Njinga's presence continued to have a devastating impact on him. He was still unable to impose his will on the *sobas* who had returned to Ndongo without relying on Portuguese military assistance; even those who gave him grudging acceptance were subject to being deprived of their positions. Some returnees did submit tribute when they were forced to, but many had precious little to hand over. During the war, the environment had been decimated; the troops had cut down palm trees and confiscated the livestock, chickens, palm oil, and hogs that comprised the expected tribute. The population, too, had been deeply affected. Portuguese troops had captured many healthy, young members of the population and taken them to Luanda, where they were either enslaved locally or sold into the Atlantic slave trade. That left few young people for Ngola Hari to send as tribute to the Portuguese king. Many *sobas* who were forced to pay up simply made do with their paltry lot, sending eighty-year-old captives who arrived in Luanda dead or so sickly that they had no value in the market. Other *sobas* who remained in the war camps on Ndongo's eastern frontier refused to send in any tribute at all and took refuge with their people in the woods when the army came after them. Some took the trek to the Kwango River in the hopes of meeting up with Njinga, while others simply disappeared into the bush.[92]

This situation was compounded by the fact that although de Sousa had invited Imbangalas such as Kasa to return to the lands from which they had been expelled and become vassals (invitations that some would eventually accept), Njinga had sympathizers in the surrounding regions such as Mbwila, Kisama, and Matamba, who continued to defy the governor. *Sobas* and other local representatives there continuously challenged Portuguese authority to impose tribute on them, avoided participating in vassalage ceremonies, and failed to communicate with Luanda.[93]

As Fernão de Sousa came to the end of his term as governor, Kambu and Funji remained hostages in Luanda. During the next few years Njinga would focus her attention on obtaining the release of her sisters while still making it difficult for Ngola Hari to rule. Although Ngola Hari retained the title of king, the real political future of the region lay with Njinga, who would soon open up a new chapter of her life.

5

WARFARE AND DIPLOMACY

Although the Portuguese had routed Njinga from her war camp in the remote Ngangela region in 1629 and captured her sisters, they had not heard the last of her, by any means. Within a few months after her daring escape, Njinga inserted herself back into the political life of Ndongo by returning to the Kindonga Islands and sending ambassadors to the new Portuguese governor in Luanda, Manuel Pereira Coutinho, who had taken over from Fernão de Sousa in August 1630. For the next two decades, not a year passed without Njinga leading her troops into battle against the Portuguese and their African allies. She also used her formidable diplomatic skills to forge an alliance with the Dutch, who conquered and ruled part of Angola from 1641 to 1648, and to build up a pan–central African alliance against the Portuguese that included the Kongo kingdom and several other nominally independent states. What contributed most to her renown, however, was Njinga's decision to adopt rituals from the Imbangala bands and combine them with Mbundu traditions, creating a new ideology that relied on the inversion of gender categories and new religious and secular rites. These bold actions so set Njinga apart that she became the stuff of legend among both Africans and Europeans, not only after her death but in life as well.

Conundrums of Portuguese Policy

Njinga's reappearance in Ndongo politics in 1630 had many repercussions for Portuguese policy. The most immediate impact was the blocking of the slave routes, which meant that *pumbeiros* (Africans trading on behalf of their Portuguese owners) were unable to travel freely to the markets beyond Ndongo to purchase slaves. As a result, merchants in Luanda had no slaves to export, and officials of the Camara (the advisory body to the governor) warned Coutinho that in light of the sorry state of the economy, he could not ignore Njinga. They suggested that he set up one of her sisters as queen of Ndongo in place of Ngola Hari. Njinga must have been apprised of the discussions taking place in Luanda, for she did not give her ambassadors slaves as ransom for her sisters, as was the custom. Instead, the ambassadors informed Coutinho that Njinga wished to return to Ndongo as queen, and that if he would not consent to this plan, then one of her sisters, preferably Kambu, should rule. She also promised to send the one hundred slaves annually that Ngola Hari had been paying in tribute.[1] With this message, Njinga made it clear to the new governor and other decision makers in Luanda and Lisbon that they would have to deal with her if they wanted to restore a flourishing slave trade.

Coutinho, who was preoccupied with subordinating *sobas* in the Dembos area who were threatening Portuguese farms, did not respond to Njinga's overtures right away; instead, he called on Fernão de Sousa, who was still in Luanda (where he would remain until the end of January 1631), to study the situation and advise him.[2] De Sousa was intent on resolving the situation in Ndongo: the continuing crisis was jeopardizing the peace and prosperity that he had hoped for after the wars against Njinga, and he wanted to protect his own legacy. He immediately began to gather additional materials with the aim of presenting Coutinho and the king of Portugal with a comprehensive plan for resolving the crisis in Ndongo. He realized that most of the *sobas* in Ndongo continued to question Ngola Hari's legitimacy to rule. Moreover, the Portuguese were on edge as a result of rumors about Njinga's association with the Imbangala leader Kasanje, the status of her two sisters, and the possibility of her attempting to rescue them. De Sousa's long letters to the king of Portugal summing up the situation provide the only account we have of these concerns and negotiations involving Njinga and her sisters.

De Sousa was right to worry that Njinga's reappearance in the region would allow her to be in contact with her sisters and would stir up more anti–Ngola Hari and anti-Portuguese sentiment. The information he gathered concerning the opinion of *sobas* and *makotas* (lineage heads) confirmed his suspicions. He realized that retaining Ngola Hari as king presented many risks to future Portuguese plans. As the situation stood, even after four years on the throne, Ngola Hari had not been able to impose his authority over the *sobas*. They had not yet sent tribute to him. And these were not just any *sobas*. Since 1627, even most of the *sobas* in his own lands of Hari had stopped paying tribute. Threats of decapitation or embarkation to the Americas as slaves did nothing to move them to obey.[3] Now Njinga's return only exposed the thorny issue of governance of Ndongo. More than his predecessors, de Sousa understood that Portuguese prosperity depended on a stable local system of governance that would allow the slave trade and tribute collection to operate smoothly. If the king, his *makotas, sobas,* and other Mbundu officials were linked through a system of clientage to the Portuguese slave markets, then slaves could be collected at the forts, and the system would work as it should.

De Sousa also knew that one of the major obstacles to the smooth operation of this system was the widespread lack of respect for Ngola Hari. In Ndongo, respect was accorded to a man who possessed a great number of slaves, musicians, and attendants. Many Mbundu *sobas* had been young men during the last years of the Ndongo kingdom, when the king had authority over hundreds of thousands of peasants and serfs and commanded massive armies. Compared with former kings, Ngola Hari lived a destitute life. In August 1633, a missionary wrote that he was distressed to find Ngola Hari "so poor in people as [to appear like] any ordinary *soba* of Ilamba."[4]

Indeed, hardly anything had changed in Ndongo since de Sousa had first nominated Ngola Hari to the throne in 1626. At the time, he threatened him with removal if he sought alliances outside the kingdom of Ndongo or disrupted the peace. Because de Sousa prohibited him from undertaking any new wars and did not give him the military assistance he needed, Ngola Hari was unable to carry out successful campaigns. Instead, de Sousa assigned him the role of chief tribute collector. Reducing both his stature and the office of king, de Sousa placed Ngola Hari in what could only be described as an unenviable situation.[5]

But it wasn't simply Ngola Hari's overall inadequacy that alienated the people. Local leaders and ordinary Mbundus alike rejected Ngola Hari because they adhered to an ideology of kingship that regarded the king not as an ordinary person but as a divinity with the ability to provide for the well-being of his people. Leadership was determined by kinship, and the legitimate ruler was the closest biological descendant of the former ruler. Although Bento Banha Cardoso had forced the *sobas* and *makotas* to elect Ngola Hari as king, they still regarded him as illegitimate. They dismissed him because his mother was a slave, and he himself had been a slave in Funji's household. More important, this lack of proper ancestry meant that he lacked the spiritual powers essential to validate him as their king. Njinga and her sisters, as the closest living kin of the former ruler Ngola Mbande, possessed the aura of divinity that legitimized their right to lead the kingdom. Indeed, this thinking was reinforced by the people's reaction to the utter devastation that resulted from the campaigns against Njinga and from the smallpox epidemic. The Mbundus connected the drought that Ndongo experienced during this period to the absence of a king, while they credited the rain that Luanda enjoyed in late December and early January 1629–30 to Kambu and Funji's presence in the capital.[6] What surprised de Sousa was that the *sobas* and *makotas* stated that their love and respect for Njinga and her sisters was such that if the king of Portugal were to allow either Kambu or Funji to return as queen of Ndongo, they would immediately obey her and work toward repopulating the kingdom. If neither sister were allowed to return as ruler, however, so intense was their distaste for Ngola Hari that they would prefer to do away with the title of king of Ndongo than allow Ngola Hari to bear it; better that the kingdom was dissolved, that they become vassals of the king of Portugal and obey the Portuguese governors in Angola.[7]

De Sousa knew this deep-seated attachment to the sisters had to be taken seriously. He discussed with the new governor, with religious and other authorities in Luanda, and with the king of Portugal the possibility of removing Ngola Hari as king and returning him to his former position as lord of Pungo Ndongo. They were divided on whether to put Kambu or Funji in his place, however, particularly since they knew that Njinga had returned to the area with a part of the army she had put together.[8] On one side was the bishop of Luanda, who argued that returning the kingdom to "these women" would be the right thing. There was no good reason to deprive them of it, he said, since Njinga had already promised to give up her right to the throne if the Portuguese nominated one of her sisters as queen. He pointed out that she had also promised to pay the Portuguese the tribute of one hundred slaves that Ngola Hari had not yet paid. On the other side were the Jesuit fathers who were serving as Ngola Hari's advisers. They were, not surprisingly, dead set against returning the kingdom to either of Njinga's sisters. They knew better than anyone that Ngola Hari had failed to deliver the population for conversion as he had promised; Christian mission work in Ndongo was almost at a standstill, as most of the population tolerated only a form of popular Christianity that was heavily influenced by Mbundu ritual practices. No matter. They argued that Ngola Hari should on principle retain the crown of Ndongo because he fully intended to pay the one hundred slaves that he owed as tribute.

De Sousa wrote to the king in Portugal that the situation had to be resolved to prevent further damage to the Portuguese crown's interests.[9] Were Ngola Hari to remain king, he explained, the *sobas* and *makotas* would continue to disobey him and would flee to other lands. He predicted that Ngola Hari would lose confidence, especially if he believed that "one of these women" could deceive him as well as the *sobas*. Even though he knew that the *sobas* and *makotas* were willing to accept one of Njinga's sisters as ruler of Ndongo, de Sousa was skeptical that either of the two sisters would be willing to work with the Portuguese. He suggested that Kambu be returned to Ndongo, since "she was loved by all," to "marry a person related to the past kings who would then become a vassal of Portugal and pay the tribute of one annually." He warned that Kambu should not be allowed to reside in the Kindonga Islands (presumably to prevent her from having easy access to Njinga), but instead should live in Kabasa. Aware that rituals to ancestors figured prominently in Mbundu ideology of leadership, he suggested that once they returned to Kabasa, Kambu and her people should not be allowed to "sacrifice to the demon, nor use the superstition of the grave," but should live as Christians, build churches, and allow the people to be baptized. There was no response from the Portuguese king. The status quo remained, and Ngola Hari continued in his role as king of Ndongo. His reputation never improved.

Becoming an Imbangala Leader

It was during the decade of the 1630s that Njinga undertook the transformation that would lead her to become known as one of the major female figures of the early modern world. This transformation built on her earlier exploits, which influenced Portuguese notions of colonial rule and even modern Angolan politics beginning with her extraordinary diplomatic coup in Luanda in 1622. At that time, she adroitly adapted Mbundu notions of leadership while shaping an economic, diplomatic, and cultural collaboration with the Portuguese that allowed her to maintain Mbundu autonomy. Her innovative political leadership further developed when she inherited the throne of Ndongo from Ngola Mbande in 1624. She governed with a style that was attentive to traditional Mbundu political and cultural notions of leadership. She clearly demonstrated this in 1626 when she invoked her brother's spirit for guidance with the sacrifice of fourteen virgins before fleeing from the island of Danji.[10]

But what really propelled Njinga's image as a leader beyond the confines of central Africa was her adaptation and implementation of other central African leadership styles into those of the Mbundu people. The new ideas came from the feared Imbangalas, whose martial traditions and rituals she first witnessed during her brother's and possibly her father's reign. In 1625, when she married the Imbangala Kasa, she came to know the ceremonies firsthand, as she had participated in some of what Cavazzi described as their "barbaric sacrifices and obscene dances."[11] She became more familiar with the intricate beliefs and rituals surrounding leadership during the initiation ceremonies she underwent to become a warrior in Kasanje's camp in Ngangela between 1629 and 1631. It was then that Njinga participated in the *cuia*, the blood oath ceremony that required the oathtaker to drink human blood to affirm friendship and alliance.[12] Njinga became an expert on Imbangala rituals, making a life-changing transformation from exiled Mbundu queen to Imbangala captain in her own right.

Adopting Imbangala ideas about leadership might have been easier for her than becoming a Christian. The Mbundu and Imbangala notions of leadership that emerged during the sixteenth century were in some respects similar, although they differed in some fundamental ways as well.[13] In Mbundu tradition, human and other sacrifices to recently deceased ancestors were practiced among the elite, but were not everyday occurrences. When Njinga sacrificed the young women to invoke her deceased brother's goodwill, she was participating in a tradition her own Mbundu ancestors had practiced. When Njinga murdered her nephew to secure the crown of Ndongo, she had as her model the legendary Mbundu queen Zundu, who had carried out the same deed.[14] The Imbangala bands also engaged in human sacrifice to honor recently deceased warriors, but such practices, as well as cannibalism, were routine occurrences.

The early Imbangala founders had developed quite different notions about leadership from those that were found among the Mbundus. As we have seen, the Mbundu people had established a state system governed by rules of inheritance based on designated lineages. According to this system, a group of electors (*makotas* and *sobas*) validated the candidate's right to the throne by certifying his or her eligibility, the most crucial aspect of which was descent from a past king. This descent ensured that the candidate possessed the spiritual grace that elevated him or her essentially to the rank of a deity.

The Imbangalas never developed a state, nor did they believe in the notion of right to rule through lineage descent. Instead, they honored a founding ancestress who they believed had bequeathed to them fourteen *ijila* (laws or prohibitions; singular, *kijila*) and a set of bloody rituals that each member of the band was required to follow. Any individual Imbangala who studiously followed the *ijila*, performed the requisite rituals, and excelled in war could become a leader of his or her own band. This seemingly democratic feature of the Imbangala system coexisted with many autocratic ones that gave the leader the right to condemn any member of his band who contravened the *ijila* to torture and death.[15] The fourteen *ijila* were not intended for settled populations but worked well for roving bands of uprooted young people who moved their *kilombos* (war camps) from place to place once they had exhausted local food supplies and destroyed local populations.

According to the traditions, some of the *ijila* had already been established when Donji, one of the original Imbangala leaders, led his band sometime in the late sixteenth century to the region of Ngangela, then a province in Matamba. Many of the *ijila* focused on the role of women: there were laws that required women to kill their children at birth, prevented women from giving birth within the *kilombo*, placed restrictions on sexual relationships, and allowed women to be sacrificed at the funerals of their deceased male concubines. Other laws ordered that women should not under normal circumstances be killed or eaten, and required elaborate festivals for girls at menarche (the first menstrual cycle). Most of the other *ijila* dealt with rituals performed at funerals, promotions or changes in status, and mechanisms for inducting young children into the *kilombo*.[16]

If Donji had already set up a system where cannibalism, rape, violence, and forcible initiation of captive children into the Imbangala lifestyle were commonplace, his concubine Mussasa, who took over the *kilombo* after his death, was reputed to have exceeded him in cruelty, training Tembo a Ndumbo, her daughter by Donji, to perfect the system she had inherited. Tembo a Ndumbo, who was credited with regularizing the *ijila,* was reported to have performed a ritual that de-gendered her, transforming her psychologically into "a man, soldier and warrior," after which she became the legislator of the Imbangala and revised the *ijila*.[17] The ritual that required the slaying of one's own child is almost unthinkable to our modern minds (though similar rituals are found in many cultural mythologies, including the Judeo-Christian tradition).[18] Tembo a Ndumbo supposedly murdered her own son by pounding him in a mortar, from which she made the oil that in Njinga's day was known as *maji a samba* (holy oil). This brutal act became the first *kijila*. From that point on, Imbangala warriors were expected to slather themselves with oil made from a human (preferably an enemy killed in battle). If this ritual couldn't be completed before battle, the soldier was required to carry a mortar and pestle in order to make the oil on the battlefield from the bodies of slain enemies.

It is believed that Tembo a Ndumbo initiated another ritual designed to either hide or transform her gender. Taking up a special military drum, she made and pounded charcoal, mixed it with the *maji a samba,* and added various herbs to produce red and white colors. She covered herself with the mixture while staring at the great bonfire she had made; then she danced and drummed to induce an altered state of consciousness, a practice that was a major part of Imbangala rituals. Drawn to her by the ritualistic drumming, her followers found her in a possessed state, and she announced to them that she should no longer be known as a woman but as a warrior. She "took a bow, arrow, and spear" and danced the war dance usually performed by male warriors. Her stated intention was to go from place to place conquering peoples, and she insisted she should no longer be considered a "lady and captain of a squadron but of an entire battalion." She demanded her followers' fidelity by requiring each of them to undergo similar rituals using the same ritual paraphernalia she had used. Tembo a Ndumbu renamed the group Muzimbo in honor of the first "father and general of the *quilombo* Zimbo," and ordered everyone to follow the fourteen *ijila* that the first captain had established.[19] The punishments that Tembo a Ndumbo inflicted on her followers who contravened the *ijila* not only increased her reputation as a powerful leader but also allowed her to mold an undisciplined ragtag group of followers into an army whose exploits and conquests became legendary in the region. Eventually murdered by her male concubine Culembe, Tembo a Ndumbo received an elaborate funeral with the requisite number of people sacrificed to serve her in the afterlife. After her death, Culembe and his new concubine helped to institutionalize the *ijila* and other customs that Tembo a Ndumbo had established.[20]

During Njinga's time, several Imbangala leaders roamed through central Africa invading the kingdoms of Matamba, Kongo, Ndongo, Portuguese Angola, and neighboring regions. Leaders such as Kasa and Kasanje assiduously imposed the fourteen *ijila* and other customs on their followers, many of them captured as children from the regions they invaded. These Imbangala leaders did not establish states; rather, they were nomadic and moved on with their *kilombos* after destroying everything in their path. The non-Imbangala population viewed them with fear, regarding them as cannibals who consumed the flesh of their dead enemies and engaged in elaborate rituals involving human sacrifice. It was because of this reputation that various Portuguese governors used them as allies in the many successful campaigns they waged against Ndongo.[21]

It was immaterial to Njinga whether the reputation of the formidable ancestress Tembo a Ndumbo was based on actual historical events or had been embellished to provide a foundational story for the Imbangalas.[22] Njinga was looking for a model for her future political life, and she chose neither the Portuguese governors, on whom she planned to wreak vengeance, nor the Kongo kings, who had only a precarious hold over their people, nor her brother Ngola Mbande, whose weakness she scorned. Instead, she chose for her model Tembo a Ndumbo and the feared Imbangalas, whose reputation for carnage, cruelty, and cannibalism made enemies and allies alike quake with terror.

Queen Njinga with bow and arrow and battle ax, by Antonio Cavazzi, ca. 1668

In deciding to adopt the traditions, rituals, and lifestyle of the Imbangalas, Njinga was rejecting the status as an exile that the Portuguese had imposed on her. Although she was familiar with the reputation of the Imbangalas and must have used some of their techniques when she fought alongside them during her brother's reign, it was only after she had become

Kasa's wife that she studied these techniques in depth and chose to make them part of her own leadership style. Later, she transformed herself into an Imbangala leader by performing ceremonies and rituals modeled on the ones that Tembo a Ndumbo had instituted, recruiting Imbangala priests to train her in the proper ways of performing the rituals and dances. The first requirement to attain the status of Imbangala leader was to kill one's own offspring and make *maji a samba* with which to anoint oneself. Since Njinga had no children and was infertile, she took an infant from one of her female concubines, crushed him in the mortar, made oil from the tissue, and pasted it on her body. (She required prospective followers to perform the same act before allowing them to join her band.) After the ceremony, Njinga assumed a new name, Ngola Njinga Ngombe e Nga (Queen Njinga, Master of Arms and Great Warrior), and took possession of the *longa* (military drum), which every Imbangala leader used to signal his authority.[23]

Njinga's tendency to adopt new names at crucial times in her life was a fundamental part of her search for an identity, a means of finding her place in a world where women were seldom major actors in war, politics, or diplomacy. In 1622 she relished the title Njinga Mbande Gambole that had been bestowed upon her by Ngola Mbande and identified her as his official envoy (literally, "referee") to the Portuguese. That same year she received the Christian name of Ana de Sousa at her baptism in Luanda and used it in all her official correspondence with the Portuguese. Her use of both her Mbundu and Christian names indicated her desire to intertwine the two cultures. After she took over leadership of Ndongo following her brother's death, she was adamant that both her people and the Portuguese address her as Ngola Kiluanje (Queen of Angola) instead of continuing to use the honorific title Lady of Angola. Now, with her adoption of the name Ngola Njinga Ngombe e Nga, she was signaling that she had come to yet another turning point in her life.

Although her Imbangala induction ceremony represented a fundamental break with much of her past, Njinga retained some symbols and rituals that were distinctly Mbundu. Just as she had done following her conversion to Christianity, she did not discard Mbundu traditions; she merely added Imbangala ideas into her belief system. She held on to her Mbundu title of Queen of Angola and incorporated Ngola Mbande as one of the

Imbangala ancestors. She also continued to use the Christian icons that she had received over the years.

Even though Njinga retained both Mbundu and Christian influences and exploited these aspects of her identity when it was to her advantage, she strongly embraced her new Imbangala identity. In particular, she immersed herself in all the requirements of the *ijila* and reshaped the laws to fit her needs. Over the years, the innovations Njinga incorporated into the original *ijila* placed her at the center of the rituals that accompanied the wars she waged, the theology she designed, and the rules she imposed on each one of her followers.[24]

Although the time is not precisely known, Njinga must have conducted the ceremony that made her an Imbangala leader sometime in the spring of 1631, shortly before or after she returned to the island of Danji and sent ambassadors to Luanda. Then she began to put together an army. Many of those who joined her *kilombo* and underwent the Imbangala initiation were disaffected Mbundus who had refused to accept Ngola Hari as their king. When the Portuguese authorities in Luanda learned of Njinga's new identity as an Imbangala leader, they were gravely concerned. The beliefs and actions of the Imbangalas contradicted the behavior the Portuguese expected of African rulers whom they considered their vassals. In 1631, a Jesuit missionary working in Kongo provided one of the first contemporary accounts of Njinga as an Imbangala leader. Although Njinga had been "reared in Luanda and cleansed by baptism," his report noted with disdain, "[she] lived an unmarried life just like the queen of the Amazons [and] she governed the army [like] a warrior female." Furthermore, she was fearlessly "going before her own people increasing the spirits of all the people." He noted that she was becoming "the best leader" and that she "offered asylum to their slaves fleeing to her with a great financial loss of the Portuguese who had deprived her of the kingdom."[25] Her personal confessor Cavazzi, relying on conversations he had with some of Njinga's followers when he lived in her court between 1657 and 1663, referred to the Imbangalas as "malefactors & thieves who were careless both of their lives and those of others."[26] By rejecting political subordination by the Portuguese and making use of Mbundu and other central African ideas of leadership, Njinga was able to reestablish herself as a major power in the region.

Njinga soon molded her army into a fighting machine and gained a reputation as a formidable Imbangala leader. Although no direct eyewitness accounts of Njinga's military exploits during the early 1630s are extant, based on conversations that Cavazzi had with Njinga and officials in her court at Matamba a few decades later, it is possible to reconstruct her movements during the period. Realizing by the end of 1631 that Governor Coutinho was not responding to her diplomatic overtures, she brought her forces into Ndongo and set them loose to ravage the territory and block the trade routes. At the same time she turned her attention to Matamba, where she had once operated and where many Mbundu *sobas* had settled with their people. After undertaking all the requisite sacrifices and ritual preparations that the *ijila* required, Njinga led her *kilombo* into the kingdom with fury. Her soldiers imprisoned some of the first groups they met, killed others, and, true to their cannibalistic practices, consumed many. As her renown grew, more Mbundus joined the ranks of her *kilombo*, and eventually she reached the capital, Mkaria ka Matamba, where Queen Muongo's court was located. A fierce battle ensued, and many of Muongo's closest followers abandoned her and fled. Njinga emerged victorious, capturing the queen and her daughter. The conquest of Matamba, which occurred between 1631 and 1635, was Njinga's first military success as an Imbangala leader.[27]

Njinga branded the defeated queen like a common slave but did not kill and eat her as required by Imbangala laws, apparently to avoid an uprising by her own Mbundu troops, who were still unaccustomed to Imbangala ways of dealing with their enemies. Even Njinga herself may not have fully come to terms with the expectations placed on her as an Imbangala leader. She banished Queen Muongo from the capital, permitting her to rule in another part of the kingdom, but the queen died soon afterward. Njinga had the queen buried in the tomb with former Matamba rulers and made sure that traditional rituals were followed during the funeral. Njinga also spared the life of the queen's daughter, also named Muongo, and reared her in the *kilombo*. In time she gave Muongo her own contingent of slaves over whom she had total control. This daughter remained at Njinga's side for the rest of her life.[28]

Njinga's conquest of Matamba gave her the political base she had lacked up until then. She became the first Imbangala leader to rule over a state and still adhere to the Imbangala lifestyle. Matamba was crucial to Njinga's plans for reconquering Ndongo. Its location on the border of the kingdom meant that she could continue to harass Ngola Hari and pressure Coutinho to release her sisters, who were still in captivity in Luanda. Njinga, ever one to capitalize on the traditions, also appears to have promoted the idea that she was a deity because of her status as a descendant of Ndongo kings. The general belief among the Mbundu people was that kings did not die but were "death itself." Indeed, as was true in many African societies, people never spoke publicly about the death of their rulers, and rulers did not tolerate anyone discussing their mortality "but wish rather to be called by the name of death itself which is *calunga*."[29] Most of her followers seem to have embraced the belief that she was immortal.[30]

Between 1631 and 1641, this aura of invincibility followed Njinga as she led her forces from one victorious campaign to another, eventually conquering lands the Portuguese had formerly claimed. During this period Njinga also adopted other aspects of the Imbangala lifestyle that allowed her to become the dominant Imbangala leader in the region.

A major transition in her evolution came when she decided that her inner circle and followers should regard her as a man, not a woman. She began her transition, oddly enough, by marrying a man, Ngola Ntombo (Lord Ntombo), and she insisted that he dress as a woman. She referred to him as female while demanding that he address her as king instead of queen. At the time of her marriage, she increased the number of male concubines she kept and ordered them to dress in the same clothing as her female bodyguards. She also required the males to sleep in the same room as her female bodyguards but demanded that they remain chaste. If one of the male concubines or female bodyguards touched someone else, even accidentally in their sleep, they would be killed or rendered impotent or infertile.[31]

Kilombo Leader and State Builder

By the time Njinga began negotiations with Coutinho concerning her sisters and the situation in Ndongo, she had become the most powerful African leader in the region. Her transformation into an Imbangala leader was largely responsible for this. She knew that she would attract large numbers of Mbundus and other peoples who for some time had been leaderless.[32] Her conquest of Matamba gave her the base she needed to launch attacks against Ndongo and surrounding areas controlled by the Portuguese.

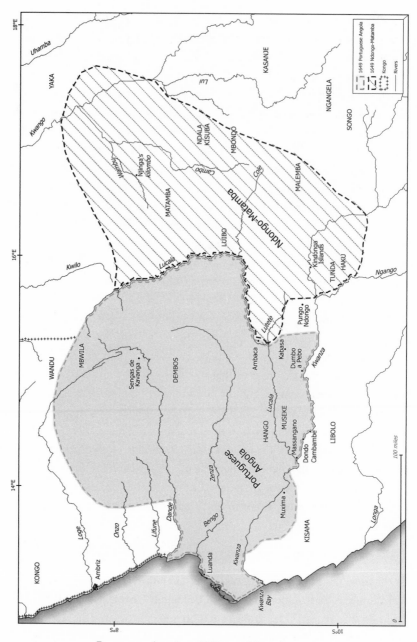

Portuguese Angola and Ndongo-Matamba, 1649

Throughout 1632 and 1633, the constant incursions of her Imbangala armies into Ndongo so terrified the *sobas* and villagers who had put themselves under Ngola Hari's authority after Njinga's 1629 flight from Ngangela that many simply joined her or attached themselves to one of the many other Imbangala bands. Others fled to the bush.[33] Njinga's activities had the disruptive effect she desired: those *pumbeiros* and Portuguese who ventured to slave markets beyond Ambaca risked being killed or imprisoned by Njinga's soldiers.[34]

An official report that the Camara in Luanda sent to the king of Portugal in July 1633 noted that "the country does not produce much since markets that were open with lots of slaves are now closed . . . because of the armies that Njinga, who wants the Kingdom of Ndongo, brings into the interior and the ones that Jagas [Imbangalas] bring."[35] With tribute in slaves and in kind having almost disappeared, and slave exports having declined from nearly thirteen thousand slaves exported in 1630–31 to almost none in 1633, Coutinho could not afford to make war against Njinga. The Portuguese also faced another threat, from Dutch forces. After the Dutch made inroads in the Luanda region, Coutinho devoted most of his attention to fortifying areas around Luanda. In Ndongo, Ngola Hari had no choice but to face Njinga's army without any assurance of reinforcements from the Portuguese. And none were forthcoming.[36]

These developments might explain why sometime during 1632–33, Coutinho decided to free Njinga's sister Kambu.[37] If Coutinho thought that her release would appease Njinga, he was sadly mistaken. Njinga's troops continued to batter Ngola Hari and the small number of people still loyal to him. In 1634, as news of the devastation wrought by Njinga and other Imbangala bands operating in Ndongo continued unabated, officials in Luanda and Lisbon began to discuss in earnest what to do about Njinga. With the governor still preoccupied by the Dutch threat from the sea, and the *sobas* in the regions near Luanda largely intimidated into submission, however, they could not muster the necessary manpower to move against her.[38]

While the Portuguese contemplated this dire situation on both fronts, Njinga spent most of 1634–35 consolidating her position in Matamba; not only did she still face opposition from followers of the deceased former queen, Muongo, but she also needed to deal with her former ally Kasa. While she was making war against Ndongo, Kasa had attacked Matamba with a large army. Only her quick return and determined resistance forced him to withdraw, although not before he destroyed many villages and succeeded in escaping with slaves and livestock that his forces had captured.[39] By 1635, Njinga was firmly in control and was leading her forces in persistent attacks against Ngola Hari and the *sobas* who lived near Ambaca and had remained loyal vassals of the Portuguese king.

By 1636, these attacks had so destabilized the area that the Portuguese could no longer ignore Njinga's presence, and the newly installed governor, Francisco de Vasconcelos da Cunha, ordered two infantry companies to Ambaca. Setting up in the same area of the Lucala River where Portuguese forces traditionally camped, the companies did not engage in battle with Njinga but were positioned to move immediately if she attacked. Njinga had no intention of fighting a conventional war against the Portuguese, and she kept her forces out of range of their guns. It would not be too long before the situation would turn in Njinga's favor, as Dutch incursions in the southern coastal port of Benguela once again distracted Portuguese attention from her and Ndongo. The governor's focus was now fixed on fortifying Luanda and other coastal regions.[40]

Even while disrupting the slave trade and making it difficult for Ngola Hari to perform his duties as a Portuguese vassal, Njinga was looking for ways to come to terms with the Portuguese. Ever one to use diplomacy even as she pursued military options, Njinga started by reaching out to the Jesuits. In 1637, she sent an official gift of ivory and slaves to their college in Luanda as an indication of her willingness to begin a diplomatic alliance. They rebuffed her overtures, rejected the presents she sent, and pointed out to their superiors that she was too corrupt for them to have any kind of relationship with. They described her as "a queen dedicated to the most horrendous customs and someone whose most appetizing meal was the hearts of boys and the breasts of girls."[41] It is possible that Njinga's overture was sincere, rather than being simply a political ploy. After the conquest of Matamba, she had broken off her relationship with Kasa, and there is reason to believe that she may have been thinking of giving up the Imbangala lifestyle in light of her success in recruiting Mbundus, many of whom were not enthusiastic about the Imbangala customs they were required to follow.

This was a missed opportunity on the part of the Jesuits, and it would be more than a decade before Njinga would again seek relations through a religious route. Njinga's army continued to operate in and around Ndongo and Ambaca until October 1639, when another governor, Pedro Cesar de

Menezes, appeared in Luanda with three hundred troops. The arrival of this well-armed governor immediately altered Njinga's strategy. Menezes imposed order in a manner that the local population had not seen since Fernão de Sousa had become governor fifteen years earlier. Shortly after settling in, Menezes sent a message to Njinga that addressed several issues he hoped to resolve, including the return of Portuguese vassals and slaves who had fled to Njinga's lands.

Njinga, aware of the large number of soldiers that Menezes had brought, but eager to capitalize on any political opening that might allow her to gain control of Ndongo, responded positively to Menezes's letter, sending ambassadors to Luanda along with gifts of slaves for the governor, the bishop, and other officials. In her letters, she indicated that she had cooperated with Menezes's command and turned over to the Portuguese emissary the slaves claimed by the Portuguese. These slaves, unlike those she sent as gifts, however, were reportedly so old and decrepit that many of them could not recall the names of their former masters.[42]

Some of the influential settlers in Luanda suspected that Njinga had sent ambassadors to Luanda to assess the strength of Menezes's forces. Others speculated that she was attempting to get news from her sister Funji, who was still being held prisoner by the Portuguese. In any case, Menezes received the ambassadors in style, with an elaborate military display. He arranged to meet them in the public plaza, where the troops stood in formation with their captains and flags. Before allowing Njinga's ambassadors to address him, he had the infantry put on a shooting demonstration with live ammunition, leaving no doubt that he had the military strength to confront Njinga's growing aggression.[43] The visual display of power had by this time become a well-developed part of political craft in the region, whether in the political sphere or in the private space of the household. After the military display, the ambassadors handed over letters from Njinga, in which she requested that a high-level Portuguese delegation visit her in her capital at Matamba to "discuss issues of interest to the two crowns."[44] By identifying herself as the ruler of Matamba, Njinga made clear to the governor that he was to deal with her as an independent sovereign and not as a returning vassal.

Menezes agreed to Njinga's proposal: he immediately nominated a respected Luanda resident named Gaspar Borges Madureira and a priest, Father Dionísio Coelho, to visit her. The two brought complementary skills to the table. Borges Madureira, a master negotiator who had lived in Angola for several years, had participated in many of the earlier wars and was an expert on local customs, and Coelho was well versed in Christian theology and was considered a humanist. The two were ordered to seek peace treaties with Njinga as well as with her erstwhile ally Kasanje and to obtain the word of both leaders that they would stop giving primacy to Imbangala rituals over Christian practices. Sometime between 1639 and 1640, the party arrived at Kasanje's *kilombo* in Ngangela. Kasanje responded favorably to the peace overtures on the condition that Njinga renounce her claims to the kingdom of Matamba, but he dismissed outright the demand that he give up his Imbangala culture.[45]

The party then traveled to Njinga's court in Matamba, where they hoped to have better success—Njinga, after all, had embraced Christianity once before. Njinga entertained the visitors lavishly, and after carefully studying the terms of the agreement that Borges Madureira had brought, she began to speak. Njinga argued that her power was based on the reputation she had gained not only in the successful wars she had fought but also among the Imbangalas, and asserted that she would not give up the ways she had learned from them. She recalled her baptism in Luanda and her exposure to Catholicism, but pointed out that the Portuguese who were now trying to attract her back to the church were the same people who had given her reason to leave it in the first place. Responding to Borges Madureira's suggestion that she should stop making wars against the Portuguese, live in peace, and accept the hand of friendship the governor had extended, she acknowledged that the Portuguese were powerful and respected enemies and noted that she would be honored to join in an alliance with the Portuguese crown. But she returned to the issue of her rights to Ndongo, asserting that only through careful judicial processes or war could there be any resolution of Portuguese claims to the provinces which her "ancestors had already possessed peacefully." His discussions with Njinga at a stalemate, Borges Madureira departed, leaving Father Coelho to convince her to renounce Imbangala practices.[46]

At this point, however, Njinga or one of her generals apparently decided to express their disapproval of the Portuguese overtures in a more pointed way. Someone, presumably at Njinga's court, gave Borges Madureira a dose of poison, and by the time he had arrived back in Ndongo, he was deathly ill. He only survived because of the quick intervention of Ngola

Hari's physicians, who administered the necessary antidote. When the governor and other officials heard of the treachery, which they assumed Njinga had perpetrated, they immediately voted to launch a military attack. But other events took precedence. As we will soon see, the Dutch conquest of Luanda in 1641 derailed any plans for moving against Njinga.[47]

In the meantime, Father Coelho remained six months longer at Njinga's court, but still he made no headway. Their daily conversations had convinced him that she remembered much of what she had learned about Christianity in Luanda, almost twenty years before. She had no difficulty in making the sign of the cross and no objection to Father Coelho leading her through the rituals of Confession prayers after she became ill. It was fine for Father Coelho to engage in such discussions with Njinga herself, but when he attempted to reach out to her followers, she drew the line, rejecting his entreaties to baptize the children who had been captured in her campaigns. If she allowed him to baptize them, she explained, she would lose her status as a true Imbangala. Father Coelho eventually left Matamba empty-handed.[48]

Njinga's encounter with Borges Madureira and Father Coelho sheds some light on the development of the leadership style that she would employ from that point on. She refused to allow the children to be baptized by Father Coelho, yet she relied on and welcomed his Christian prayers and blessings. As time went on, she would impose on her followers new, even more elaborate religious ideas and rituals. It appears that Njinga had become an expert at manipulating religious ideology and rituals to maintain power. She knew exactly what she needed to do to retain control over her followers. The arbitrary cruelties she exacted against those who contravened the *ijila* laws or against enemies who resisted her demands, which sometimes resembled the actions of a deranged tyrant rather than those of an aggrieved ruler seeking to regain the kingdom that had been unjustly taken from her, were necessary to rebuild her power base.

Alliance with the Dutch

In 1641, a new player arrived on the scene in central Africa. A Dutch armada, comprising twenty-two ships, two thousand soldiers from the Netherlands and elsewhere in Europe, and Native Americans from Brazil, sailed into Luanda on April 20. The city was soon captured.[49] Njinga was ecstatic when she received the news of the Dutch invasion and held many celebrations even before sending her ambassadors to propose an alliance.[50] Her aims, of course, differed fundamentally from those of the Dutch. Whereas she was determined to expel the Portuguese, regain her ancestral lands, and become the most powerful African ruler in the region, the Dutch were mainly interested in having a reliable source of slaves for sup-plying northeastern Brazil, which they had conquered from the Portuguese in 1630. Njinga was not the only African ruler in the region to welcome the Dutch, however, and her plan to build a Dutch-African coalition to oppose the Portuguese would depend on her skills at dealing with another major central African contender, the kingdom of Kongo. Kongo would prove her greatest ally but would also pose a major threat to her goal.

Kongo's attempts to expel the Portuguese from the region went back several decades. In 1622, when Njinga began her quest to establish Ndongo autonomy, Kongo kings were claiming Ndongo as a vassal state. Kongo rulers had long envisioned a time when they could reassert political domi-nance over Ndongo and other regions that the Portuguese had conquered. In fact, in 1622, Pedro II of Kongo had written to the Estates General in Amsterdam, inviting the group to send troops to form a Kongo-Dutch mili-tary alliance to attack Portuguese Angola. When the Dutch finally did invade Luanda in 1641, Kongo's then-ruler, King Garcia II, immediately confiscated goods and slaves from the Portuguese merchants in the capital of São Salvador and forced them to leave. Rulers in several of Kongo's prov-inces even killed some Portuguese residents. Garcia also sent troops to the southern provinces straddling the Bengo and Dande Rivers, where the Portuguese governor and other officials had gone after Luanda was taken. Kongo troops assisted the Dutch in military operations in Luanda and the surrounding regions, which resulted in Portuguese officials and thousands of Mbundu free people and slaves fleeing the region and taking refuge in the more secure forts at Cambambe, Muxima, Massangano, and Ambaca. Besides rulers in Kongo, other Africans who aided the Dutch included several leaders in the Dembos region, more than thirty *sobas* in the Libolo region, rulers in the province of Kisama (who had never accepted Portu-guese rule), and hundreds of *sobas* who had nominally been vassals of the Portuguese.[51]

To create a successful coalition, Njinga would also have to bring on board the many Mbundu leaders who, although opposed to the Portuguese, had no intention of becoming Imbangalas or being her subjects. Many of these leaders welcomed the Dutch, providing them with local assistance and intelligence. The Portuguese were aware of the dire political consequences of any kind of Dutch/Mbundu alliance, especially among the seasoned and loyal *kilambas* (Mbundu soldiers under Portuguese command) who had been so crucial to Portuguese military successes in the interior. One such soldier defended Mbundu collaboration with the Dutch by arguing that they were "soldiers of fortune" who had "wives to feed," and who, moreover, were "offended by the bad treatment they received [from the Portuguese] in front of their wives and children who were nearby."[52]

The Dutch were not surprised when Njinga's ambassadors arrived in Luanda in November 1641, some seven months into their conquest. They had already collected intelligence on potential allies among local rulers and had identified "a certain woman called Nzinga [with whom] the Portuguese have never had peace neither friendship as they have with the other inhabitants."[53] The ambassadors had committed to memory the entire text of Njinga's message and recited it to Pieter Moortamer, the Dutch West India Company's representative in Angola. They began by expressing the "joy the queen felt about the progress of [the Dutch] victory" and emphasized her interest in trading with them. Although Moortamer noted that he did not quite know what to make of those "savages" and their queen, who "did not have anyone who knew how to read and write," he sensed that the relationship would benefit the company, since Njinga had indicated her willingness to trade with them, and this was "something she had never voluntarily done with the Portuguese."[54] Moortamer welcomed Njinga's initiative, as it promised to enhance the company's major goal: to defeat their Catholic enemy Spain (Portugal and Spain were under one crown from 1580 to 1640) in the protracted Thirty Years' War that had spread from Northern Europe to Brazil and Angola.[55] Despite the "savage" appearance of Njinga's ambassadors, Moortamer immediately sent Dutch soldiers back to her court in Matamba with the envoys, supporting her plans to broaden the alliance against the Portuguese.[56]

Njinga was also putting other pieces of her plan into action. While her ambassadors were in Luanda, her troops were operating in eastern Matamba, Ndongo, Ambaca, and surrounding areas. Between April 1641 and 1642, the Portuguese governor was not only confronting Kongo forces who had joined with the Dutch and invaded Portuguese-occupied lands in the regions of the Bengo and Dande Rivers, but he was also coming up against popular resistance among Portuguese slaves and free Mbundus who lived in the vicinity of the forts at Cambambe, Muxima, Massangano, and Ambaca. Governor Menezes, realizing that he did not have enough ammunition or troops to confront these new threats, retreated to Massangano, which became his new base of operations. From there he sent out small contingents of troops and spies against some of the *sobas* as well as against Dutch and Kongo forces.[57] Seeing the Portuguese thus pinned down, Njinga's troops were able to operate with impunity in the African villages around the fort at Ambaca, and many of the *sobas* there and elsewhere once again began to recognize her authority.[58] Eager to press her advantage, Njinga ignored appeals for reconciliation in a letter sent by Governor Menezes in October 1641. Ngola Hari remained her main target, and her troops harassed him without fear of a Portuguese counterattack.[59]

At the same time, Njinga's spies in the Dembos region were passing on to her crucial information concerning the popular uprising that was going on there against the Portuguese. Portuguese troops suffered a terrific rout after they attacked the Dembos ruler Nambu a Ngongo, who was able to repel them with the aid of two hundred Dutch soldiers. Njinga was then emboldened to move her eighty-thousand–strong *kilombo* to the middle of the Dembos region, while still maintaining her headquarters in Matamba. This area was in the region of Sengas de Kavanga in the lands of one of her supporters, the *soba* Kavanga. The site had many advantages. Not only was it strategic from a military point of view, but it was well-watered, fertile, and pleasant, located near the Dande, Zenza, and Lifune Rivers and containing many small streams where Njinga and her entourage could go for recreational baths. The *kilombo*, set on a plateau, was so large that it took two days to go from one end to the other, and, unlike *kilombos* of other Imbangala leaders, which were barebones, easily moveable structures that allowed quick retreats, it was a large, complex center, containing palm trees and livestock of all kinds. The *kilombo* provided lodging for her large army, and Njinga would later build residences for herself, her sisters, and her courtiers and other officials, including her many religious advisers and the local rulers who were her allies. As she captured more people, she built more residences where they could stay and work. The *kilombo* also featured common areas in which she could receive dignitaries.[60]

Although the move was a direct threat to Kongo, which bordered the Dembos region, Njinga now had access to her two closest allies, the Dutch and the Dembos *sobas*. From this base she had no difficulty intimidating any *sobas* who dared to oppose her, particularly Kitexi ka Ndambi, the only local ruler who had refused to join her. Njinga attacked him with Dutch support and set his capital on fire, and he was finally forced to submit. By the end of 1642, Njinga had been able to compel all the *sobas* of the Dembos region to recognize her authority, a feat that neither the Portuguese nor the Kongo kings had ever managed to achieve.[61]

While Njinga was extending her influence beyond Matamba, reconquering or subordinating territories that had formerly paid tribute to Ndongo, the Portuguese were huddled in their four forts, Massangano, Muxima, Cambambe, and Ambaca, and some of the islands in the Kwanza.[62] Although they regularly ambushed Dutch forces and organized punitive expeditions against the *sobas* who lived in the vicinity of the forts, most of these *sobas* had switched their allegiance to Njinga or the Dutch.[63] At this point Njinga was meeting little direct resistance from the Portuguese.

The situation changed in January 1643, however, when the Dutch and Portuguese authorities signed a truce in Lisbon. The truce was meant to end the fighting and force the Portuguese to concede Luanda and certain other areas to the Dutch. In exchange, the Dutch would allow the Portuguese to return to their farms along the Bengo River and travel freely to Luanda to sell slaves and other goods. Satisfied with the terms, Governor Menezes felt that the situation had stabilized sufficiently to return, with many of the Portuguese who had fled, to the Bengo region. By May, however, Dutch officials had broken the truce. They secretly sent troops to the areas the Portuguese had reoccupied, killing up to forty soldiers and officials, taking more than 180 Portuguese prisoner, including the governor, and occupying Portuguese forts in the Bengo and Hango regions. Those Portuguese fortunate enough to survive the attack made their way back to Massangano.[64]

While tensions between the Portuguese and the Dutch persisted, Njinga's troops continued to make life difficult for Ngola Hari. In March 1643, he wrote to the new Portuguese king, João IV, to complain about the "persecutions that I have suffered as a result of Njinga's actions."[65] But Njinga had more than Ngola Hari on her mind. After she learned about the

Dutch-Portuguese truce, she became suspicious of the Dutch. Would they maintain their alliance with her? Indeed, there might be some truth to Cadornega's contention that once Njinga had used the Dutch alliance to defeat the Portuguese she would then "throw the Dutch out of Angola."[66] It would have been foolhardy for Njinga to believe that they were totally committed to her interests. Although she certainly didn't trust the Dutch completely, neither did she regard them as a major threat to her plans. The Portuguese were still of much greater concern. Njinga may have believed that if she defeated the Portuguese and gained control of all of the lands from Luanda to Matamba, she would be able to dictate the terms of the relationship with the Dutch in a way she had never been able to do with the Portuguese.[67]

After the breakdown of the truce, Njinga was relieved, believing that this signaled the possible demise of Portuguese rule in Angola.[68] While her troops occupied themselves with their continued harassment of Ngola Hari, stopping short of engaging the Portuguese troops that had been stationed at the fort in Ambaca, Njinga turned her attention to Kongo. To the horror of King Garcia II, Njinga dispatched most of her forces, some estimated eighty thousand Imbangala soldiers, to Wandu, an eastern province of Kongo.[69] The ruler of the province of Wandu had revolted against Garcia, and Njinga took the opportunity to send in her army. Although Garcia was partial to Njinga's war against Portuguese, he was fearful of Njinga's expansionist activities, and such a large-scale attack against Wandu threatened Kongo itself.[70]

Njinga's growing military power led to a slew of diplomatic initiatives by Kongo, the Portuguese, and the Dutch. In September 1643, two of Garcia II's ambassadors arrived in The Hague to request Dutch military assistance. Although some reports suggest that Garcia needed troops to put down a rebellion in the coastal province of Soyo, it is more likely that his fear of Njinga led him to make the request. The Portuguese, for their part, feared that he was requesting help to dislodge them from the area. Undoubtedly Njinga's military successes were forcing Garcia, the Portuguese, and the Dutch to reassess their dealings with her. Portuguese officials conjectured that having more Dutch troops in the area could be disastrous for them because Garcia could consolidate the inroads he had made in northern Angola, and they advised the king of Portugal to send troops to Angola under the guise of assisting Njinga.[71] Dutch West

India Company officials, while wanting to help Kongo, were reluctant to jeopardize the relationship they hoped to build with Njinga. One report from Luanda noted that Njinga controlled an enormous region that stretched from the borders of Dutch-occupied Luanda to some 300 leagues (about 900 miles) inland, and that between two thousand and three thousand slaves per year came from her lands. The report went on to speculate that she could potentially supply the Dutch with "all that we need."[72]

Officials in The Hague thus rated friendship with Njinga very high and cautioned local representatives not to take any action that would antagonize her. Instead of helping Garcia, they pressed local company officials to send a high-level embassy to Njinga to persuade her to maintain her alliance with them.[73] The Portuguese were even more concerned about Njinga. For the time being, Njinga's alliances with Kongo and with the Dutch survived, but as she pursued plans to end Portuguese rule in the region, she knew that she could not count heavily on Kongo's support. Njinga was unquestionably making herself a key player, whose decisions could change the political fortunes of the Portuguese, the Dutch, and the Kongolese.[74]

As resentment of the Portuguese increased among the African population between 1644 and 1646, Njinga did not hesitate to capitalize on her growing military and diplomatic dominance. She strengthened her ties with Imbangala leaders and with *sobas* who had joined her cause, and their troops attacked the populations in the vicinity of Ambaca and Pungo Ndongo, where many were still loyal to the Portuguese. Njinga's forces also came to the aid of enemies of the Portuguese, whom she considered her allies. For example, in early 1644, Njinga dispatched troops to help her ally the *soba* Ngolome a Keta when he sent for help. Ngolome a Keta, who had been destroying villages around Ambaca, had been attacked by an army made up of Portuguese soldiers from Massangano, troops commanded by the Imbangala Kabuku Kandonga, and the army of Ngola Hari's son. These combined forces succeeded in encircling and trapping Ngolome a Keta and his troops in their mountainous hideout. Some of his troops had managed to escape and traveled to Njinga's headquarters at Sengas de Kavanga, where they asked for her assistance. Njinga immediately sent a detachment of her most experienced soldiers, headed by Njinga a Mona. When she learned that his forces had suffered heavy losses and failed to break through Portuguese ranks, Njinga raised another detachment and led the charge herself. Encouraged by her admonition to stand up against "these few *mundeles* [whites]," her soldiers engaged the Portuguese in a day-long bloody conflict. Njinga emerged victorious, her troops having killed seventy Portuguese officers and soldiers. Many Imbangala troops and numerous *kilambas, sobas,* and their soldiers were also wounded, killed, or captured. Njinga had told her soldiers not to kill the Portuguese officers they captured, but they disregarded her and beheaded most of the captives. In the end, only seven Portuguese captives remained alive, including the priest Father Jerónimo Sequeira, whom Njinga imprisoned in her *kilombo* along with the others. Njinga's troops also captured the Imbangala Kabuku Kandonga, a Portuguese ally, along with his concubine Coamza, and some officials of his *kilombo,* as well as a number of *sobas* from the Ambaca region who had been supporting the Portuguese.[75]

Although Kabuku was an ally of the Portuguese, Njinga ordered his release, adhering to the Imbangala oath which prohibited an Imbangala leader from killing a fellow leader. What Njinga did not know was that her very success as an Imbangala leader had harmed her reputation among the other Imbangalas. Kabuku, for example, who regarded himself as a true Imbangala and claimed descent from the original group, had more prestige among many Imbangalas than Njinga did. Many viewed her as an upstart. Setting Kabuku free allowed him to rejoin the Portuguese and continue the war against her.[76] Njinga had her revenge against another Imbangala leader named Kalandula, a number of years later, when he refused to turn himself over to the Portuguese to fulfill her part of a proposed peace treaty. As we will see in the next chapter, Njinga could not tolerate this act of defiance. Nearly seventy-five years old, she donned her war outfit and led her soldiers in a rigorous war dance in the middle of the main square before leading them in a confrontation with Kalandula. Scoffing at the compliments of Father Gaeta, who witnessed the dance, Njinga retorted: "Excuse me father, . . . when I was young I conceded nothing to any Jaga [Imbangala] in ability and in fearlessness. . . . I never feared facing a group of 25 armed soldiers, except if they had muskets. . . . When it came to other arms where anyone could demonstrate their courage, agility and valor, [I was ready]."[77]

It was this fearlessness that allowed Njinga to instill dread in Africans and Europeans alike. She also was a careful strategist. One of her greatest successes from the 1644 victory in support of Ngolome a Keta was her capture of many *sobas* from Ambaca who had accompanied the Portuguese forces, including a close blood relative named Ngola Kanini. Ngola Kanini was the same *soba* who had been forced to pay an annual tribute to the Portuguese for the construction and upkeep of the Church of our Lady of the Assumption in Ambaca when Mendes de Vasconcelos built the fort there in 1619 (see Chapter 3). Although Ngola Kanini had been a Portuguese vassal for all those years, Njinga treated him kindly, allowing him to remain in her camp and later at her court, bestowing on him the respected title of *mwene lumbo*.[78]

Because her aim was to build up Mbundu political institutions in Matamba, the capture of the *sobas, makotas,* and others who were connected to Mbundu ruling lineages, who had knowledge of the traditions already, was vital to her plans. Relying on what she remembered of the Ndongo of her youth, Njinga was in the process of putting together an intricate court system in Matamba, even as she constructed *kilombos* when she was in the field. She spared no expense on housing, clothing, and material objects for her inner circle. She built houses from local materials, all richly decorated with imported carpets, silks, and cloths of various patterns for herself, her personal attendants such as the *mwene lumbo* Ngola Kanini, her sister Kambu, the Matamba princess Muongo whom she had adopted, and her many concubines.

When she had moved her *kilombo* to the Dembos region in 1641, she painstakingly recreated the court system she had built at Matamba. Here she made some interesting additions to her temporary residence. Like the Ndongo kings of old, who had several courts, she made sure that her sister and officials had their own quarters. She also built accommodations for the Dutch soldiers and their families who had fought alongside her soldiers. The Portuguese looked on all of this with suspicion. They believed that part of the Dutch strategy was to send Dutch women to live in Njinga's *kilombo* so that the local population would see her giving orders to whites and would be more willing to join in the campaign against the Portuguese. Several rulers from Dembos had residences in the camp, and it also served as a prison for the Portuguese and Africans she captured.[79]

Njinga used most of the income she received from the sale of the slaves she captured, the presents and tributes she received from the Dutch and her African allies, and the booty she took from her military campaigns to purchase guns and ammunition, as well as cloths and jewels. Since she considered Kongo's King Garcia II her only equal in the region, she went to elaborate lengths to ensure that she had a public space built where she could receive his ambassadors, as well as others. The meeting place, located in the center of the *kilombo*, was a covered structure containing two elevated daises with a wall at the back, and it served as a place of both business and pleasure. She entertained diplomats and visitors here, and also adjudicated cases. For visiting Kongo or European diplomats, Njinga covered both the wall and the daises with rich velvets and silks and placed several sets of imported cloths and tapestries on the grounds of the entire plaza. To meet a visiting delegation, she would always dress for the occasion, wrapping herself in brightly colored cloths, wearing several sets of gold jewels and pearls, and displaying on her legs and arms the traditional bracelets from her youth. On these occasions, her personal mate and female attendants, surrounding the dais on which she sat, were similarly decked out. Perhaps recalling the days when she sat at her father's feet as he received delegations, Njinga would have Kambu and Muongo elaborately dressed as well, and she made them sit in front of her on carpets. Her officials, Dutch soldiers, and *sobas*, as well as members of the visiting delegation, would sit on carpets set out in front of the daises.[80]

Njinga's success in establishing political centers in both Matamba and the Dembos region and her continuing military successes were a cause of serious concern to King João IV of Portugal and his Overseas Council. Although the council members still supported her rival, Ngola Hari, the focus now shifted to how to stop Njinga's advance.[81] The news the council received from Angola was not good. In the months following Njinga's 1644 rout of Portuguese forces near Ambaca, the Portuguese situation had deteriorated; the army was laid low by sickness and lack of military supplies, while Njinga's forces operated seemingly everywhere with apparent impunity. Her troops roamed about, intimidating the *sobas* and raiding Ngola Hari's lands, and she continued to make new allies with *sobas* in the Dembos region. Moreover, her invasion and destruction of Wandu in eastern Kongo had left Kongo's King Garcia stunned. Her actions had even intimidated the powerful forces of Kasanje, who, with other Imbangalas, had invaded Matamba but made no headway against her. In July 1644, officials on the Overseas Council expressed frustration at Njinga's military successes and advised the king of the need to "exterminate her," referring to her as that "infernal woman in her customs who links herself with all the rebels." She couldn't be more unlike Ngola Hari, who, they wrote, "has retreated to his land and is faithful."[82]

As New Year 1645 dawned, it became evident that something needed to be done. King João IV finally decided to nominate Francisco de Sotomaior, the governor of Rio de Janeiro, to the post of governor general of Angola. He ordered Sotomaior to put together an army to reconquer Angola. Njinga's successful campaigns against the Portuguese made her the center of discussion as plans unfolded for the invasion.

Sotomaior arrived in Angola on July 25, 1645, with 260 soldiers, and in December, he submitted a report to João IV that revealed how much Njinga's military successes had changed the political and military landscape in the region. Sotomaior noted that many Portuguese experienced in local warfare, as well as one hundred soldiers who had come earlier from Brazil as reinforcements, had been killed by Njinga's Imbangalas. Moreover, the Dutch conflicts with the Portuguese had led to the Dutch banishing to Brazil hundreds of Portuguese who had participated in many of the earlier wars.[83] At the time, he calculated that the number of available white Portuguese troops amounted to a scant eighty soldiers who protected the forts at Massangano and Muxima, while at Cambambe and Ambaca the Portuguese might be able to muster 130 soldiers and about eight thousand Mbundu bowmen. The pathetic military state of the Portuguese forces had encouraged Njinga to be even more aggressive, and her army had taken up positions all around the forts and the villages of the Mbundu *sobas* who were vassals of the Portuguese, making it impossible for them to help Sotomaior, and even threatening Ngola Hari, who it seemed had survived only because he was able to rely for defense on the natural fortress in Pungo Ndongo, where his capital was located. Although recognizing the role the Dutch played in the dire military and political crisis the colony faced, Sotomaior identified Njinga as the main enemy, acknowledging that the regular slave trade she carried on with the Dutch guaranteed her supplies of ammunition to sustain her eighty-thousand–man army, while damaging Portuguese trade and power.[84]

Yet Sotomaior, like previous Portuguese governors, was initially reluctant to believe that Njinga possessed the necessary military and leadership skills to challenge Portuguese power in Angola. After six months laid up with his sick troops in Massangano, he still hesitated to move against her, blaming the delay on the precarious situation at the forts and the bad climate, which was affecting the health of his soldiers. Although eventually identifying Njinga as "the most powerful adversary that has ever existed in this Ethiopia [Africa]," noting that she was widely reputed to be responsible for the Portuguese defeats and vowing to bring an end to her insolence, he still blamed the Dutch for fomenting the situation and for indoctrinating Njinga with anti-Portuguese sentiments. He admitted, nevertheless, that he was unable to confront Njinga at the moment; she was too popular, too admired by the Africans for him to be able to get any of the local people to join in the campaign against her.[85]

Defeat in Dembos

After Sotomaior's arrival in Luanda, Njinga's spies, among them her sister Funji, whom the Portuguese still held as a prisoner in Massangano, sent her regular updates about the Portuguese military plans. She was aware that Sotomaior had appointed Gaspar Borges Madureira, the ambassador who had visited her in Matamba in 1640, to lead a unified force against her. The army was to include the usual array of Portuguese soldiers and settlers, some of their former slaves, Mbundu soldiers, and Imbangala soldiers supplied by the Imbangala leader Kabuku. Even as the preparations were underway, Njinga had received word that Estácio de Sá Miranda, the Portuguese captain of the cavalry, was already in the village of a man named Gregório, a prosperous former Mbundu slave who lived not far from Ambaca. From her *kilombo* in the Dembos region, located some eight days from Ambaca, she ordered one of her Imbangala generals, Gaspar Akibata, to lead a contingent of Imbangala soldiers to attack Gregório's village and to capture and bring the captain to her. Akibata made the trip to Gregório's village in record time, guided by the expert scouts Njinga had provided, but when he arrived, he discovered that Sá Miranda had left. Determined not to disappoint Njinga, his soldiers attacked and imprisoned or killed most of the population. They carried off all the cattle and other provisions and destroyed whatever they couldn't carry, setting the village on fire as they made their victorious departure.[86]

Sotomaior, who was at Ambaca, soon received news of the assault and rounded up the troops for a counterattack. In an impassioned speech to the soldiers, he rehearsed the outrageous actions their enemy Njinga had committed against a Portuguese vassal and explained the importance of responding with immediate force to preserve the integrity of Portugal. He then led them in a successful attack on Akibata's *kilombo*. The attack happened just after Akibata's men had returned to their base and built a bonfire to feast on their human and animal spoils. The Portuguese army succeeded in killing Akibata and most of his soldiers, although a few escaped to Njinga's *kilombo*. After receiving news of the defeat from the lucky few survivors, she ordered them beheaded; she considered it bad luck that they had brought such horrible news to her and had expected them to die along with their comrades. This defeat was disheartening for Njinga's Mbundu supporters, many of whom fled from the *kilombo* and resubmitted themselves to the Portuguese. The shock of the defeat created such a sense of foreboding and dread among those who remained that they spent several days performing *tambos,* the solemn Mbundu rites that occurred at funerals. Perhaps it was at this point that many Mbundus who had looked to Njinga as a goddess realized that even she could not protect them from the Portuguese.[87]

This setback did not deter Njinga, however. Her troops were soon attacking *sobas* loyal to the Portuguese whose populations were located some distance from Ambaca. She must have had some successes, since she sent a great number of slaves to the Dutch and asked for their help in moving against Ambaca. The Dutch were receptive to her overtures; a delegation had already been sent to Njinga with the hopes of improving relations.[88] Njinga believed that despite this recent reversal, her forces still outnumbered the Portuguese and that the Dutch alliance would help her regain her military edge and improve her sagging prestige among the local population.[89]

What she had not anticipated was that Sotomaior was intent on breaking her alliance with the Dutch and would soon follow up with a larger and more coordinated attack against her base in Dembos. Unlike previous governors, who had been satisfied with the status quo, organizing targeted campaigns to force loyal *sobas* to pay tribute and ensuring that the slave markets and slave routes remain open, Sotomaior realized that before long, the status quo might cease to exist: Njinga's alliance with the Dutch and her military successes against the Portuguese posed a very serious threat to it. The governor knew that he had to bring the war to Njinga's *kilombo* at Sengas de Kavanga to prevent her from launching further attacks. Sotomaior's ambitions were grand: he planned to destroy Njinga and defeat the

Dutch at the same time. Njinga would be shown no mercy. He ordered that upon her capture she should be immediately killed. It would be "unnecessary to bring her" with the other captives, and they should destroy "everything else of her *kilombo*; and that even the fruit trees should be turned upside down, and that everything with her name should be destroyed forever."[90]

Sotomaior calculated that his troops stood a better chance of defeating Njinga now, while she was closer to Massangano and not hundreds of miles in the interior at her court in Matamba. He recognized that he could neutralize the Dutch by fighting on two fronts—a river war in which vessels would block the Dutch from using the Kwanza River to bring supplies to Njinga, and a land war in which a large Portuguese-African force would head for her *kilombo*.[91] In fact, Dutch and Kisama soldiers had recently attacked Portuguese troops in Muxima, which was only thirty miles from Massangano, and in the process had killed eighty soldiers and taken many captives. The fear was that these same forces would soon overrun Massangano.[92]

In March 1646, Borges Madureira put together the largest land force that Njinga had ever faced and led the troops into what would be an epic battle, with equally epic goals of capturing and killing her, destroying her *kilombo,* and ending her alliance with the Dutch. The force, assembled at Ambaca, comprised more than four hundred Portuguese military officers and soldiers; two hundred armed mulattos; sixteen cavalry; field artillery; thirty thousand African soldiers, including archers; more than two thousand scouts; troops led by Ngola Hari; Imbangala troops; troops of sympathetic *sobas* and freed slaves of the Portuguese; and thousands of porters, who carried all the supplies and food, since the army expected no supplies to get through along the way. To describe Borges Madureira's army as formidable would be an understatement.[93]

Marching north from Ambaca, Borges Madureira's troops crossed the Zenza River and finally arrived at the Dande River, where they eventually spotted Njinga's *kilombo* from some nearby hills. Njinga apparently had prepared for the invasion, building three bridges with the expectation that the Portuguese would use them to cross the Dande River. She calculated that the soldiers and carriers would make excellent targets for her bowmen and the thousands of her soldiers who had guns. But Borges Madureira would not allow Njinga to dictate the conditions of the attack and dissuaded the leaders of his squadrons from crossing over the bridges. Instead, his army took a longer and more dangerous route, crossing at a deeper part of the river and arriving much closer to Njinga's *kilombo*. But she was also prepared for a surprise attack, having placed around the perimeter of the *kilombo* troops provided by the ruler Mbwila, of the Dembos region, as well as some Dutch troops. She had ordered the soldiers to hide in tall bushes, and as soon as the Portuguese troops entered, they were supposed to set the bushes on fire to prevent the Portuguese advance. But this strategy failed: Borges Madureira was able to arrange the vanguards in such a way that the porters carrying the supplies were in the middle, and thus the supplies were protected. As the Portuguese troops neared the camp, they had to contend with Dutch soldiers and the troops led by feared general Njinga a Mona as well as by Njinga's *mwene lumbo* and other generals. Njinga herself didn't stay out of the fray; Portuguese spies spotted her standing on a hill, surrounded by her loyal core of youthful Imbangalas and dressed in her war outfit.

The two sides fought a bloody battle from about nine o'clock in the morning until late afternoon, when the Portuguese troops finally succeeded in breaking through Njinga's defenses. Njinga sent soldiers armed with guns to charge down the hill against the surging Portuguese, but they failed to prevent the advance. Dutch soldiers provided support, but they lacked heavy artillery, which would have been much more effective against the invaders. In the end, even with stiff resistance from the Dutch and Njinga's Imbangalas, the Portuguese troops prevailed, and the vanguard reached the *kilombo*.[94]

Njinga had stationed various battalions of her army at strategic distances from the *kilombo*, but once the Portuguese vanguard had broken the perimeter and entered, she realized that the small number of bodyguards would be incapable of defending it. She and her close associates made a quick escape. Her sudden departure was obvious to the victorious Portuguese, who met no resistance upon entering the *kilombo*. They quickly discovered that Njinga and her bodyguards had not even had time to gather items from her residence or the residences of her officials. Everything was left behind. Sacking the houses of Njinga and her main advisers, they found five hundred firearms and stores of rich fabrics and jewels. Ngola Hari now claimed every possession in the house, coming away with "many rich pieces of silk and other valuable things."[95]

The hasty retreat meant that the many noncombatants who had remained in the *kilombo*, waiting to celebrate the anticipated victorious return of Njinga and the army, had not been warned and were shocked to see Portuguese troops entering their residences. Among them were several officials and other *sobas* from Dembos who had set up residence in the *kilombo* but who were not physically fit to join in the battle.

The Portuguese were most surprised to discover in one of the residences an obviously pregnant "Flemish woman." Through hysterical tears, she explained to the bewildered soldiers that her husband was among the group of Dutch troops who lived in the *kilombo*. The young woman did not know where her husband was but thought he might have either died or abandoned her, fleeing with the couple's son.[96] The presence of Dutch soldiers with their families in the *kilombo* is a clear indication that Njinga had successfully made these northern European foreigners her dependents. The presence of these foreigners helped her pressure the powerful rulers of Dembos and independent *sobas* to join her cause. Learning the details of how Njinga ran her *kilombo*, the Portuguese grew even more hostile. The soldiers physically and verbally abused the African rulers they captured for the affront they believed Njinga had committed against their fellow Europeans.[97]

Of all the riches they amassed, of all the *kilombo* residents they captured or killed, by far the most valuable to the Portuguese was Njinga's sister Kambu. Whether Njinga had abandoned her, or whether Njinga planned to later bargain with the Portuguese for Kambu's release, her appearance when the enemy troops entered her residence suggested that she was resigned to becoming their prisoner once again. The Mbundu *kilambas* (soldiers allied with the Portuguese) found her sitting in regal splendor with forty ladies-in-waiting attending her, seemingly unperturbed by the intrusion. Kambu remained so calm that the military chronicler Cadornega, who fought in the campaign, later credited her deportment to "majesty and sovereignty." Despite horrific treatment—she was sexually abused during the night by the Mbundu soldier who found her and held her captive—Kambu comported herself with the same royal dignity when she was handed over to Borges Madureira the following morning. To prepare for her appearance before the captain, Kambu had her ladies-in-waiting dress her elegantly. They decorated her hands with gold rings, placed beautiful jewels on her head and chains around her neck, and wrapped her hair with cords that cascaded from her head to her hips. Indeed, although Kambu was well over sixty years old at the time of her second capture, she appeared so much younger that Borges Madureira, to avoid another situation where she might be assaulted by Portuguese guards, took over her supervision, keeping her in his quarters until he could transfer her to Massangano.[98]

Borges Madureira knew that Njinga had been holding several Portuguese prisoners, including the priest Jerónimo Sequeira, in the *kilombo;* not finding them in the inner area where Kambu and the other officials were housed, he learned that, before fleeing, Njinga had sent these prisoners, along with some of her valuables, to the *soba* Kitexi ka Ndambi, whose lands were about one day's journey from the *kilombo,* demanding that he guard them in the forests surrounding his lands. Kitexi ka Ndambi had remained a reluctant ally since Njinga and a hundred Dutch troops had invaded his lands a few years before, and now he was only too willing to turn over the twelve soldiers and the priest to Borges Madureira's envoys.

Kitexi ka Ndambi's betrayal meant that if Njinga had had plans for a prisoner exchange, she now had to give them up. Borges Madureira promptly sent the freed soldiers and priest to Massangano and publicly killed twelve *sobas* and some of the Dembos rulers in the *kilombo.* The Portuguese troops freed a number of their African allies whom Njinga had kept prisoner, including Coamza, the concubine of the Imbangala Kabuku. After allowing their own soldiers and those of their Imbangala allies to pillage the residences, storehouses, and passageways of the *kilombo* and take whatever valuables and supplies they could get their hands on, the Portuguese set fire to the camp, destroying most of the residences and public buildings as well as hundreds of small, scattered temples where Njinga's priests conducted their rituals.[99]

Njinga's quick retreat had other serious repercussions. The Portuguese found letters written to Njinga by her sister Funji hidden under the altar in the small chapel she had built for the Catholic priest. The letters revealed much about Njinga's spy network and put Funji's life at risk. During her more than fifteen years of captivity, Funji had fed Njinga news about Portuguese military operations. This explained why Njinga had been able to move against the Portuguese with such ease. The Portuguese also discovered letters that Njinga had received from her African allies, including Garcia II of Kongo. In one letter, Garcia had congratulated Njinga for her 1644 victory against the Portuguese. Kongo would pay dearly for Garcia's alliance with Njinga.[100]

With this victory, the Portuguese destroyed the strategic base in Dembos that Njinga had built, but, more important, they handed her a humiliating personal defeat. They once again held both her sisters prisoner. In addition, Borges Madureira conjectured that her flight would damage her alliance with the Dutch, destroy the relations she had cultivated with King Garcia II, and weaken the prestige she had acquired throughout the region. But, as in the past, Njinga remained undaunted. In fact, her ability to escape unharmed from the *kilombo* even though the Portuguese had brought in several Imbangala allies to capture her, including her old nemesis Kasanje, showed that Njinga still retained a great deal of popular support in the area. Although she realized that her enemies had taken some important prisoners and that her army had suffered great losses, the strategy Njinga had employed of spreading her troops throughout and around the *kilombo,* where they could hide between the tall bushes and palm trees, ensured that many of her soldiers and porters had been able to escape along with her. Borges Madureira and his army realized this after their search of the *kilombo* turned up the baggage that her porters had abandoned as they retreated. No porters were to be found, though. When the Portuguese troops arrived at the foot of the hills, all they found were thousands of footprints that the departing soldiers and porters had left behind.[101]

Dutch Betrayal

Within a few months of her flight, Njinga was again planning a counterattack. This time the Dutch were fully involved. Months after the rout, Njinga's envoys had gone to Luanda with a large supply of slaves, a gift to Dutch West India Company officials that demonstrated her firm commitment to the alliance.[102] They responded accordingly, and in April 1647 they sent an embassy led by Ferdinand van Chapelle, the company's commissioner for trade, to Njinga's *kilombo.* She had relocated her *kilombo* to Kunsi, in the northeastern region of Ndongo, near the upper Bengo River. Before van Chapelle's arrival, Njinga had been reassessing her military strategy and reconstituting her army. Instead of attacking the Portuguese with all her troops, as before, she instead sent out small guerrilla forces that ceaselessly pillaged the lands of *sobas* friendly to the Portuguese around the forts of Ambaca and Massangano. Van Chapelle told Njinga that the company was formally inviting her "to celebrate by written agreement with his Majesty

[Willem] a solid offensive and defensive agreement." Njinga graciously thanked the director, declaring that she was ready to celebrate the "act and contract," and van Chapelle left the meeting elated. A formal signed contract was not long in coming. On April 23, 1647, Njinga's *mwene lumbo* placed her seal on a provisional agreement, and on May 27 he ratified it on Njinga's behalf, the directors Cornelis Ouman and Adriaen Lens signing for the company.[103]

The terms of the agreement called on the Estates General, the Prince of Orange, and the West India Company on the one hand, and Queen Njinga on the other, "to help each other with their people, counsel and actions" in order to "exterminate the Portuguese." The pact directed Njinga to send to Luanda half of all the slaves she captured. It also stipulated that neither party could have dealings with the Portuguese and their allies without the prior knowledge of the other, and that each party would have to support the other party in the event of such negotiations. This was not the sort of agreement made during the height of colonial conquest in the later nineteenth century between European explorers and merchants scheming to deceive illiterate, primitive African "chiefs"—it was a formal pact between equals. Both parties solemnly bound themselves, under oath, "to maintain, respect and sacredly comply with the agreement, and to revenge any treachery, betrayal and attacks committed against the alliance." To demonstrate their good faith, the Dutch sent seventy soldiers from Luanda to Njinga's *kilombo* to help her in her forays against the Portuguese and their allies.[104]

The formal signing of the agreement was a diplomatic coup for Njinga. Although she did not know it, the directors of the company in The Hague had been committed all along to making a formal alliance with her, despite the frustrations they had faced in communicating with her directly. The officials had high regard for Njinga's military leadership and looked on her as someone who could advance their cause in Angola. Indeed, from the time of their conquest of Luanda in 1641, company directors had hoped that a solid alliance with Njinga would so alarm the Portuguese that they would give up their holdings in Angola.[105] In 1645, they had actually sent correspondence to Njinga laying out the terms for a closer alliance, but Kongo's Garcia II, who had already signed a treaty with them, was suspicious of their outreach to Njinga and intercepted the message.[106]

For Njinga as well as for Dutch officials, political considerations were at the heart of the move to finalize a formal relationship. Since the March 1646 destruction of her *kilombo* and the capture of Kambu, Njinga had been seeking ways to exact revenge on the Portuguese and rescue her sisters. But in 1647 she was hit with terrible news: Funji was dead, drowned by the Portuguese in the Kwanza River as punishment for spying. Kambu was still alive, though, and Njinga became so intent on saving her remaining sister that she showered the Dutch with gifts and promised to come in person with her army to fight alongside them.[107] Van Chapelle's embassy must have buoyed her spirits: she became convinced that the Dutch also wanted to avenge the recent successful attacks by the Portuguese against their bases in and around Luanda and against the *sobas* from Kisama who supported them.[108] The Dutch were frustrated that all their military and other efforts had failed to break the Portuguese resolve. By September 1647, the situation was threatening the Dutch hold on the capital and along the Dande, Bengo, and Kwanza Rivers and the island of Nsandeira, in the mouth of the Kwanza River, where their troops were stationed. Dutch soldiers had started deserting to the Portuguese, revealing secrets of the sorry state of affairs in the capital. Their allies in the Dembos region, fearing a Portuguese attack, pleaded with the Dutch for military assistance.[109]

Between September and October of 1647, the Dutch, the *sobas* in Dembos, and Njinga prepared for a general attack on the Portuguese. As plans for the attack developed, Njinga's prestige improved considerably. This time, no one leaked the details of her preparation to the Portuguese. Perhaps they feared for their own lives and chose not to antagonize Njinga unnecessarily, or perhaps they believed that this time Njinga would be successful. Even King Garcia II, her inconsistent ally, calculated that he might gain by joining in the attack. The plan was that Garcia could raise an army comprising troops from his provinces, as well as from a people called the Kongos who lived on the island of Luanda. Njinga would lead her contingent of Imbangala forces, and Njinga a Mona and other captains would lead others along with *sobas* from Ilamba and parts of Ndongo and Matamba. Njinga was to meet up with the Dutch as they made their way from Luanda. This Dutch-African alliance would also include many "rebel *sobas*" who were scattered throughout the region with their own soldiers.[110]

On October 25, before the Dutch could assemble at the appointed camp, however, the Portuguese army, numbering some twenty-five thousand men divided into three groups, attacked on three fronts. Although the troops from Dembos made a valiant defense, succeeding in killing three hundred Portuguese, it was Njinga's arrival on October 27 that turned the tide. She arrived two days before she was supposed to meet the rest of the Dutch army with her four thousand men, half of whom were battle-seasoned archers, along with the seventy Dutch soldiers under their own captain who had been sent to join her forces. All told, the army numbered three hundred Dutch led by Ouman, ten thousand men from Dembos, and four thousand Imbangalas under Njinga. They immediately marched to Kumbi, an area north of the Lucala River, where one of the Portuguese battalions under Borges Madureira had set up camp.[111] They immediately launched a ferocious attack against Borges Madureira.

The Portuguese were caught off-guard by this attack of the combined Dutch/Njinga forces. Before the battle ended, more than three thousand of the enemy lay dead, and the survivors, mulatto and African soldiers and carriers, fled in disarray. Borges Madureira himself was one of the victims, having suffered a fatal wound to his leg. Thousands were taken prisoner.[112]

The victorious armies then made their way to Massangano. Njinga had selected Njinga a Mona to lead the charge against the fort to free Kambu, and he was able to get the local *sobas* to relay messages among the three armies and to allow embassies to move easily between one location and the other. Indeed, many of these *sobas* who had earlier rejected Njinga suddenly demonstrated their loyalty by giving the Dutch free passage through their lands, allowing them to come within a quarter mile of the Massangano fort. For eight days, Njinga's forces together with the Dutch torched more than two hundred villages of *sobas* who had joined with the Portuguese and razed the surrounding farms and plantations on which the 1,500 Portuguese who were living at the fort relied.[113] A Portuguese spy who reported on the advancing army described it as being so large it covered "mountains and valley." Yet the army failed to penetrate the defenses of the fort.

The Portuguese knew that should Massangano fall, that would signal the end of their presence in the region. To avoid this calamity, they had taken precautions to upgrade the fort's defenses. Massangano had become the intelligence center for Portuguese administrative and military officials and was a refuge for both African and Portuguese soldiers and for the thousands of carriers who accompanied the army. The fort also housed priests, women, and children who had fled the Dutch-controlled regions near the Bengo and Dande Rivers. Some of them had in fact spilled out of the fort and built villages near the Lucala River, which they protected with trenches.[114] By the time Njinga's and Ouman's troops arrived, the fort was so overcrowded that houses had to be destroyed to accommodate the artillery, and every man was armed, priests included.[115]

Njinga's guerrillas did their utmost to break through the fort's defenses, but Ouman's presence helped little because he lacked the heavy artillery so crucial to a successful bombardment of the well-constructed fort. The Portuguese strategy of fighting both a land and river war was critical here, as the blockades the Portuguese had erected all along the Kwanza River had prevented the Dutch from bringing heavy artillery near enough to the fort to bombard it. Njinga a Mona, following Njinga's orders, attempted a different approach. Njinga had him send the troops to set fires in several locations to distract the Portuguese guards in the hopes that some soldiers could force their way through. Even if only a few soldiers gained access to the fort, Njinga hoped they would be able to determine the exact location of the arms and ammunition and, not least of all, the whereabouts of her sister. Njinga's strategy came to naught, however, since the guards discovered the plot. When one of their former allies, the *soba* Pedro Bamba Atungo, was caught, the guards arrested him and sounded the alarm, despite his claims that he was assisting the Portuguese. He was later beheaded.[116]

A dejected Njinga a Mona, disappointed by the inability of the Dutch to break through the Portuguese defenses and unable to free Kambu, returned empty-handed to Njinga, who had remained at a strategic location. In the meantime, Ouman and the remaining Dutch troops headed back to Luanda, leaving Njinga to reassess her position. Njinga continued to attack *sobas* who supported the Portuguese and regularly dispatched messengers to Luanda with crucial information about Portuguese troop movements. One of the messages she sent, in April 1648, informed the Dutch that a Portuguese army made up of 133 white soldiers and 280 specially trained soldiers armed with guns was located a short distance from Massangano; they were on their way to Ambaca to relieve the fort there, in response to Njinga's relentless attacks on all Portuguese settlements in the region. The Dutch sent Major Thyn Pieterszoon and three hundred soldiers, along with thousands of Africans, to meet Njinga at the camp where she had brought her own troops. This time, the Dutch made the trip in record time; they had secretly built a canal in the region of Muxima that allowed them to bypass the heavily fortified fort.[117]

By August 1648, Major Pieterszoon's three hundred soldiers had taken their positions alongside Njinga's four thousand troops on the Ambaca plateau. There, the two armies waited for the Portuguese troops. When the African troops supporting the Portuguese finally appeared, Njinga's Imbangalas pounced from their hideouts, taking them totally by surprise. The attack was so sudden that the porters fled in panic, leaving their cargoes along the way. Although the Portuguese fought heroically, they had to divide their forces so that some of them could fight Njinga's Imbangala soldiers and others the Dutch.[118] They were overwhelmed by the combination of artillery fire from Dutch guns and the ferocity of Njinga's Imbangalas. More than one hundred Portuguese lost their lives, and only eleven remained alive to surrender. Dutch forces and Njinga's plundered whatever they could, burned the rest, killed innumerable Africans, and captured three thousand Africans who would be sold as slaves. Included among the Africans who were killed was Ngola Hari's son Francisco.

By the second week of August, the Dutch-Njinga alliance seemed unstoppable. Njinga was planning to move against Ngola Hari in Pungo Ndongo to remove him from power and then lead her troops with those of her Dutch allies to finish off the Portuguese, who had tenaciously clung to Massangano. By this time, the people in Massangano had lost all communication with the other forts and were destitute and starving. The survivors could only anticipate what was in store for them, as none of their local allies dared send provisions and reinforcements. It was too great a risk.[119]

What Njinga did not know was that the Portuguese king had nominated a new governor, Salvador Correia de Sá, and that in June 1647, he had left Rio de Janeiro with an armada of fifteen ships and nine hundred men. In August 1648, Correia de Sá and his armada thundered into Luanda's harbor, sending a shiver through the heart of the Dutch director Ouman. Although he had no idea that one of Correia de Sá's ships had sunk, he knew his numbers, and they weren't reassuring. He had barely 250 men under arms and hoped that he would be able to hold out until the arrival of reinforcements under the command of Major Pieterszoon. But Correia de Sá had heard from some local fishermen that Pieterszoon was in the interior, so he immediately bombarded the city with cannons and sent negotiators with an ultimatum to Ouman: give up Luanda in three days and receive safe conduct, or face more bombardment. Ouman sent word to Njinga and Pieterszoon to dispatch troops to Luanda immediately. The disconcerting message could not have come at a less opportune moment for Njinga and Pieterszoon, who were leading their troops in what they believed would be the final assault against Massangano. In the meantime, anticipating the quick arrival of Njinga and Pieterszoon's forces, the Dutch West India Company officials tried in earnest to drag out the negotiations. Here again, however, the company's directors were outmaneuvered. They had left the entrance to the port completely unprotected, having ordered their soldiers to gather in the larger forts, especially the well-protected Fort Ardenburg (Portuguese Fort São Miguel), where all the company books and other valuable items were stored. On August 15, Correia da Sá, not waiting any longer for the Dutch response, bombarded the city from all points and continued night and day until his troops arrived at the walls of the forts. Realizing that Correia de Sá's forces were now joined by tumultuous groups of Portuguese who still lived in the city, Ouman lost heart and within a few days sued for peace.[120]

Njinga, arriving with Pieterszoon in late August, was ignorant of the fact that before her arrival, Ouman and other officials had signed a treaty of capitulation, turning over their positions in Angola to the Portuguese and agreeing to leave Luanda. She had positioned her troops a few miles outside Luanda, preparing to move them in at the first sign from Pieterszoon, who had gone on ahead. No word came. Pieterszoon had arrived just in time to board the ships with his departing compatriots. What Njinga couldn't miss, however, once she approached the city, was the Portuguese flag flying high above the fort of São Miguel. Njinga was left to ponder if there were any Europeans left that she could trust. Once again, a major betrayal forced her to retreat back to her base in Matamba.[121]

As she joined the rest of her Imbangala forces, who were carrying out operations beyond Massangano, the last thing Njinga wanted to do was to give her enemies the impression that she was crawling back to Matamba in defeat. Although she knew that she had to return to Matamba, where Kasanje had taken advantage of her long absences to make several incursions into the eastern parts of the kingdom, she wanted to demonstrate that she was still the major African power in the region.

On September 23, 1648, a little over two weeks after her retreat, Njinga sent a contingent of her troops to invade Kongo's eastern province of Wandu, where her Imbangalas had been operating. Njinga might have sent her troops to help Garcia II discipline the still rebellious provincial ruler as part of an agreement she had made with Kongo. She also had personal reasons for ordering the invasion. She wanted to avenge the death of some of her captains and soldiers who had died at the order of the ruler; she also wanted to punish him for having dismissed her as a mere woman who was "cleverer with a distaff than a sword."[122] Njinga gave the order to destroy the province and unleashed fifty thousand of her troops, which included female units whose soldiers were integrated into the general army. The fighting began in early October and lasted three days, with the provincial ruler himself and five hundred of his soldiers losing their lives. Most of the women and children fled the capital for the safety of the mountains. By the time another contingent of Njinga's soldiers arrived, the city lay in ruins. Two Spanish Capuchin missionaries hid in the ruins of the church during the fighting. After the battle was over, Njinga, who had remained some distance outside of the city, sent two hundred men, "their heads decorated with various feathers, their bows and arrows flexed," to carry out mop-up operations. The church was a convenient place to start, since most of the residents had fled, carrying everything they could. After desecrating the altar and taking the vestments and other religious items, they found the missionaries, whom they captured and abused physically and verbally but did not kill. They also captured the missionaries' Kongo companion and interpreter, Calisto Zelotes dos Reis Magos, also a priest, who would later join Njinga's court.[123]

After the priests were taken before Njinga, and she looked at them standing before her temporary throne, perhaps she was thinking about whether these priests were different from the other white men who over the years had betrayed her. Could she use them and the spiritual bond that she shared with them to obtain what she most desired: the freedom of her sister, an end to the Imbangala life that she had been forced to adopt to survive militarily, and recognition of her right to rule an independent Ndongo-Matamba state? Although the Wandu campaign would not be the last war Njinga fought, it created a turning point in her strategy. From the time she met the two missionaries to the day of her death fifteen years later, Njinga was preoccupied with using diplomacy and spirituality to achieve the goals that had eluded her for so many years.

6

A BALANCING ACT

At the end of 1648, when Njinga was in her mid-sixties, she found herself having to formulate a new strategy. The Dutch had broken their agreement with her and sailed away, and she had had to give up her plans to attack the Portuguese fort of Massangano. She realized that to achieve her chief goals—obtaining her sister's release from Portuguese hands and pressing her claims for the return of the Ndongo lands—she would have to adopt strategies other than military ones. Although she continued to fight wars, she focused now not on expelling the Portuguese entirely but on ensuring that they could make no political or economic headway in the interior unless they dealt with her.

To maintain a strategic advantage over the Portuguese, Njinga adopted a three-pronged approach between 1648 and 1656. First, she reestablished firm political control over Matamba and the lands between Matamba and Ndongo, areas that were the primary source of slaves. As a result, despite the successes of Governor Correia de Sá's campaigns against the Imbangalas and *sobas* who had joined the alliance between Njinga and the Dutch, he and later governors were forced to reopen political relations with Njinga to resolve the slave trade question. Second, Njinga initiated direct relations with the Capuchins, a religious order whose missionaries would come to serve as her political intermediaries not only with Portuguese governors in Angola but with higher officials in Europe as well. Third, Njinga developed plans to put Catholic Christian beliefs and rituals in place of the Imbangala religious ideas and rituals that had been the unifying ideology binding her together with her followers.

Njinga's successful implementation of her new strategies would allow her to achieve all of these goals. By the end of 1656, she had secured her sister's release, confirmed her right to rule Matamba as an independent kingdom with definitive borders recognized by the Portuguese, and put in place the conditions for transforming Matamba into the Christian kingdom she envisioned. In fact, Njinga's success in blending military, religious, and political diplomacy into an effective strategy of governance so amazed her detractors and admirers alike that during the last five years of her life, both groups were already praising her as having no equal in all of Africa. To follow Njinga during the decade or so after she returned to Matamba, we will look first at her continuing military operations, then at her religious diplomacy, and finally at the political diplomacy that eventually resulted in the signing of a peace treaty with the Portuguese in 1656.

Njinga's Continuing Military Campaigns

Even though Njinga's new strategy no longer envisioned military defeat of the Portuguese, she continued to use war as an essential element of her leadership. A 1650 report by a Portuguese observer listed more than twenty-nine invasions that Njinga's armies undertook between 1648 and 1650, noting that the rulers of the lands Njinga invaded were either killed or had become her tributaries, who recognized her as their "natural lady." She had not lost any of her ferocity: in one campaign against the Imbangala Caheta, Njinga's forty thousand troops faced Caheta's ten-thousand–man army and so overpowered his troops during a dawn attack that Caheta was paralyzed with fear, not knowing whether to fight or to flee. She came away with more than six hundred prisoners and destroyed everything in Caheta's *kilombo*, "up to the trees." Describing the Njinga he observed during these years, the writer noted, "I have seen Njinga dressed like a man, armed with a bow, arrows, and already old and of small stature. Her speech is very effeminate."[1]

After her quick departure from Luanda in August 1648, Njinga's first act had been to quarter her army near Massangano and send troops out to force the *sobas* in the region to recognize her as their ruler. With 139

Imbangala regiments under her control, she had no difficulty in getting *sobas* to comply with her demands.[2] The invasion of the Kongolese province of Wandu in September of that year, described in Chapter 5, had come out of Njinga's desire to demonstrate to the local ruler there that she could still impose her will in the regions bordering Ndongo.

Njinga continued to use her army to intimidate local *sobas* in the regions that bordered Kongo, Matamba, and Ndongo to illustrate that she still had formidable forces under her control, despite the military setbacks she had suffered. In the months following the Wandu invasion, she even undertook several military operations near the Portuguese forts of Massangano and Ambaca. She knew that the governor was preoccupied with strengthening military reinforcements in the forts in and around Luanda in his efforts to bring rebellious *sobas* in the region back to the Portuguese fold and would think twice about engaging her in direct battle.

As she was heading back to Matamba, she ordered invasions on the east side of Matamba, as far as the borders of the Kwango River, in an attempt to reestablish a strong military presence in the region. This area had formerly been under Njinga's control but had been overrun by her enemies during the years that she had been fighting around Ambaca. Her greatest military opponent here was the Imbangala Kasanje, who had established his *kilombo* in a part of Matamba that Njinga claimed as her own.[3]

It is important to note that Njinga's armies during these campaigns of the early 1650s were made up of both men and women. A French traveler to Angola in 1652 observed that the women who accompanied Njinga's army were numerous and that each had "four or five officers in their service and for their pleasure." Like Njinga, these women were trained to fight, and either fought battles alongside the men or went on their own campaigns.[4]

Njinga did not restrict her military activities to eastern Matamba. In March 1655, for example, she ordered Njinga a Mona to invade the Mbwila region in eastern Kongo; despite strong resistance, he succeeded in conquering the province. Njinga must have wanted to demonstrate to the Portuguese that she was still capable of fielding military operations even though she was at the same time seeking peace with them.[5] Njinga now controlled lands that extended from the eastern side of Ndongo to Matamba and northward along the Kwango River.[6] Njinga always maintained that she had a right to Angola and Ndongo, but even after having been defeated and forced to flee the Dembos region, the kingdom she ruled still included parts of Ndongo, the entire kingdom of Matamba, territory that Kongo claimed, and parts of the Yaka kingdom (in present-day Democratic Republic of the Congo).[7]

Njinga not only sent her captains out to war but even took the helm herself sometimes during this period. In December 1657, just before leading her troops in a campaign against the Imbangala captain Kalandula, Njinga prepared herself for battle by leading the soldiers in the customary, rigorous military exercises with arrows and spears. Most of the soldiers participating in the exercise were young enough to be her great-grandchildren. On the way to Kalandula's camp, Njinga gave orders to block all possible routes of escape, and the army clandestinely encircled his base during the night. In the morning, she had a soldier put her flag high up in a tree and challenged Kalandula to fight. Realizing that Njinga had him cornered, Kalandula immediately sent an emissary who swore that he considered Njinga "his queen and goddess" and that in the future he wished to obey and serve her. When four hundred of his troops attempted to flee upon hearing his declaration, Njinga immediately sent some of her troops after them and captured most of them. Many of the captives were sent to Ambaca and sold as slaves. She then led her troops in a ferocious attack against Kalandula's remaining forces, in which 1,500 soldiers were captured and many were killed. Kalandula himself died; his head was severed and presented to Njinga, who would send the grisly trophy to the Portuguese governor.[8]

Although this battle was to be the last that Njinga personally led, she never disbanded the army, and she continued to rely on warfare as part of her strategy to maintain control over territories she had subordinated, to help allies, or to punish neighbors who presented a threat to her rule.[9] Njinga's sergeant general informed her of any movement of enemy armies, and she kept a group of military scouts who could be deployed at any time to assess the danger. She was prepared to order troops into the field whenever necessary.[10] For example, in March 1658, four months after her return from the battle against Kalandula, Njinga received news that the Yaka army had taken advantage of her absence and made several incursions into Matamba's northeastern border. Njinga attempted to negotiate with the Yakas' king, but when he made it clear that he regarded this as a sign of weakness, she abandoned diplomacy and ordered an attack. The captain of the operation succeeded in capturing the king, who immediately sued for pardon. Njinga obliged; the war and pardon ensured an appropriate level of respect and fear for her, as well as peace in the far northeastern part of Matamba.[11]

To demonstrate that war remained a core aspect of her leadership, Njinga continued to welcome into her ranks many Imbangalas and *sobas* who had been her former allies during the Dutch occupation but who had shifted their loyalties back to the Portuguese as a result of Correia de Sá's military campaigns against them from 1648 to 1650. Correia de Sá had beheaded fourteen *sobas* identified as rebels who had joined the Dutch, as well as four of the five Imbangalas his troops had captured during operations in Kisama. Many of the remaining *sobas* and Imbangalas soon became disaffected by the Portuguese policy of promoting the interests of the settlers. In fact, they had lost most of the fertile lands they farmed along the Dande, Zenza, and Kwanza Rivers to Portuguese settlers who moved following the reconquest. As a result, they switched their allegiance once again to Njinga.[12]

One of these leaders was the Imbangala Kabuku Kandonga (a different person with the same name as the Kabuku we met in Chapter 5). In February 1653, he decided to break his alliance with the Portuguese and make a secret arrangement with Njinga to join his *kilombo* with hers in Matamba. Njinga sent emissaries to him early in 1654, but the Portuguese governor, who described Njinga at the time as "the capital enemy of the Portuguese," learned of the plan and gave the order to imprison everyone in Kabuku's *kilombo*. The following year, the new governor, Luis Martins de Sousa Chichorro, invaded Kabuku's lands, captured him, and sent him off to Brazil.[13] A few days later, Sousa Chichorro organized a major campaign against the *soba* Kambambe, one of Njinga's former allies who had reemerged as a major threat to the Portuguese, attracting some ten thousand enslaved Ndongos whom Portuguese settlers claimed as their own. Sousa Chichorro continued operations in the region for eighteen months, with both sides amassing major casualties.[14] Kalandula, the Imbangala whom Njinga later killed in battle, was also implicated in plans to join Njinga, but he managed to escape capture and flee with a large number of slaves and one thousand soldiers. He placed himself and his people under Njinga's control and settled six miles from Ambaca in lands that she claimed.[15]

Njinga's military strategy relied not only on the successes of the armies she led or on the Imbangalas and *sobas* that she attracted to Matamba or other parts of her lands. She also remained actively involved in the local politics of Ndongo, which meant that she often used her army to resolve succession disputes in favor of candidates she supported. One such case was that of João Muquila. João contested the selection of his brother as *soba* to take their father's place and assassinated his brother and several of his uncles. When the Portuguese recognized the brother's son, Sebastião Kiluanje, as ruler in 1656, João recruited Njinga to aid him in ousting Sebastião. Although Njinga's army made three attempts against Sebastião, Portuguese troops repelled the assaults and killed the three captains who had led them.[16] Although she did not succeed in toppling Sebastião, the case illustrates that even as Njinga was negotiating a peace treaty with the Portuguese, she was prepared to move against *sobas* in the area around Ambaca. This region would continue to be the center of resistance for the rest of her life, and Portuguese officials, although they were able to consolidate some level of control over the area, had no choice but to recognize that Njinga's military strength would be a major hindrance to their plans for expanding beyond the Ambaca fort.[17]

Even in the last years of her life, when she was no longer leading her army, she continued to oversee military campaigns. For example, in October 1661, Njinga sent her army into battle against the Imbangala leader Kasanje after he led his army in an attack against a *soba* in her lands, killing all the men and infants and taking the women and children prisoner. Although another *soba* repelled a second attack, forcing Kasanje to retreat, Njinga still decided to counterattack immediately. Before gathering combatants, she went to church to make a private confession explaining the reasons for her decision to go to war. She then went to the public square, accompanied by her female bodyguards, armed with their bows and arrows, and her male soldiers, who also served as protection for her. She roused the people with passionate words, and soon she had gathered a massive army to fight Kasanje. Following the retreating army, her troops successfully routed Kasanje's forces, killing many, taking others prisoner, and delivering to Njinga sixteen flags of the officers who had drowned while trying to escape across the Kwango River. Even though this occurred after Njinga had fully accepted Christianity as the official religion of Matamba, the victory celebration included Imbangala rituals along with a Christian service in which the captured flags of the enemy were offered to the Virgin Mary in thanks for the victory.[18]

Queen Njinga smoking in front of a shrine, by Antonio Cavazzi, ca. 1668

Njinga's strategy of using military might to demonstrate her continuing power so vexed the Portuguese governors that they frequently asked permission of the king of Portugal to make war against her again. In July 1652, Bento Teixeira de Saldanha, an official in Luanda, noted in a letter to King João IV that the principal adversaries of the Portuguese in Angola were the king of Kongo, Njinga, and the ruler of the completely unconquered province of Kisama. All three rulers, he explained, were able to stop the slave trade to Luanda, "so vital to the economy," because "they persecute and attack the vassal *sobas*." He requested permission to recruit African soldiers to defend the *sobas* and to make war against the three rulers. In December 1652, the issue was partially resolved when the Overseas Council, in a split decision, advised the king not to agree to the request.[19] Njinga's continuing military strength likely influenced the council's decision. Members warned him that he should caution the authorities in Luanda not to go to war against Njinga or the other leaders, reminding him that earlier governors who used war as a means for capturing slaves had brought ruin to the territory. To pardon Njinga and her two fellow African leaders for their betrayal during the period of the Dutch occupation, the council suggested, would be advantageous to the Portuguese. A renewed friendship would mean a return to slave trading.[20]

In a letter dated September 16, 1653, Portuguese officials in Lisbon ordered officials in Luanda to undertake a war against Njinga in the interior only if they were certain they had enough troops to protect Luanda. The city must under no circumstances be subject to "an invasion by the enemies." In 1654, João IV warned Governor Sousa Chichorro against acceding to Ngola Hari's demands to make war against Njinga. Instead, Sousa Chichorro should work to "conserve that queen" so that her army would not invade and ruin the colony.[21] Although João IV died later that year and Sousa Chichorro undertook other military operations against Kongo and Kisama, the royal directive of the deceased king continued to inform dealings with Njinga. As late as 1657, after Njinga had signed a treaty with the Portuguese, of the "three enemies" the Portuguese identified in Angola, Njinga was the only one with whom they felt the need to pursue peace.[22] While other regions would continue to see their share of fighting, Matamba would not be subjected to Portuguese military aggression thanks to Njinga's powerful persona as much as to her military preparedness.

Religious Diplomacy Revisited

Even as her army engaged in campaigns all over the regions east of Ndongo between 1648 and 1656, Njinga was looking for a diplomatic solution. As a first step, instead of dealing directly with the Portuguese, she made use of the priests and Capuchin missionaries captured by her armies. Njinga's first attempts at religious diplomacy came as early as 1643, at her *kilombo* in Sengas de Kavanga in the Dembos region. Here, Njinga began a long-term campaign to gain the confidence of the missionaries coming from Rome so that they would be willing to plead her case in Europe. From the outset, she treated captured missionaries differently from other Portuguese soldiers or civilians. Instead of holding captured priests as hostages, Njinga often released them; if she did keep them as prisoners, as she did Father Jéronimo de Sequeira, she afforded them considerable freedom. She captured Father Sequeira in 1644, along with twelve soldiers, yet she gave him the run of her *kilombo* and even built a small altar for him to use and required him to say mass for her. She treated him respectfully, addressing him as *nganga ngola* (priest of the *ngola* [king]), to which he responded "*kalunga, kalunga queto*" (Heaven, Our Heaven). Not surprisingly, the Portuguese who captured the *kilombo* in 1646 were scandalized to find that the altar was located alongside a "diabolical house" she had built for her own *ngangas*.[23]

The capture by her army of two Spanish Capuchin missionaries and a Kongo priest during the invasion of Kongo's Wandu province in 1648 provided her the opening she was looking for to initiate formal diplomatic relations with the Catholic Church. The Spaniards, Father Bonaventura de Cordella and Father Francisco de Veas, along with their Kongo companion and translator, Father Calisto Zelotes dos Reis Magos, had been given permission by King Garcia II to go to the rebellious province of Wandu to carry out missionary work, and the group arrived a week before Njinga's army attacked the province and looted the capital. Njinga's personal guards rounded up the Capuchins, who had taken refuge in the church and were hiding under the altar. Njinga's soldiers remembered her order that Christian *ngangas* were not to be killed, so they delivered the Spanish priests to her. She reassured them that they need not fear her, but they worried that they would be required to consume human flesh. Njinga put their minds at ease by having one of her servants prepare venison for their meal, the skin and bones of the animal still showing to indicate the source of the meat. Njinga also spent many hours conversing in Portuguese, a language she knew well, with the Spaniards. When Njinga learned that Father Zelotes was among the prisoners slated to be killed and eaten by the victorious soldiers, she demanded that the Imbangala captains turn him over. It was only then that she realized he was the priest who had first introduced her to Christianity a quarter-century earlier in Luanda. Al-

Queen Njinga with captured missionaries

though she could not prevent him from being branded and having his two front teeth extracted (indicating that he was to be a slave in the *kilombo*), Njinga cared for him by tending his wounds and bringing him back to health. He would later become her personal secretary and would play a crucial role in her reengagement with the church.[24]

But Njinga had other motives for treating Father Cordella and Father Veas as well as she did: she wanted to test them to see whether she could use them as her conduits to Rome. In the many conversations she had with the two Capuchins, she made a spirited defense of her lifestyle. Although she sidestepped their attempts to persuade her to change her ways, she indicated nevertheless that she was serious about developing closer ties to · the church. It was well known that missionaries and the church were appalled by the Imbangalas' ritual cannibalism. Njinga denied that she was a cannibal, asserting that she and her captains *"no comemos carne humana* [do not eat human flesh]."[25] She admitted that she tolerated the custom among her Imbangala soldiers, but what could she do? "It was their custom," she said, resignedly, and it was impossible to stop.

Njinga fought hard to secure an alliance with the Roman Catholic Church. She gave the two priests a letter addressed to the pope, in which she promised to return to Christianity and invite Capuchin missionaries to her kingdom as soon as the war with the Portuguese was over and her kingdom restored. As was customary, she gave the priests gifts to show her sincerity, offering them slaves and other "valuable goods." She was completely taken aback—and pleasantly surprised—when they refused her offers, including that of the slaves. Impressed, she allowed them to leave in the company of a Kongo embassy that King Garcia II had sent bearing gifts for her.[26]

Although this meeting with the two Spanish Capuchins in 1648 was Njinga's first exposure to missionaries in this order, her reputation was already well known among them. In March of the same year, the Capuchin father Giovanni Francesco da Roma had written a letter to the Propaganda Fide in Rome (the Congregation of the Holy See, founded for the purpose of evangelizing areas of the globe where Christianity had not yet taken hold) concerning the state of the church in Kongo. In the letter, he made reference to Njinga, noting that her lands bordered Kongo and that she had been baptized as a Catholic but had abandoned the faith because of the "cruelty of the Portuguese" who "had made a war against her and dispossessed her of her kingdom."[27] Although she did not know it at the time of her meeting with Father Cordella and Father Veas, the Capuchins were regarded with suspicion by the Portuguese and the Jesuits, and, as a result, the Spanish priests were predisposed to be sympathetic to her. The letters she sent to the Capuchins indicating her willingness to develop formal diplomatic contacts with Rome garnered the kind of attention she would never have received from the Jesuits. The Jesuits had played a central role as the religious arm of the Portuguese conquest of Angola from the time of Dias de Novais's 1575 arrival in Luanda, and they still represented the official Portuguese colonial order in Angola.

Njinga nevertheless faced obstacles in her outreach to the Capuchins, who were still uneasy with some of what they knew about her. In February 1651, some two years after Njinga had freed the two Capuchin priests in Wandu, Father Serafino da Cortona, the head of the Capuchins in Luanda, received a letter from Njinga in which she indicated that she wanted him "to come and baptize her people."[28] He didn't respond immediately, but he was certainly intrigued. It would be a full four months before he wrote to the Propaganda Fide. In this letter, he explained that he could not address Njinga's request until King Garcia II of Kongo and the Portuguese resolved their long-standing dispute concerning where the bishop of Kongo and Angola should reside, which stemmed from Portuguese attempts to move the see from the capital of Kongo to Luanda as a way of punishing Kongo for having supported the Dutch. Father Cortona was reluctant to let the opportunity go by, though, and he encouraged officials in Rome to send at least two Capuchins to work in Matamba, convinced that their presence "would be a great service to God to help her." Njinga's reputation as an apostate who consumed human flesh and took the lives of innocent children was by then so well established that the Capuchins in Angola knew they would need the full support of Rome before they could make any commitment to follow up on Njinga's request. In fact, in his letter, Father Cortona referred to Njinga as a ruler who went to war every year, who condoned the "barbarous customs" of killing newborns, burying them alive, or leaving them to be eaten by wild beasts, and lived by pillage, with no settled place of residence.[29]

In April 1651, Father Cortona was joined in Luanda by a second Capuchin priest, Father Antonio Romano. Father Romano had come directly from Rome, and the two priests were assigned to work in the Portuguese fort of Massangano. In addition, they traveled around the countryside, bringing the sacraments to many of the inhabitants of the regions surrounding the fort. Most significantly, Father Cortona had become confessor to Njinga's sister Kambu, now known by her Christian name Barbara, and he seems to have persuaded Barbara, then living as a prisoner in Luanda, to write a letter to Njinga to encourage her to give up her Imbangala lifestyle and return to Christianity. Perhaps inspired by this letter or by a short visit from Father Cortona and Father Romano, Njinga wrote a letter on August 15 of that year (which she gave to Father Cortona) directly to the Propaganda Fide. In it, she thanked the cardinals for their concern about her own salvation and that of her people, and for sending the Capuchin father Antonio Romano to her lands. She confessed that because of the visit, she at last had knowledge of the "true God" and now realized she had been "deceived by our idolatrous beliefs, possessed by the devil." Asking forgiveness for her transgressions, Njinga promised that any other missionaries would be welcomed with open arms, because there were "many people in our kingdom ready to receive the Holy Baptism."[30]

Although the wars in which Njinga was engaged at the time and the Imbangala practices she condoned suggest that she was not ready for a complete transformation, her missionary diplomacy was making some headway. The Capuchins' favorable stance toward Njinga, bolstered by Father Roma's sympathetic letter of 1648, certainly helped her cause.[31] Through sheer persistence, Njinga seems to have convinced the Capuchins that there was some truth to her contention that the Portuguese had unjustly invaded her lands.

Suddenly she had a voice at the Vatican. A letter from Father Cortona to the head of the Capuchin order in Tuscany in 1651 makes this clear. Citing Njinga's request for missionaries, Cortona accused the Portuguese of dissuading him from responding to her and demanding instead that he send missionaries to Massangano.[32] Furthermore, he wrote, the Portuguese had taken Angola "by force" from Queen Njinga.[33] A few months later, another Capuchin priest in Angola once more raised the issue of Njinga's request for missionaries, reminding the Propaganda Fide that Angola, which was under Portuguese jurisdiction, had been taken "by force of arms from Queen Njinga, a heathen."[34]

Their sympathy notwithstanding, the Capuchins were reluctant to reach out to Njinga because they found it difficult to explain why she had given up Christianity and adopted practices that went against everything their religion stood for. Njinga soon realized that she would have to try another tactic. Simply proclaiming that she would eventually return to Christianity was no longer enough: it was time to act. In early 1652, Njinga dispatched an ambassador directly to Luanda. Njinga wanted the Capuchins to baptize him, he told the Portuguese officials, and he assured them of her desire to have Capuchin missionaries work in Matamba. After some deliberation, Father Cortona refused to baptize the ambassador. Even after Njinga's two letters, even after her promise to welcome missionaries in Matamba, Father Cortona was convinced that the ambassador would simply go back to his heathen ways upon his return home. The Capuchins praised Njinga's kindness to Father Cordella and Father Veas, but they were well aware that Njinga wanted to dictate the terms of their relationship, and they were not ready to trust her entirely.[35]

Njinga's overture to the Capuchins paid off in other ways, though. The Capuchins, who up to that point had concentrated most of their missionary efforts on the kingdom of Kongo, realized that Matamba and the other territories Njinga claimed—including parts of Ndongo—were extremely populous and would be rich and rewarding for missionary work.

Anticipating this possible change in focus, Father Cortona, in a letter written in 1652, advised the authorities in Rome that prospective candidates to the region should learn Kimbundu, the language of Njinga and her people, instead of Kikongo, the language of the Kongos.[36] A few weeks later, one of the candidates in a contentious nomination for head of the Capuchin order in Luanda asked permission to travel with a companion to the "heathen country" because they had received "renewed requests" for missionaries from Queen Njinga. Even though Njinga had been "continuously at war" and had committed "innumerable cruelties, condemned not only by the law of God but by natural law," he set out for Matamba, armed with a copy of her letter. (The extant records are silent as to whether he achieved his goal.) The missionaries knew that they faced challenges in bringing into the church a ruler whose many wars and Imbangala practices made her in equal parts feared and fascinating. They, like their secular counterparts, could not understand why Njinga made the choices she did.[37]

Father Cortona and other Capuchins continued to press the Vatican regarding Njinga's request for missionaries, sending letters to the Propaganda Fide and their Capuchin colleagues in Rome and elsewhere in Italy. Njinga's letters had succeeded in convincing the Capuchins in Luanda that she was far too important a ruler to ignore, and despite their revulsion at aspects of her lifestyle, they pushed her case. The fact that her sister Barbara was living an exemplary religious life in Luanda during her imprisonment by the Portuguese gave the Capuchins hope that Njinga would find in her sister a Christian role model.[38]

Although it would take some months for Njinga to receive the news from Rome, a breakthrough in her missionary diplomacy occurred in March 1653, when Father Cortona dispatched Father Antonio Maria de Monteprandone to Rome to make the case for founding a prefect of Matamba that would be separate from that of Kongo. While not downplaying Njinga's "sinfulness" or the fact that her subjects were "pagans [who] eat human flesh," Father Monteprandone stressed Njinga's repeated requests for missionaries. When the house of cardinals met in May 1653, they finally approved the request, and by October they had selected missionaries to go to Matamba.[39] Among the missionaries were Father Antonio da Gaeta and Father Antonio Giovanni Cavazzi. Along with other Capuchins, they arrived in Luanda in November 1654. Four days later the Vatican published the official decree establishing the mission in the kingdom of Queen Njinga. After the group arrived in Luanda, Father Cortona wrote to Njinga. She responded immediately. At long last, by early 1655, one part of Njinga's missionary diplomacy had borne fruit. In the coming years, Fathers Gaeta, Cortona, and Cavazzi would become crucial players in Njinga's political and missionary diplomacy and, finally, in her own religious transformation.

Political Diplomacy Revisited

Njinga had not given up on political diplomacy, and she still had one more strategy to pursue before all her plans could fall into place. Realizing she had to reach a formal agreement with the Portuguese to secure Barbara's release and to resolve her claims to lands that she believed the Portuguese governors had wrongfully taken from her, Njinga looked for an opening to deal directly with officials in Luanda. An opportunity had presented itself immediately after her return to Matamba in 1648, when she received an envoy from Governor Correia de Sá. Njinga knew that Correia de Sá's military operations had allowed the Portuguese to regain the allegiance of all the *sobas* in parts of the Dembos region that she had once controlled, as well as some in the provinces of Libolo and Kisama and around the fort of Massangano. Indeed, many *sobas* who had once pledged their allegiance to her had begun sending embassies to Luanda to ask the Portuguese for friendship and peace.[40] She calculated that Correia de Sá did not have sufficient troops to send against her, however, and was not surprised when, after she returned to Matamba, she began to receive letters and envoys from Correia de Sá as well as from the king of Portugal.

Njinga guessed that because of her military successes, Correia de Sá would be reluctant to threaten her with war, in contrast to the situation with King Garcia II of Kongo. She guessed correctly. King Garcia's communications with Correia de Sá were fraught with tension and accusation. Unlike Njinga, Garcia himself sent Correia de Sá a letter after the Dutch had left in 1648 in which he outlined conditions for peace. Correia de Sá's response the following year was to threaten Kongo with military invasion if Garcia did not agree to pay reparations. Correia de Sá accused Garcia of betraying the king of Portugal and warned that if Garcia didn't agree to pay nine hundred slaves, Correia de Sá would invade his kingdom. It didn't end there: in addition to several other onerous conditions, Correia de Sá told Garcia that he would lose the rights to the island of Luanda and to the silver mines that were supposedly located in lands that Kongo claimed.

While Correia de Sá was involved in this hostile exchange with Njinga's neighbor, he was at the same time trying to appease Njinga by opening diplomatic relations with her. Njinga responded favorably to embassies from the governor that came to Matamba between 1648 and 1650, but these chiefly had to do with trade and other minor issues. Beginning in early 1650, Correia de Sá began to send messages offering to pardon her in the name of King João IV, and even indicating that the king would welcome her back under Portuguese protection. But these messages did not mention the issues of greatest concern to her: Barbara's release and Njinga's longstanding claims to lands in Ndongo.[41]

About two years after she received the first letters, Njinga responded to the olive branch Correia de Sá extended in December 1650. Believing that the governor was genuinely interested in peace and that she might finally secure Barbara's release, she sent him "slaves and two hundred *banzos*" (a *banzo* was a set of trade items equivalent to one slave) to encourage him to send a more formal embassy. Correia de Sá did as she asked; a few months later, he sent an embassy headed by Rui Pegado da Ponte, a Portuguese with long years in Angola and fluency in Kimbundu. Pegado brought with him a letter from Correia de Sá, dated April 13, 1651, in which he addressed her as "queen." He flattered her and told her she was descended from "the royal blood of kings and emperors" and that she was different from the Imbangalas, who were "thieves" who had no "fathers or mothers or lands," so despised that "God cannot help such people." He implored her to give up her Imbangala ways and return to the church, and he hoped she would allow Pegado or any baptized white or lord of her country to "baptize the children."[42]

Before Njinga responded to the governor, she consulted with her counselors, who fully supported her efforts to solve the impasse through diplomacy. Noting that Correia de Sá's letter did not make any reference to Barbara's release or to the question of her land claims, she made these the central issues in her response. Thanking Pegado for the gifts and the favorable words expressed in the letters, she stressed that everything rested on the release of her sister Barbara. She then detailed the long history of the conflict with the Portuguese, and as she had done on so many occasions in the past when meeting with representatives of the Portuguese crown, she blamed the beginning of all her problems on former governor Fernão de Sousa. She accused him not only of oppressing and invading her state, but of taking her kingdom from her and transferring it to her vassal Ngola Hari. Intent on capitalizing on the diplomatic opening that Correia de Sá had initiated, Njinga took the opportunity to ask for his assistance in recovering the parts of Matamba that the Imbangala Kasanje had claimed, promising in return to give up Imbangala practices. Finally, as to the question of Christianity, she put him off, promising to discuss it at a later date.[43]

Pegado assured Njinga that Correia de Sá would make peace with her and would release Barbara, so Njinga sent more presents to seal the arrangement. This might explain why on October 6, 1651, Correia de Sá wrote to King João IV that he had made Njinga "a vassal of his majesty" and made her fearful of the "arms of your majesty."[44] She was not so easily cowed, though, and continued to demand a number of conditions for peace. Working out the details of the agreement would last from 1651 to 1656, with many starts and stops in the negotiations.

During the three years that Correia de Sá remained in Angola (1648–1651), and in the following three years, during which time two additional governors served, Njinga attempted on several occasions to capitalize on diplomatic openings to push for Barbara's release and to obtain Portuguese assistance in consolidating her control over Matamba. By the end of 1654, Njinga had become convinced that the Portuguese governors had no intention of serious diplomacy—that they were only out "to discredit her in the world's eyes and the opinion in which she was held by the black people."[45]

By the time Governor Luis Martins de Sousa Chichorro began his term in October 1654 and indicated that he wished to reopen peace negotiations, Njinga was ready to welcome Portuguese overtures. She felt she was in a good position, both politically and personally. Her armies had succeeded in consolidating her hold over Matamba and its frontiers, despite the fact that the country was still largely depopulated, and the Capuchins had contacted her and indicated that they were ready to begin work in Matamba. From a personal perspective, she was delighted to learn that Sousa Chichorro was related to João Correia de Sousa, the former governor who had served as her godfather at her baptism in 1622. She seized the connection as an opportunity to get the stalled negotiations she had started with Correia de Sá moving again. Njinga sent an ambassador to

Luanda with a letter congratulating Sousa Chichorro on his safe arrival and extending other customary pleasantries. The rest of the letter, however, was a request for the release of her sister Barbara, with promises to pay the appropriate ransom. She also promised to return to the church and abandon her Imbangala lifestyle. She requested Capuchin priests to come to her court to "reconcile her with blessed God, baptize her people, and found a church at her court."[46] Although it would take fourteen months of negotiation before she would receive a positive response, the political climate in Luanda was shifting in Njinga's favor.

Sometime in December 1654 or early January 1655, she arranged (through the Capuchins in Luanda) to have Barbara—still imprisoned in Luanda—and an envoy meet with the governor. Once the meeting was set, both Njinga and Sousa Chichorro prepared for an elaborate public event, with each side planning to stage a traditional display of political drama. Governor Sousa Chichorro arranged to have one thousand armed soldiers in military dress stand at parade rest in the square around the governor's palace. He waited inside the palace for Barbara and her retinue to be announced, seated on his chair in the official meeting room and surrounded by military captains and other officials. Njinga, not one to squander the opportunity to make any public space hers, had prepared her representatives for what amounted to a public showdown. The embassy she assembled was led by Barbara and the envoy, both of whom were "richly and pompously dressed and attended by many Christian blacks from the city." In fact, Barbara's attendants were so impressive and appeared "so much like Christian gentlemen" that honor guard soldiers greeted the party with volleys of gunshots. Sousa Chichorro was openly taken with the appearance of Barbara, the ambassador, and the rest of the party. As they entered the room, the governor forgot himself and "right away got up from his chair and went to greet and honor Barbara." He did not neglect the envoy, greeting him and introducing the two to his entourage.[47]

At this point the two parties began negotiations. The governor directed Barbara and the envoy to their seats, cushions placed on the floor. Unlike Njinga, who three decades before had refused to sit on the floor, Barbara and the envoy sat where they were told, and in a businesslike manner Barbara presented Njinga's letter to the governor. The envoy then took over, informing Sousa Chichorro in Kimbundu of the reason for the audience. He explained that his queen, Njinga, had sent him to welcome the governor officially to Luanda and to let him know that she and all her court rejoiced at his arrival, and that she hoped they would have a cordial and productive relationship. It was essential to Njinga that she establish publicly the connection between her godfather and the current governor, and the envoy informed the governor, as Njinga had instructed him to, that his uncle had stood as Njinga's godfather in 1622, and that she retained the family name. Then the envoy relayed to Sousa Chichorro Njinga's fervent desire that he would assure the release of her sister Barbara, who had lived as a prisoner in Luanda for nine years. Njinga was old, the envoy noted, and she wished to have someone related by blood nearby in the last years of her life. How many captives would Njinga have to send, the envoy asked on her behalf, to ransom Barbara? At the end of the discourse the envoy presented Sousa Chichorro with ten slaves as a gift from Njinga.

Sousa Chichorro accepted the slaves and told Barbara and the envoy that although he could not give them an answer before consulting with his council, they should let Njinga know that he was willing to negotiate. He promised that since his uncle had played a role in Njinga's baptism, he would certainly do everything in his power to free Barbara.[48] The governor signaled the end of the meeting, and Barbara and the envoy, along with their attendants, exited with the same pomp and pageantry they had displayed during their entrance.

While negotiations with Sousa Chichorro were moving forward, Njinga sent two ambassadors for further discussions with the governor.[49] In addition to bringing letters of credentials, the ambassadors also transmitted to the governor an oral message that "they had well studied," which they "spoke [in] their own Ambundu [Kimbundu] language." By February 1655, negotiations in Luanda were in full swing.[50] Njinga remained hesitant about bringing the Capuchins directly into the picture until the talks were further advanced. She also continued her military operations, knowing that Sousa Chichorro had recently launched a major offensive against Kisama and had written to the king of Portugal to inform him that once those operations were over, he would be free to move against Kongo and Njinga. For this reason Njinga had begun the secret negotiations with the *sobas* Kabuku and Kalandula two years earlier. But Njinga also realized that continuing negotiations with the governor was essential, and did not let up in her communications with him.[51]

And the negotiations were indeed going somewhere. The two ambassadors whom Njinga had sent to discuss peace with Sousa Chichorro had made some progress. Meanwhile, the envoy who had accompanied Barbara to the meeting with the governor had returned to Matamba and relayed to Njinga the details of the encouraging meeting he and her sister had had with the governor. Sousa Chichorro was very pleased with the gift, the envoy reported, and despite the difficulties, the governor was favorably disposed to freeing Barbara. Njinga sent the envoy immediately back to Luanda, this time with twenty slaves to present to the governor in her name, as well as another six for the auditor general, one of the members of the Luanda bureaucracy who adamantly opposed any settlement with her. Njinga again directed the envoy to bring up the issue of Barbara's release, and also to request that Sousa Chichorro permit one of the Capuchins to come to her court in Matamba to help move the negotiations forward.

Njinga's decision to have her envoy ask the governor to include a Capuchin priest in the discussions paid off. Governor Sousa Chichorro wrote to the head of the order in Luanda and requested that he identify a priest who could be included in the negotiations. Portuguese officials in Luanda strenuously debated the merits of the decision to negotiate with Njinga and to free Barbara, and many of them came out against it.

Njinga was making somewhat different demands in her discussions with the Capuchins; in her correspondence with Father Cortona, who had not yet traveled to the interior after his election as the prefect to establish the station in Matamba, she suggested that a Capuchin missionary should accompany Barbara to Matamba after her release. He had become Barbara's confessor at a crucial point in the negotiations, and in the early months of 1655, Njinga sent him three very "courteous letters," an indication of how much she had come to trust him. Father Cortona had essentially become another link to the governor for Njinga, another voice arguing for Barbara's release. Since his election, he had been eager to travel to Matamba, and in February, before leaving the city with Father Gaeta, he contacted Barbara, undoubtedly to apprise her of the progress of the negotiations. He arrived in Ambaca in early May and immediately wrote Njinga two letters advising her that he would soon be in Matamba. Despite his close relationship with Barbara and his contact with the governor on her behalf, during the delicate months of negotiations, Njinga had refused to give him permission to enter Matamba—except under one condition. In response to his letter of May 5, 1655, Njinga sent a reply stating in no uncertain terms that he was to come to Matamba only if Barbara accompanied him. After waiting in Ambaca for two months, he returned to Massangano and wrote to Sousa Chichorro, explaining his predicament and encouraging him once again to free Njinga's sister.[52]

Njinga's strategy to prohibit the Capuchins from entering Matamba until the negotiations over Barbara were complete had the desired effect. By the end of the summer of 1655, negotiations were back on track. Even as she was blocking the entry of the missionaries, she was engaged in secret negotiations with Governor Sousa Chichorro, receiving his messages, exchanging opinions on the war in Kisama that he was planning, and thanking him for the presents he sent her. He always selected items he knew she liked. In September, Sousa Chichorro reported to King João IV on his discussions with Njinga. She had asked him to free Barbara, he told the king, and the governor was waiting for her response to see whether she and her officials would agree to the conditions for peace he had put forth. Yes, Barbara was nearly as old as Njinga, but she was a "good Christian," "well instructed in the things of the faith"; surely her return would facilitate Njinga's reconciliation with the church. For both the governor and Njinga, Barbara's release had become the central issue in the negotiations.[53]

Njinga must have agreed to Sousa Chichorro's conditions, because on December 2, 1655, she welcomed the formal embassy he sent to Matamba. The embassy was led by a well-respected settler named Manuel Frois Peixoto, who came armed with a list of demands that would become the core elements of the final agreement.[54] Within two weeks, Njinga was persuaded that Sousa Chichorro was serious about freeing Barbara and making peace. As a result of her discussions and the increasing faith she came to place in Peixoto, Njinga wrote a long letter to the governor on December 13, responding to the demands that Peixoto had presented. She took the opportunity to review the history of her dealings with the Portuguese, in order to explain why she and her officials remained suspicions of Portuguese calls for peace, and she spelled out exactly what she required before any meaningful settlement could take place. To begin with, Njinga accused Correia de Sá and other former governors of reneging on earlier promises they had made to release Barbara—and as if that wasn't enough, they had cheated her out of the slaves she had sent as ransom. The bulk of the letter, however, was a point-by-point discussion of the conditions Sousa Chichorro set for Barbara's release, along with Njinga's expectations for the transfer. Using a similar strategy as in previous negotiations, Njinga situated these negotiations in the context of past Portuguese actions, while at the same time attempting to convince the governor that it was in both her own interest and that of King João to reach an agreement. She stated outright at the beginning that she wanted the Portuguese king to know that she was serious about making peace. But, still distrustful that local officials and settlers would derail the agreement, she took the opportunity to lay out a roadmap. She praised Governor Sousa Chichorro for sending Peixoto, whom she referred to as a seasoned and poised negotiator who had convinced her and her officials of the seriousness of the Portuguese commitment to peace. She was particularly impressed that Peixoto spoke Kimbundu ("the language of my kingdom") and stressed that she hoped he would remain the main negotiator. Why change course now, since all her officials were pleased with him, and they all believed that he was following the king's instructions and "speaks the truth and reports everything"? This was no small feat amid such a skeptical crowd, and Njinga did not want it to go without saying. Njinga was also adamant about getting assurance that any agreement she signed should be signed by the king's hand; no documents should originate with local officials, whom Njinga dismissed as having always turned past governors against her. This was the only way that she and her officials would be convinced that the document was genuine. Additionally, well aware of the benefits of personal connections, she reminded Sousa Chichorro that her godfather, João Correia de Sousa, was his distant relative.[55]

Njinga also included a detailed plan for Barbara's return, ever mindful that a grand public display of status was essential to her people. She asked the governor to make sure that Barbara arrived in Matamba in the company of two priests, the Capuchin Father Cortona and Father João, a Carmelite missionary, both of whom would provide her with "good and accredited company." She had selected Father João because "I am told that he is a good preacher and knows the language of Ndongo." She also demanded that the governor provide Barbara with a secular escort who should be "a soldier with knowledge of fireworks so I can celebrate my sister's arrival with them." Now, for the first time, Njinga referred to her own mortality (at the time of the negotiations she was seventy-four years old), noting that because she was "quite old," she wanted to settle her affairs once and for all and live out her remaining days in peace. Barbara's safe return was a key part of Njinga's plans to maintain the integrity of the lands she had conquered. She still fervently believed that her descent from the founders of the Ndongo kingdom gave her (and Barbara) the right to rule, as opposed to others (Ngola Hari and the Imbangala captains, particularly Njinga a Mona), whose non-royal descent, she believed, excluded them from ruling. Njinga discussed her future plans for her lands and how Barbara fit into them. She would leave her lands to Barbara and not to her "slaves"; they would not know how to rule. Njinga worried that if an Imbangala captain such as Njinga a Mona inherited Matamba upon her death, "great ruin would happen because they would not know how to obey his Majesty." Barbara's birthright and the many years she had lived among the Portuguese as a good Christian made her the best candidate to continue the balancing act that Njinga envisioned as a result of the peace. She believed that Barbara would at least keep the Portuguese at bay while retaining the respect and admiration of her people in an independent Ndongo-Matamba.

Njinga included in the letter detailed instructions for the governor to follow in exchange for her agreeing to the conditions that Peixoto had presented. For example, Njinga indicated that she would "immediately endeavor to allow women to give birth and to raise children [in the *kilombo*]" only after Barbara and the two missionaries had arrived safely in Matamba. As it stood, women were not allowed to deliver or rear children in the *kilombo*, and most fetuses were either aborted or, if full term, left to die outside the camp. Also, aware that some government officials and other religious congregations in Luanda were suspicious of her relationship with the Capuchins, and in fact had gone so far as to block Father Gaeta (who had taken over from Father Cortona) from leaving Massangano to travel to Matamba, she reiterated that she would give up her "warlike practices as long as I have clergymen (specifically Fathers Gaeta and Father João)" to provide "me and my officials good examples and teach them to live in the Holy Catholic faith." Njinga believed that it was critical for maintaining the integrity of her kingdom and people to have a priest like Father João who knew how to speak Kimbundu.

The promise of Barbara's safe return seemed to cast everything in a different light for Njinga. Some of the conditions she agreed to now she had formally rejected before. One such condition required her to turn over to the Portuguese the Imbangala Kalandula, whom she had imprisoned because he had destroyed her lands. She stated in the letter that she would do so, her desire to see Barbara so great that as soon as Peixoto delivered her, she would allow Kalandula to leave "and place himself at his [Sousa Chichorro's] orders." Njinga was not only willing to betray this sometime ally for peace and the return of her sister; in addition, she volunteered to send one of her captains with a large army to help Sousa Chichorro conquer Kisama, which the Portuguese had not succeeded in bringing fully under their control. She was willing to take these drastic steps to show how sincere she was in her response to the Portuguese offer of peace, how ready she was to give "obedience" to the king of Portugal. Njinga knew that the restoration of peace would strengthen her slave trade markets and allow them to become better integrated with the Portuguese trading network. The Portuguese would certainly benefit, and she anticipated purchasing imported goods at a cheaper price.

There was one condition that Njinga would not agree to: Sousa Chichorro's demand that she pay two hundred slaves to ransom Barbara. The number was too high, she argued. After all, over the years she had given numerous slaves to various governors and their envoys, as well as sending many gifts to secretaries and servants. Her counteroffer was for 130 slaves. She would send one hundred when she could confirm that Barbara had arrived in Ambaca, and she would hold Peixoto as a hostage in Matamba until "I can see with my own eyes my sister arriving in my court." Njinga pleaded with the governor not to interpret her behavior as strange. He must know that she had been deceived time and again by the Portuguese, and she refused to be gullible this time. But it wasn't just Njinga: even though she herself believed that Peixoto's delegation was genuine, her officials remained suspicious of their motives.

The envoys who had delivered Njinga's long letter to the governor were still in Luanda when another envoy from her arrived, in February 1656. This envoy made a verbal presentation to the governor in which he noted that Njinga was ready to sign the treaty. It was this envoy who returned to Njinga with the first copy of the several articles that would form the final peace agreement. Sousa Chichorro, convinced that Peixoto had gained Njinga's confidence, wished to move quickly to conclude the negotiations. He faced rising opposition, however, from two sources—the first being the Jesuits, who had been part of the conquest apparatus since Dias de Novais's time. Jealousy raged among the various orders of priests, and members of the Jesuit order (and others, mainly Portuguese) with head-quarters in Luanda resented the fact that the Capuchins (mainly Italians) had been given permission to open up a new outpost in Matamba. They did everything they could to sabotage the Capuchins' plans to send some of their members to Matamba. (By this time Father João, the Carmelite, had died.)

Even stronger opposition came from the Camara, the official advisory body in Luanda made up of settlers, which was openly acrimonious. The members sent two letters directly to the king, one written in March and the other in July 1656, complaining about Sousa Chichorro's leadership and requesting that he stop the governor from proceeding with plans to free Barbara. Like Njinga, the settlers had deep-seated memories of the Angolan wars, and in their letter they included a long list of reasons as to why Sousa Chichorro's decisions should be overruled. They went over the history of their dealings with Ndongo, beginning with Njinga's brother Ngola Mbande, and reminded the king of how much the wars had cost them in lives and property. Njinga was even worse than her brother, they wrote, and all the governors since Mendes de Vasconcelos's time, four decades previously, had been forced to take up arms against her. Their advice to the king: Continue to keep Barbara as a prisoner. If she were released, there was no guarantee that Njinga would honor the treaty. If she were kept, and there was no treaty, then Njinga would have no one in her line to inherit the kingdom of Ndongo, which they claimed was "justly taken from Ngola Mbande," and the kingdom would disappear.[56]

But Njinga's shuttle diplomacy was too far advanced for it to come off the rails now, and Sousa Chichorro was increasingly convinced that he had to free Barbara and make peace with Njinga for the colony to prosper. Njinga had convinced him that peace would result in the end of the Imbangala system of wars and bring stability to the lands beyond Ndongo, stability he realized was essential for Portuguese traders. On April 1, 1656, Sousa Chichorro wrote to the Capuchin prefect in Luanda informing him of his decision, noting that he believed that Njinga's cause was just—and would be beneficial to "the King & Lord." Furthermore, he believed that Njinga was genuinely interested in returning to the Catholic faith. He also pointed out that he had requested two hundred slaves in return for Barbara's release, and that once everything was settled, the colony would have peace and trade, and commerce with Matamba would reopen. He also announced that he was going to release Barbara in a few days.[57]

Governor Sousa Chichorro was true to his word, and in early April, the process of making Barbara a free woman began. Barbara left Luanda under armed escort to travel to Massangano, where, on April 9, 1656, she received a military welcome. She remained in Massangano for a week with Father Gaeta by her side; with numerous escorts, they left for Ambaca. Father Cortona had given Father Gaeta a long list of instructions regarding what he needed to do to speed the end of Imbangala practices in Matamba. On May 20, after a long trip broken up by brief stops where the local Mbundu population showered Barbara with enthusiastic greetings, Barbara and Father Gaeta finally arrived in Ambaca, where Barbara received another military welcome. After the formalities, Barbara was taken to the house of one of the missionaries, where she was supposed to stay a short time before she and Father Gaeta, along with the military escort demanded by Njinga, would continue on to Matamba. Father Gaeta kept Njinga abreast of the progress of the party and wrote to her as soon as they arrived in Ambaca, letting her know that he and Barbara would be on their way shortly.

Within three days of their arrival in Ambaca, however, the outrage among officials in Luanda, furious that Sousa Chichorro had actually released Barbara, was overwhelming. Still awaiting word from the king, they passed a resolution ordering the governor to halt the release. The resolution ordered the governor to send word to Captain Giuseppe Carasco, who was supposed to serve as Barbara's military escort from Ambaca to Matamba, to prevent Barbara from leaving Ambaca. He was ordered to arrest her immediately and imprison her in the fort to prevent the people from helping her to escape. The order stipulated that Barbara should be escorted to Matamba only after the governor had received the two hundred slaves that he had demanded as ransom. This new development caused an uproar. Father Gaeta was livid, convinced this was all part of a scheme to prevent the Capuchins from finally beginning their work in Matamba. The many attendants and courtesans Njinga had sent to accompany Barbara were distraught. The local Mbundus who had gathered to welcome her and wish her well on her trip to Matamba were irritated and disappointed. Before long, rumors spread that the Portuguese had tricked Njinga again—that the governor didn't intend to return Barbara to Njinga at all, but instead wanted to send her back to Luanda and imprison her.[58]

Njinga had spent months preparing for her sister's return, and she had planned an elaborate public ceremony to mark the occasion. When news reached her of events in Ambaca, now embellished by rumors that the Portuguese had lied to her and tricked her into agreeing to sign the treaty, her anger and disappointment knew no bounds. The information so incensed her and her officials that she immediately turned on Peixoto, who was still at her court, and threatened him with "cruel murder" if Barbara was not turned over to her. She was quoted as saying to him, "If we here cry because of the imprisonment of our sister, we will do so, and in Luanda they will mourn your death."[59] Imprisoning Barbara in Ambaca threatened to derail all the preparations and put Peixoto's life in grave danger. It was at this point that Njinga's religious diplomacy paid off, as Father Gaeta realized that only his intervention could prevent the deal from collapsing. Njinga knew that threats to Peixoto's life and public outrage were the only means she had to move the process along, and although she did not want to endure another set of wars and stalemates, she was willing to do anything to obtain the release of her sister. A pleading letter from Father Gaeta, coupled with news of an unlikely spiritual encounter of Imbangala Njinga a Mona with a Christian crucifix ended up saving the day.

Father Gaeta, who was anxious to arrive in Matamba and begin building a church, advised her to keep believing. He reassured her that everything would be all right. Calmed considerably by his encouraging words, Njinga responded to Father Gaeta immediately. His letter had lifted her spirits, she wrote, and made her happy that God had sent a missionary of his stature to her. She reiterated her commitment to follow through with her promise to allow him to work in Matamba and assured him that when he arrived, he would find everything he had requested for the church he intended to build. She again indicated her readiness to give up the Imbangala lifestyle. In conclusion, she explained how much she was looking forward to greeting him, her sister, and her sister's military escort, Captain Carasco, at her court in Matamba. Njinga had one hundred slaves sent to Ambaca, and ninety-nine of them arrived in July 1656, one having died on the way.[60] Njinga hoped was that once the slaves arrived in Ambaca, the commandant of the fort would free Barbara and she could be on her way to Matamba.

When Father Gaeta received Njinga's letter, he was still unsure whether she was intending to send the additional one hundred slaves the Portuguese had demanded. Father Gaeta feared that if he couldn't persuade Njinga to meet all the conditions for the agreement, his missionary work in Matamba could not proceed, and all the investment the Capuchins had put into it would be for naught. Father Gaeta decided to go directly to Matamba to discuss the issue with Njinga, face to face. Both Barbara and Carasco initially supported his decision, but Carasco tried to dissuade him from going. What if Njinga became so incensed upon seeing Father Gaeta without her sister, Carasco argued, that she took revenge on him, as she had threatened to do with Peixoto? Like most Portuguese, Carasco demonized Njinga; he tried to impress on Father Gaeta that she was evil, so steeped in her Imbangala practices that she and her officials would think nothing of killing him, an innocent priest. Father Gaeta remained resolute.[61]

At this point, Njinga's religious and political diplomacy had drawn both Sousa Chichorro and Father Gaeta too deeply into the process for them to give up. Father Gaeta wrote to Father Cortona and informed him of his decision to travel alone to Matamba. Cortona forwarded Gaeta's letter to the governor. It elicited a quick response. Sousa Chichorro thanked Cortona for all he had done to advance the process and told him that he approved the plan. Father Cortona could now urge Father Gaeta to travel to Matamba immediately to assure Njinga that he was committed to freeing Barbara.[62]

Religious Miracles and Political Peace

In addition to keeping the negotiations with the governor on track, Njinga also had to prepare her suspicious counselors and army captains for the peace process and the Christianization to which the peace agreement had committed her. Even as she was corresponding with Father Gaeta and the governor, she was anxiously awaiting Njinga a Mona's return from operations against the Christian ruler Pombo Samba in the province of Mbwila. As it turned out, the highlight of his return to court revolved not around his military successes or the spoils of war he brought with him, but a four-foot-tall crucifix that he sent to Njinga. It was, he told her, "the image of her old Nzambi [God]."[63]

Njinga a Mona later told Father Gaeta where the crucifix came from. During the operations against Mbwila, he explained, six months before Father Gaeta's arrival in Matamba, Njinga a Mona's soldiers had desecrated the church there. The damage to its large crucifix was severe, and Njinga a Mona ordered his soldiers to throw it in the bush. During the night, however, his sleep was disturbed by a dream in which the crucifix appeared to him in a scolding manner and ordered him to retrieve it. It spoke the following words: "Take me to your queen or I will see that you will not leave this place." Njinga a Mona was so bewildered by the dream that early the next morning he sent soldiers to look for crucifix. They found it, wrapped it in an animal skin, and delivered it to him.

Njinga a Mona carried the crucifix triumphantly to court, where he presented it to Njinga. Some of the soldiers who had gone about with the white people, he said, had explained to him that this was "the figure of God that Christians adore." He also related his dream to her. Njinga seemed overcome by a wave of emotions, and she was said to have shouted in a loud voice: "God searches for me and comes in person to find me." She then kissed the crucifix and placed it on an altar in a room in the palace that she had specially built for it. Njinga visited the room every day, praying to have "peace and quiet" so that she would not have to continue leading her armies in battle from place to place.[64]

Perhaps the dream happened just as Njinga a Mona said it did. It is also possible that the crucifix story was a ruse, one which Njinga concocted to make the negotiations and conversion more palatable to her counselors and captains. Whichever is true, Njinga a Mona's encounter with the crucifix happened at an opportune moment. In late August 1656, Father Gaeta was within two days of Njinga's court after a harrowing twenty-day journey and sent one of the Mbundus in his party ahead with a letter informing the queen of his imminent arrival.[65] Learning that Father Gaeta was nearby, Njinga prepared a public performance in his honor. According to his report, when he was just one mile away from the court, his eyes fell on a procession made up of Njinga's army captains, court officials, and one thousand bowmen, all "pompously dressed," who knelt on the ground before him, asking to kiss his hand as they approached him. The captains and officials then led Father Gaeta to Njinga, who was waiting in a large plaza surrounded by her bodyguards and attendants. Always aware of the impression she was making, Njinga walked regally toward Father Gaeta, knelt in front of him, and then kissed with deep devotion a crucifix which he extended to her. Still kneeling, Njinga uttered the words, "Now yes I will live in peace and joy." But Njinga's extravagant avowal was far from over. After she stood up, she welcomed Father Gaeta and addressed him as the "priest of God" who had come to bring her rest at a time when she wanted to stop fighting. After Father Gaeta responded with words of comfort, she signaled to her guards to fire volleys of welcome. The entire crowd then followed the party to Njinga's residence. Her musicians played horns and drums and other instruments while the people sang and the women ululated loudly. Njinga led the party to the courtyard of her residence, where she had built a platform with elaborate wooden columns, where her archers, dressed in silks and cloths of different colors, stood at attention. In the middle of the courtyard, Njinga had set up three seats, one under a white canopy for herself, a second seat not far from hers for Father Gaeta, and a third for Peixoto. All of her other attendants and people stood while Njinga listened to Father Gaeta deliver his political and religious messages.[66]

But the deep reverence Njinga showed to Father Gaeta and her outward appearance of sincere piety and willingness to listen to the religious messages was not the end of what she had planned. Following the formal meeting, she led Father Gaeta to the room where she had placed the crucifix from the Mbwila campaign. She had hung it over the altar, which was "dressed with various silks" and where candles were lit and torches burned. After they both kissed the feet of the crucifix, Njinga confessed to Father Gaeta that even though Portuguese actions against her had driven her away from the church, she was ready to "stop adoring idols." "All my people," she said, "will follow my example and convert to the same faith." Within a few days she issued orders for the people to bring construction materials to build the first simple church.[67]

Njinga's newfound devotion, however, did not guarantee that she would sign the treaty. In fact, when she became ill a few days after the church was built, the anti-Christian elements in her court wasted no time in blaming her illness on her passion for the crucifix and Christian worship. As her illness worsened and the herbal remedies and ritual marks and objects that her medical and religious practitioners prescribed failed to improve her health, the chances increased that Njinga would not survive to oversee the political and religious transformation that she hoped to bring about in Matamba. In fact, her illness provided an opening for some of her traditional practitioners, many of whom felt marginalized, to assert themselves and move to regain some of their ebbing power.

But Njinga survived this ordeal, just as she had so many others.[68] After her recovery she placed even greater faith in Father Gaeta. During the worst part of her illness, he had prayed with her and had even encouraged her to remove and burn the ritual objects that her religious men had placed on her neck. He replaced them with a card hanging from a silk chain, which had a picture of the Holy Virgin Mary and the words "In your conception, Virgin, Immaculate you were; Pray for us to your Father, whose son you brought forth." Father Gaeta put the silk chain around her neck and instructed her to hold the card lovingly in her hand and invoke the name of the Virgin Mary as often as she could. Her recovery a few days later convinced Njinga that her decision to renounce Imbangala/Mbundu rituals for Christian ones was the right one.[69]

Njinga's recovery and newfound devotion to Catholic rituals in no way lessened her desire to ensure that the Portuguese not cheat her out of her kingdom. In the closing days of September, as her strength returned, she led her counselors in marathon discussion sessions with Peixoto, Father Gaeta, and other Portuguese representatives. She and her advisers studied every word in the draft of the peace treaty. They strenuously objected to language that called on her to pay an annual tribute to the Portuguese king. In fact, Njinga found the Portuguese presumptuous for including that condition and lashed out at it. In the end, she calmly told Peixoto and the Portuguese delegation that if the Portuguese king returned to her the kingdom of Ndongo which he had taken from her by arms, he would be acting like a gentleman; but if he gave her all of Ndongo along with the lands of Angola which he had taken from her, he would be acting like a good Christian. She was returning to Christianity of her own free will, she explained, and she wanted to build not one church but many in Matamba. She would be "a friend of the friends and enemies of your enemies" of the Portuguese, as the treaty called for, as long as there was "true and genuine peace." Turning to the issue of paying tribute to the Portuguese king, Njinga explained at some length that it was out of the question:

> In regard then to paying the tribute that you claim from me,
> there is no reason to do so, because having been born to rule

my kingdom, I should not obey or recognize another sovereign, and to go from absolute Lady to become a servant and slave would be a great embarrassment. Now that I have embraced the faith of Christ to live quietly and finish my life in peace, I do that which I had not wished to ever do in the past while I was an Imbangala, and at the height of my many troubles and persecutions. If the Portuguese want a gift from me every year, I would give it to them voluntarily as long as they equally give me one so that we both would deal with each other courteously.[70]

Njinga prevailed. The treaty that was eventually signed made no mention of payment of an annual tribute to the Portuguese king.[71] During the final stages of negotiations, Njinga also convinced Peixoto and the other Portuguese representatives to agree that the Lucala River would be the boundary between the Portuguese kingdom of Angola and her kingdom of Matamba.[72]

At this stage both Peixoto and Father Gaeta were convinced of Njinga's seriousness and sent word to the governor to vouch for her. Father Gaeta had already told Father Cortona of the changes he had witnessed. Shortly after his arrival, he wrote to Cortona that he found Njinga "completely different from what has been presented to me, I say and affirm that she is not what she was; she has become someone else, peaceful, pious, and devoted."[73] The governor heeded the opinions of Father Gaeta and Peixoto. Now confident that Njinga's change was genuine, Sousa Chichorro issued the order for Barbara to be released from Ambaca and gave permission for her to leave for Matamba, even before he received the additional slaves.

Accompanied by some Portuguese escorts and Father Ignazio de Valsassina, the Capuchin who had arranged Barbara's lodging in Ambaca, Barbara left Ambaca on October 1, 1656. Father Ignazio would remain in Matamba with Barbara for four years.[74] When the party crossed the Lucala River and stepped onto the soil of Matamba, the rush of the crowd was overwhelming as people who had traveled from all parts of the country strained to catch a glimpse of her. Many of them did not return to their villages, but simply joined the party all the way to Njinga's court, where Barbara and her entourage arrived on October 12.

A week earlier, Njinga's envoys had arrived in Luanda and turned over to Governor Sousa Chichorro the articles for peace. Njinga waited impatiently for the governor's response. She knew that she would not be able to see Barbara until the governor had confirmed the contents of the agreement and made it public. Once the governor's response came back, Njinga and her officials wasted no time in getting the final proceedings underway.[75]

Throngs of people, including members of the military and court officials, greeted Barbara upon her arrival at the court. As soon as Njinga laid eyes on her sister, her emotions erupted. She threw herself on the ground in front of Barbara, rubbing herself in the soil as was customary when a person received a favor or when dependents paid homage to masters or superiors. Given permission to approach Barbara, Njinga kissed her sister's hand and knelt once more, letting her face drop to the ground once again. After this ceremonial greeting the two sisters embraced and for a long time held on to each other tenderly, not speaking a word, but kissing each other repeatedly.[76]

Once the highly charged emotional greeting ended, Njinga and her officials immediately had an audience with Peixoto, Captain Carasco, Barbara, and the official scribe, as well as Father Gaeta. Both parties listened as an official read aloud in Kimbundu each of the conditions for peace. The formal language of the agreement was the same that Njinga had agreed to. As the terms were read, the Portuguese scribe recorded the following articles: Njinga agreed to reconcile with the Holy Catholic Church, to immediately ask for priests and fathers, to build a church for Father Gaeta, and to allow him to baptize all children born after the signing of the treaty. Njinga would also have to make a public announcement letting her people know that Father Gaeta had the authority to get rid of all Imbangala rites and practices in Matamba. In addition, Njinga must now obey King João IV and would have to send her army to any part of Angola whenever a request came from the king's representative. Njinga also agreed to send her army to discipline rebel *sobas,* to allow Portuguese traders free access to her markets, to hand over the Imbangala leader Kalandula to Sousa Chichorro (which she did when she presented his severed head to the Portuguese), and to pay 130 slaves to free Barbara. The treaty promised that the governor would restore to Njinga the lands of Kituxela, which she claimed as her patrimony, and agreed to order Kasanje and Ngola Hari to repopulate it so that Portuguese traders could use it to reprovision themselves and travel directly to her court. As it happens, Sousa Chichorro had already forced Kasanje to return people that he had captured from Njinga.[77] The agreement also committed Portuguese troops to protect Njinga's people against Kasanje or Ngola Hari if they contravened the treaty.

After everyone heard all the terms of the agreement, Njinga and her officials clapped their hands, indicating in the formal Mbundu manner that they understood and accepted the treaty. Njinga verbally ratified the agreement yet another time in a second ceremony while her attendants, officials, onlookers, and the Portuguese party and others waited. After the formal ceremony, her officials and all the people who had joined Barbara made their way to Njinga's court. There, a crowd of people who had witnessed the ceremony began to clap, indicating their agreement with Njinga's verbal acclamation. Once Peixoto and Carasco heard the applause of the population, they knew that the formal part of the ceremony was over. They handed Barbara over to Njinga. At that point Njinga and all her officials placed their mark on the document, and Father Gaeta, Peixoto, and Carasco signed it as well.[78] The long wait was over. The peace that had taken over a year to negotiate was finally signed on October 12, 1656.

Once the treaty was signed and Barbara was officially free, Njinga announced the beginning of the celebrations in honor of her sister's return. For the next several days and nights Njinga and her people rejoiced with enthusiasm. Father Gaeta complained mightily about the nightly revelry and bemoaned the fact that no one had bothered to come to the church to celebrate. Njinga and her people did not mind the many sleepless nights, and public celebrations weren't limited to her court in Matamba. When Sousa Chichorro announced in Luanda that Njinga had agreed to the terms of the treaty, he publicized it to the sound of trumpets, and the Mbundus there celebrated the long-sought peace.

Not everyone in Luanda was as elated, the euphoria there tempered by the fact that members of the Camara who had opposed both Barbara's release and the treaty were still awaiting a reply from the king concerning their request that Sousa Chichorro be stopped from freeing Barbara and making peace with Njinga. By December 12, 1656, when the Portuguese regent, Queen Luisa de Gusmão, finally acceded to the Camara's request and sent a royal decree ordering Governor Sousa Chichorro not to prolong Barbara's imprisonment, the die had already been cast. The peace was underway. The ninety-nine slaves that the governor had received from Njinga as ransom for Barbara's release had been transported to Pernambuco in Brazil, and another thirty had been sent to fulfill the terms of the treaty.[79] Most important, Barbara was enjoying the life as a Ndongo princess in the kingdom of Ndongo-Matamba that her sister had established as her legacy.

As Njinga entered the next and last chapter of her earthly life, she proved that she was willing to go to the same fanatical extreme in embracing her new religious and political life as she had done years before when she became an Imbangala and survived a lifetime of war and rapine. Her dealings with the Portuguese set her apart from her fellow central African leaders, especially from Ngola Hari, whom the Portuguese continued to marginalize and humiliate until his death. While she was dictating the terms of her relationship with the Portuguese king and his representatives in Angola, Ngola Hari was begging them to recognize the sacrifices he had made on their behalf, including the loss of his son in the war against the Dutch. His 1652 complaint that he was "molested by people every day who ask me to carry the loads of private people to the *pumbo* [market]" and to favor him with "arms when I ask it against Njinga" was in stark contrast to the diplomatic coup and military success that Njinga had pulled off.[80]

Yet Njinga could never be complacent. She steeled herself for the significant challenges she knew she would face as she moved to align Ndongo-Matamba's relationship to the Portuguese and to Rome, to ensure her kingdom's political independence.

7

....

ON THE WAY TO THE ANCESTORS

Having finally achieved peace with the Portuguese after decades of protracted wars and tortuous diplomacy, Njinga spent the last seven years of her life on an unprecedented, once unthinkable spiritual and political journey. During this time, she put her efforts into institutionalizing Christianity within her kingdom of Ndongo-Matamba, reasserting the concepts of nobility with which she had grown up, and preparing to pass an independent, Christian kingdom on to her sister Barbara. Although many of her opponents, both inside and outside her kingdom, opposed this program, the reputation Njinga had gained as the dominant political figure in central Africa guaranteed that few would openly question or oppose her campaign to build a new Ndongo in Matamba.

Becoming a Christian Ruler

Although Njinga had privately confessed to Father Gaeta her deep desire to return to the Catholic faith, her spiritual rebirth was a process that unfolded slowly. It began during the final phase of the peace negotiations when, in truth, she would have said anything to secure her sister's release. Once Barbara was freed, Njinga did not stop to bask in the euphoria of success. The next step in Njinga's program was to transform her followers into Christians and to build a Christian community in Ndongo-Matamba,

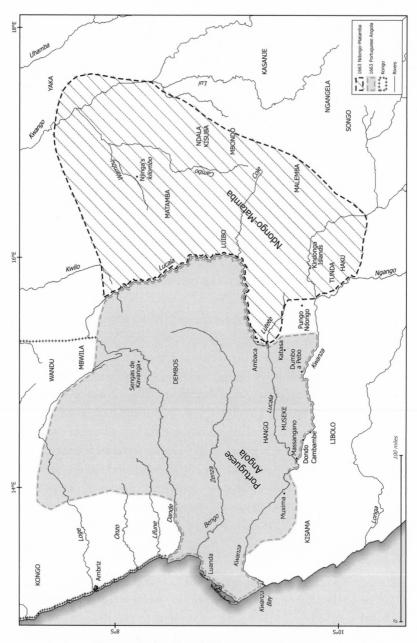

Portuguese Angola and Ndongo-Matamba, 1663

on her terms and under her royal leadership. Although she was sincere about her yearning to become a devout Christian, her spiritual quest was strongly linked to her notions of royalty, and she did not intend to let the Capuchins dictate the pace and nature of Christian conversion in her kingdom. As a queen of Ndongo and Matamba descended from Ndongo royalty, she held on to the political ideals and symbols that were central to royal rule.

She articulated this idea of her destiny to rule a Christian community as a Christian queen after her reunion with Barbara, when in a conversation with Father Gaeta she commented that the Sousa family "gave me life, death, and resurrection."[1] If by life Njinga meant the baptism she underwent in Luanda in 1622, when João Correia de Sousa was governor, and by death she meant her transformation into an Imbangala as a result of Fernão de Sousa's wars, then by resurrection she was probably referring to the freeing of Barbara, as part of the peace treaty she signed with Luis Martins de Sousa Chichorro. But that resurrection, more significantly, also involved replacing Imbangala customs with traditional Mbundu notions of royalty.

Njinga's views of how an Ndongo queen should live had much to do with her desire to settle down after her retreat from Luanda in 1648, and she embraced the trappings of royalty partly as a means of garnering the respect of both the Portuguese and her neighbors. Even as she led her armies herself or sent her Imbangala troops to battle in the immediate aftermath of her retreat, she was at the same time overseeing the rebuilding of her court in Matamba. Because large areas to the east and west had been destroyed during the previous twenty years of war, Njinga had selected for her new court a location in the middle of the country. Much of Matamba would remain unpopulated until as late as 1658, but the city and the court Njinga built were bustling centers of royal rituals and diplomacy.[2]

Njinga never missed an opportunity to make an impression. The residence in which she welcomed Father Gaeta in August 1656, with its large courtyard and many wooden columns, remained a center of pomp and official business long after the peace-treaty celebrations had ended. On the occasion of his first meeting with her, when he came to discuss details of the treaty, she had sent word to her captains to gather a thousand bowmen to serve as his honor guard when he entered the city. This massive display was essential, she believed, because Gaeta's presence would "increase her prestige."[3] Following the signing of the treaty, there were many occasions on which she welcomed visiting delegations, entertaining them in what had become her trademark elaborate ways. Her court was always full of people requesting audiences with her, and she could be counted on to give them a show.[4]

Njinga paid particular attention to the dress and behavior of her armed female and male bodyguards. Again, she was mindful of first impressions: they were the first group to greet visitors approaching the outskirts of the city, and they were responsible for escorting visiting delegations into the city.[5] Njinga always sat on a throne when she welcomed official visitors. According to Father Gaeta, who lived in Matamba for a total of more than three years, Njinga paid special attention on these occasions to her own wardrobe, not only that of her guards. "When she received foreign ambassadors," he observed, she "was always elaborately dressed in silk drapes, velvet and brocades imported from Europe, wearing a crown, and she always wore on her hands, feet, and arms several rings made of gold, silver, copper, iron, corals, and various imported beads." She also wore the best of the local wraps that women valued, and used these occasions to showcase the rich rugs, mats beaded with silver, and other precious items that she had acquired. Her court was held to the same standard, and she made sure that her many pages and three hundred personal female attendants were also "richly dressed according to the Portuguese manner."[6]

During her years as an Imbangala, Njinga had either downplayed her royal identity or simply did not have the opportunity to express it. Since the peace treaty granted her authority over part of the former kingdom of Ndongo and legalized her position as queen of Matamba, she found other opportunities to reinforce her long-hidden royal status. She insisted that she possessed special spiritual attributes, and she always appeared in the courtyard of her residence at a designated hour to dispense the "*lunene real* [royal word] which the people believed was 'the best luck in the world.'"[7] Njinga expected deference, and her free subjects, whether they were nobles or commoners, were required to work three times a week on her royal lands.[8] On public occasions she displayed royal symbols that held great significance for her and her people, and she revived many rituals as well. The battle ax, a traditional royal symbol, was a weapon that Njinga wielded with tremendous skill. After signing the treaty, according to Portuguese and missionary reports, Njinga publicly threw down her battle ax and informed the soldiers that the Portuguese king had defeated her. In the years after that, she always displayed the ax and a bow on public occasions. She was heard to boast that the ax could not be defeated because it was "a royal weapon."[9] Even after Njinga no longer participated personally on the battlefield, her soldiers believed that if they received their bows directly from her hand, they would hit their targets and would be invincible.[10]

Although her desire to maintain some Ndongo rituals and privileges did not fundamentally contradict the expectations the missionaries had of her as a Christian monarch, she faced challenges from her own people when she attempted to discard certain Mbundu/Imbangala religious ideals and ritual practices. Her first attempts to implement a new policy began during the negotiations in 1656, when she had no choice but to demonstrate her sincerity about returning to the Catholic faith. As she had done in the past when making major decisions, Njinga staged her transformation in a public meeting with traditional priests.

Njinga's preservation of the crucifix that Njinga a Mona had brought back from the battlefield, and her practice of praying to it daily, posed a threat to the relationships she had cultivated with religious and political advisers during her Imbangala days. She needed their confidence to avoid rebellion by her followers, especially the powerful Imbangala captains. She orchestrated a rupture with traditional spiritual beliefs in a public setting in October 1656, a few days before Barbara arrived in Matamba, calling together the council of nine advisers on whom she relied to enforce her authority: the five powerful *xingulas* (*ngangas* possessed by ancestral spirits) and her four highest political councilors. She would call on the *xingulas* to contact her honored ancestors. She had organized a similar ceremony in 1626, when she fled from the island of Danji. At that time, the priests had brought out the sacred *misete* (reliquary chest) in which she had stored some of Ngola Mbande's bones and possessions; invoking the spirit of her brother, they had sought the spirit's approval for her flight.

On this occasion, the *xingulas* invoked a pantheon of five ancestors. In addition to Ngola Mbande's *misete*, there were four others which held the bones of four revered Imbangala captains who had achieved ancestor status after their death. Njinga knew that she had to obtain the ancestors' approval as well as that of her council if she was to successfully replace the Mbundu/Imbangala religious ideology and practices with Christianity.

Father Zelotes, the Kongo priest whose life Njinga had saved after his capture in the 1648 Wandu campaign and who had since become one of her court favorites, attended the ceremony. He was the only eyewitness to the event, and he later related to Father Gaeta how Njinga conducted the meeting. Njinga stood in front of the members of the council and addressed each of them in turn. She told them that Father Gaeta, a Christian *nganga*, would teach them the "law of Christ." Christ, she explained, was believed by Christians to be "the God of the Sky and of the land." She announced that she intended to follow Christian law, since she had been baptized in Angola as a young woman when she went to Luanda as her brother's ambassador. But before giving up her Mbundu / Imbangala beliefs, she needed to know their opinion. This was terribly important, she said, because once she embraced Christian law, she would have to remove the *misete* dedicated to "our dead," and she would no longer be permitted to conduct any of the sacrifices that had been part of their rituals. She ended by asking, "What about it, what is your sentiment?"[11]

Once Njinga finished speaking, Father Zelotes later told Father Gaeta, each of the *xingulas* became possessed by the spirits of the deceased Imbangala captains and Ngola Mbande, and each spirit gave Njinga its permission. Once the priest arrived, Njinga explained, he would baptize all the children born in Matamba, and they would have to be allowed to live instead of being killed or left to die, as had been done in the *kilombo*. A lively debate followed among the spirits in the form of the possessed priests. One of them told Njinga that she could dispose of the *misete*, she could reject all Imbangala rituals, but there would always be others to honor them in other regions.

In the end, the four Imbangala spirits affirmed that they had been raised as Imbangalas and had followed Njinga, who had given them a home. If she wanted to live as a Christian, they said, as queen she was free to do so. Njinga listened particularly closely to the priest through whom the spirit of her brother, Ngola Mbande, spoke. When he lived in the world, he said, neither he nor a single one of his ancestors was ever an Imbangala. He reassured Njinga that he was pleased with everything she had done so far, and he appreciated the sacrifices she had had to make. Yes, he would prefer she live according to the ancient traditions of Ndongo, in the way of her ancestors, but if receiving Christian law and living as a Christian meant that the whites would no longer make war and would allow her to live in peace and quiet in the kingdom, then he accepted her decision. The four political councilors then gave their approval for Njinga to proceed with her ideological transformation.[12]

Njinga was now ready to begin the process of Christianization. This meant directing Father Gaeta and working alongside him. Njinga's preparation for the transition had been carried out so skillfully, enhanced by Barbara's arrival and the acceptance of the peace settlement, that she had no difficulty generating excitement among the population. Now, instead of first consulting the *xingulas,* Njinga turned to Father Gaeta and, later on, to Father Cavazzi.

The mass baptisms that soon followed, which took place in the plaza in front of the newly built church on days Father Gaeta selected, had more in common with a military fall-in formation than with one of the most sacred events in the church. But Njinga was present for them all at the beginning. In a short time, six of the principal courtiers and many army officers were baptized. A few baptisms were special affairs, and Njinga made sure that she recognized them appropriately. When Njinga a Mona was baptized, for example, squadrons of soldiers appeared in the plaza in front of the church with their flags flying, drums beating, and musical instruments blaring before the actual religious ceremony. Njinga hosted banquets at her residence after each of these special, heavily attended baptisms. Once the city's populace saw her officials agreeing to baptism, they crowded the church to learn the catechism and undergo the rite as well. The majority of the ordinary people receiving baptism were soldiers who had had nomadic lives until then, remaining no more than three or four years in one place before being sent to another campaign at the whim of Njinga and her captains. As many as eight thousand soldiers and a thousand children who were born after Father Gaeta's arrival later underwent the ceremony.[13]

Christian Marriage

Before Njinga was accepted into the church as a full member, she went through a long period of soul-searching and personal transformation. Although Njinga and her nobles had accepted Christian teachings and baptism with relative ease up to this point, the sacrament of monogamous marriage was a much tougher sell. The lengthy and heated debates that Father Gaeta conducted with her nobles and soldiers did little to help and ended only in finger-pointing. The ordinary soldiers declared that they would give up their concubines only if the nobles did so first, and the nobles said they would do so only if their social superiors acted as examples and gave up theirs. The highest courtiers had only to point at Njinga. It was unfair to ask them to give up their concubines—a sacred custom that they had inherited from their ancestors—while "the queen our Lady even though she is baptized . . . has more husbands and more lovers than we have wives."[14]

Njinga had to admit this was a dilemma. She reached a decision, as she always did, after calculating how her actions would advance her goals. Since the death of her newborn and the incident that led to her inability to bear children so many years ago, Njinga had exhibited a complicated relationship with men. During her years as an Imbangala, possibly to compensate for the loss of her child, she would publicly humiliate men and often ordered both men and young boys to be killed in ritual sacrifices. At the same time, she surrounded herself with hundreds of virile young men and boys who served as her lovers, concubines, and soldiers. Yet, even as she welcomed her sister back and designated Barbara as her successor, she still yearned for a son. She even stated on one occasion that only a son would ensure Matamba's survival. One day she broached the topic with Father Gaeta, asking him to pray to God to help her conceive a son. Doing all he could to control his surprise that a seventy-five-year-old woman would consider it possible to bear children, he took the opportunity to bring up the issue of Christian marriage. If she wanted such a gift from God, he said, she would first have to give up her lovers and concubines and marry just one husband in a Catholic ceremony. This would provide no guarantee that she could conceive a son, of course; if she proved unable to, he did not want her to blame God. Regardless, marriage to one man would enhance her status, earning her "great credit and reputation in the world" for setting an example for her people, and "glory and honor" in heaven. Convinced by these arguments, Njinga agreed to a church wedding, aware that her upcoming nuptials would encourage her people to follow suit. She selected from among her courtiers a young boy named Sebastião, "graceful, robust . . . and of most beautiful features" to be her husband.[15]

On January 30, 1657, five days before her wedding was scheduled to take place, Njinga sent out an order to all her court officials, attendants, and thousands of her soldiers to assemble in the plaza in front of the church, now called Santa Maria de Matamba. Dressed in her war attire, she ordered them to perform the military dance that they usually held before they went on a campaign. After the exercise, they assembled in their squadrons, anxiously awaiting her announcement. Njinga stood on a large chair placed in the middle of the plaza. In a dramatic gesture, she picked up her bow and turned to her vassals and the troops. At the top of her voice, she shouted, "Listen, my dear vassals, who can ever defeat this bow and arrow of your Queen Njinga?" They responded: "No one has ever done that because thousands of men would come to your defense." Njinga continued: "I want to tell you that the *maniputo* [Portuguese king] has won, and because I am already old I no longer wish to go to war against his people. I am already living in peace with him, and more glory will come to me through the Fathers who have come from Rome and who will reconcile us with the Holy Roman Church. . . . I will embrace the Holy Catholic faith which before I had professed, and in which I will die." She acknowledged that she had delivered slaves to the Portuguese to redeem her sister, and all was as she wished. As Njinga stopped speaking, Barbara came out and threw herself on the ground in front of her, turning herself over in the dust in a display of gratitude, as Njinga herself had done when Barbara had been presented to her, finally free.[16]

The ceremony was all about setting examples. She addressed the crowd again, proclaiming that Njinga a Mona, the captain of the army, had accepted baptism. Most important, she herself had selected a man to marry who was already baptized. She announced that Barbara was also to be married, to the *mwene lumbo* Ngola Kanini, now known by his baptismal name João Guterres Kanini, as soon as it could be confirmed that his first wife was dead. She called on everyone assembled to give up their multiple partners and adopt monogamous unions, attend catechism classes, and agree to baptism.[17]

On February 4, 1657, after having dismissed the more than forty husbands or concubines she had kept, Njinga married Sebastião in a church wedding.[18] Although her spouse was decades younger than she and not of noble blood—he was the son of a slave who had fled Luanda and enlisted in her troops—she honored him immediately with the title "husband of Njinga" (not "king") and granted him five hundred slaves so that he could live as a nobleman.[19]

Barbara's marriage proved more complicated. Njinga had selected João Kanini because he was a blood relative of theirs and thus eligible to rule. She had captured him at the battle in support of Ngolome a Keta in 1644, and instead of having him killed, she had made him her *mwene lumbo*, or keeper of the household. He had all the qualities she favored. Besides being a close relative, he owed her loyalty for having freed him after she had taken him prisoner. Furthermore, he was already a Catholic. She hoped that by selecting one of her own relatives, the throne would remain within her lineage. When news arrived from Massangano that João Kanini's first wife was still alive, Njinga was forced to cancel the betrothal. Reluctantly, she gave permission for Barbara to marry Njinga a Mona, now called Antonio Carasco Njinga a Mona. Barbara's elaborate Catholic wedding ceremony took place on September 9, 1657. Although neither Njinga nor Barbara trusted Njinga a Mona—after all, he was not of royal lineage, and indeed was an Imbangala and a slave—she recognized that over the years he had served her faithfully. As a result, she honored him not only with her sister's hand but also with a noble title.[20]

Njinga's bold decisions had an immediate impact. By early March 1657, her capital, whose name she had changed to Santa Maria de Matamba in honor of the church she had built, boasted 2,506 baptized Christians, and many of her subjects were attending catechism classes. Among the earliest converts were many of Njinga's officials, including eighty *makotas* (lineage heads) and their wives. During this period, both Njinga and Barbara devoted all their attention to the church, attending services three times a week and participating in the Holy Procession, a weekly Friday event in which the people joined Father Gaeta as he carried the Holy Crucifix around the plaza. During these processions, six young Mbundu men did penance by beating themselves with iron chains.[21]

Njinga, the Portuguese, and the Vatican

After she and Barbara held their Christian marriage ceremonies, Njinga began a systematic campaign to ensure that a European-style Catholic Christianity would spread among her people by pushing her court representatives to get baptized and live as Christians. She had political motives for spearheading this Christian transformation of Ndongo-Matamba. Even though the peace treaty had ceded to the Portuguese certain lands around

Ndongo and in the Dembos region that Ndongo had traditionally controlled or that she had conquered, she still had to ensure that Matamba and the areas of Ndongo still under her control remained independent. Between January and September 1657, she reopened the political and religious diplomacy with Rome that she had begun almost a decade before, sending nearly ten letters to Governor Sousa Chichorro, to King João IV in Portugal, and, most important, to officials in Rome. As we shall see, she even went so far as to nominate one of her councilors to head an official embassy to the Vatican. By this time, Father Gaeta had become her personal confessor and political adviser and advocate, and she did not hesitate to use him to relay her messages and to arrange for the details of her ambassador's travel to Portugal and Rome.

Njinga's letters and embassies to the Portuguese and to officials in Rome all contain elements that display her political and religious motives. In the letters her ambassadors delivered to the governor in Luanda, for example, Njinga used her royal title (queen) to refer to herself, along with her given Kimbundu name (Njinga) and her Christian name (Dona Ana). These letters always noted her compliance with the terms of the peace treaty, meant to reassure the skeptical Portuguese officials of her commitment to adhere to all of its conditions. She stressed in her letters how serious she was about her new religion and provided details of its spread among her followers. Her goal was to assure Portuguese officials in Luanda and in Lisbon, too, not only that she was serious about peace, but that her newfound faith had put her on equal spiritual ground with them. In January 1657, less than three months after signing the first copy of the treaty, she sent a letter to Governor Sousa Chichorro that spoke of her acceptance of Christianity. In it, she said she had become his "spiritual relative."[22] Three days later, she wrote him yet another letter, this one of a more political nature, in support of the chief negotiator Peixoto, who had been so instrumental in guiding the peace negotiations to their successful conclusion. She praised him for the commitment and passion he showed, and for having such an in-depth knowledge of Kimbundu: he was "the best linguist in my kingdom because he was born in Angola and raised by his grandparents."[23]

In March 1657, she sent her courtiers again to the governor with news of her Catholic marriage and also with a young slave as a present. Governor Sousa Chichorro was eager to pass on to officials in Lisbon the good news of the rapid spread of Christianity in Matamba. In his letter of congratulations to Njinga, he called her his "daughter" and sent her as a gift a piece of jewelry made of many pearls, in the middle of which was set an image of the Virgin Mary. The governor also sent detailed letters to the king on developments in Matamba.[24]

Njinga did whatever she could to demonstrate that she was now a strong Portuguese ally. In response to his wedding gift, she had sent the governor another young slave, intended to serve as one of his porters. Later that year, in August, Njinga wrote to Sousa Chichorro yet again, this time offering to send her army to join in a war against the king of Kongo, whom the Portuguese had accused of harboring runaway slaves. Upon learning of the death of King João IV, who had died in November 1656, not long after peace had finally come to Ndongo-Matamba, Njinga declared a period of public mourning in his memory, and, following Portuguese custom, wore mourning clothes herself.[25]

Njinga's written and verbal contacts with the Portuguese in Luanda in the five years following this spate of letters in 1657 focused largely on her growing unease about their military operations. She made it a point of responding to their persistent requests for her to settle commercial disputes that arose between the many Portuguese merchants and their representatives, who had increasingly started moving to Matamba in the wake of the peace settlement. One of these letters was written in response to one she had received from the Portuguese soldier/chronicler António de Cadornega, who had become a judge in Luanda and wrote to Njinga after a meeting with Father Gaeta. Eager to build a church modeled on those she had seen in Luanda, she had asked Father Gaeta to recruit skilled craftsmen, carpenters, stonemasons, masons, and ironworkers. She had given him an account to pay slave owners up front for the rental of their slaves' services so that they could be sent to Matamba. Once word got around that Njinga was planning a major building project, slaves owned by the Portuguese in Massangano ran away and tried to reach the region. Cadornega wrote to Njinga to resolve the issue. In her response, Njinga denied that her people had either taken in or sold Portuguese slaves who had run away. She pinned the accusations on individuals who wanted to disrupt the peace she and her people were enjoying. She challenged him to question all the *pumbeiros* (Africans who traded for slaves on behalf of their Portuguese owners) in her court about the merchandise their owners had given them to purchase slaves. She ended the letter by noting that when she sold slaves to Portuguese agents, she always warned them to lock the slaves up; but instead, it seemed that most let the slaves out to go about their own business. They were taking a chance.[26]

Despite the many letters to the governor and her public display of friendship, Njinga's mistrust of the Portuguese never subsided. She continued to cultivate her relationship with the Capuchins, who she knew would facilitate the diplomatic relations she wanted with the pope. While her ambassadors were in Luanda delivering her letters and reporting to the governor the many wonderful things Njinga was doing to advance Christianity in Matamba, she continued to push ahead with her religious diplomacy. Njinga had become disenchanted with the quality of the parish priests who had come to Matamba from Luanda, and indeed had already dismissed several of them. She decided instead to appeal directly to Rome for Capuchins.

In August and September of 1657, Njinga wrote several letters to the pope and to the Propaganda Fide in Rome. At last she had come to knowledge of the true God, she wrote, and she was relieved to no longer be living an idolatrous life in the power of the devil. She said that any priests who might be sent would be received with goodwill in her kingdom, since so many of her people were eager to be baptized.[27]

Relying on Father Gaeta's advice, by August of that year, she had come up with an elaborate plan to have the papacy recognize her as a Christian monarch and Matamba as a Christian state. One of her counselors, João, who could speak and write Portuguese, would head an official embassy to Lisbon and Rome. She gave him one of the highest titles of her court—*mwene makau* (chief cup bearer)—and selected her *tendala* and a *makota* to accompany him. She also put at João's disposal a number of slaves so that he could travel in the style associated with royalty.[28] On August 8, 1657, João left Matamba with letters entrusted to him by Njinga and which he was supposed to deliver personally to the authorities in Luanda, Lisbon, and Rome. One of the letters was addressed to Portugal's Queen Luisa, widow of King João IV, who was acting as regent for her young son and the future king, Afonso VI. Njinga's letter expressed to the queen her deep condolences on the death of her husband and respectfully thanked her for finalizing the peace treaty.

Njinga hoped the letter would convince Portuguese officials in Luanda that her sole purpose in sending João to Portugal was to convey her condolences personally to the queen. Of course, this was far from the truth. Her real aim was to have Father Serafino da Cortona and other Capuchins in Lisbon arrange for João to travel to Rome so that he could deliver the letters she had written to the Propaganda Fide and to the pope. Confident that they would be able to help him navigate the bureaucracy in Luanda and Lisbon, she entrusted João's arrangements to Father Gaeta and to Father Cortona, the prefect of the mission headquartered in Massangano.

Njinga swore Father Gaeta to secrecy after discussing the plans with him. She feared that if news reached the Portuguese traders in Matamba or members of other religious orders in Luanda, they would try to derail the embassy. She wrote to Father Cortona on August 15, sharing all the details with him, and asking him for his help. She stressed to the priest that it was imperative that João travel to Rome to present her letter personally to the pope. She wanted the pope to know that she had accepted him as the "universal Father of all Christians," and she hoped that in her name João would "kiss his feet and ask for his blessing as the daughter that I am of the church." Leaving nothing to chance, she told Father Cortona that she had "signed with my sign of the cross and seal" to prove to everyone that João was indeed her ambassador.[29]

Njinga trusted Father Gaeta implicitly, knowing how deeply committed he was to her Christian project. In the one year he had been at her court, he had not only become her spiritual adviser but also her political confidant. Father Gaeta, seeing an opportunity for the Capuchins to spread the news in Rome and throughout "all Christianity" of the conversion of a "heathen queen" who pledged her total allegiance to the pope, served as the conduit between Njinga, her ambassador, and Father Cortona.[30] On August 20, he wrote a letter to Father Cortona providing him with further details about the embassy and swore him to secrecy, as he himself had been. Njinga's ambassador needed a teacher to give him lessons in European etiquette before he left for Lisbon, and Father Gaeta implored Father Cortona to find one. Njinga was aware of the importance of appearance, and she intended to provide João with slaves, "so that good vests and clothes are made for him to wear during the trip to Lisbon," as well as an umbrella (to indicate his status) and five or six attendants. João would take one or two of the party along with him to Rome, and the others would wait for him in Lisbon. The Capuchins involved in furthering Njinga's papal diplomacy knew that they could strengthen her case if they could show that Portuguese officials were obstructing the missionary outreach

Njinga's letter to Father Serafino da Cortona, August 15, 1657 of the papacy. Father Gaeta told Father Cortona that if Portuguese officials in Luanda prevented Njinga's ambassador from leaving, he should spread word in Lisbon and Rome that the Portuguese had prevented the ambassador from carrying her letter of condolence to King João's widow and young son. This would bolster the cardinals' sympathy for Njinga's requests.[31]

But João never left Luanda. The newly nominated governor, João Fernandes Vieira, who replaced Sousa Chichorro in May 1658, prevented his departure. Governor Sousa Chichorro had given his approval, and, in fact, João was set to travel on the same vessel the governor was taking on his return trip to Lisbon. Governor Vieira announced his decision to stop the ambassador's departure for Lisbon at a public hearing where João had made a presentation to officials detailing the reasons why Njinga wished him to go to Lisbon. Vieira based his position on a royal decree that stipulated that "no Ethiopian [African] Lord should travel or send an embassy to Europe." Even as her counselors threatened to break the peace over the insult, Njinga had no choice but to recall her ambassador. This was a tremendous blow to Njinga. She remained outwardly unruffled, however, since she had already designated Father Cortona as her envoy and representative to Rome. Before returning to Matamba, João turned over to Father Cortona the letters he was supposed to have delivered, along with the verbal instructions Njinga had given him.[32]

Njinga's energetic outreach to Rome was in stark contrast to her dealings with the Portuguese. After she had achieved her goals of freeing her sister and settling the western borders of Matamba, the Portuguese were less central to her plans. She still maintained contact with officials in Luanda, but the number of letters she wrote began to decline considerably. Moreover, her responses lacked the details, the urgency, and the desperation of the pre-1658 letters. She wrote chiefly about the still contentious issue of her political relationship with *sobas* whom she had formerly subjugated and over whom the Portuguese now claimed sovereignty, or those who had been her allies during the war. Njinga was aware that the treaty had not resolved all the political disputes with her former rivals, and they knew that she still had the ability to mobilize an anti-Portuguese alliance. In fact, in August 1658, Vieira, the new governor, had written in a report to Lisbon that one of these *sobas* refused outright to comply with his requests and had even sent him a letter asserting that he would swear allegiance only to "the king of Kongo and Queen Njinga." He was ready to do whatever these rulers ordered, but would do no such thing for the king of Portugal.[33] The letters Njinga received from officials in Luanda often came after demands from Lisbon to allow missionaries from Rome to travel to Matamba to baptize the people and convert Njinga's lords. Officials in Luanda were also ordered to maintain open correspondence and friendship with Njinga so that "after her death her officials would remain under the obedience of the king."[34]

Njinga still maintained official relations with the sovereigns of Kongo and regularly entertained envoys from and exchanged letters with them. This situation led Governor Vieira to declare war against Kongo in March 1659. The governor contended that he had received news that King Garcia II had renewed his alliance with Njinga, "our capital enemy," and warned that if he did not declare unilateral war, Kongo and Matamba would again become allies and take with them many *sobas*, "some willingly and others because of fear."[35]

At the same time that she was maintaining the status quo with the Portuguese, Njinga continued efforts to initiate direct contact with the papacy. She wrote countless letters to Capuchins in Rome and to the Vatican, expressing her deep desire for Capuchin missionaries and official recognition. Her letters to officials in the Vatican include information she had gathered from the Capuchins about Rome's treatment of European Christian monarchs and the role of the church in society. They represent a veritable campaign to persuade Vatican authorities that she was worthy of being treated the way they would treat any Christian ruler, from Europe or elsewhere.

The letters were also intended to persuade officials to recognize Matamba as a Christian kingdom. In a letter written in September 1657, which Father Cortona took to Rome on her behalf, she indicated that the priest had permission in her name to swear allegiance and obedience to the pope as Christ's vicar on earth, as well as to give him thanks for sending Capuchins to her. She proudly declared that she and all her court had been cleansed by baptism and had built a church. In conclusion, she asked the pontiff to help her continue along the path she had chosen and to send her missionaries, indulgences, and blessings.[36]

Njinga would have to wait several years before she received responses from Rome. Although officials of the Overseas Council in Lisbon supported the missionary work of the Capuchins in Matamba, they were adamantly against the order establishing religious institutions there; doing so, they feared, would allow Njinga to find new opportunities to challenge the Portuguese. In January 1659, the councilors warned Queen Luisa that she should never allow the Capuchins to build a permanent base in Luanda devoted only to their work in Matamba, but merely a hospice where they could rest after their trips.[37]

With Portuguese officials erecting such obstacles, it proved difficult for Rome to address Njinga's requests for Capuchins to come to Matamba. Njinga's letter-writing campaign persisted with or without responses. The fact that Father Gaeta and Father Romano were also sending letters and reports to officials in the Vatican on her behalf, pointing out the impact that Njinga's conversion had had on neighboring polities, kept the campaign alive and drew more Capuchins to her cause.[38] Njinga never gave up hope that she would receive a positive response from the Vatican, and after each lengthy discussion she had with Father Gaeta and Father Cavazzi, she would write a letter to whichever Vatican official they suggested. In December 1659, for example, she wrote a letter to Cardinal D'Este, thanking him for sending Father Gaeta to her. She credited Gaeta with saving the souls of herself and her vassals and pointed out that his presence had allowed her to know the "true God," as a result of which she was at peace "in body and soul." She ended the letter, as she had done many times before, by pleading for other Capuchins to come to Matamba, so they could confer holy baptism on the many people in her kingdom desperate to receive it.[39]

In March 1661, Njinga finally received the letter she had so desperately craved: one written in the hand of the pope. Dated June 19, 1660, it had taken nine long months for the letter to arrive. In it, Pope Alexander VII responded favorably to every one of Njinga's requests. He addressed her as "Dearest in Christ our Daughter Anna Queen Nzinga," welcomed her into the true Christian religion, and indicated that he was praying that her country would be prosperous and virtuous. The pope also wrote of his hope for her specifically—that as a daughter of Christ, she would grow in virtue and generosity and that the Supreme God would admit her into the elect.[40]

In her response, dated August 25, 1662, less than a year and a half before her death, Njinga acknowledged to the pontiff that she would not live to see the full flowering of Christianity in Matamba and that the religious transformation she envisioned could not be done in a day; it had to develop slowly. She swore, however, that as long as God gave her life, she would "leave the new Christianity in a good state" so that after her death, her replacement would rule a kingdom that was truly Christian. Njinga pleaded with the pontiff to think kindly of her kingdom. She admitted that it was in great need of spiritual treasures of the Holy Church and requested that he send her two indulgences, one for Saint Anna's Day, which she promised to "read in the church that I have made in my court dedicated to the said Saint Anna" and the other for another church she had built, which was dedicated to the Holy Crucifix and to Our Lady.[41] She had signed her first letters to the pope simply as "Queen Dona Anna" or as his "most obedient and submissive" daughter; she had not yet included the cross as her official seal. But when she responded to the letter in which he had offered her his official acceptance of her as a Christian monarch, she inserted the cross as her official seal in front of her name.[42]

In what would be the waning months of her life, Njinga's letter writing escalated. In March 1663, she wrote to the Capuchin father Crisostomo de Genoa requesting that he hand deliver a letter to the pope, as well as a second one addressed to the Procurador of the Capuchins. She asked Father Genoa to greet the pope in her name and kiss his feet, and to receive on her behalf the pontiff's blessing, as well as to spread the word about the progress of Christianity in her kingdom.[43]

Just eight months before her death, in April 1663, she wrote another letter to the prefect of the Propaganda Fide, again giving it to Father Genoa to deliver. As usual, she thanked the prefect for sending her Capuchins, noting that they had brought her the "true light" and that they were fulfilling all their duties. She also noted that as a Christian monarch, she humbly kissed the pontiff's sacred robe and asked him for a blessing. The main point of her letter, however, was to bemoan the fact that the death or sickness of several Capuchins in Matamba had left her land lacking missionaries to carry out evangelical work. Without more Capuchins, she feared, the situation would turn dangerous. She also took the opportunity to announce that she was building another new church. Additionally, she had given permission to build a school where new priests could teach the children.[44] As in her letter to the pope, Njinga's signature reflected her new status: she inserted "Daughter in Christ" and placed the Christian cross before her name, "Queen Dona Anna."[45]

Letter from Pope Alexander VII to Njinga, June 19, 1660

54

Dominus rediens Patri ... et matrem ...
... animo ... Ade igitur ...
filia Nestor generis, atque constanter ...

... Die 19 Juny 1662 ...

71

Laying the Groundwork for Transformation

Njinga's new spiritual passion was not limited to letter writing or maneu-
vering to get diplomatic recognition by the Vatican. Even as she anxiously
awaited assurances from Rome that more missionaries would be sent, she
worked with the Capuchins who were already in Matamba to begin laying
the groundwork for its Christian transformation. She had by this time
abandoned her Imbangala practices but had not given up the techniques
she had employed as an Imbangala leader. Just as she had reshaped Imbangala laws when she became a captain, she began the Christianization effort
by initiating a campaign of church building so that Fathers Gaeta, Valsassina, and Cavazzi and the few parish priests in Matamba would be able to
preach and teach the catechism to the people. She learned everything she
could from the Capuchins about church celebrations and organization in
Europe, sometimes lamenting that she was unable to have such elaborate
festivals. She took the information to heart, however, and attempted to put
in place some of the public trappings expected of a Christian monarch.

By late 1658 she had built three locations for altars; four cemeteries just
beyond the four entrances to the city; and four new churches, one of which
was for the exclusive use of her sister Barbara.[46] Other, smaller churches
followed, along with small Christian altars, and a larger cemetery inside
the city.[47]

In 1659, Njinga decided to relocate her capital city about six miles away,
to the banks of the Hamba River, a tributary of the Kwango River. Njinga
chose an excellent location for the new city, in a valley surrounded by a
variety of trees. Early in 1660 she began preparations for the move, ordering her people to build a temporary church and houses for her court.
Using traditional materials for its construction, the builders completed the
church quickly. Her own residence, a house for the Capuchins, and houses
for her court officials and attendants soon followed. (Although she initially intended to allow only people who had been baptized to live in the
city, she eventually rescinded that order.)

Njinga made a momentous decision before the move that signaled
a growing distance between her new spirituality and the old Mbundu/
Imbangala beliefs. It was during this time that she decided to turn over to
Father Gaeta the silver *misete* that held the remains of her brother and other
ritual objects. The decision was made partly in response to pressure exerted

by Father Gaeta and her interpreter Calisto Zelotes, the former Kongo priest whose life she had spared in 1648. They insisted that she could not really be considered a Christian if she still believed the *misete* offered her protection. She didn't disagree, but she also realized that she could not simply turn over the *misete* to Father Gaeta without risking a possible revolt by the *ngangas* (priests), who still exercised tremendous spiritual power over the population despite Njinga's turn to Christianity. As in 1656, she knew that she had to get the backing not only of the *ngangas* and *xingulas* but also of other officials whose public support was vital for the ideological revolution she was trying bring about. To counter any public opposition, she organized one of her famous public discourses, where the leading factions hotly debated the issue. The outcome of the debate was as expected: there was no room for the *misete* in Njinga's new Matamba. Afterward, Njinga carried it to the church, and, kneeling reverently before the Holy Crucifix, surrendered it to Father Gaeta.[48] Once again, she had succeeded in defusing a potentially volatile situation by using a seemingly democratic discussion to advance another step in her cultural revolution. In a final break with her Imbangala lifestyle, she agreed to allow the *misete* to be melted down and made into a Christian lamp for use in her new church.[49]

After the handover of the *misete*, Njinga and the Capuchins led the population in a solemn parade to the temporary church where her new court, called Kabasa (the traditional title for the seat of Mbundu rulers), as well as by its Christian name, Santa Maria de Matamba, was to be located. They viewed the spot where she had decided to undertake a major building project, the construction of a large stone church, along with a hospice for the priests and a school.

The new church would be 122 by 42 feet, with porches on all sides. She wanted the church to replicate the European-style churches she had seen in Luanda, and she took every opportunity to educate herself by questioning Portuguese merchants in Matamba about how to go about building such an edifice.[50] With Father Gaeta assigned to recruit skilled tradesmen from among the slaves in Massangano, Njinga had to mobilize men, women, and children to begin the laborious work of digging up and transporting stones and wooden beams to the location that had been selected. At some points during the operation Njinga recruited everyone, no matter what their station—from the Capuchins to her nobles to her household attendants—to dig and transport stones. Most of the builders, of course, were slaves, who numbered in the thousands, but more than seventeen thousand free people, including women and children, took part, too. Even Njinga herself carried some stones, as well as providing meals and other incentives to the workers. She paid close attention to ensure that Christian rituals surrounding construction were followed to the letter, placing two gold rings in the ground before the builders laid the foundation stones.[51]

Although it would take three years to complete, Njinga succeeded in constructing a church made entirely of stone in a place where building materials were scarce and skilled workers were hard to come by. After its completion in 1663, it was the largest structure ever built in the interior of Angola. Beside the main church were two side chapels, one containing the Holy Crucifix that Njinga a Mona had brought from Mbwila, and the other a picture of Our Lady, which was dedicated to the Holy Rosary. This chapel was very important to Njinga. She built it specifically for the use of the brotherhood of Our Lady of the Rosary, which she had encouraged the Capuchins to organize. She provided the funds for building the chapel and for the upkeep of the brotherhood.

Not content with having foreign Capuchins as the only conveyors of the religion, Njinga pressed the missionaries to build a seminary to prepare her own people for the priesthood. She also had a school built next to the church. Although she did not live to see local men become priests, before her death, forty children received a rudimentary education at the school, learning to read and getting religious instruction.[52] At the same time that she was building the large church, she built a smaller one in her court that she dedicated to Saint Anna. As she had done for the big stone church, she laid a gold ring in the foundation of this one, too. When the church was complete, she paid what would have been considered at the time a small fortune—125 Italian ducats—for a beautiful rendering of Saint Anna, and she also ordered several silk and brocade decorations.[53]

During the period of construction of these churches, Christianity was beginning to take root in Matamba largely because of Njinga's efforts. She encouraged people to attend services, to learn the main tenets of the new religion, and to get baptized and married. She also expected them to have their newborn infants baptized in the church and to live as Christians. To help achieve this goal, she called on the services of Father Zelotes to help catechize the adults. Before long, teams of young men who had learned the catechism were teaching others. She herself did not miss an occasion to bring people to the church, encouraging them to attend the catechism classes—sometimes using threats (this was Njinga, after all), but also providing prizes as incentives. Njinga became a teacher herself, putting young girls through the litanies of the Holy Virgin and explaining to them the virtues of virginity.

When Njinga realized that her initial campaign had not resulted in a significant increase in the number of people the Capuchins believed were sufficiently prepared for baptism, she took more draconian steps, going from house to house and entreating families to give up their concubines and attend church. Within five months of her own marriage, as many as three thousand people, including children, were baptized. When Father Cavazzi, who would become Njinga's main confessor and would remain in Matamba until after Njinga's death, and the other missionaries arrived in October 1658, many people were eager to have their children baptized, and fourteen nursing mothers greeted him, requesting baptism for their babies, asserting that the infants had been born after Father Gaeta had left Matamba earlier that year. Although Cavazzi thought that some of the adults whom he examined had sufficient familiarity with the catechism to receive the Holy Sacrament, the number of people who had been baptized up to that date and who were eligible to take Communion represented a minuscule percentage of the population.

The Battle for Souls

The numbers were simply not in Njinga's favor. It could be argued that the small number of Christians in Matamba derived from the fact that there were never more than two Capuchins present at the same time, and on their own they were unable to reach such a large population, estimated at about two hundred thousand throughout the kingdom of Ndongo-Matamba. But Njinga knew where the real root of the problem lay. Those two Capuchins and the handful of secular priests were no match for the thousands of *ngangas* who continued to practice the rituals and provide the spiritual services that most of the population depended on. Some of the *ngangas* and *xingulas* publicly challenged Njinga and the Capuchins; one of them even declared, when possessed by spirits, that he was Ngola Mbande, the creator of the heavens and earth.[54]

These traditional spiritual leaders were found all over Matamba and formed a powerful counterforce to the Christianity that Njinga was pushing. In 1659, after an Easter service where only a small group of people took communion, she decided it was time to move against the *ngangas*. Soon after the service, she sent out a proclamation requiring everyone to kneel and demonstrate proper devotion or face arrest when the church bell rang in the morning, at midday, and in the late evening. Another proclamation soon followed, ordering the *ngangas* to close all their initiation camps.

Soon Njinga entered into controversial discussions with her counselors, urging them to push to end the custom of *tambos*, the elaborate ceremonies for the deceased that included traditional Imbangala and Mbundu practices, including human sacrifice. In a dramatic move, she made them promise that they would not conduct *tambos* after her own death. Many people resented these proclamations, hiding their ritual objects and continuing to perform the traditional rites in secret at the graves of their ancestors. But an official policy was introduced that all religious veneration had to be done in the Christian churches through the mediation of the priests. By November 1659, Njinga's efforts had had some success. The total number of people who were baptized had grown to four thousand, still a small percentage of the population.[55]

Wanting to root out Imbangala practices and to plant Christianity in regions beyond her court, in June 1661, Njinga sent a letter to Father Gaeta in Luanda, in which she informed him of her efforts to exhort the *sobas* to embrace the Catholic faith and encourage their people to listen to and obey the missionaries. She wanted the *sobas* to help the Capuchins burn the houses where the *ngangas* kept their religious icons and instead build churches and erect crosses.[56] Sending the missionaries out to the countryside was an even more direct approach. On two occasions, in 1661 and then again in 1663, she sent Father Cavazzi with her officials to tour her kingdom and gave him permission to go to the courts of all her regional rulers to convert them and their people.

From late 1661 to early 1662, Cavazzi traveled to the western provinces of Matamba, some ten days from Njinga's court. This area had been the core part of the Ndongo kingdom and the location of her court before she fled in 1629, after the Portuguese sent their troops to the area. Njinga's secretary (most likely the Kongo priest Zelotes) and a page accompanied Cavazzi. The page acted as an interpreter, delivering the message to the local rulers in Kimbundu. When Father Cavazzi, the secretary, and the page arrived at the Kindonga Islands, where Njinga's court had formerly been located, Cavazzi sent out an order for all the *sobas* of the islands to appear to listen to Njinga's proclamation, and the page announced Njinga's message in Kimbundu. He informed them that Njinga had sent the Capuchin priest and her secretary to baptize them and the children, to marry them as the Holy Mother Church ordered, and to urge them "to imitate her example." Njinga demanded that each of them build a church in their court as she had done in hers and "erect Crosses and other things as the Priest shall see."[57] These demands, he concluded, required strict compliance by all Mbundus.

For those listeners who were not Mbundus—the local population included refugee slaves and other foreigners—Njinga had a different set of rules. If they refused to obey her instructions to give up their traditional customs, they must leave the islands. The secretary ended with the demand that the assembled people turn over to Cavazzi "all their relics." By way of example, he explained to the people that Njinga had given up Mbande Ngola's *misete*, which she had had with her when she fled the islands, and which contained the deceased ruler's remains. Through the translator, Cavazzi also provided directions for how to build a church.[58] Cavazzi baptized 440 children on this occasion and destroyed many altars and small temples built by local fishermen along the banks of river. The popular belief was that the river spoke to the ancestors, and these temples were a sign to the ancestors to bless them with an abundant haul of fish.[59]

For Father Cavazzi's second tour, in September 1663, Njinga sent the priest to an area in the southeast region of Matamba, some five days away from her court, and gave him permission to burn all the altars where the people honored their local deities and erect crosses in their place. In no time he had baptized 330 infants and several adults, and also burnt several altars. He planted many crosses on the road "to remember as shrines, [and] gave each a saint's name."[60] The campaign ended after only six weeks. In spite of his success, he had to return to Matamba because Njinga had taken ill, and (as we shall see) he was needed at her court.

In her own capital city, Njinga allowed Father Cavazzi and the other Capuchins to arrest the *xingulas* and other traditional religious practitioners, to confiscate and burn their ritual objects and temples, and to turn them over to her for a special trial. Many of the condemned were immediately sold to Portuguese merchants and sent to Luanda for transport "across the salt water." This was the situation an eighty-year-old priest called Nganga ya Matamba faced in 1661. Though he was an extremely popular man—known, respected, and feared by Capuchins and Portuguese officials alike—Njinga nevertheless sentenced him and a companion to a public whipping after finding them practicing Imbangala/Mbundu religious rituals. Following the public humiliation, she sold them to Portuguese merchants. Nganga ya Matamba ended up in Luanda and was transported to Rio de Janeiro, where he was questioned by Jesuits. Realizing that he was a notorious *nganga* of Matamba, and knowing the reputation he had in Angola, they feared he would quickly have a following among the slaves in Brazil. They sent him back to Angola, but he died on the return journey.[61]

Soon after the incident with Nganga ya Matamba, Njinga arrested seven people suspected of being involved in divining and condemned them as well. She confronted the *xingulas'* defenders at court, demanding that they turn over those they were protecting. The money from the sale of the condemned practitioners went to the Capuchins, who used it to buy religious ornaments for the church.[62]

By the summer of 1662, Njinga's efforts began to pay off, as the number of Christians in Matamba had increased significantly. Although no exact numbers are available, a month after the dedication of the large stone church in August 1663, the number of baptized adults stood at eight thousand, in addition to the thousands of children who had also been baptized. More than six hundred Christian marriages had also been consecrated by this time.[63]

Njinga's push to transform Matamba into a Christian society was visible in other ways as well. Just as it had in the kingdom of the Kongo, the cross became ubiquitous throughout Matamba and replaced many of the traditional symbols that formerly dominated public assemblies. Crosses were found in every house in the city, and Njinga's armies now added the symbol to the flags and banners they carried on military campaigns. Human sacrifice had no place in war rituals anymore. Captives who wished to be baptized were sent to the Capuchins, who used them to build churches as well as to work with the poor. The lure of Christianity had spread out from Njinga's residence and core population to the surrounding countryside miles away, and people came to the capital to have their children baptized, to hear the Capuchins preach, or to receive spiritual counseling.[64]

The impact of Njinga's Christian revolution was not limited to Matamba and the regions she controlled but had already had reverberations throughout the kingdoms of allies and enemies alike. The Imbangala Kasanje, who had struck fear into the Capuchins by feasting on human flesh while they were in his lands during their earlier attempts to convert him, demanded that a Capuchin come to him. Father António Seravezza would baptize Kasanje and twenty-eight of his sons. Ngola Hari, who had largely neglected to promote Christianity during his reign, pressed Governor Sousa Chichorro to send Capuchins and had everything ready for them when they arrived. The news of Njinga's conversion and active promotion of Christianity also spread to Libolo, a region whose rulers had consistently resisted Portuguese armies and who had been among Njinga's strongest allies. They wrote twice to Governor Sousa Chichorro requesting priests. Although she could not have known it, her Christian revolution took Portuguese officials by surprise; whenever a Capuchin passed through Lisbon, he was invariably peppered with questions about the miraculous conversion of the person who to them had represented the epitome of evil and barbarity.[65]

The Public Face of Christianity

Although her royal status allowed her to implement the social revolution that was beginning to transform Matamba into a Christian kingdom, Njinga knew that for her Christian project to reach the population at large, she, not the missionaries, must be its public face. She was well prepared for the challenge: all along she had contended that if the Portuguese stopped making wars against her, she would return to the Christian religion. She threw herself into all her tasks with equal zeal, and just as she had done when she transformed herself into a feared Imbangala leader, she became a devout adherent of the faith. Immediately after her marriage, she set about to learn, understand, and incorporate into her daily life all the elements of the Catholic faith. Three times a week she went to the chapel she had built for the Brotherhood of the Rosary, and in the company of her sister, her court officials and military leaders, and her female attendants and other courtiers, she made her devotions.[66] Before long she had not only learned to say all the devotions and prayers in Kimbundu but had also memorized the Latin words to some hymns. She demanded that her female attendants learn to sing along with her "The Canticles of the Madonna."[67] She achieved her biggest spiritual victory in 1660 when, on the Sunday of Pentecost, she received Holy Communion for the first time.[68] From then on Njinga was a model of Christian piety, so fervent in her observation of the rituals that she often spent hours in the church, especially after communion. In fact, she once declared Saturdays to be "the day of the Queen" and did nothing the entire day but perform devotional prayers to the Virgin Mary, admitting to Father Cavazzi on one occasion that spending the day in devotion to the Holy Mother was nothing to her, so great was her desire to "honor her."[69]

If the missionaries are to be believed, Njinga also observed the Christian virtue of being generous to the less fortunate. She passed out alms to the people and distributed provisions at Christmas, Easter, Pentecost, and on saints' days. She always made sure that the Capuchins had enough resources to purchase the wine, candles, and other items vital for mass. She seized every occasion that the church calendar offered to demonstrate her munificence and public piety. When she gave Father Gaeta the *misete* with her brother's bones to take to Luanda to be melted down, she also sent along four slaves to be sold to cover the cost of the container she wanted to have made for the holy water.

In April 1662, during the dedication ceremony for a small church she built called Saint Anna, Njinga showed the depth of her religious transformation by writing a prayer herself to Saint Anna and reciting it aloud in the church. In the prayer, Njinga confessed to Saint Anna that although she was a sinner unworthy of her name, she had built the poor little church to honor her. Acknowledging that the Holy Mother knew her feelings and intentions, since God had revealed everything to her, she admitted that for years she had been a Christian in name only, having abused the faith through idolatry and the taking of innocent blood, but through his priests, God had given her the opportunity to make penance. The prayer called on Saint Anna to intercede with Jesus Christ and seek pardon for all her grave sins. She wanted to repair the immense harm she had done to her soul and the souls of so many creatures for whom he had died. Njinga sensed that she was nearing the end of her life, and she expressed genuine contrition. She prayed that Saint Anna would accept the small offering of the little church and consider her among the least of her slaves, so that "by your intervention in my name God fill my soul with grace and his eternal blessings." According to Cavazzi's account, she showed such sincere remorse when reciting the prayer that all who heard it felt that the prayer had come from deep in her soul. Tears flowed from everyone, including the missionaries.[70]

Njinga had many other opportunities to publicize her newfound piety and generosity. One of these came after Father Gaeta's death in Luanda on July 9, 1662. At a ceremony for the commemoration of the souls of the dead that she held in his honor two months later, Njinga and members of her court held an elaborate requiem mass for his soul, dressing in the appropriate Portuguese mourning clothes.[71] The next day she sent provisions to the hospice for the Capuchins to distribute to the poor, making sure that there was more than enough left over to hand out to the people who lived in the city and the neighboring area.[72]

Her grandest public display of both her piety and her largesse came on August 12, 1663, when she dedicated the large stone church in an elaborate ceremony to the Virgin Mary. The church was a spectacular achievement, the tallest building ever constructed in the area. A massive gathering of onlookers, ranging from *sobas* from lands near and far to Europeans anxious to glimpse this unlikely masterpiece in the middle of the wilderness, stood before Njinga. She announced that the first service was dedicated to Our Lady, which was also to be the name of the church. On the high altar Njinga placed a painting that was a copy of one in the church of Santa Maria Maggiore, which had been sent to her from Rome, and statues of Saint Francis and Saint Anthony of Padua, gifts from Portugal.[73]

As Njinga's Christian spirituality deepened, she continued to discard other elements of her non-Christian life, at times referring to herself simply by her royal title and Christian name, "Lady Queen Anna," in her official correspondence instead of using her given name of Njinga. At one point she changed her entire manner of dress. She shed the elaborate cloths and silks she so loved, along with the dresses made from the local bark cloth that was a sign of her royal status. She also set aside Portuguese fashion, as well as the numerous bracelets that had long been her royal trademark. Instead she used only two cloths to cover her body, one as a skirt and the other as a blouse, and wrapped her shoulders with a finely made shawl. In place of the elaborate ornaments that had adorned her neck and legs, she wore instead a necklace with "a Holy Cross and Crown in relief."[74] It appeared to be a total transformation, inside and out.

Solidifying Succession and Royal Status

Although Njinga's personal engagement with Christianity during her last years represented a genuine expression of her spiritual renaissance, her motives were also, as always, deeply political. Her greatest fear was that if Christianity did not take root in Matamba and the parts of Ndongo under her control, Barbara would not be able to hold on to the kingdom after her death. Certain that the only way to guarantee her royal legacy was to ensure that Rome regard Matamba as a legitimate Christian kingdom, she pressed on with the Christian revolution.

She had reason to fear what would become of Matamba when Barbara became queen. Her primary worry still revolved around the Portuguese, who she knew would not hesitate to take over Matamba given the opportunity. In fact, the military operations that they were constantly undertaking against *sobas* who lived in the lands that bordered Ndongo and Matamba convinced her that they were bent on breaking the peace and pushing her back to war and insecurity. She also suspected that they were displeased that she had bypassed them and was instead seeking an official alliance directly with the Vatican.[75] It was the September 1663 operations that Governor André Vidal de Negreiros conducted against areas formerly under her control that troubled her most.[76] These operations had resulted in the Portuguese installing their own candidate in a region that they had taken over from Njinga and capturing, imprisoning, and deporting to Brazil some of her former allies, along with more than four thousand other captives.[77] Njinga knew that this did not augur well for Matamba.

She also spent many sleepless nights fretting over the domestic political situation in Matamba. It was obvious by 1663 that the approval she had received from the powerful *xingulas* and her four councilors, in which they supported her decision to give up the silver *misete* and, by extension, the Mbundu/Imbangala rites and practices in favor of Christianity, had not been enough to guarantee full popular support for her religious revolution. Opposition was increasingly evident, as court officials hid *ngangas* whom the missionaries had caught practicing their arts, and some of them re-sented the growing power that Njinga had bestowed upon the Capuchins.[78]

The leader of the opposition was none other than Njinga a Mona, her trusted confidant, and the husband she had reluctantly selected for Bar-bara. Njinga a Mona and Njinga's relationship was a complicated one and became even more so as her Christian spiritual journey escalated. Born in Ndongo, Njinga a Mona had been captured by one of Njinga's Imbangala armies as a child and raised by them in their ways. Njinga had taken a par-ticular interest in the young captive, perhaps at one point seeing him as a replacement for her murdered son. Indeed, his very name, Njinga a Mona—"child of Njinga"—reflected the closeness of the relationship be-tween the two. Some in the court thought of him as Njinga's foster brother, since local lore identified him as the son of the woman who had served as Njinga's wet nurse.[79] During Njinga's Imbangala days, Njinga a Mona had moved up quickly through the ranks and achieved the distinction of gen-eral of Njinga's armed forces. Throughout all these years he had never openly challenged her, not even during the early years of her return to Chris-tianity. In fact, the rumor in the court was that the story of the mystical crucifix he had rescued during the Mbwila campaign in 1655 was some-thing of a contrivance, and that Njinga had actually sent Njinga a Mona to locate it and bring it to her in an effort to help her through her difficult political crisis.

But he harbored a certain level of resentment and jealousy against her: he had no doubt that she valued his military skills and that he was her most trusted counselor, yet she never fully regarded him as her equal because of his plebeian background. And although he regarded himself as the natural inheritor of the *kilombo* (now the kingdom of Ndongo-Matamba), Njinga had announced that it was Barbara—now his wife—who would take over after her death. The bond between the two became more frayed as Njinga a Mona realized that Njinga's Christian journey also came with a renewed interest in royal lineage that clearly barred him from consideration as the future leader of Matamba. Njinga, for her part, feared and respected Njinga a Mona, but as she drew closer to Christianity, the distance between them was growing. Although Njinga a Mona openly went along with Njinga's Christian program, he was at the same time quietly cultivating the support of the disaffected *ngangas* (even being identified as their leader and a secret practitioner).[80] Njinga a Mona also attracted other factions in the court who felt that the queen was giving up too many of the democratic principles that had prevailed in the *kilombo,* where merit more than birth allowed individuals, even humble slaves, to rise into positions of leadership. She still engendered fear in them, and certainly she still commanded their respect as queen, but these people now felt powerless.

Njinga realized that Njinga a Mona would not play second fiddle to Barbara. Because of this, she kept him in her confidence, not only because his outstanding military skills afforded Matamba protection, but also because he submitted to her will, not hesitating to follow her instructions and never questioning her actions. He was the first official in the court to step forward to be baptized, and he basked in the public praise and adulation that she showered on him. He always stood by her side at her public appearances. But still, Njinga had some inkling of Njinga a Mona's growing alienation regarding her turn to Christianity. It became quite evident following her public announcement in 1659 that there should be no more *tambos* (human sacrifices and other rituals performed at burials), even for her. For the first time, Njinga a Mona contradicted her publicly, stating that sacrificing in her honor would make people very happy. Angered by this show of independence, Njinga lashed out at him, suggesting that her nobles would be the first to be sacrificed, and he would be at the front of the line. He never again opposed her publicly, but he secretly continued to cultivate the *ngangas,* and instead of suppressing Mbundu/Imbangala rituals, he promoted them.[81] Despite Njinga a Mona's opposition, Njinga continued to push ahead with the Christian program. Her aim was to win official papal recognition for Matamba as a Christian state; she was convinced that this was the only guarantee for securing a powerful political and ideological counterweight against the Portuguese and Njinga a Mona's partisans.

But the threat extended beyond Njinga a Mona, for most of Njinga's people still held on to the traditional beliefs with which they had grown up. Indeed, Njinga's royalist program was in part responsible for this, because she had integrated many of the conventions of Ndongo royalty into her Christian rituals. Ironically, the more she moved to orchestrate a smooth transition away from the Imbangala militaristic traditions, the more she allowed her Mbundu royalist ideology to inform the Christian revolution. This bias gave Njinga a Mona ample opportunity to attract the support of other powerful and increasingly alienated Imbangala members of her court. By choosing Barbara and not Njinga a Mona to inherit her throne, Njinga made official the idea that her descent (and Barbara's) from the founders of the Ndongo state made them the rightful rulers of Matamba. Even though she may not have heard about the notion of divine right of kings, she viewed the alliance with Rome as the guarantor that would allow her to hand over Matamba to Barbara.

This attitude was already evident in 1657, during Njinga's intensive period of letter writing to Portuguese officials in Luanda, to the pope, and to other officials in the Vatican. At that point she gave up the title Ngola Njinga Ngombe e Nga (Great Lady, Queen of Arms and Great Warrior), which she had taken when she became an Imbangala, and instead used Queen Njinga Anna. Moreover, instead of referring to her residence as the *kilombo* of Njinga, she called it "our kingdom of Matamba" or "my court at Matamba."[82] Njinga never gave up two core elements of her Mbundu identity, however. She held on to the idea, first, that as a descendant of the rulers of the Ndongo kingdom she had an inherent right to rule and, second, that she had an obligation to preserve core elements of her people's culture and traditions. Even in her last letters to the Vatican, in which she announced her absolute allegiance to the pope and identified herself as Dona Anna, she always used the title of queen.[83]

Njinga's royalist leanings were geared to her domestic and secular agenda. Her commitment to royalty increased as she grew deeply enmeshed in her Christian faith. Her belief in her own superiority colored every argument she made. When she learned of the Portuguese army's operations in 1659 in the parts of Ndongo still under her control, she immediately summoned Father Gaeta to demand explanation. Without allowing him time to respond, she launched into a long diatribe against the Portuguese governors and the settlers. Even though she had signed the peace treaty, she fumed, they were jealous of the peace that she had brought to Matamba and were attempting to goad her into returning to war so that she would lose her kingdom. She put up a spirited defense of her right to rule, asserting that she had "never provoked" the Portuguese nor was she even the first "to take up arms against them." She accused them of trying time and time again to "take my kingdom from me" and blamed the governors and settlers for all the wars she had fought. She explained away her conquest of Matamba by blaming the Portuguese, who had taken away her kingdoms of "Angola and Ndongo" and had forced her to occupy a land that "was not mine." At the end of the tirade, she emphatically asserted that "I was born a queen and I have to act as a queen in everything that I do." Because of the way she perceived the idea of royalty, she insisted that no one should question her authority as queen, least of all the Portuguese governors, whom she derisively dismissed as mere officials who were "born subordinate in Europe." She accused them of coming to Angola only because of ambition and greed, noting that all of them wanted to "live like kings in Africa to the disadvantage of the country."[84]

Njinga was always ready to defend her right as queen, and she used every available opportunity to reinforce her royal status. The wars her army fought after 1658, when she was no longer an active participant on the battlefield, still afforded her opportunities to appear before her people as a military leader and a queen. Church festivals also provided opportune settings at which to display her royalist and militaristic orientation. She chose January 6, 1661, the feast of Epiphany, less than a year after she had received her first Holy Communion, to hand over to the church the lamp that had been made from the melted silver of the *misete* in which she had kept her brother's bones and other relics. She had her musketeers and musicians play military music and shoot off rounds of gunfire as she walked from her court to the steps of the church. Dressed in various wraps and silks, she received the holy water before entering the church. In Njinga's party were Njinga a Mona, who carried the lamp; one of her other senior advisers, who carried the container she had had made for the holy water; her *tendala,* who carried a carpet made of gold; and her sergeant general, who carried a piece of the same golden carpet. Njinga led the procession to the altar. Taking the lamp from Njinga a Mona, she gave it to Father Cavazzi, along with the other items.[85] Not long afterward, she requested that Father Cavazzi organize a procession around the houses in her court with the Blessed Sacrament. She explained that she wanted to do this because she had so much love for the divine mystery that she wanted all her subjects to see it and learn how to show the proper veneration and respect. On the morning of the procession, she arrived dressed in feathers, jewels, and a richly designed blanket, all items associated with royalty in the Mbundu tradition. As the procession approached an altar she had had built at the center of the plaza, Njinga rose from where she was sitting, handed a candle to one of her pages, and, taking her arrows and a bow, did a war dance in front of the altar. She knelt down three times in front of the altar, then began to perform a stately dance. This was typical of Njinga's ability to blend Mbundu and Christian traditions. Her outfit and the war dance she performed came from the royal traditions she had learned at the courts of her father and grandfather, whereas the dance around the Christian altar was a tradition for which the Portuguese in Luanda were famous, and which she had picked up during her stay there in 1622.[86]

Njinga had some success in skillfully blending the symbols and rituals from her royalist past with elements of popular Christianity. What was remarkable was that she clearly saw that the Christian rituals worked well with Mbundu religious and political ideas about kingship and tried to institutionalize them. In fact, the more she developed Christian piety and deportment herself, the more she insisted that court officials and others maintain the traditional deference and respect that her royal person demanded. She expected this deference whether she was working alongside her people when they were building churches, attending mass, or doing penance. She also encouraged them in the belief that monarchs did not die. Njinga had outlived most of her peers by several decades, so it was easy for people to maintain the old Mbundu belief that rulers were immortal and reject the Christian teaching about earthly death. Njinga reinforced traditional belief by forbidding people from discussing her death.[87]

Even though Njinga became more spiritually devout in the last few years of her life and sometimes donned simple clothing, she continued to pay attention to her dress and deportment. She always attended church service wearing clothes specifically designed for her, some even imported from the Yoruba region of Ijebu. Everyone understood that only Njinga and Barbara could wear the "silks, velvets, and brocades" that came from Europe. The royal crown obviously set her apart from everyone, and she always wore it to church and religious celebrations. Before 1660 she also wore many rings made of "gold, silver, iron, copper, corals and glass" on her hands, feet, and legs, all of them legitimizing her status to her Mbundu followers and proving that she was still the queen of Ndongo.[88] With the attention that Njinga lavished on her appearance, it's no wonder that she was so reluctant to part with the arm bracelets that the xingulas had blessed, which she wore in the belief that they would protect her from illness and physical harm. She had gotten rid of some of them in 1657 because of her illness, but the others only came off later in her spiritual journey.[89] Nineteen iron rings remained. Covering her arms and legs, these rings had been dedicated to her ancestors by the priests. Njinga until the very end believed these had even more power to protect her from illness than did the Christian objects. As dedicated to Christianity as she became, she continued to tolerate many Mbundu/Imbangala rituals.

Pomp and Pageantry

While there was a clear distinction between the attire and adornments worn by Njinga and her nobles and attendants, those who served in her court were always elaborately and appropriately dressed. At festivals, she was often accompanied by as many as a thousand magnificently dressed attendants who jumped to respond to her orders.[90] She went so far as to send some of her female attendants to Luanda to learn lace making and sewing, and they were responsible for making many of the dresses, scarves, and other items of dress common among the high-status women in Luanda. On state occasions when she entertained Portuguese officials, Njinga and her attendants dressed in these clothes.[91]

Pageantry remained central to everything Njinga did. She retained the traditional military entourage, singers, and musicians of Mbundu/Imbangala culture and expected them to be ready to perform on command, whether it was firing off their muskets when the occasion called for it, entertaining her with new songs they had composed in her honor, or playing the traditional music she favored. When she left the court to make the rounds of the city or to attend church festivals, the musicians accompanied her. She always saw herself as ruling over all things, including the law. She never gave up the idea that as queen she had the right to adjudicate cases, and her royal court was a beehive of activity, as she listened attentively to the various criminal cases argued before herself and her counselors. Although she never failed to consider the opinion of her counselors, she ultimately made the final decision as to the plaintiffs' guilt or innocence.[92]

During the early years of her transition to Christianity, most celebrations had many Mbundu/Imbangala elements, with only a veneer of Christianity. Christian rituals began to gain in influence, and by 1662, public festivities were characterized by a unique blend of Christian and Mbundu rituals. This mixing was already evident following her marriage, when the church and the plaza replaced the *kilombo* as the site for both secular and religious celebrations. By then the two traditions had become indistinguishable. At mass her musicians played Mbundu musical instruments; her soldiers discharged muskets at the raising of the host and held holy vigils the night before a feast day. She participated with the people in various dances, communal singing in Kimbundu, and the like.[93]

Her receipt of Pope Alexander VII's letter in 1661, in which he called her his daughter, was an event that called for celebration. All the elements of Mbundu royal traditions and Christian theater came together gloriously. Cavazzi had translated the letter from Latin into Kimbundu. The day before he was to read the letter to the gathered crowd, she went to the church and spiritually ratified it with a public profession of her Christian faith; Cavazzi then placed the document in her hands. After this formal religious ceremony in the church, Njinga carefully placed the letter in a leather pouch that hung around her neck. The next day she appeared with Father Cavazzi in the square, where a large crowd was waiting. They greeted her with the customary Mbundu "clapping of hands, shouting and daubing themselves with earth," the kind of greeting inferiors always gave to their superiors. She announced to them that she had finally received a greeting from the pope. Father Cavazzi then read aloud the Kimbundu version of the letter, after which Njinga led the crowd, including Father Cavazzi, other religious personnel, and her attendants away from the square and to the open area in front of her residence, where she had prepared a great feast. She sat on the chair under the canopy her officials had prepared and ordered them to open large casks of European wines, which she made available to the people. The attendants poured the wine into large wooden Mbundu vessels and called on the people to drink "to her greatness."[94] On this occasion she broke with her long-standing habit of eating with her fingers in Mbundu fashion. When Father Gaeta had asked her why she preferred to eat this way, she had proudly and simply stated that she preferred to follow "the ancient custom of her ancestors."[95] But for this special feast, she used European-style utensils and serving dishes.

The feast equaled anything the governor could have prepared in Luanda. The day was one long celebration. Njinga gave out titles and other honors to her courtiers and even freed some of her slaves. Later in the day, she participated in the military dance expected of a queen, showing all the maneuvers she had perfected as a child, skillfully wielding her bow, arrow, and sword.[96] Njinga became a devout Christian, but she remained a royalist and a traditionalist to the end. She wanted Barbara to preserve it all.

Her desire was clear in the thank-you letter she wrote to Pope Alexander VII. She provided a detailed account of the events she staged on receipt of his letter, noting that everyone was happy with the letter and that the celebrations lasted "many continuous days." By then she had succeeded in getting two additional Italian Capuchins to join Father Cavazzi to carry on the work of Christianizing her people, but the numbers of priests remained small.[97]

As she had done in earlier letters, Njinga pleaded with the pope not to forget her kingdom. She knew that the decision makers in her court, particularly Njinga a Mona, remained suspicious of the missionaries and their religion, and she feared for the future of the kingdom.[98]

Death of a Queen

Njinga's courtiers and even Njinga a Mona's faction knew that Njinga was deeply committed to her royalist ideas. Those members of her inner circle who were born as Imbangalas, who longed for the heady days when upward mobility rested on military prowess and inhumane rituals, anxiously awaited for the momentous event they sensed was imminent. Beginning in 1662, Njinga's impending death began to unleash mounting tensions. Until that time, while she was in good health, Njinga had largely kept the tensions between the Christians and royalists on one side and the Mbundu/Imbangala faction on the other in check, but her illness prevented her from doing so anymore. This first became evident in 1656 during her bout with a dangerous inflammation in her throat and a high fever, which threatened to end her life. Her advisers had at first called on the *xingulas* to treat her, and Father Gaeta only intervened after their medication and procedures failed.[99] In the first years of her spiritual rebirth, Njinga tolerated Mbundu/Imbangala rituals at the passing of high-status officials. Such was the case in 1658, when one of her prominent officers died, and Father Gaeta refused to give him the Christian burial she demanded. Stung by the refusal, she organized and participated in *tambos* that included the human sacrifice that she had condemned and declared illegal. To the casual observer looking at Matamba in the three years after her Christian rebirth, Njinga remained firm in her new beliefs, but only when everyone enjoyed good health. When illnesses erupted or unexplained deaths occurred to Mbundus or Capuchins on whom she relied, she allowed the traditionalists some space. The sequence of events that occurred from the end of March 1662 to her death on December 17, 1663, illustrates this quite clearly.

In March 1662, Father Gaeta fell ill in Matamba; by the beginning of April, he had recovered to some extent. Njinga herself became sick just a few days later. During her illness, news arrived from Luanda that the pope and his cardinals had responded to her recent letters. On top of that, a new group of six Capuchins had arrived in Luanda and were slated to be sent to work in Matamba. Although still feeling unwell, she found the strength to orchestrate the sort of elaborate public celebration at which she could share the exciting news and demonstrate that she was a powerful monarch. Not all the news was good, though. Njinga became despondent as she learned that Father Gaeta was to be transferred from Matamba to Luanda to become head of all the Capuchins in central Africa. Her spirits were lifted when he gave her his old, worn-out Capuchin robe. He also agreed to remain long enough to oversee the dedication of Saint Anna's Church, which was near completion. Father Gaeta left Matamba after the dedication service in April 1662. In the nineteen months between Father Gaeta's departure and Njinga's death, she would implement several policies to strengthen Christianity throughout Matamba, many of which revolved around her heightened letter-writing campaign to the pope and intensified routing of the *ngangas*.

After receiving news of Father Gaeta's death in Luanda on July 9, 1662, her spirits were bleaker than ever, and her health remained poor. She and her attendants paraded in mourning clothes and held an elaborate requiem mass for his soul. The Christian mourning rituals, however, only added to her sense of foreboding and doom.

A little more than a year later, in August 1663, a double death that occurred within the span of a few hours presented her with the most serious challenge to date from the pro-*xingula* faction. First, Njinga a Mona's brother Kabanga died unexpectedly. His sister arrived to mourn just a few hours later. In great pain, she collapsed on the corpse and died instantly. The fact that the two deaths occurred on the night before the dedication service for the stone church cast a shadow over the impending celebrations. Father Cavazzi suspected that the two had taken poison in a suicide pact orchestrated by the *xingulas* to undermine Njinga's Christian project. However, it was Cavazzi's refusal to give the deceased a Christian burial that incensed the population. Their leaders retorted that the deceased should have both a Christian burial and a *tambo:* their suicide was an act of love, but they were still Christians. In the heated discussion that followed, some leaders of the pro-*xingula* faction threatened to boycott the dedication and have the *tambo*. In the end, the people only got part of their wish. They were able to bury the dead brother and sister near the church, but the *tambo* was forbidden. Njinga prevailed in this crisis but knew that if she did not take renewed steps to stamp out the *xingulas,* they would act again. On September 2, less than two weeks after this volatile incident, Njinga gave Father Cavazzi permission to travel four days away from the court so that he could work with local officials to convince them to join in the campaign to root out *ngangas* and *xingulas* and destroy their altars and other ritual objects.[100]

She might have been triumphant this time, but the unexplained deaths and the disappointment she felt at the open resistance of the pro-*xingula* faction bothered her. Although she continued with her religious campaign, the exuberant mood that she often displayed was replaced by a sense of doom and silent reflection. Sometime between September 2 and October 14, 1663, about two months after Njinga a Mona's siblings' deaths, sickness hit again. Two Capuchins who were in her court fell ill, and shortly afterward she herself became gravely ill. On October 14 her health deteriorated despite the interventions of the *xingulas* whom her counselors had called in to divine the cause of her ailment. Her throat and chest had become so inflamed that she could only utter a few words in a labored voice. Between October 14 and December 14, Njinga remained bedridden, running high fevers that on some days made her delirious. Whenever she had the strength to speak, she would reflect on the disappointments she had experienced, seeing the deaths of Kabanga and his sister as a warning to herself about her own impending mortality. When she could find her breath, she warned those around her that, although she appeared to be improving, she felt that she was going to die. An abscess that appeared on the right side of her throat at this point was a bad sign, as it confirmed that the infection was spreading. On December 14, the abscess burst, and the infection spread to her lungs. Her doctors bled her several times, but her condition only worsened. Indeed, she remained in this acute state for three days, with high fevers and shortness of breath that waxed and waned as her lungs deteriorated further.[101]

The drama between the pro-*xingula* faction and Father Cavazzi played itself out in Njinga's private quarters during her final days. Father Cavazzi had returned to the court from his trip on October 14. Njinga's four councilors, who had stood vigil outside her private quarters from the moment she had taken ill, had immediately summoned traditional doctors to attend her once the illness appeared. The priest and these doctors were together with Njinga during her last days. While the doctors applied their various remedies and bled her, Father Cavazzi provided for her spiritual needs, saying masses in the church for her health, placing the image of the Virgin Mary on her chest, delivering Holy Communion to her, and encouraging her to confess her sins. Realizing she did not have long to live, in her customary way she attempted to take charge of the situation, since she feared that the councilors would not follow her instructions without hearing directly from her. On December 11, before receiving communion, she mustered all the energy she could and told them exactly what she wanted them to do after her death.[102] Njinga had them send word to Father Cavazzi to inform him of her deteriorating state and to request his immediate presence at court. Once Father Cavazzi returned, the councilors seem to have taken a back seat to the medical practitioners and the Capuchin. The traditional practitioners continued to use various remedies to relieve her symptoms, to no avail.

Three days before she died, Njinga had Father Cavazzi call the four councilors into the room again. Between bouts of acute shortness of breath, she gave what would be her last orders. Njinga wished to die a Catholic, she said, and she wanted them to continue to promote Christianity in Matamba. Her only regret was that "she did not leave a son because she desired that someone of her lineage inherit her kingdom." Stopping several times to regain her breath, and speaking in a barely audible voice, she rested her eyes on her senior councilor (the *tendala*) and told him that after she died, he would become the interim viceroy. She cautioned him to make sure the kingdom remained at peace and encouraged him to work with her interpreter to defend the Christianity she had brought to the country. Finally, Njinga uttered one last command: not to interfere with the funeral and burial arrangements she had already made with Father Cavazzi.[103]

During the communion service that Father Cavazzi conducted soon afterward, she found the strength to ask forgiveness several times, and to say "Amen" at the end of the prayers. As death drew near, she was at her most repentant, begging the councilors and Father Cavazzi to intercede for her soul. These were her last words. For the next thirty-six hours, Njinga lingered at death's door, finally entering a calm sleep. Father Cavazzi administered the last rites just before she died peacefully in her sleep at eleven o'clock on the morning of December 17, 1663.

The ramifications of Njinga's royalist and Christian revolution began to play out even as she was in the throes of death. As the last breath left her body, her councilors were already sending out soldiers to reinforce the guards around the court to prevent slaves and servants who anticipated being sacrificed from fleeing. Some had already made their escape before the guards assembled, and many were brought back to the court by force. To avoid the pandemonium they feared would erupt after news of her death became public, her councilors tried to keep it a secret by closing the gates to the court. They could only keep this up for the twenty-four hours immediately following her death. At that point they had to make her passing public.

Their concerns had not been misplaced. Neither they nor anyone in Matamba, including the Capuchins, could envision a Christian burial for Njinga without the accompanying traditional funeral rites, including the *tambos* and human sacrifice she had banned. Her personal attendants, particularly her female attendants, were the first to show their fear of what her passing augured. During the previous six years, they had followed her on her Christian and royalist journey, living as Njinga did, exhibiting, as she did, a deep Christian spirituality and disdain and suspicion for the pro-*xingula* faction. The arrangements for her burial promised drama and dread for all concerned.

Competing Traditions and a Royal Funeral

Even before she took her last breath, Njinga's Christian revolution was already unraveling. Tensions over the royalist notions at the core of Njinga's governing ideology surfaced within hours of her death, when her councilors had to decide what kind of burial she should have. Although on her deathbed she had gathered the strength to admonish them to respect her wishes and bury her in Father Gaeta's simple Capuchin habit, her officials had other plans. As soon as she died, they instructed her personal attendants to prepare her corpse for a royal send-off. Simplicity would not come into play.

Njinga's attendants lovingly washed her body, rubbing it down with powders, herbs, and perfumes. After the embalming, they dressed it in all the finery that bespoke her royal status. The items they chose reflected the Mbundu royal traditions Njinga had so revered. She would be royal in death as in life, from head to toe. The attendants covered her head with an exquisite cap, over which they placed her crown of corals, pearls, and other jewels. They also carefully arranged four feathers, two red and two white, under the front of the crown—only royals were allowed to wear feathers at official ceremonies. Honoring her love of personal adornment, the women arranged her hair with corals and pearls, and they put two large pearl earrings in her ears. They covered her limbs with bands of silver and gold, placing between each set of bracelets another symbol of royalty, an arrangement of elephant hair. They placed on her feet an elegant pair of velvet slippers with glass buttons and covered her body with two rich brocade wraps, one for her top half and the other covering her down to the ankles. Finally, they draped a scarlet cape embroidered with gold over her shoulders and clasped the two sides together with a large brooch.[104]

With the body so lovingly and elaborately dressed, the attendants and counselors were intent on ensuring that people would view Njinga's corpse in all its royal splendor. They blatantly ignored Father Cavazzi, who had been hovering in the room the entire time, attempting to remind them of the vow they had made to their queen: they must honor her deathbed wish and bury her in Father Gaeta's habit. They knew he was right, but they consented only after Cavazzi promised that they would be allowed to dress her corpse in all the royal regalia following the Christian service. Now began the careful process of undressing and re-dressing their queen, wrapping her body in the Capuchin habit, placing a crown on her head and a rosary and crucifix in her hand.

In the meantime, the councilors had agreed that Barbara should be crowned queen before the people were informed of Njinga's death. At exactly eight o'clock in the morning of Thursday, December 18, 1663, some twenty-four hours after Njinga's death, the councilors announced Barbara's election and gave her the "bow and arrow, which are the royal symbols."[105] Only after this did they publicly announce Njinga's death, as her attendants were preparing her body for the official lying in state.

The funeral party left Njinga's quarters at two o'clock on Thursday afternoon, less than six hours after Barbara had been crowned queen.

Njinga would have been proud of the members of the funeral procession who made the short walk, bearing her corpse on a stretcher-like bed or tabletop from her living quarters to the plaza, where during her life she had made so many official pronouncements, participated in numerous religious pageants, and bade farewell to troops, or, after successful campaigns, welcomed them back. At this point, the funeral procession bore greater resemblance to that of a Christian monarch than of an Mbundu/Imbangala leader. A member of the Brotherhood of the Rosary, dressed in a white cape and carrying a large cross, led the procession, with forty additional members of the Rosary, dressed in similar outfits and carrying lighted candles and rosaries, following him. Father Cavazzi and the two other Capuchins who were working in Matamba at the time had prominent places directly in front of the bier, while twelve brothers of the Rosary served as pallbearers. Also accompanying the procession were a military band with more than ninety players as well as many of the one thousand men, women, and children who formed Njinga's personal entourage.[106]

At this point Njinga's corpse had not yet been placed in a coffin but was still covered with piles of beautiful *jabu* (imported cloth from Ijebu, Nigeria). The corpse lay on its back on the table; a young page sat on the table at Njinga's head and held it in an upright position. When the procession reached the plaza, they placed the table on the raised portico in the area called the "audience room." Njinga had delivered so many speeches here on so many occasions; now the twenty thousand soldiers and others had gathered in the plaza to view the corpse of their queen, to see Njinga for one last time.[107] During the several hours that the body was on display, the young page sat motionless, holding up the crowned head, while Njinga's adoring subjects passed by the portico to pay their respects.

The fact that a mixture of Christian and Mbundu traditions were evident while her body lay in state is not surprising, given that Njinga had died before her Christian revolution was complete. Formal Christian burial rituals took place at this point even as Njinga's corpse lay covered with colorful Nigerian fabric. Father Cavazzi and the other Capuchins, joining members of the Brotherhood who were literate in Portuguese, stood around the body and took turns reading the Catholic prayers of the Office of the Dead. The people who had gathered in the square passed by respectfully, many of them returning several times.

While this vigil would be familiar to any Catholic of the time, the ceremony that followed was distinctly Mbundu. As the councilors announced that Njinga's burial would take place that very afternoon so as not to delay Barbara's coronation, the military musicians began to play music that Cavazzi described as "so strange and barbarous and not meant to invoke compassion"; it signaled to the members of the army present in the square that it was time to get in parade formation. The soldiers immediately formed an honor guard on both sides of the square and placed their arms on the ground. As soon as the twelve Catholic pallbearers took up the bier and moved slowly through and around the plaza, the soldiers picked up their arms and suddenly began to dance joyfully at the sight of the deceased queen.

As the cortege moved slowly toward Saint Anna's Church for the Christian service, reality sank in. When the people realized that Njinga would no longer be there to give the customary blessings, they were overcome with grief, wailing that the queen they had lost was irreplaceable. The soldiers discharged their firearms while men, women, and children stretched their arms up into the air. The mourners fell to the ground, spat in the dust, and plastered themselves with a mixture of saliva and earth, some using ashes and herbs they had brought along to put on their bodies as well. In this ultimate act of subordination before the corpse, they showed the same level of respect, in the same manner, to a deceased Njinga as they had when she was alive. Njinga would have expected nothing less.

The intersection of Christian and Mbundu cultural elements continued during the actual burial in the grave that had been dug just outside the church that Njinga had built, and was also evident in the rituals that occurred before and after the interment. Before the body was placed in the twelve-by-eighteen-foot tomb, Father Cavazzi and the other Capuchins conducted a Catholic funeral with an oration no different from that heard at Catholic funeral services for deceased European rulers. After the oration was over, Njinga's officials prepared the grave to receive the corpse. Mbundu custom dictated that all the clothing and other items that the deceased wore be placed in the grave so that no living person could use them. In accordance with this custom, they lined the sides of the grave with Njinga's favorite items—silk laces trimmed with gold, various wraps, and beautiful rugs—giving the tomb the appearance of an opulent, cushioned royal chest. Led by Njinga a Mona, the councilors and attendants then added Njinga's personal belongings, including large quantities of wraps, royal crowns,

Queen Njinga being taken to her sepulcher, by Antonio Cavazzi, ca. 1668

corals, silver vessels, fine Dutch cloth, imported silks, capes, pieces of linen from Germany, velvets, poles, shields, bows, arrows, and a large number of elephant skins that she had acquired during her long life. Njinga's request to be buried in Gaeta's Capuchin habit was apparently not honored, as she was redressed in all her finery.

Also in keeping with custom, Njinga a Mona ordered some of Njinga's female attendants and pages to enter the grave to receive the body. Fearing they would be buried with their mistress, they cowered together and then ran away screaming. During the pandemonium, one of the priests, with the assistance of Njinga a Mona and other court officials, wrapped the body in three cloths, one red, one yellow, and one black, on each of which a Portuguese tailor employed by Njinga had embroidered a white cross. They also placed on the corpse the many silks Njinga had worn. Before placing the body into the velvet- and crimson-lined wooden coffin, Father Cavazzi put under Njinga's head a lead plaque with an epitaph inscribed in Latin. Father Cavazzi, Njinga a Mona, and the other officials nailed the coffin shut and were ready to lower it into the grave—but there were no attendants to receive it. They had all vanished. Two of the Capuchin priests agreed to step in for the missing women. They arranged the coffin securely on the objects that had been placed in the grave before scrambling out.[108] The value of the items entombed with Njinga amounted to some sixteen thousand *scudi romani,* according to Cavazzi. This was the equivalent of the entire estate of a nobleman living in Rome at that time.[109] Despite being buried with so many valuable worldly goods, the only objects that identified the place as Njinga's gravesite were stones marked with the cross that surrounded the grave and another cross at the head of the grave.[110]

During the burial, it was Njinga a Mona, and not Barbara, who supervised and participated in the burial rituals as protocol demanded. He identified the body, helped nail the coffin, and threw the first dirt into the grave. Although he was angry that the attendants did not fulfill their duty, he chose not to reprimand them, and the group reappeared after the grave had been covered, having assured themselves that the danger had passed. At this point the city residents joined in the all-night vigil around the grave. The mourning activities consisted of Christian prayers, soldiers discharging their firearms, and the performance of other acts around the grave.

The burial was only the beginning of a long period of mourning held in Njinga's honor, as ceremonies during the days, weeks, and months following occurred not only in the capital city of Matamba, but throughout the rest of the kingdom, where *sobas* and regional powers over whom Njinga had ruled held services in her honor. The Portuguese also held a service in Luanda to honor her.

The capital remained the official mourning center. The morning following the burial, the Capuchins held an elaborate requiem mass in Saint Anna's Church with Barbara, her entire court, and members of the various militias in attendance. Cries and wails from the mourners interrupted the long service several times. Indeed, the people's public expressions of grief were so strong that the soldiers pressed their captain to obtain permission for a *tambo*, flagrantly disregarding Njinga's outlawing of this practice. The soldiers believed it unjust to deprive one so revered of so high an honor, the captain explained to Father Cavazzi and Barbara. He also cautioned that it might be dangerous to deny the soldiers the *tambo:* there was no guarantee what would happen if their request was refused. Barbara agreed to their request because she feared a revolt and hoped that by relenting, she would win them over. She placed several conditions on it, however, stipulating that the *tambo* be limited to a military ceremony and there should be no spilling of "blood, whether men, women or animals." She also warned them not to engage in any "immodest dances."[111]

For the following six days, the twenty thousand–plus soldiers and civilians who had come to witness Njinga's interment remained in a temporary village they had constructed in the middle of the city and put on an elaborate play that portrayed every aspect of their queen's long life. Among the highlights were reenactments and skits of her military strategies, which depicted Njinga's way of calling the troops to formation, her surprise attacks, her actions in battle, her treatment of enemies, and the behavior of captives. At the end of each performance, the soldier/actors stood in front of their officers, held out their bows and arrows, and shouted, "Long Live the Queen, I am ready to give my life to defend her from her enemies." Njinga's advisers also reenacted scenes from the many debates and discussions they had had with her. Her personal attendants did their part as well, enlivening the *tambo* by dancing vigorously and suggestively, attempting to dress themselves as they had when Njinga was alive, mimicking her royal walk, imitating their ways of serving her, and presenting a variety of amusing and entertaining sketches that demonstrated their deep devotion and the depth of their loss at the queen's passing. At the end of each day's performance, Barbara provided a sumptuous meal for the participants, while she received tribute from the many *sobas* and provincial lords who came to the city to pay their respects to the dead queen and to swear obedience to the new one. Some people were dissatisfied with this modified *tambo* ritual, however, fearing it was not sufficiently solemn and wondering aloud whether Njinga would come back and "take revenge."[112]

The efforts of the people to honor Njinga's life according to Mbundu traditions and the fervor of the Capuchins to pray for her soul meant that Mbundu and Catholic traditions continued to work together but at cross-purposes even after the *tambo* formally ended. To try to return the population to the church, which had not held any services since the *tambo* rituals had begun, Father Cavazzi announced immediately after the last set of performances that the church would hold prayers to honor Njinga's memory. For the next eight days, he and the other Capuchins led the people in reciting the Offices of the Dead, celebrating High Mass, and performing the usual blessings at the grave for the repose of Njinga's soul. The services were elaborate affairs: the altars and other parts of the church were decorated in black; lighted candles were placed on the altars and on the walls; palms were prominently displayed throughout the church; and incense was used liberally. Each day Barbara and members of her court, followed by great crowds, filled the church and participated in the rituals at Njinga's tomb, where the priests and civilians poured holy water on the grave and recited funeral orations.

Perhaps it is not surprising that conflicts erupted. Although the Capuchins planned to restrict the activities at the grave to purely Catholic rituals, the people had other ideas. When Father Cavazzi insisted that they restrain themselves and do only what the church permitted—to begin with, only saying prayers on behalf of Njinga's soul, since God would take care of everything else—they largely ignored him and mourned in Mbundu fashion, crying loudly and demanding permission to place lighted torches around the grave. They explained to him that this was what they did at the graves of their kings. Njinga had greater need of their cries than their prayers, they argued, and their sole purpose was to honor their royal mistress. In the end, her followers were allowed to place only two candles on the grave. The courtiers, however, made a ceremony out of this event, immediately selecting two young pages to carry the two candles from the church to the grave. Before the pages left the church, several of Njinga's female attendants thoroughly cleaned the passageway where the young men were to walk, and in keeping with the Mbundu tradition of honoring their kings, the women sprinkled the pavement with large amounts of perfume and powder.[113]

Evidence of this intersection of Mbundu and Christian traditions was not confined to the events that took place in the city where Njinga had lived. It was also visible in areas of the kingdom far beyond the court. Indeed, as soon as news of Njinga's death reached the more distant parts of Matamba and even Luanda, the services in her honor ranged from those that conformed entirely to Mbundu / Imbangala traditions, to a formal Catholic ceremony in Luanda. Whereas in areas near the court, the people had reluctantly honored Njinga's prohibition on human sacrifice, in some of the frontier parts of the kingdom, the celebrations included such Imbangala practices, involving sacrifices of both humans and animals.[114] In Luanda, the governor held a High Mass to mourn Njinga. Joined by his cabinet, members of the council, and other high-standing members of Luanda society, the Capuchins led religious dignitaries, public officials, and merchants in the procession, carrying candles to pray for Njinga's soul. Mbundu slaves and freemen in the city likely commemorated Njinga's death with a mix of Catholic and Mbundu rituals, but the documents are silent on exactly what took place outside the official service.

Even as Njinga lay dying, many aspects of her long life were already shaping every conversation and marking every face in her court and beyond the boundaries of Matamba. In the months and years following her death, the political strategies and competing ideas of the people closest to her—Barbara, Father Cavazzi, Njinga a Mona, Portuguese officials, her opponents and her devotees—all claimed the right to her legacy and contributed to the evolution of her memory.

Epilogue

A fter Njinga's death, her memory lived on in the stories people told about her. Those stories developed in very different ways in the traditions of Europe versus those of Africa and the Americas, as illustrated by two contrasting poems about Njinga.

The first poem was written by Antonio Cavazzi, the Capuchin missionary who lived in Njinga's court during the last years of her life. It was included in the manuscript version of Cavazzi's 1687 book *Istorica Descrizione de' tre' regni Congo, Matamba et Angola* (Historical Description of the Three Kingdoms of Congo, Matamba, and Angola). The poem did not appear in the published version, however, and it remained hidden for more than three centuries within the unpublished manuscript, which Cavazzi completed between 1666 and 1668, two years after Njinga's death.[1]

Although Cavazzi witnessed Njinga's conversion to Christianity and was present at her deathbed, he was never convinced of her sincerity and indeed, in his poem, presented her in the company of women, such as Medea, who had gained notoriety for their alleged use of the black arts, their cunning, and their cruelty. To Cavazzi, Njinga bested them all, because she outsmarted heaven by robbing it of her soul:

> *Under this thrice-folded cloth*
> *In this dark tomb that you see*
> *Ginga, who made herself Queen of Dongo and Matamba*
> *Lies buried, a dry corpse*
> *In this dark tomb that you see*

. . .

Here lies the one who lived to die
Here lies the one who by dying lives
In this dark tomb she hid herself.

. . .

Because of Agrippina, Rome rebelled
Because of Helen, Greece rebelled
Because of Uxodonia, Germany rebelled
Because of Hecuba, Spain rebelled
But Ethiopia did not rebel for Ginga
Instead, Ginga overturned, destroyed, and ruined Ethiopia.
Ginga in death
stole from Heaven's treasury
In this tomb
Her body is locked up
Therefore we can sing to a most cunning thief
A most cunning thief has stolen from the treasury of Heaven.[2]

A little more than three centuries after Cavazzi wrote this poem, the Yoruba-descended Afro-Cuban poet and journalist Georgina Herrera wrote a very different poem about Njinga. Herrera resurrected in poetic language a Njinga far removed from Cavazzi's construction. In her 1978 poem "Canto de amor y respeto para doña Ana de Souza" (Song of Love and Respect for Lady Ana de Souza), Njinga becomes the "holy lady and queen" as well as the "mother of all beginnings." Herrera reclaims Njinga, sanctifying her memory in the African diaspora and bringing life and legitimacy to her, bridging the divide Cavazzi had put between the ruler and "mother Africa":

. . .

Oh! Doña Ana, grandmother
of anger and kindness. So many
years of battle against the enemy

. . .

make you an inimitable woman.
It is lovely to close my eyes, looking
at you through the centuries
and circumstances, speaking
to your people . . .[3]

Herrera's poem, published three years after the 1975 United Nations' First World Conference on Women, not only spoke for women of the African diaspora, but reclaimed Njinga for all women. This Njinga burst out from the dark tomb where Cavazzi had encased her to take her place as a remarkable historical figure.

•

This recuperation was sorely needed, because over the centuries, Njinga's memory had fallen captive to the version of her story that the missionaries Antonio da Gaeta and Antonio Cavazzi had fed to the European public. These two men, whose legitimacy was never questioned because they lived in Njinga's court during her final years, had much to do with the image of Njinga that reached Europeans. They had collected oral traditions while serving as her confessors and advisers and ministering to her people. They recorded the various contradictory elements that Njinga had creatively combined to guarantee her political, cultural, spiritual, and physical survival. Their private letters and reports sent to the Vatican informed the biographical, historical, and psychological retelling of Njinga's story. They and their editors at the Vatican shaped the story that reached the public.

The author of the first published biography of Njinga was Antonio da Gaeta, the first Capuchin who ministered to her in Matamba and who claimed success for her conversion to Christianity. The biography appeared in 1669, only six years after Njinga's death, with the laudatory title *La Maravigliosa Conversione alla Santa Fede di Cristo della Regina Singa e del suo Regno di Matamba nell'Africa meridionale* (The Marvelous Conversion to the Holy Faith of Christ of Queen Njinga and of Her Kingdom of Matamba in Central Africa). The work gave muted praise to Njinga, referring to her as a "highly noble lady."[4] Gaeta placed Njinga in the company of all the women of antiquity who had become famous, or infamous, for their ability to gain renown in a man's world. His list included, among others, Minerva, Artemisia, Semiramis, Hippolyta, Cleopatra, Saint Catherine, Mariana of Austria, and Saint Apollonia.[5] In Gaeta's biography, what stood out was the incredible achievement of the missionaries who were able to penetrate the heart of this "warlike Amazon."[6] Divine providence had used Gaeta as the conquering archangel who subverted the devil and turned monstrous Njinga, a "pagan idolater" who had been steeped in "rituals and diabolic ceremonies," into a "devout Christian."[7]

A second biography of Njinga appeared as part of Cavazzi's book, which was published in 1687. The manuscript had gone through several revisions at the hands of the editorial committee at the Vatican, which excised the poem and removed other fanciful references that Cavazzi had included. The printed version included information from letters written to the Vatican authorities by Cavazzi's contemporaries.[8] Although the editors left out the poem in which he castigated Njinga for daring to rob Heaven of her soul, and declared that her fate was to lie forever hidden in her "dark tomb," the book he and his handlers published actually liberated Njinga from that tomb.

Publications about Njinga that appeared after Gaeta's and Cavazzi's books gave her faint praise as a "wild genius" or a reluctant convert. Writers focused chiefly on Njinga's barbarity, bloodthirsty nature, wanton sexuality, and cannibalism. Dutch and French writers produced translations of Cavazzi's book that presented only selected aspects of Njinga's life. The French Jesuit Jean-Baptiste Labat, a brother of the Dominican Order who had traveled to the West Indies to do missionary work, published his expanded French translation of Cavazzi in 1732 to highlight the successes of Catholic missions among primitive peoples. For him, Njinga's history illustrated the power of the European state and the Catholic Church to colonize and spread Christianity to pagan lands. Labat thus transformed Njinga into a conquered colonial subject who became subordinate to European arms and the church.[9]

Later authors writing during different times and in different genres produced their own versions of Njinga's story. Ignoring Gaeta's portrayal of a leader whom the church had finally converted, or Cavazzi's less complimentary but still complicated portrait of an astute political leader, French, Dutch, and German writers during the eighteenth and nineteenth centuries relied largely on Labat's doctored version of Cavazzi as well as on a 1668 book by Olfert Dapper that described African peoples and societies based on the reports of Dutch traders and officials.[10] At the time, the only Portuguese publication available on Njinga was an eight-page pamphlet printed in 1749. But Portuguese publications on Njinga continued to appear until well into the twentieth century.[11] The lengthy work by Portuguese historian and soldier António de Oliveira Cadornega, written between 1670 and 1681 and containing extensive details on Njinga's military and diplomatic dealings with the Portuguese, did not appear in print until 1940.[12]

Labat's translation of Cavazzi provided the fodder that eighteenth- and nineteenth-century European intellectuals used to create their own versions of Njinga's life. Although some writers linked Njinga to the fables about man-eating African monarchs and other strange tales included in the popular travelogues and historical geographies that had gained wide circulation in Europe by the mid-eighteenth century, they also created a Njinga who showed all the foibles of a complex leader.[13] Jean-Louis Castilhon's 1769 *Zingha, reine d'Angola* (Zingha, queen of Angola) stands out as the first fictional work with Njinga as its subject. Castilhon's Njinga is by nature cruel but not a cannibal; it was her desire to wreak vengeance and to dominate that made her overcome the horror of consuming human flesh and to become an Imbangala.[14] Castilhon's Njinga is a leader intelligent enough to formulate strategies to oppose Portuguese claims to her land. In the end, she repents and is saved by conversion despite her crimes.[15]

The overwhelming interest of European writers in Njinga's life was to use her as the stand-in for the African other.[16] It was as a cannibal queen that Njinga dominated the libertine novels that appeared in the years leading up to the French Revolution. During this period, writers spurned the established church and political hierarchy and instead explored, among other things, the world of the erotic. Writers created their own salacious and gory details about Njinga, using images by European painters that pictured her as an erotic figure. The Marquis de Sade's 1795 *La Philosophie dans le Boudoir* (Philosophy in the bedroom) used the example of Njinga to illustrate the tendency of women to be driven by their sexuality to commit horrendous deeds. His "Zingua, Queen of Angola," whose life story he claimed he had come to know from "a missionary source," was presented to his readers as "the cruelest of women," who exercised total domination over men. This queen, he wrote, "killed her lovers as soon as she had her way with them." Njinga's evil spirit and sexual disposition was such that she treated men as the Romans did their gladiators. Like the Romans, she had warriors fight to the death with the "victor's prize" not money or freedom, but she herself. Sade created a Njinga who had no respect for ordered life, only a desire for pleasure. She went so far as to establish a law promoting prostitution, and thought nothing of grinding in a mortar "every pregnant woman under the age of thirty."[17] This Njinga confirmed European notions of the exotic other.[18] When Njinga appeared in an 1817 review of *The Histories of the Discoveries of Africa* published in the *London Quarterly*

Review, the reviewer, well acquainted with Cavazzi's book as well as with the other publications, bought into the existing narrative about Njinga. He concluded that she was "one of the most horrible monsters that ever appeared on the face of the earth in female shape."[19]

This image of Njinga as an icon of sexual deviance, evil, and brutality was not limited to the French libertine writers or to English reviewers. The philosopher G. W. F. Hegel also propagated a similar portrait. In lectures delivered at Berlin University in the early 1800s, he used the portrayals of Njinga circulating in European religious and literary circles to illustrate that Africa was "outside of history." For Hegel, Njinga (whose name he chose not to use, perhaps knowing that a name marks the person as a subject of history), together with other African leaders, represented an aberration of history. She ruled a "female state," where gory scenes of blood prevailed as adult men and male children were routinely massacred. Moreover, the men who survived had no power as men, since the woman warriors (Hegel refers to them as "the furies") who surrounded Njinga used male captives as lovers. These women were so unnatural that they did not cultivate or nurture anything, destroying settled lands and going outside the camp to give birth to the babies they conceived. Their hatred of men was such that they abandoned male babies outside of the camps, leaving them to die. Thankfully, Hegel concluded, the state disappeared.[20]

Published in 1834, three years before Hegel's work, a chapter on Queen Njinga appeared in the book *Les femmes célèbres de tous les pays* (Celebrated women of all countries) by Laure Junot, Duchess of Abrantès, and Joseph Straszewicz, which portrayed Njinga as a paragon of lust and cruelty and contributed to an image of Njinga that fed Europe's repressed sexual fantasies as well as the emerging image of the primitive.[21] Junot placed Njinga alongside the likes of "Lady Jane Gray, Maria Letizia Ramolino [Napoleon Bonaparte's mother], Marie Antoinette and Catherine I of Russia," all notorious women of their time. As an English reviewer at the time noted, the author focused on these women to illustrate "horrid portraits of human nature." Junot's Njinga, like Hegel's, was "one of the most insatiable furies of her period." This Njinga could never be the loving "grandmother" whom a diasporic granddaughter like Herrera yearned to gaze upon.[22] Instead, Junot presented an evil, bloodthirsty fiend who at her father's funeral killed and had consumed two hundred men, women, and children. These innocent people were dispatched by Njinga herself, who then drank the blood of one of the victims. Junot's image of Njinga was widely propagated in English publications. For example, long excerpts and reviews were published in magazines such as *Royal Ladies Magazine, Literary Gazette,* and *The Britannica Magazine.*[23]

Decades after Junot's work appeared, snippets of distorted information on Njinga continued to surface in newspapers, journals, and magazines published in Europe. By that time, Portuguese and Brazilian essayists and pamphleteers were competing to present their own versions of Njinga. The Portuguese writers had several aims. In particular, they wanted to correct what they denounced as "the absurd legend of the missionary Cavazzi," which provided foreigners with distorted images of Portuguese conquests in Angola and Njinga's place in these events. These Lusophone writers were eager to point out that European writers were not privy to any of the Portuguese eyewitness accounts and therefore could not present unbiased histories of Portuguese activities in Angola during these years. Despite claims that they were correcting history and thus reclaiming a less distorted image of Njinga, what they did was to create their own distortions. Over the nineteenth century, the image of Njinga that Portuguese readers consumed retained many of the elements that had made her an attractive figure for French libertine writers. In one version she was painted as a "manly queen" who took pleasure in performing the "most cruel" acts, while in another, she appears as a cannibal "who ate the chest of her victims because that was where the heart was."[24] During the course of the twentieth century, when Portuguese officials used colonialist propaganda as the ideological arm in their attempt to extend and consolidate the Portuguese state in Angola, Njinga was "a black savage" who, despite possessing a "superior indigenous intellect," was ultimately conquered by superior Portuguese military power and willingly submitted to Christianity.[25]

•

The traditions of colonized Angolans and enslaved Africans sent to the Americas during Njinga's life paint a very different image of the African ruler. In Angola, Portuguese textbooks either had told the story of Njinga as a pagan who eventually became subordinate to the Portuguese or had erased her name altogether. As Africans in the colony began to wage a nationalist struggle against Portuguese colonialism, voices in the rural areas Njinga once controlled presented a very different version. The story of Njinga that people in rural regions of Kimbundu-speaking Angola passed on orally to their children and grandchildren was that of a proud ruler who conquered lands, won many wars against the Portuguese, and maintained the independence and traditions of her people.[26]

This image of Njinga that the oral traditions preserved took on a new dynamic in the 1960s, when Angolans increasingly looked to history to frame their own resistance struggle against the Portuguese. Facing a racist and exploitative colonial regime whose policies divided Angolans along race, class, ethnic, regional, and linguistic lines, the descendants of Mbundu elders who had absorbed the oral traditions about Njinga's resistance brought back the heroic Njinga. In the revolutionary poems and histories they published in Western sources and used as propaganda to encourage young Angolans to join the struggle, they placed the example of Njinga's resistance at center stage. Their Njinga was not the sexual deviant or the cruel cannibal who filled the pages of earlier European publications. Instead, Angolans made Njinga into a revolutionary hero who united her people in an epic struggle against Portuguese aggression. This Njinga provided the model for remaking colonized Portuguese subjects into revolutionary guerrillas whose duty, like hers, was to gain the independence of Angola and keep the people united.[27]

Since attaining independence in 1975, the MPLA (People's Movement for the Liberation of Angola) government has been promoting Njinga's history and image. Besides publishing poems, books, and histories on Njinga and Angola's history during her era, the government set about making Njinga into a national heroine. The new government, now headed by former prisoners and leaders of the resistance, moved to undo the colonial legacy that had excluded Njinga from textbooks and required teachers to punish African students who spoke Kimbundu, in which they might share the traditions about Njinga's exploits that they had picked up in villages. The new leaders chose to root the history of the new nation in the seventeenth-century history of Njinga. The first step in making her a symbol of the nation was to require that all schools and military recruitment centers use a revised edition of a textbook, *History of Angola,* that placed the resistance story of Njinga at the center of the nation's history.[28] Moreover, the government supported the publication of historical novels and other works about Njinga and the period she lived in.[29]

This focus on nationalism took on special importance because of the bloody civil war that began a few months before independence in 1975 and did not end officially until 2002. Although the war was in part a byproduct of the Cold War struggle between the USSR and the United States, it was also shaped by the ethnolinguistic divisions that Portuguese colonial policies had encouraged.

After the end of the civil war, officials in the MPLA-run government who had used Njinga's history of resistance to motivate young Angolan guerrillas appropriated her history as a symbol to unify the nation. Although other historical figures were recognized for their contribution to the founding of the modern Angolan nation, Njinga received special attention. In 2003, the government unveiled a monumental statue of her in Kinaxixe, a central thoroughfare in Luanda that had featured prominently in Angola's pre-colonial and colonial history. During the seventeenth-century Portuguese wars against Ndongo, Kinaxixe had served as a slave market, and it continued to be the site where rural Mbundus brought their products for sale. In 1937, the Portuguese had turned it into a place of colonial glory when officials unveiled a monument honoring Portuguese dead in World War I. In 1975, the MPLA government removed that monument and replaced it with a massive military vehicle symbolizing victory over the Portuguese. By the time Njinga's monumental statue replaced the military vehicle, millions of Angolans who had fled the countryside during the civil war were now living in Luanda. Njinga's statue in this symbolic and revered site attracted Angolans of all linguistic and ethnic backgrounds who came to regard her not only as a symbol of resistance but as a stern mother nurturing her children in the new nation. Njinga's statue, located in the cleanest space in the capital, became a place where, for example, wedding parties congregated to take photographs. During the decade that her statue graced the historic Kinaxixe roundabout, Njinga was truly the "Mother of the Nation" as many young Angolans in Luanda asserted.[30]

The many symposia, forums, and international gatherings that the Angolan government sponsored on Angolan history only reinforced Njinga's standing as an exemplary figure of the Angolan past with contemporary relevance.[31] One of the major initiatives of the government was to identify Njinga as the "mother of the modern Angolan nation." This national campaign did much to rescue the image European writers had perpetuated

Author Linda Heywood at the side of Njinga's towering statue, Luanda, Angola

about Njinga. By 2013, when Angolans celebrated the 350th anniversary of Njinga's death with a number of exhibits and books in her honor, Njinga's image had changed to that of a prominent leader in Angola and the world. She was a figure of history, memory, and myth. In the academic symposia the government held in both Angola and Europe, Njinga's wars of resistance held equal space with Cavazzi's depiction of her conversion. This Njinga was a queen, "a woman of arms who fought in the African interior in defense of her people."[32]

The effort by the Angolan government that had the most impact in transforming Njinga's status was to commission a film, *Njinga, Rainha de Angola/Njinga: Queen of Angola*, which premiered in Angola in the 350th anniversary year.[33] Starring the beautiful Angolan actress Lesliana Pereira, the film created a new Njinga for a new Angolan nation and the world. Instead of a sexualized Njinga with one breast exposed, as depicted in a painting used in Castilhon's book (and that still remains the iconic image of Njinga), the new Njinga was a fearless guerrilla leader. Attired in a traditional bark outfit that could be mistaken for a bandolier, sporting a hairstyle patterned after the politicized Afros of the nineteen sixties and seventies, this Njinga was determined to keep Angola independent.[34]

Njinga also had a renaissance in Brazil, where millions of African captives from Ndongo, Matamba, and Kongo, enslaved before, during, and after her life, had been sent. On the plantations and in the mining regions of northeast Brazil, Rio de Janeiro, and elsewhere, they fused elements of their central African languages and culture with Brazilian traditions to develop a unique Afro-Brazilian culture. The earliest visitors to Brazil's northeast recorded the secular and religious celebrations in these slave communities. Their language, religious practices, dances, and songs all contained references to historical and cultural events from the central Africa of Njinga's day. In time, these celebrations, especially the election of kings and queens, came to include enslaved Africans from other parts of Africa who were also brought to Brazil. Despite this, however, the central African contribution remained dominant; for example, the king and queen elected during festivities were always called the king of Kongo and Queen Njinga.

By the twentieth century, when the central African–inspired pageant parades, the *lundus, maracatus, cucumbis, congadas, umbandas,* were on their way to becoming synonymous with Afro-Brazilian culture, Njinga's history, and especially her wars against the Portuguese and the Kongo kings, was the focal point in dramas that communities all over Brazil staged. From the Pernambuco region in the northeast, where during the annual celebrations of the *cucumbis* the woman carrying the title "Njinga" sat alongside the "King of Kongo" and was assured of the veneration of the community for the entire year, to public performances of the *congados* in the early twentieth century, where Njinga's ambassador tried to get an audience with the "King of Kongo" but was prevented from proceeding because of the king's fear of Queen Njinga, her name has been kept alive in Brazil. Njinga's history was also captured in the terminology of the *capoeira* martial art, where the term *njinga* came to signify the stealthy movements reminiscent of the training that Njinga's soldiers received in preparation for battle. However, as the term evolved in impoverished Afro-Brazilian urban centers, reporters and police authorities came to stigmatize the physical actions associated with these movements as dangerous or criminal.[35]

But Njinga was in Brazil to stay. During the middle decades of the twentieth century, as African countries gained their independence, Brazilian scholars tentatively looked to Africa to explore the roots of Afro-Brazilian culture. It was at this time that the first Portuguese-language biography of Njinga was published in Brazil. By the 2000s, Njinga had become the darling of poets of the Samba schools of Rio de Janeiro. They wrote songs praising her bravery and what they interpreted as her promotion of women's rights and black power. Afro-Brazilians led the public interest in the history of Njinga, believing they could now present to the nation the long-hidden part of their identity. By 2013, when the Angolan film *Njinga: Rainha de Angola* premiered in Brazil, Afro-Brazilians welcomed its revolutionary focus, which they saw as linked to their life in Brazil. Afro-Brazilian women, especially those connected to the Samba schools whose dances, food, and religious traditions demonstrated their resilience and independence, viewed Njinga as their hero. They saw themselves as "royal heirs of Queen Nzinga of Angola."[36]

The Angolan government's strategic appropriation of Njinga's life to represent colonial resistance and national unity was only the first step in the rehabilitation Njinga's image has undergone in the last half century. The interest in Brazil in cultural roots also brought the story of Njinga into the consciousness of a new generation of Afro-Brazilians anxious to reconnect to a glorious African past. But Njinga's impact also extended to other Afro-descended populations in the Americas. In places like Cuba, Jamaica, and the United States, interest in Njinga's story has generated an outpouring of poems, plays, paintings, and even a children's book.[37] Njinga's cultural renaissance has also reached a larger global audience. In 2013, at the request of the Angolan government and with the generous financial support of the

Republic of Bulgaria, UNESCO commemorated the 350th anniversary of Njinga's death by profiling her in the UNESCO series "Women in African History." The fifty-six–page comic strip, intended for use in elementary schools, includes important incidents in Njinga's life, and a pedagogical section focusing on themes such as "Resistance" and "Governance by a Woman."[38] In addition, UNESCO added Njinga's name to a list of nineteen important women leaders of Africa it has honored so far.

Njinga's resurrection, however, is still underway.[39] She has yet to take her place in popular history alongside her near contemporaries Queen Elizabeth I and Pocahontas in the ranks of "famous women in history," although the UNESCO honor is a step in that direction. Njinga no longer represents the other, but a powerful woman with few contemporary equals who did what was necessary to maintain the independence of her lands. She served as an inspiration for her people during her life and for Angolans and Brazilians centuries after her death. Njinga demands to be presented as the complex human being that she was, and given her rightful place in world history.

Glossary

feiticeiro	wizard, or non-Christian religious practitioner
ilija	laws or prohibitions of the Imbangala (singular: *kijila*)
kijiko	serf
kilamba	Mbundu soldier under an African commander, fighting with the Portuguese
kilombo	war camp, or military unit housed in such a camp
kimbare	Mbundu soldier serving with the Portuguese
makota	leading man of Ndongo; lineage head or hereditary noble
makunze	messenger, low-level representative
misete	reliquary
mubika	slave
murinda	territorial division smaller than a province
mwene lumbo	official in charge of the royal residence
nganga	Ndongo priest or religious practitioner
ngola	king or ruler
pumbeiro	African slave working as a merchant for the Portuguese in the slave markets
soba	local leader or provincial lord
tambo	Mbundu funeral rite
tendala	chief administrative officer of the Ndongo court
xingula	spirit medium; a *nganga* who has been possessed

Names

Rulers of Ndongo

Ngola Kiluanje kia Samba (reigned 1515–1556). Founder of Ndongo.
Ndambi a Ngola (reigned 1556–1561)
Ngola Kiluanje kia Ndambi (reigned 1561–1575)
Ngola Kilombo kia Kasenda (reigned 1575–1592)
Mbande a Ngola Kiluanje (reigned 1592–1617). Son of Kasenda.
Ngola Mbande (reigned 1617–1624). Son of Mbande a Ngola, brother
    of Njinga.
Ngola Hari (installed as king by Portuguese in 1626). Rival of Njinga.
Njinga (b. 1582; d. 1663; reigned 1624–1663). Daughter of Mbande a
    Ngola and sister of Ngola Mbande. Sisters Kambu (Barbara) and Funji
    (Graça).

Selected Portuguese governors of Angola, with dates in office

Francisco de Almeida (1592–1593)
Manuel Cerveira Pereira (1603–1606)
Bento Banha Cardoso (1611–1615)
Manuel Cerveira Pereira, second term (1615–1617)
Luis Mendes de Vasconcelos (1617–1621)
João Correia de Sousa (1621–1623)
Pedro de Sousa Coelho (1623)
Bishop Simão de Mascarenhas (1623–1624)

Fernão de Sousa (1624–1630)
Manuel Pereira Coutinho (1630–1635)
Francisco de Vasconcelos da Cunha (1635–1639)
Pedro Cesar de Menezes (1639–1645)
Francisco de Sotomaior (1645–1646)
Salvador Correia de Sá (1648–1651)
Luis Martins de Sousa Chichorro (1654–1658)
João Fernandes Vieira (1658–1661)

Chronology

1515	Founding of Ndongo under Ngola Kiluanje kia Samba
1556	Ngola Kiluanje kia Samba dies; Ndambi a Ngola becomes king
1560	Portuguese mission arrives in Luanda
1561	Ndambi a Ngola dies; Ngola Kiluanje kia Ndambi becomes king
1575	Portuguese armada arrives in Luanda under command of Paulo Dias de Novais
	Ngola Kiluanje kia Ndambi dies; Kasenda becomes king
1582	Njinga is born
1592	Kasenda dies; Mbande a Ngola becomes king
1617	Mbande a Ngola dies; Ngola Mbande becomes king
1622	Njinga heads a diplomatic delegation to Luanda and is baptized
1624	Ngola Mbande dies; Njinga becomes queen
1626 (July)	Portuguese rout Njinga's forces from the Kindonga Islands; Njinga flees
1626 (Oct)	Portuguese install Ngola Hari as puppet ruler of Ndongo
1629	Njinga is attacked by the Portuguese and flees from the Ngangela region
	Portuguese capture Njinga's sisters, Kambu and Funji

1631	Njinga becomes an Imbangala leader and begins conquest of Matamba
1632–33	Kambu is released
1641	Dutch forces capture Luanda from the Portuguese
1646	Portuguese destroy Njinga's *kilombo* in the Dembos region
	Kambu is recaptured
1647	Njinga and Dutch sign agreement to become allies
	Portuguese kill Njinga's sister Funji (Graça) for spying
1648 (Aug)	Portuguese retake Luanda, Dutch withdraw
1648 (Sept)	Njinga attacks Wandu province, Kongo
	Njinga establishes a court in Matamba and reigns as ruler of Ndongo-Matamba
1654	Rome approves sending Capuchin missionaries to Matamba
1656 (April)	Portuguese release Njinga's sister Kambu (Barbara) from captivity
1656 (Oct)	Barbara arrives in Matamba
	Njinga signs peace treaty with the Portuguese
1661	Njinga receives a letter from Pope Alexander VII
1663 (Dec 17)	Njinga dies

Notes

....

Abbreviations

AHU	Arquivo Histórico Ultramarino, Lisbon
Cavazzi, MSS Araldi	Giovanni Antonio Cavazzi da Montecuccolo, "Missione evangelica nel Regno de Congo" (1668), volume A. Private collection, Araldi Family, Modena, Italy. Cited by book and page number. For more on this source, see http://www.bu.edu/afam/faculty/john -thornton/cavazzi-missione-evangelica-2/
Cx.	Caixa (Box)
FHA	Beatrix Heintze, ed., *Fontes para a História de Angola do Século XVII*, 2 vols. (Wiesbaden: Franz Steiner, 1985–1988)
fol.	folio
JAH	*Journal of African History*
MMA	António Brásio, ed., *Monumenta Missionaria Africana: Africa Ocidental*. 15 vols. Lisbon: Agência Geral do Ultramar, Divisão de Publicações e Biblioteca, 1952–1988
MS	Manuscript
para.	paragraph

Introduction

1   See, for example, Patrick Graille, "*Zingha, Reine d'Angola, Histoire Africaine* (1769) de Castilhon, Premier Roman Historique Africain et Anticolonialiste de la Littérature Occidentale," in Inocência Mata, ed., *A Rainha Nzinga Mbandi: História, Memória e Mito*, 2nd ed. (Lisbon: Edições Colibri, 2014), 47–56.

2   "Carta do Rei do Congo ao D. João III, 28 January 1530," *MMA* 1:540.

3   "Apontamentos do Padre Sebastião de Souto" (1561), *MMA* 11:479.

4   For a thorough overview of the organization of Ndongo in the sixteenth century, see Beatrix Heintze, "O Estado do Ndongo no Século XVI," in Heintze, *Angola no Séculos XVI e XVII: Estudos sobre Fontes, Métodos e História* (Luanda, 2007), 169–242.

5   "Carta do Irmão António Mendes," 29 October 1562, *MMA* 2:511.

6   For a more detailed discussion of the administrative arrangements in Kabasa, see Linda M. Heywood and John K. Thornton, *Central Africans, Atlantic Creoles, and the Foundation of the Americas, 1585–1660* (New York: Cambridge University Press, 2007), 72–79.

7   For the issue of legitimacy and power in Ndongo, see John K. Thornton, "Legitimacy and Political Power: Queen Njinga, 1624–1663," *JAH* 32 (1991): 25–40.

8   John K. Thornton, "The Art of War in Angola, 1575–1680," *Comparative Studies in Society and History,* 30 (1988): 360–378.

9   [Baltasar Barreira], "Informação acerca dos Escravos de Angola" (1582–1583), *MMA* 3:227–229.

10   Cavazzi, MSS Araldi, book 2, p. 3.

11   Pierre du Jarric, *Histoire des choses plus memorables advenues tant ez Indes Orientales, que autres païs de la descouverte des Portugais,* 3 vols. (Bordeaux, 1608–1614), 2:98.

12   Brother António Mendes to the Father General, 9 May 1563, *MMA* 2:509.

13   Letter of Brother António Mendes, 29 October 1562, *MMA* 2:489.

14   Father Francisco de Gouveia to the Father General, 1 November 1564, *MMA* 15:231–232.

15   Giovanni Antonio Cavazzi da Montecuccolo, *Istorica Descrizione de' tre' regni Congo, Matamba et Angola* (Bologna: Giacomo Monti, 1687), book 2, para. 131. All references to Cavazzi's *Istorica Descrizione* are cited by book and paragraph number. A Portuguese translation was published as João António Cavazzi de Montecúccolo, *Descrição Histórica dos Três Reinos do Congo, Matamba e Angola,* trans. Graciano Maria [Saccardo] de Leguzzano, 2 vols. (Lisbon: Junta de Investigaçoes do Ultramar, 1965).

16   "Carta do Irmão António Mendes ao Padre Geral," 9 May 1563, *MMA* 2:500.

17   "Carta do Irmão António Mendes," 29 October 1562, *MMA* 2:508. See also Heywood and Thornton, *Central Africans,* 80–81.

18   For the story of Hohoria and Zundi, see Cavazzi, MSS Araldi, book 2, pp. 2–10; Antonio da Gaeta, *La Maravigliosa Conversione alla Santa Fede di Cristo della Regina Singa,* ed. Francesco Maria Gioia (Naples, 1669), 136–139.

19   For a discussion of the several lineages that were descended from the concubines of Ngola Kiluanje kia Samba, see Cavazzi, MSS Araldi, book 2, p. 10. See also Cavazzi, *Istorica Descrizione,* book 2, paras. 129–133; Beatrix Heintze, "Written Sources, Oral Traditions, and Oral Sources as Written Sources: The Steep and Thorny Way to Early Angolan History," *Paideuma* 33 (1987): 263–287.

20   Cavazzi, MSS Araldi, book 2, pp. 13–14.

21   Father Diogo da Costa to the Provincial of Portugal, 31 May 1586, *MMA* 3:333.

22   Ibid., *MMA* 3:336–337.

23   "Informação dos Casamentos de Angola" (1582–1583), *MMA* 3:231.

24   Ibid., *MMA* 3:231–232. See also António de Oliveira de Cadornega, *História Geral das Guerras Angolanas,* ed. José Delgado, 3 vols. (1940–1942; repr. Lisbon: Agência-Geral do Ultramar, 1972), 1:30–32.

25   Cavazzi, MSS Araldi, book 2, p. 14.

1. The Ndongo Kingdom and the Portuguese Invasion

1   For an overview of contemporary European sources that provide details of the Ndongo-Portuguese relationship, see Linda M. Heywood and John K. Thornton, *Central Africans, Atlantic Creoles, and the Foundation of the Americas, 1585–1660* (New York: Cambridge University Press, 2007), 79–82.

2   Giovanni Antonio Cavazzi da Montecuccolo, *Istorica Descrizione de' tre' regni Congo, Matamba et Angola* (Bologna: Giacomo Monti, 1687), book 2, para. 130.

3   Cavazzi, *Istorica Descrizione*, book 2, para. 130.

4   For a reconstruction of this early history see Cavazzi, MSS Araldi, book 2, pp. 4–12; Antonio da Gaeta, *La Maravigliosa Conversione alla Santa Fede di Cristo della Regina Singa*, ed. Francesco Maria Gioia (Naples, 1669), 135–145.

5   Farinha Torres, "Campanhas contra o Rei de Angola," *Mensário Admininstrativo* 26/27 (1949): 97–99.

6   Ibid., 97–101.

7   For the details of this visit, see Brother António Mendes to the Father General, 9 May 1563, *MMA* 2:498–500.

8   Brother António Mendes to the Father General, 9 May 1563, *MMA* 2:509, 511.

9   Andrew Battel, *The Strange Adventures of Andrew Battell in Angola*, ed. E. G. Ravenstein (London: Hakluyt Society, 1901), 26–27, notes that tame peacocks were regarded as sacred and were kept on the grave of the provincial ruler Shillambansa, the uncle of the king of Ndongo.

10   For a description of this attire see Cavazzi, MSS Araldi, book 2, p. 3.

11   Brother António Mendes to the Father General, 9 May 1563, *MMA* 2:509. See also Heywood and Thornton, *Central Africans*, 81; David Birmingham, *Trade and Conflict in Angola: The Mbundu and Their Neighbours under the Influence of the Portuguese, 1483–1790* (Oxford: Clarendon Press, 1966), 33–38.

12   Manuel Ruela Pombo, *Angola-Menina, 1560–1565* (Lisbon, 1944), 18.

13   Cavazzi, MSS Araldi, book 2, p. 6; Brother António Mendes to the Father General, 9 May 1563, *MMA* 2:508–509; Garcia Simões to the Provincial of Portugal, 20 October 1575, *MMA* 3:134.

14   Brother António Mendes to the Father General, 9 May 1563, *MMA* 2:499–503.

15   These events are detailed in Brother António Mendes to the Father General, 9 May 1563, *MMA* 2:499–503.

16   António Mendes wrote that Ngola Kiluanje had received word from the king of Kongo alerting him that the Portuguese were only interested in determining whether Ndongo had silver and gold, so that Portugal could "take the land." See ibid., 2:502.

17   Ruela Pombo, *Angola-Menina*, 28. This scenario comes from a document written by Captain Garcia Mendes Castelo Branco, who accompanied Dias de Novais on his 1575 voyage and who served for half a century as a soldier in Angola. See "Relacão do que faz o Capitão Garcia Mendez das cousas tocantes ao Reyno de Angola," *MMA* 6:453–467 (dated to 1620 by the editor of *MMA*).

18   Francisco de Gouveia to Father Diogo Mirão, 1 November 1564, *MMA* 2:528; Francisco de Gouveia to Father General, 1 November 1564, *MMA* 15:231–232.

19   Cavazzi, *Istorica Descrizione*, book 2, para. 131.

20 Brother António Mendes to the Father General, 9 May 1563, *MMA* 2:508–509; Francisco de Gouveia to Father General, 1 November 1564, *MMA* 15:230.

21 Father Garcia Simões to the Provincial, 20 October 1575, *MMA* 3:135. Traditions I collected between 2008 and 2011 in the modern province of Malange, where Njinga's state and capital were located, and where people called Gingas live, attribute many miracles to Ngola Kiluanje kia Ndambi.

22 For a discussion of this issue see Heywood and Thornton, *Central Africans*, 85.

23 Cavazzi, *Istorica Descrizione*, book 2, para. 132.

24 Letter of Father Baltasar Barreira, 14 May 1586, *MMA* 3:321.

25 Diogo da Costa to the Provincial of Portugal, 31 May 1586, *MMA* 3:337.

26 Ruela Pombo, *Angola-Menina*, 29. See also Captitão Durão Paias, "Efemérides Angolanos em Mais de 4 Séculus," *Mensário Administrativo* 26/27 (1949): 16.

27 Garcia Simões to the Father Provincial, 20 October 1575, *MMA* 3:131.

28 Torres, "Campanhas contra o Rei de Angola," 98–101.

29 Ruela Pombo, *Angola-Menina*, 29.

30 Pero Rodrigues, "História da Residência dos Padres da Companhia de Jesus em Angola," 1 May 1594, *MMA* 4:572. A Spanish league was approximately 2.6 miles. Remembrances of Jerónimo Castanho to the King, 5 September 1599, *MMA* 4:606–607; Letter of Donation of Paulo Dias de Novais to the Fathers of the Company, 26 August 1581, *MMA* 15:265–267, 279. The slaves were said to number 1,000.

31 Dias de Novais to King, 13 March 1582, *MMA* 4:335.

32 Letter of Father Baltasar Afonso, 31 August 1582, *MMA* 3:219.

33 Letter of Father Baltasar Afonso, 3 January 1583, *MMA* 3:233; Letter of Father Baltasar Afonso, 3 October 1583, *MMA* 3:248.

34 Letter of Diogo da Costa, 20 July 1585, *MMA* 3:320.

35 Father Baltasar Afonso to the Provincial of Brazil, 27 August 1585, *MMA* 3:323–325.

36 Father Diogo da Costa to the Provincial of Portugal, 31 May 1586, *MMA* 3:336.

37 Father Baltasar Afonso to Father Miguel de Sousa, 4 July 1581, *MMA* 3:202.

38 Letter of Father Baltasar Afonso, 3 October 1583, *MMA* 3:248.

39 Ibid. For the various reports of the campaigns see Letter of Pero Rodrigues, 20 November 1583, *MMA* 4:567–568; Letter of Baltasar Afonso, 3 October 1583, *MMA* 3:248.

40 Letter of Baltasar Afonso, 3 October 1583, *MMA* 3:248.

41 "Mémorias de Jerónimo Castanho a El-Rei," 5 September 1599, *MMA* 4:606–607.

42 The army that Sebastião Manibama, brother-in-law of King Alváro of Kongo, sent in 1579–80 was said to number almost sixty thousand men. See Felippo Pigafetta, *Relazione del Reame di Congo e circonvincine contrade* (Rome, 1591), 27.

43 Pierre du Jarric, *Histoire des choses plus memorables advenues tant ez Indes Orientales, que autres païs de la descouverte des Portugais*, 3 vols. (Bordeaux, 1608–1614), 2:87; Father Baltasar Barreira to the Father General, 3 January 1582, *MMA* 15:269.

44 Paulo de Novais to the King, 3 May 1582, *MMA* 4:342.

45 Rodrigues, "História da Residência," *MMA* 4:587.

46 Father Baltasar Barreira to Father Sebastião Morais, 31 January 1582, *MMA* 3:208.

47 Letter of Diogo da Costa, 4 June 1585, *MMA* 3:316; Pero Rodrigues, *MMA* 4:574.

48 Annual Letter of the Mission of Angola, 15 March 1890, *MMA* 3:482–483.

49 Du Jarric, *Histoire,* 2:102.

50 Section of a letter of Fernão Martins, 1591, *MMA* 3:433–434; "Desbarato dos Reis da Etiópia e Descobrimento da Islha de Luanda," 1591, *MMA* 4:534–540; "Memória intitulada O Livro Primeiro da Monarquia Angolana . . . e os fatos occiridos dos anos de 1580 até 1590," Instituto Histórico e Geografico Brasileiro, Rio de Janeiro, África/Angola Col., DL41, doc. 13, fol. 8.

51 Section of a letter on Angola and Congo, 1591, *MMA* 3:431–432.

52 Elias Alexandre da Silva Corrêa, *História de Angola,* ed. Manuel Múrias, 2 vols. ([1792] Lisbon: Editorial Ática, 1937), 1:211.

53 Father Baltasar Afonso to Father Miguel de Sousa, 4 July 1581, *MMA* 3:200.

54 Du Jarric, *Histoire,* 2:89.

55 Cavazzi, *Istorica Descrizione,* book 2, para. 132.

56 Brother António Mendes to the Father General, 9 May 1563, *MMA* 2:509.

57 Remembrances of Jerónimo Castanho to the King, 5 September 1599, *MMA* 4:606–607; Letter of Donation of Paulo Dias de Novais to the Fathers of the Company, 26 August 1581, *MMA* 15:265–267, 279.

58 Letter of Seismaria of Paulo Dias de Novais, 2 April 1587, *MMA* 4:461–464.

59 Rodrigues, "História da Residência," *MMA* 4:554.

60 Rodrigues, "História da Residência," *MMA* 4:578.

61 Garcia Simões to the Provincial, 20 October 1575, *MMA* 3:138–141.

62 Father Baltasar Barreira to the Father General, 3 January 1582, *MMA* 15:270–272.

63 Rodrigues, "História da Residência," *MMA* 4:578–581.

64 Father Dioga da Costa to the Provincial of Portugal, 31 May 1586, *MMA* 3:332–333.

65 Father Baltasar Afonso to Father Miguel de Sousa, 4 July 1581, *MMA* 3:202–203, 206.

66 Father Baltasar Barreira to the Father General, 3 January 1582, *MMA* 15:276.

67 Du Jarric, *Histoire,* 2:90.

68 Ibid. In 1622, Njinga would challenge this custom when she went to Luanda to negotiate peace on behalf of her brother.

69 Paulo Dias de Novais to King, 3 July 1582, *MMA* 4:342.

70 Father Baltasar Barreira to the Provincial, 20 November 1583, *MMA* 3:258–259.

71 Father Baltasar Barreira to the Father General, 3 January 1582, *MMA* 15:270–274.

72 Father Baltasar Afonso to Father Miguel de Sousa, 4 July 1581, *MMA* 3:204–205.

73 Letter of Diogo da Costa, 31 May 1586, *MMA* 3:339.

74 Du Jarric, *Histoire,* 2:91–92, 99.

75 Letter of Father Diogo da Costa, 20 July 1585, *MMA* 3:319–320.

76 Father Diogo da Costa to the Provincial of Portugal, 31 May 1586, *MMA* 3:339.

77 Father Baltasar Barreira to the Father General, 3 January 1582, *MMA* 15:274.

78 Father Baltasar Barreira to the General of the Company; see also du Jarric, *Histoire*, 2:89.

79 Du Jarric, *Histoire*, 2:89.

80 Cavazzi, MSS Araldi, book 2, pp. 9–10, 15, 18; "Estado Religioso e Politico de Angola" (1588), *MMA* 3:376.

81 Letter of Father Baltasar Barreira, 14 May 1586, *MMA* 3:329–331. Descriptions of the appearance of spectral beings during major battles occur often in Portuguese religious and military descriptions of the time. See, for example, John Thornton, *The Kongolese Saint Anthony: Donna Beatriz Kimpa Vita and the Antonian Movement, 1684–1706* (Cambridge University Press, 1998), 32–35.

82 Father Diogo da Costa to the Provincial, 31 May 1586, *MMA* 3:332–333.

83 Cavazzi, *Istorica Descrizione*, book 2, para. 132.

84 Pero Rodrigues (1580), *MMA* 4:66. See also Heywood and Thornton, *Central Africans*, 86–87.

85 Father Baltasar Afonso to Father Miguel de Sousa, 4 July 1581, *MMA* 3:202–203.

86 "Estado Religioso e Politico de Angola" (1588), *MMA* 3:376. Kafuxi ka Mbari lived in the region of Kisama, which later became a magnet for runaway Mbundu freemen and slaves. See Beatrix Heintze, "Historical Notes on the Kisama of Angola," *JAH* 13 (1972), 407–418.

87 "Estado Religioso e Politico de Angola" (1588), *MMA* 3:376.

88 Brother António Mendes to the Father General, 9 May 1563, *MMA* 2:509.

89 Father Diogo da Costa to the Provincial of Portugal, 31 May 1586, *MMA* 3:333.

90 Cavazzi, MSS Araldi, book 2, pp. 7–8.

91 Gaeta, *La Maravigliosa Conversione*, 171–172.

2. Crisis and the Rise of Njinga

1 Pero Rodrigues, "História da Residência dos Padres da Companhia de Jesus em Angola, e Cousas Tocantes ao Reino e Conquista," 1 May 1594, *MMA* 4:569–571.

2 Garcia Mendes Castello Branco, "Relação," *MMA* 6:465; Andrew Battel, *The Strange Adventures of Andrew Battell, in Angola and the Adjoining Regions*, ed. E. G. Ravenstein (London: Hakluyt Society, 1901), 27.

3 Pierre du Jarric, *Histoire des choses plus memorables advenues tant ez Indes Orientales, que autres païs de la descouuerte des Portugais*, 3 vols. (Bordeaux, 1608–1614), 2:103.

4 See David Birmingham, *Trade and Conflict in Angola: The Mbundu and Their Neighbours under the Influence of the Portuguese, 1483–1790* (Oxford: Clarendon Press, 1966), 57–63.

5 "Missão dos Jesuitas em Angola" (1602–1603), *MMA* 5:53–55, 82–83; António de Oliveira de Cadornega, *História Geral das Guerras Angolanas*, ed. José Delgado, 3 vols. (1940–1942; repr. Lisbon: Agência-Geral do Ultramar, 1972), 1:217–218.

6 "Missão dos Jesuitas em Angola" (1602–1603), *MMA* 5:51.

7 Ibid., *MMA* 5:54. See also Linda M. Heywood and John K. Thornton, *Central Africans, Atlantic Creoles, and the Foundation of the Americas, 1585–1660* (New York: Cambridge University Press, 2007), 91–92.

8   Battel, *Strange Adventures*, 26.

9   For the most recent discussion of the Imbangala, see Heywood and Thornton, *Central Africans*, 93–95.

10 Elias Alexandre da Silva Corrêa, *História de Angola*, ed. Manuel Múrias, 2 vols. ([1792] Lisbon: Editorial Ática, 1937), 1:219.

11 Andre Velho da Fonseca to the King, 28 February 1612, *MMA* 6:64–70.

12 Letter of Bento Banha Cardoso, 28 June 1614, *MMA* 6:178.

13 Devassa de Bento Banha Cardoso, 21 August 1615, AHU, Cx. 1, doc. 40.

14 For the Portuguese slave trade during these years see Birmingham, *Trade and Conflict in Angola;* Heywood and Thornton, *Central Africans.*

15 Du Jarric, *Histoire*, 2:79–80; [Barreira], Information on the Slaves of Angola (1582–1583), *MMA* 3:228. Heywood and Thornton, *Central Africans*, 77–79, stated that *mubikas* could be sold but *kijikos* could not be. However, Baltasar Barreira (in "Information on the Slaves of Angola," 228–229), states that both *mubikas* and *kijikos* were sold and exchanged. Giovanni Antonio Cavazzi da Montecuccolo, *Istorica Descrizione de' tre' regni Congo, Matamba et Angola* (Bologna: Giacomo Monti, 1687), book 1, para. 330, recalling the situation that existed in the 1650s to 1660s, noted that ordinarily, *kijikos* were not sold.

16 Father Francisco de Gouveia to the College of Arts, 19 May 1565, *MMA* 2:530.

17 [Barreira], Information on the Slaves of Angola (1582–1583), *MMA* 3:230.

18 Ibid., *MMA* 3:228.

19 Antonio da Gaeta, *La Maravigliosa Conversione alla Santa Fede di Cristo della Regina Singa*, ed. Francesco Maria Gioia (Naples, 1669), 169.

20 "Mémorias de Jerónimo Castanho a El-Rei," 5 September 1599, *MMA* 4:606–607. See also Heywood and Thornton, *Central Africans.*

21 Letter of a Father to the Provincial of Portugal, 15 December 1587, *MMA* 3:354.

22 Graziano Saccardo, *Congo e Angola: Con la storia dell'antica missione dei cappuccini,* 3 vols. (Venice, 1982–1983), 1:102–103.

23 Heywood and Thornton, *Central Africans,* 95.

24 Ibid., 113.

25 "Memorias de Pedro Sardinha ao Conselho de Estado" (1612), *MMA* 5:103–106.

26 Andre Velho da Fonseca, 4 March 1612, "Devassa que tem direito sobre as Causas," AHU, Cx. 1, doc. 18.

27 "Processo de Justificação dos Actos de Bento Banha Cardoso," in Alfredo de Albuquerque Felner, *Angola: Apontamentos sobre a Ocupação e Inicio do Estabelecimento dos Portugueses no Congo, Angola e Benguela* (Coimbra: Imprensa da Universidade, 1933), 437–439.

28 Consulta 31 October 1616, AHU, Cx. 1, doc. 58.

29 Guerreiro, *Relação* (1602–1603), *MMA* 5:57.

30 Guerreiro, "Das Coisas da Missão de Angola" (1606–1607), *MMA* 5:238–240.

31 For a thorough discussion of these developments see Heywood and Thornton, *Central Africans,* 102–105. See also John K. Thornton, "Religious and Ceremonial Life in the Kongo and Mbundu Areas, 1500–1700," in Linda Heywood, ed., *Central Africans and Cultural Transformations in the American Diaspora* (Cambridge: Cambridge University Press, 2002), 71–90.

32 Du Jarric, *Histoire*, 2:103.

33 Missão dos Jesuitas em Angola (1602–1603), *MMA* 5:55–56; "Relaçion del Governador d'Angola sobre el Estado en que tem Aquella Conquista . . . ," 28 May 1603, *MMA* 5:60–62.

34 Saccardo, *Congo e Angola*, 1:168.

35 Regimento do Governador de Angola, 26 March 1607, *MMA* 5:269.

36 Regimento do Governador de Angola, 22 September 1611, *MMA* 6:26.

37 Andre Velho da Fonseca to the King, 28 February 1612, *MMA* 6:65.

38 Ibid., *MMA* 6:66; Andre Velho da Fonseca, 4 March 1612, "Devassa que tem direito sobre as Causas," AHU, Cx. 1, doc. 18.

39 Regimento do Governor de Angola, 3 September 1616, *MMA* 6:258–259.

40 Ibid.

41 "Catalogo dos Governadores do Reino de Angola" (1784), in *Collecção de Noticias para a Historia e Geografia das Nações Ultramarinas*, vol. 3, part 1 (Lisbon, Academia Real das Sciencias, 1825), 361–362; João Carlos Feo Cardoso de Castello Branco e Torres, *Memórias Contendo a Biographia do Vice Almirante Luiz da Motta Feo e Torres* (Paris: Fantin, 1825), 151–152.

42 Ibid.

43 Cavazzi, *Istorica Descrizione*, book 2, para. 134 [258].

44 Ibid., book 2, para. 23.

45 Cavazzi, MSS Araldi, book 2, p. 23.

46 Feo Cardoso, *Memórias*, 155.

47 Gaeta, *La Maravigliosa Conversione*.

48 Cavazzi, MSS Araldi, book 2, p. 23.

49 Saccardo, *Congo e Angola*, 1:169; Cavazzi, MSS Araldi, book 2, p. 15.

50 For Cavazzi's life and travels, see the introduction by Francisco Leite de Faria to the Portuguese translation of his book, *Descrição Histórica dos Três Reinos do Congo, Matamba e Angola*, trans. Graciano Maria [Saccardo] de Leguzzano, 2 vols. (Lisbon: Junta de Investigaçoes do Ultramar, 1965).

51 Feo Cardoso, *Memórias*, 156.

52 Luis Mendes de Vasconcelos to the Conde de Faro, 9 September 1617, *MMA* 6:286.

53 Ibid.

54 Cadornega, *História Geral*, 1:86; see also Heywood and Thornton, *Central Africans*, 117–118.

55 Cadornega, *História Geral*, 1:86.

56 "Informação de Manuel Vogado Sotomaior a Sua Majestade El-Rei" (c. 1620), *MMA* 15:476. See also the accounts of Bishop Manuel Baptista Soares, "Relata a elRei os excessos que presenciara no Governo de Angola," 7 September 1619, *MMA* 6:378–381; Manuel Severim da Faria, "História portugueza e de outras provincias do occidente desde o anno de 1610 até o de 1640," in Cadornega, *História Geral*, 1:88n1; and Fernão de Sousa, "Lembrança do estado em que achej a El Rey de Angola," ca. October 1624, *FHA* 1:195.

57 "Informação de Manuel Vogado Sotomaior a Sua Majestade El-Rei," *MMA* 15:476.

58 Saccardo, *Congo e Angola,* 1:170.

59 Letter of Baltasar Rebelo de Aragão (1618), *MMA* 6:334. Located in the province of Kwanza North.

60 Saccardo, *Congo e Angola,* 1:171.

61 Soares, "Relata a elRei," *MMA* 6:380; Cadornega, *História Geral,* 1: 94–95.

62 Feo Cardoso, *Memórias,* 157.

63 Cadornega, *História Geral,* 1:91–92.

64 Ibid., 1:94–95; see also Beatrix Heintze, *Angola nos Séculos XVI e XVII: Estudos sobre Fontes, Métodos e História* (Luanda, 2007), 286.

65 "História Política de Angola (1622–1623)," *MMA* 7:78; Cavazzi, MSS Araldi, book 2, p. 23; Cavazzi, *Istorica Descrizione,* book 5, para. 106; Cadornega, *História Geral,* 1:88–89n1, 90; Feo Cardoso, *Memórias,* 157; Saccardo, *Congo e Angola,* 1:171.

66 Cadornega, *História Geral,* 1:135.

67 Cavazzi, MSS Araldi, book 2, p. 23.

68 "Informação de Manuel Vogado Sotomaior a Sua Majestade El Rei" (ca. 1620), *MMA* 15:479.

69 Feo Cardoso, *Memórias,* 157.

70 It seems unlikely that Ngola Mbande would have agreed to make an annual payment of this magnitude to the Portuguese crown and accept Portuguese overlordship, as some later documents claimed. For that refusal see Cavazzi, MSS Araldi, book 2, p. 25; Feo Cardoso, *Memórias,* 159.

71 Felner, *Angola,* 209.

72 Cadornega, *História Geral,* 1:155n.

73 "Informação de Manuel Vogado Sotomaior a Sua Majestade El Rei" (ca. 1620), *MMA* 15:476. See also Saccardo, *Congo e Angola,* 1:171.

74 Gaeta, *La Maravigliosa Conversione,* 148; Bento Banha Cardoso to the King, 2 February 1626, *MMA* 7:414.

75 See David Birmingham, "Carnival at Luanda," *JAH* 29 (1988): 96. For the original description see "Relação das Festas que a Residença de Angolla fez na Beatifição do Beato Padre Francisco de Xavier da Companhia de Jesus," in Felner, *Angola,* 531–541.

76 Sottomaior, "Papel sobre as cousas de Angola" (ca. 1620), *MMA* 15:476; see also Heywood and Thornton, *Central Africans,* 159–160.

77 "Catalogo dos Governadores," 364; Feo Cardoso, *Memórias,* 158; Cavazzi, MSS Araldi, book 2, pp. 24, 25.

78 Cavazzi, MSS Araldi, book 2, p. 24.

79 Ibid.; Cavazzi, *Descrição Histórica,* vol. 2, book 5, para. 106.

80 Cavazzi, MSS Araldi, book 2, p. 25; "Catalogo dos Governadores," 364.

81 "Catalogo dos Governadores," 364–365; Feo Cardoso, *Memórias,* 158; Cavazzi, Araldi MSS, book 2, p. 25; "Relação do Padre Mateus Cardoso" (1623), *MMA* 7:177.

82 Cavazzi, MSS Araldi, book 2, p. 25; Feo Cardoso, *Memórias,* 159.

83 Cavazzi, MSS Araldi, book 2, p. 24; Feo Cardoso, *Memórias*, 159.

84 The church was called Igreja Matriz.

85 Cadornega, *História Geral*, 1:156n.

86 Cavazzi, MSS Araldi, book 2, pp. 28, 29.

87 "História Política de Angola" (1622–1623), *MMA* 7:79.

88 "Carta do Colector Apostólico ao Cardeal Barbnerini," 30 December 1623, *MMA* 7:172–173; Cavazzi, *Descrição Histórica*, vol. 5, book 5, para. 106.

89 Correia de Sousa himself described this campaign in a report he sent to Lisbon: "Carta de Correia de Sousa ao Marques de Frecilha," 3 June 1622, *MMA* 7:17–24. See also Heywood and Thornton, *Central Africans*, 136–137; Saccardo, *Congo e Angola*, 1:176.

90 Heintze, *Angola nos Séculos XVI e XVII*, 308.

91 Ibid., 310.

92 Silva Corrêa, *História de Angola*, 1:219.

93 Cavazzi, MSS Araldi, book 2, p. 32.

94 Ibid.; Cadornega, *História Geral*, 1:161.

3. A Defiant Queen

1 Cavazzi, MSS Araldi, book 2, p. 20; Giovanni Antonio Cavazzi da Montecuccolo, *Istorica Descrizione de' tre' regni Congo, Matamba et Angola* (Bologna: Giacomo Monti, 1687), book 5, para. 106; Antonio da Gaeta, *La Maravigliosa Conversione alla Santa Fede di Cristo della Regina Singa*, ed. Francesco Maria Gioia (Naples, 1669), 146.

2 Cavazzi, *Istorica Descrizione*, book 5, para. 106.

3 Ibid.

4 Interview, *Rei Ginga* (King of the Gingas), Royal Court, Marimba, Angola, July 22, 2011. After the 1670s, the Portuguese addressed the ruler of Ndongo-Matamba as Rei Jinga, or King Jinga. By the nineteenth century, the name "Njinga" became associated with people living in the area of Matamba (today the province of Malange) where Njinga's last capital, Marimba, was located. The title is still in use today. In 2011 I visited Marimba to locate Njinga's burial site and interviewed Rei Jinga, who was called King Cabombo.

5 Cavazzi, MSS Araldi, book 1, p. 21.

6 Gaeta, *Maravigliosa Conversione.*

7 Cavazzi, MSS Araldi, book 2, pp. 94–95.

8 Cavazzi, MSS Araldi, book 2, pp. 82–85.

9 Cavazzi, *Istorica Descrizione*, book 1, para. 314.

10 António de Oliveira de Cadornega, *História Geral das Guerras Angolanas*, ed. José Delgado, 3 vols. (1940–1942; repr. Lisbon: Agência-Geral do Ultramar, 1972), 1:58. Although the editor of the *História Geral* and historians such as Beatrix Heintze have discounted all of Cadornega's references to Njinga during the years before she became queen, arguing that Cadornega mixed up the dates regarding Njinga, I disagree with this conclusion. I contend that although Cadornega did indeed confuse his dates, throughout the text

he referred to Njinga as Queen Njinga because that was her status when he arrived in Angola in 1639. I believe that Cadornega was right when he identified Njinga as being a participant in the wars before 1624, since he consulted now-lost field notes describing the situation on the ground that commanders and governors left at the fort in Massangano. It seems likely that his many references to Njinga mobilizing the population to fight against the Portuguese in the years before she became queen were based on descriptions of the battles from these accounts, and Cadornega would not have inserted Njinga into the action without substantiation. See, for example, Cadornega's reference to the campaigns of João Mendes de Vasconcelos, in which he noted that he had consulted "some service papers of the ancient conquistadores" who had accompanied Mendes de Vasconcelos and had actually spoken to some of the participants: Cadornega, *História Geral*, 1:95.

11 Cadornega, *História Geral*, 1:59.

12 Ibid., 1:61.

13 Cavazzi, *Istorica Descrizione*, book 5, para. 106.

14 Cadornega, *História Geral*, 1:94.

15 Cavazzi, *Istorica Descrizione*, book 5, para. 106.

16 Cadornega, *História Geral*, 1:53–54.

17 Ibid. Cadornega refers to the governor's letter as containing *palavaras imperiosas* (imperious words), intended to indicate that he was the superior and Ngola Mbande was inferior to him. Cadornega had access to documents generated at the time, including the governor's outgoing correspondence to Ngola Mbande. Many of these documents are no longer extant.

18 At least the Portuguese believed this; see Cadornega, *História Geral*, 1:53–54.

19 Cavazzi, *Istorica Descrizione*, book 5, para. 106.

20 Gaeta, *Maravigliosa Conversione*, 174.

21 Cavazzi, MSS Araldi, book 2, pp. 24–25; Cavazzi, *Istorica Descrizione*, book 5, para. 106.

22 Cavazzi, MSS Araldi, book 2, p. 25; Cavazzi, *Istorica Descrizione*, book 5, para. 106.

23 Cavazzi, *Istorica Descrizione*, book 5, para. 106.

24 Cavazzi, MSS Araldi, book 2, p. 25; Cavazzi, *Istorica Descrizione*, book 5, para. 106.

25 "História das relacões entre a Angola portuguesa e o Ndongo 1617–Septembro de 1625," *FHA* 1:199.

26 Cadornega, *História Geral*, 1:126.

27 Cavazzi, MSS Araldi, book 2, p. 33; "Carta de Fernão de Sousa ao Governo," 15 August 1624, *FHA* 2:85.

28 Cavazzi, MSS Araldi, book 2, p. 33.

29 For a discussion of how Njinga handled challenges to her eligibility to the throne of Ndongo see John K. Thornton, "Legitimacy and Political Power: Queen Njinga, 1624–1663," *JAH* 32 (1991): 25–40; see also Joseph C. Miller, "Nzinga of Matamba in a New Perspective," *JAH* 16 (1975), 201–216; Adriano Parreira, *Economia e Sociedade em Angola na época da Rainha Jinga, século XVII* (Lisbon: Editorial Estampa, 1990), 177–183.

30 Cadornega, *História Geral*, 1:142.

31 Cavazzi, *Istorica Descrizione,* book 5, para. 107; "História das relacões entre a Angola portuguesa e o Ndongo 1617–Septembro de 1625," *FHA* 1:199.

32 "Carta de Fernão de Sousa ao Governo," 15 August 1624, *FHA* 2:85–86.

33 Ibid.

34 Ibid.

35 "O Extenso Relatório do Governador a Seus Filhos" (s.d., 1625–1630), *FHA* 1:223.

36 "Carta de Fernão de Sousa sobre os tributos de vassalagem dos sobas," 8 July 1626, *FHA* 1:363.

37 Ibid., 1:363–364.

38 Ibid., 1:364.

39 "Governador a Seus Filhos," *FHA* 1:227.

40 "Carta de Fernão de Sousa ao Governo," 19 March 1625, *FHA* 2:129; "Governador a Seus Filhos," *FHA* 1:227.

41 "Carta de Fernão de Sousa a El-Rei," 22 August 1625, *MMA* 7:366.

42 "Carta de Fernão de Sousa ao Governo," 2 August 1627, *FHA* 2:183.

43 "Carta de Fernão de Sousa sobre os tributos de vassalagem dos sobas," 8 July 1626, *FHA* 1:364.

44 "Carta de Fernão de Sousa a El-Rei," 22 August 1625, *MMA* 7:365–368.

45 Cadornega, *História Geral,* 1:141–142.

46 Ibid., 1:116–117, 146.

47 "Carta de Fernão de Sousa ao Governo" (s.d., 9 July 1626), *FHA* 2:166–167.

48 "Governador a Seus Filhos," *FHA* 1:229–230.

49 "A ilegitimidade do novo rei do Ndongo, Angola Aire" (s.d., between 20 July and 14 September 1629), *FHA* 1:209. For the background of the Hari lineage, see Cadornega, *História Geral,* 1:141–142.

50 "Governador a Seus Filhos," *FHA* 1:229–230.

51 Ibid., 1:240.

52 "Carta de Fernão de Sousa a El-Rei," 21 February 1626, *MMA* 7:417–420; see Beatriz Heintze, *Angola nos Séculos XVI e XVII: Estudos sobre Fontes, Métodos e História* (Luanda, 2007), 321–329, for the most recent reconstruction of the sequence of these events.

53 "Governador a Seus Filhos," *FHA* 1:241.

54 "Carta de Fernão de Sousa a El-Rei," 21 February 1626, *MMA* 7:417. This issue has generated extensive discussion in the secondary literature. See, for example, Thornton, "Legitimacy and Political Power"; Miller, "Nzinga of Matamba in a New Perspective."

55 "Carta de Fernão de Sousa a El-Rei," 7 March 1626, *MMA* 7:426.

56 Heintze, *Angola nos Séculos XVI e XVII,* 328.

57 Ibid., 331.

58 "Governador a Seus Filhos," *FHA* 1:242–243.

59 Ibid.; Heintze, *Angola nos Séculos XVI e XVII,* 340–341.

60 "Governador a Seus Filhos," *FHA* 1:242–243.

61 Ibid.

62 Ibid.

63 Queen Njinga to Bento Banha Cardoso, 3 March 1626 [misdated 1625], as quoted in "Governador a Seus Filhos," *FHA* 1:244–245. Portugal was under the Spanish crown.

64 Ibid., 1:245.

65 "Governador a Seus Filhos," *FHA* 1:245.

66 Ibid., 1:261.

67 For details see Cavazzi, MSS Araldi, book 2, p. 26; João Carlos Feo Cardoso de Castello Branco e Torres, *Memórias Contendo a Biographia do Vice Almirante Luiz da Motta Feo e Torres* (Paris: Fantin, 1825), 160.

68 Cavazzi, MSS Araldi, book 2, p. 100.

69 Ibid., book 2, p. 27.

70 Cavazzi, *Istorica Descrizione,* book 5, para. 106.

71 Ibid.

72 Ibid., para. 108.

73 "Carta de Fernão de Sousa a El-Rei," 15 August 1624, *MMA* 7:249.

74 "Carta do Padre Péro de Novais aos Govenadores de Portugal," 11 June 1624, *MMA* 7:240–242. See also *MMA* 7:491.

75 "Carta do Governador de Angola a El-Rei," 16 January 1628, *MMA* 7:530–531; Graziano Saccardo, *Congo e Angola: Con la storia dell'antica missione dei cappuccini,* 3 vols. (Venice, 1982–1983), 1:170–171.

76 "Carta de Fernão de Sousa ao Governo," 10 December 1624, *FHA* 2:117.

77 Cadornega, *História Geral,* 1:137–138; Heintze, *Angola nos Séculos XVI e XVII,* 341.

78 "Carta de Fernão de Sousa A El-Rei," 22 August 1625, *MMA* 7:361, 365.

79 "Notícias da África Ocidental (1624–1625)," *MMA* 7:300.

80 "Governador a Seus Filhos," *FHA* 1:242; "Carta de Fernão de Sousa a El-Rei," 21 February 1626, *MMA* 7:419.

81 "Governador a Seus Filhos," *FHA* 1:242; "Carta de Fernão de Sousa a El-Rei," 21 February 1626, *MMA* 7:418–419.

82 "Governador a Seus Filhos," *FHA* 1:245–247.

83 Ibid., 1:247–248; see also Heintze, *Angola nos Séculos XVI e XVII,* 342.

84 "Governador a Seus Filhos," *FHA* 1:251.

85 "Carta de Fernão de Sousa ao Governo" (s.d., 9 July 1626), *FHA* 2:167.

86 "Governador a Seus Filhos," *FHA* 1:248.

87 "Carta de Fernão de Sousa ao Governo" (s.d., 9 July 1626), *FHA* 2:167.

88 Ibid.; "Governador a Seus Filhos," *FHA* 1:252.

89 "Governador a Seus Filhos," *FHA* 1:252.

90 Cadornega, *História Geral,* 1:132–134.

91 Ibid., 1:135–136.

92 Ibid., 1:136–139; "Governador a Seus Filhos," *FHA* 1:252.

93 "Governador a Seus Filhos," *FHA* 1:252.

94 Ibid.

95 Cadornega, *História Geral,* 1:138–139; see also "Governador a Seus Filhos," *FHA* 1:254; "Carta de Fernão de Sousa ao Governo" (s.d. 9 July 1626), *FHA* 2:167.

96 Cadornega, *História Geral,* 1:139–140; see also "Governador a Seus Filhos," *FHA* 1:254; "Carta de Fernão de Sousa ao Governo" (s.d. 9 July 1626), *FHA* 2:167.

97 "Governador a Seus Filhos," *FHA* 1:254; "Carta de Fernão de Sousa ao Governo" (s.d. 9 July 1626), *FHA* 2:167.

98 Cavazzi, MSS Araldi, book 2, p. 38; Heintze, *Angola nos Séculos XVI e XVII,* 344, 348.

4. Treacherous Politics

1 "O Extenso Relatório do Governador a Seus Filhos" (s.d., 1625–1630), *FHA* 1:254.

2 For Ngola Hari's lineage, see Fernando Campos, "Conflitos na Dinastia Guterres através da sua Cronologia," *África* (São Paulo) 27–28 (2006–2007): 23–43, at 27–28.

3 "Governador a Seus Filhos," *FHA* 1:256–257.

4 Ibid., 1:254. For insight into the debates about Njinga's legitimacy, see John K. Thornton, "Legitimacy and Political Power: Queen Njinga, 1624–1663," *JAH* 32 (1991): 25–40; Joseph C. Miller, "Nzinga of Matamba in a New Perspective," *JAH* 16 (1975), 201–216.

5 "Governador a Seus Filhos," *FHA* 1:255–257. For the terms imposed on Hari a Kiluanje, see "Regimento de Fernão de Sousa a Bento Banha Cardoso" (s.d., ca. January 1626), *FHA* 1:204–205.

6 "Governador a Seus Filhos," *FHA* 1:256.

7 Graziano Saccardo, *Congo e Angola: Con la storia dell'antica missione dei cappuccini,* 3 vols. (Venice, 1982–1983), 1:220.

8 António de Oliveira de Cadornega, *História Geral das Guerras Angolanas,* ed. José Delgado, 3 vols. (1940–1942; repr. Lisbon: Agência-Geral do Ultramar, 1972), 1:158.

9 "Governador a Seus Filhos," *FHA* 1:256; Cadornega, *História Geral,* 1:139.

10 "Governador a Seus Filhos," *FHA* 1:256, 258.

11 Ibid., 1:260.

12 Ibid., 1:256.

13 Ibid., 1:256–257.

14 Ibid., 1:258.

15 Ibid., 1:258; Beatrix Heintze, *Angola nos Séculos XVI e XVII: Estudos sobre Fontes, Métodos e História* (Luanda, 2007), 352–353.

16 "Fernão de Sousa ao Governo," 2 August 1627, *FHA* 2:183–184.

17 Ibid., 2:183–185; Relação dos successos de Angola [1]623 a [1]624, Biblioteca Nacional de Rio de Janeiro (BNRJ), Seccão Manuscrito, I-33-33-11, Codice Manuel Severim de Faria, fols. 1–10.

18 "Governador a Seus Filhos," *FHA* 1:258; "Relação do Governo Fernão de Sousa ao Secretario de Estado," 30 January 1627, *MMA* 7:497–489.

19 "Governador a Seus Filhos," *FHA* 1:282; Saccardo, *Congo e Angola,* 1:224.

20 "Estado Religioso do Reino de Dongo," 27 March 1627, *MMA* 7:505.

21 "Governador a Seus Filhos," *FHA* 1:282–288.

22 Ibid., 1:284.

23 Ibid., 1:282–283.

24 Ibid., 1:26, 282–285.

25 Cadornega, *História Geral,* 1:141–142.

26 "Governador a Seus Filhos," *FHA* 1:287.

27 Ibid., 1:284.

28 Ibid., 1:290, 298.

29 Ibid., 1:298.

30 Ibid.

31 Ibid., 1:293–294.

32 Ibid., 1:294.

33 Ibid.

34 Ibid.

35 Ibid., 1:298.

36 Ibid., 1:299–300.

37 Ibid., 1:298–299, 314

38 Ibid., 1:300.

39 Ibid., 1:297.

40 Ibid., 1:297–299.

41 Ibid., 1:300.

42 Ibid., 1:301.

43 "Carta de Fernão de Sousa ao Governo," 10 July 1628, *FHA* 2:198.

44 See, for example, Merry Wiesner-Hanks, *Women and Gender in Early Modern Europe,* 3rd ed. (New York: Cambridge University Press, 2008); Sharon L. Jansen, *Debating Women, Politics, and Power in Early Modern Europe* (New York: Palgrave Macmillan, 2008).

45 The exception to the rule in Europe was found not in de Sousa's Catholic Iberian Europe but in post-Reformation England, with the unmatched Queen Elizabeth I, who was a half century into her seventy-year reign (1533–1603) in the year of Njinga's birth. See Christopher Haigh, *Elizabeth 1,* 2nd ed. (New York: Longman, 1998).

46 "Governador a Seus Filhos," *FHA* 1:316.

47 Ibid., 1:325, 328.

48 Ibid., 1:328–329.

49 Ibid., 1:316.

50 Ibid.

51 Ibid., 1:314–315.

52 "Carta de Fernão de Sousa ao Governo," 10 July 1628, *FHA* 2:198–199; "Carta de Fernão de Sousa ao Governo não enviado" (s.d., end of July or beginning of August 1628), *FHA* 2:201.

53 "Carta de Fernão de Sousa ao Governo," 10 July 1628, *FHA* 2:197–199.

54 Ibid.

55 Ibid., 2:198–199.

56 Ibid.

57 Ibid., 2:197–199.

58 "Governador a Seus Filhos," *FHA* 1:306.

59 Ibid, 1:305.

60 "Carta de Fernão de Sousa ao Governo," 10 July 1628, *FHA* 2:197–199.

61 "Carta de Fernão de Sousa ao Governo não enviado" (s.d., end of July or beginning of August 1628), *FHA* 2:200.

62 "Governador a Seus Filhos," *FHA* 1:303–305.

63 Ibid., 1:303, 305.

64 Ibid., 1:316.

65 Ibid., 1:322.

66 Ibid., 1:330.

67 "Queixa dos *Tendalas* e *Macotas* de Ndongo," 28 February 1629, *FHA* 2:286; "Carta de Fernão de Sousa a Paio de Araújo de Azevedo," 20 March 1629, *FHA* 2:287–288.

68 "Governador a Seus Filhos," *FHA* 1:326.

69 Ibid., 1:328–329.

70 Ibid., 1:328–329.

71 Ibid., 1:327–328.

72 Ibid., 1:331, 334.

73 Ibid., 1:334.

74 Cadornega, *História Geral,* 1:148.

75 "Governador a Seus Filhos," *FHA*:331–332; Cadornega, *História Geral,* 1:149.

76 "Governador a Seus Filhos," *FHA* 1:332; João Carlos Feo Cardoso de Castello Branco e Torres, *Memórias Contendo a Biographia do Vice Almirante Luiz da Motta Feo e Torres* (Paris: Fantin, 1825), 166.

77 "Governador a Seus Filhos," *FHA* 1:333.

78 Ibid., 1:332.

79 Ibid., 1:333–334.

80 Ibid., 1:335.

81 Ibid., 1:335; Cadornega, *História Geral,* 1:150–152.

82 "Governador a Seus Filhos," *FHA* 1:334–335.

83 "A Ilegitimidade do Novo Rei do Ndongo, Angola Aire" (s.d., between 20 July and 14 September 1629), *FHA* 1:209–210.

84 "Governador a Seus Filhos," *FHA* 1:336.

85 Ibid.

86 Ibid.; "Catalogo dos Governadores do Reino de Angola" (1784), *Collecção de Noticias para a Historia e Geografia das Nações Ultramarinas,* vol. 3, part 1 (Lisbon, Academia Real das Sciencias, 1825), 369–370; Feo Cardoso, *Memórias,* 166.

87 "Governador a Seus Filhos," *FHA* 1:346.

88 Ibid., 1:345.

89 Ibid.

90 Ibid., 1:345–346.

91 Ibid., 1:346.

92 Ibid., 1:339, 346.

93 Ibid., 1:346–347.

5. Warfare and Diplomacy

1 António de Oliveira de Cadornega, *História Geral das Guerras Angolanas,* ed. José Delgado, 3 vols. (1940–1942; repr. Lisbon: Agência-Geral do Ultramar, 1972), 1:166n; Ralph Delgado, *História de Angola,* 2nd ed. (Banco de Angola, n.d.), 140.

2 João Carlos Feo Cardoso de Castello Branco e Torres, *Memórias Contendo a Biographia do Vice Almirante Luiz da Motta Feo e Torres* (Paris: Fantin, 1825), 69; "Carta de Fernão de Sousa ao Governo," 8 January 1630, *FHA* 2:244–245.

3 "O Extenso Relatório do Governador a Seus Filhos" (s.d., 1625–1630), *FHA* 1:326–327.

4 "Carta e Verdadeira Relação do Padre Pedro Tavares . . . as suas Missões dos Reinos de Angola e de Congo," Biblioteca Pública de Évora, Évora, Portugal, Codex CXVI/2–4, fols. 21, 23.

5 "Relação do Governador Fernão de Sousa," 1624–1630, *MMA* 7:653.

6 "Carta de Fernão de Sousa ao Governo," 8 January 1630, *FHA* 2:244; "Relação de Fernão de Sousa," 23 February 1632, *MMA* 8:138.

7 "Carta de Fernão de Sousa ao Governo," 8 January 1630, *FHA* 2:244–245; "Relação de Fernão de Sousa," 23 February 1632, *MMA* 8:138.

8 Cadornega, *História Geral,* 1:166n; "Carta de Fernão de Sousa ao Governo," 8 January 1630, *FHA* 2:244; "Relação de Fernão de Sousa," 23 February 1632, *MMA* 8:138.

9 "Carta de Fernão de Sousa ao Governo," 8 January 1630, *FHA* 2:244; "Relação de Fernão de Sousa," 23 February 1632, *MMA* 8:138.

10 For more on human sacrifice and Mbundu death rituals, see "Carta do Padre Pedro Tavares ao Reitor do Colégio de Luanda," 14 October 1631, *MMA* 8:71–72.

11 Giovanni Antonio Cavazzi da Montecuccolo, *Istorica Descrizione de' tre' regni Congo, Matamba et Angola* (Bologna: Giacomo Monti, 1687), book 5, para. 107.

12 Cavazzi, MSS Araldi, book 2, p. 95.

13 For the various ideas that have been posited for the origin of the Imbangalas, see Joseph C. Miller, *Kings and Kinsmen: Early Mbundu States in Angola* (Oxford: Clarendon Press, 1976). See also Paulo Jorge de Sousa Pinto, "En Tourno de um Problema da Identidade: Os 'Jaga' na História do Congo e Angola," *Mare Liberum* 18–19 (1999–2000): 193–246.

14 See Cavazzi, MSS Araldi, book 2, pp. 1–40.

15 Ibid., book 1, pp. 15–25.

16 Ibid., book 1, pp. 26–30.

17 Ibid., book 1, p. 4.

18 Cavazzi, who provides the full story of Tembo a Ndumbo, may have embellished the story for his seventeenth-century readers.

19 Cavazzi, MSS Araldi, book 1, p. 23.

20 Ibid., book 1, pp. 37–40.

21 Ibid., book 1, p. 23.

22 For a discussion of the lineage principle and the place of the Imbangala in central African politics, see Miller, *Kings and Kinsmen*, 144–150, 162–164, 234–235.

23 Cavazzi, MSS Araldi, book 2, pp. 35–39.

24 Ibid., book 2, pp. 35–39.

25 Antonio Franco, *Synopsis Annalium Societatis Jesu in Lusitania* (Augsburg: Vieth, 1726), doc. 1632, para. 7 [p. 260].

26 Cavazzi, MSS Araldi, book 2, p. 37.

27 Ibid., book 2, pp. 42–43. See also Cadornega, *História Geral*, 1:194.

28 Cavazzi, MSS Araldi, book 2, pp. 42–43; Cadornega, *História Geral*, 1:414.

29 Cavazzi, MSS Araldi, book 2, p. 196. In Kimbundu, *kalunga* means "sea" or "death."

30 Cavazzi, MSS Araldi, book 2, p. 3.

31 Ibid., book 2, pp. 42–43, 103; Cadornega, *História Geral*, 1:405.

32 Cadornega, *História Geral*, 1:153.

33 "Carta do Padre Gonçalo de Sousa en Nome da Camara de Luanda," 6 July 1633, *MMA* 8:242–243.

34 "Relação de Fernão de Sousa a El-Rei," 2 March 1632, *MMA* 8:161–162.

35 "Carta do Padre Gonçalo de Sousa en Nome da Camara de Luanda," 6 July 1633, *MMA* 8:242–243.

36 Franco, *Synopsis Annalium*, doc. 1632, para. 7 [p. 260]; "Carta de Fernão de Sousa a El-Rei," 31 March 1634, *MMA* 8:261.

37 Cadornega, *História Geral*, 1:415.

38 "Carta de Fernão de Sousa a El-Rei," 31 March, 1634, *MMA* 8:261.

39 Cavazzi, *Istorica Descrizione*, book 5, para. 112.

40 Cadornega, *História Geral*, 1:193–194.

41 Franco, *Synopsis Annalium*, doc. 1637, para. 19 [p. 273].

42 Cadornega, *História Geral*, 1:209–210.

43 Ibid., 1:209–210.

44 Ibid., 1:210.

45 Cavazzi, *Istorica Descrizione*, book 5, para. 113; Cavazzi, MSS Araldi, book 2, pp. 44–45.

46 Cavazzi, *Istorica Descrizione*, book 5, para. 113; Cavazzi, MSS Araldi, book 2, pp. 44–45.

47 Cadornega, *História Geral*, 1:222–224.

48 Cavazzi, MSS Araldi, book 2, pp. 44–45; Cavazzi, *Istorica Descrizione,* book 5, para. 113.

49 For details of the Dutch conquest, see Linda M. Heywood and John K. Thornton, *Central Africans, Atlantic Creoles, and the Foundation of the Americas, 1585–1660* (Cambridge: Cambridge University Press, 2007), 145–152.

50 Cavazzi, MSS Araldi, book 2, p. 53.

51 Feo Cardoso, *Memórias,* 175.

52 Cadornega, *História Geral,* 1:247–248.

53 Louis Jadin, *L'Ancien Congo et l'Angola, 1639–1655: D'Après les Archives Romaines, Portugaises, Néerlandaises et Espagnoles,* 3 vols. (Brussels: Institut Historique Belge de Rome, 1975), 1:158. This book provides French translations of the original Dutch documents.

54 Jadin, *Ancien Congo,* 1:255.

55 For the central African dimension of the Thirty Years' War and for the kingdom of Kongo's initiatives for furthering commercial and political relations with the Dutch, see John Thornton and Andrea Mosterman, "A Re-Interpretation of the Kongo-Portuguese War of 1622 according to New Documentary Evidence," *JAH* 51 (2010): 241–242. For a more far-ranging analysis of this period, see John K. Thornton, "The Kingdom of Kongo and the Thirty Years' War," *Journal of World History* 27 (2016): 189–213.

56 "Pièces d'un dossier . . . Éstats-Généraux," 20 January 1649, in Jadin, *Ancien Congo,* 2:1102; Klaas Ratelband, *Os Holandeses no Brasil e na Costa Africana: Angola, Kongo e São Tomé, 1600–1650* (Lisbon: Vega, 2003), 161–162.

57 "Carta do Governador de Angola a el Rei de Portugal," 9 March 1643, *MMA* 9:28–31.

58 Cadornega, *História Geral,* 1:261, 286–287.

59 Jadin, *Ancien Congo,* 1:124; Cadornega, *História Geral,* 1:293; Cert. de Francisco de Fonseca Sarvaiva, 29 November 1642, MS 1505, Papeis sobre Angola, Biblioteca da Universidade da Coimbra (BUC), Coimbra, Portugal.

60 Cadornega, *História Geral,* 1:422–423.

61 Ibid., 1:290–294.

62 Cavazzi, *Istorica Descrizione,* book 5, para. 115.

63 Jadin, *Ancien Congo,* 1:124.

64 Feo Cardoso, *Memórias,* 174; "Catalogo dos Governadores do Reino de Angola" (1784), in *Collecção de Noticias para a Historia e Geografia das Nações Ultramarinas,* vol. 3, part 1 (Lisbon, Academia Real das Sciencias, 1825), 374; "Sucessos do Arraial do Bengo entre Portugueses e Holandes," 17 May 1643, *MMA* 9:46–54.

65 Jadin, *Ancien Congo,* 1:416–417.

66 Cadornega, *História Geral,* 1:393–394.

67 Although we do not have direct evidence of Njinga's view, the Portuguese did believe this, according to Cadornega, *História Geral,* 1:394.

68 Cadornega, *Historia Geral,* 1:326.

69 Ibid., 1:326–328. For Garcia's desperate attempt to gain Dutch support to move against Njinga, see "Carta de Sousa Coutinho a El-Rei," 6 September 1643, *MMA* 9:64.

70 Cadornega, *História Geral,* 1:327–328.

71 "Carta de Sousa Coutinho a el Rei," 6 June 1643, *MMA* 9:64; "Carta de Sousa Coutinho ao Conde da Vidigueira," 1 October 1643, *MMA* 9:81.

72 "Rapport de Pieter Moortamer au Conseil du Bresil," 14 October 1643, in Jadin, *Ancien Congo*, 1:346–347.

73 Ratelband, *Os Holandeses*, 253.

74 "Les XIX aux directeurs du district de la côte sud d'Africa," 30 November 1644, in Jadin, *Ancien Congo*, 1:597.

75 Cadornega, *História Geral*, 1:352, 404.

76 Ibid., 1:396.

77 Cavazzi, *Istorica Descrizione*, book 6, para. 32.

78 Cadornega, *História Geral*, 1:350–353; "Carta do Nuncio em Madrid á Propaganda Fide," 27 September 1645, *MMA* 9:380.

79 Cadornega, *História Geral*, 1:412–413.

80 Ibid., 1:412–414.

81 "Consulta do Conselho Ultramarino," 17 August 1644, *MMA* 9:133.

82 "Avis du Conseil d'Outre-mer sur le Rapport au Roi d'António de Abreu de Miranda," 23 July 1644, in Jadin, *Ancien Congo*, 1:556.

83 "Carta do Nuncio em Madrid a Propaganda Fide," 27 September 1645, *MMA* 9:380.

84 "Carta de Francisco de Sotomaior a El-Rei D. João IV," 4 December 1645, *MMA* 9:406–407; Cadornega, *História Geral*, 1:387.

85 "Carta de Francisco de Sotomaior a El-Rei D. João IV," 4 December 1645, *MMA* 9:402, 406, 407.

86 Cadornega, *História Geral*, 1:387–388.

87 Ibid., 1:387–389.

88 Ratelband, *Os Holandeses*, 275.

89 Cadornega, *História Geral*, 1:395.

90 Ibid., 1:395

91 Ibid., 1:394.

92 "Carta de Antonio Teles da Silva a El-Rei D. João IV," 18 December 1646, *MMA* 9:470–471.

93 Cadornega, *História Geral*, 1:394–395.

94 The descriptions of the sequence of the battle and other details all come from Cadornega, *História Geral*, 1:393–432. Cadornega participated in the battle.

95 Cadornega, *História Geral*, 1:412; "Carta de António Teles da Silva a El-Rei D. João IV," 18 December 1646, *MMA* 9:471.

96 Cadornega, *Historia Geral* 1:412–413, 418; "Informação do piloto Manuel Soares sobre do Reino de Angola," 1647, *MMA* 10:69.

97 Cadornega, *História Geral*, 1:413–415.

98 Ibid., 1:415–416.

99 Ibid., 1:421–422. As a sign of their indebtedness to the Imbangala soldiers, the Portuguese allowed them to strip the residences before the other soldiers. They wasted

no time in selling or exchanging the gold rings, silks, and other valuables to the Portuguese, since they did not use such "adornments and gaities." Cadornega, *História Geral,* 1:421.

100 Cadornega, *História Geral,* 1:418–419.

101 Ibid., 1:421–422.

102 Ibid., 1:490.

103 See the entries for 17, 24, and 27 May 1647, in "Extract uyt het register der resolutien gehouden in Angola," MS 5759, West–Indische Compagnie Archiven (West India Company Archives), Nationaal Archief, The Hague; Ouman and Lems to Queen Ana Njinga, 10 June 1647, ibid.; as excerpted by Ratelband, *Os Holandeses,* 302–303, 334–335. I have consulted the original Dutch as well.

104 Ibid.

105 "Les XIX au Directeurs de Luanda," 1 August 1646, in Jadin, *Ancien Congo,* 2:827–828.

106 Jadin, *Ancien Congo,* 2:765.

107 Cadornega, *História Geral,* 1:507–508.

108 Ibid., 1:521–523.

109 Ratelband, *Os Holandeses,* 223–224, 331.

110 Cadornega, *História Geral,* 1:491–492.

111 Ibid., 1:491–492; Letter from São Paulo de Loanda, 16 December 1647, in Jadin, *Ancien Congo,* 2:938–940.

112 Cadornega, *História Geral,* 1:430, 434.

113 Letter from São Paulo de Loanda, 16 December 1647, in Jadin, *Ancien Congo,* 2:938–940; Cadornega, *História Geral,* 1:498–500. See also *Arquivos de Angola,* 2nd series 2 (1945), pp. 149–164, for testimony of Portuguese survivors; Ratelband, *Os Holandeses,* 304–306; *Extract van seeckeren Brief, gheschreven uyt Loando St. Paulo, in Angola, van weghen de groote Victorei die de Onse verkregen hebben tegen de Portugesen onder 't beleydt van onsen Directeur Ouman* (The Hague: Ludolph Breeckevelt, 1648).

114 Cadornega, *História Geral,* 1:444.

115 Ibid., 1:501.

116 Ibid., 1:501–505. The Portuguese had some farms in his lands, but Atungo had joined the Njinga-Dutch alliance and had fought alongside Njinga's captain-general Njinga a Mona.

117 Jadin, *Ancien Congo* 2:883n1, 1053.

118 Cadornega, *História Geral,* 3:89–91; 462. See also Jadin, *Ancien Congo* 2:883n1, 1053.

119 Ratelband, *Os Holandeses,* 318–321; Cadornega, *História Geral,* 1:521–528.

120 Ratelband, *Os Holandeses,* 330–335.

121 Ibid., 330–336; Jadin, *Ancien Congo,* 2:883n1.

122 Cavazzi, MSS Araldi, book 2, p. 76.

123 For details of the Wandu operations, see de Tereul, "Descripcion Narrativa," pp. 85–90, in MS 3533, Biblioteca Nacional de España, Madrid; Cavazzi, MSS Araldi, book 2,

pp. 78–80; J. B. Labat, *Relation Historique de l'Ethiopie Occidentale,* 4 vols. (Paris, 1732), 3:118–226; Cavazzi, *Istorica Descrizione,* book 4, paras. 21–22.

6. A Balancing Act

1   "Araldi Ms. Informazione sopra la Regina Jinga, Ambaca, 20/10/1650," Congo, Angola, Documenti, vol. 2 (1646–1653), p. 234, Saccardo Collection, Archivio Provinciale dei Cappuccini di Venezia, Venice, Italy (hereafter cited as Saccardo Collection). This report was written either by Rui Pegado da Ponte, an ambassador sent to Njinga by the Portuguese in 1648, or by Father Dionísio Coelho, a member of the 1640 Portuguese embassy to her court in Matamba who tried and failed to move her away from Imbangala practices and toward Christianity.

2   Giovanni Antonio Cavazzi da Montecuccolo, *Istorica Descrizione de' tre' regni Congo, Matamba et Angola* (Bologna: Giacomo Monti, 1687), book 6, para. 138.

3   Cavazzi, MSS Araldi, book 2, p. 2.

4   "Relação de uma Viagem a Angola," *MMA* 11:249.

5   António de Oliveira de Cadornega, *História Geral das Guerras Angolanas,* ed. José Delgado, 3 vols. (1940–1942; repr. Lisbon: Agência-Geral do Ultramar, 1972), 2:128–132.

6   Cavazzi, *Istorica Descrizione,* book 6, para. 32.

7   Antonio da Gaeta, *La Maravigliosa Conversione alla Santa Fede di Cristo della Regina Singa,* ed. Francesco Maria Gioia (Naples, 1669), 99. Njinga, in describing to Father Gaeta her long years of living as an Imbangala, claimed that the Portuguese "turned me out of my kingdoms of Dongo and Angola."

8   Cavazzi, *Istorica Descrizione,* book 6, paras. 31, 32.

9   Ibid., book 6, para. 93.

10   Cavazzi, MSS Araldi, book 2, pp. 151–152.

11   Graziano Saccardo, *Congo e Angola: Con la storia dell'antica missione dei cappuccini,* 3 vols. (Venice, 1982–1983), 2:507; Cavazzi, *Istorica Descrizione,* book 6, paras. 4, 33.

12   João Carlos Feo Cardoso de Castello Branco e Torres, *Memórias Contendo a Biographia do Vice Almirante Luiz da Motta Feo e Torres* (Paris: Fantin, 1825), 180–184; Saccardo, *Congo e Angola,* 2:75–79, 498.

13   Cadornega, *História Geral,* 2:128, 347, 355.

14   "Consulta do Conselho Ultramarino," *MMA* 11:498n30, 514–517; Luis Martins de Sousa Chichorro to João IV, *MMA* 11:509; Cadornega, *História Geral,* 2:103–126.

15   Cavazzi, *Istorica Descrizione,* book 6, paras. 31, 32; Cadornega, *História Geral,* 2:75–79; "Consulta do Conselho Ultramarino," *MMA* 11:497–498; AHU, Angola, Papeis Avulsos, 9 December 1656, Cx. 6, doc. 681; Saccardo, *Congo e Angola,* 1:516.

16   "Avventimenti della 'Morinda' o sobato Gunza-Moisa (1670)," Africa, Angola, Congo, Documenti, vol. 4 (1664–1674), p. 234, Saccardo Collection.

17   Treslado de Paz con Congo (transcript), "Auto de Devaça que mandou obrar o Cappitam-Mor Luis Lobo de Sequeira," 25 August 1664, AHU, Cx. 5, doc. 15. Although Njinga died a few months before this investigation, Portuguese officials suspected Spanish missionaries of promoting a pro-Spanish agenda and reported several rumors of Spanish–central African

alliance throughout the 1650s. Witness no. 4, Manuel Afonso Salgado, said that the Kongos were waiting for a Spanish fleet that was going to come and destroy the Portuguese. He wanted the help of the Dembos and also "Raynha ginga" (n.p.).

18 Cavazzi, MSS Araldi, book 3, pp. 30–32.

19 "Consulta do Conselho Ultramarino," 14 December 1652, *MMA* 11:245; Bento Teixeira de Saldanha to the King of Portugal, 13 July 1652, in Louis Jadin, *L'Ancien Congo et l'Angola, 1639–1655: D'Après les Archives Romaines, Portugaises, Néerlandaises et Espagnoles*, 3 vols. (Brussels: Institut Historique Belge de Rome, 1975), 3:1428.

20 "Consulta do Conselho Ultramarino," 14 December 1652, *MMA* 11:246.

21 "Carta do Rei ao Governador Chichorro," 22 February 1654, *MMA* 11:355.

22 Letter from Governor Sousa Chichorro, 11 January 1657, AHU, Cx. 6, doc. 92.

23 Cadornega, *História Geral*, 1:415–418.

24 Filippo da Firenze, "Ragguagli del Congo, Succinta Relazione de i tre Regni di Congo, Matamba e Angola" (1711), fols. 88–90, Archivo Provinciale dei Cappuccini di Toscana, Florence; see also Jadin, *Ancien Congo*, 2:818; Saccardo, *Congo e Angola*, 1:507.

25 António de Teruel, "Descripción Narrativa de la Mission serafica de los Padres Capuchinos en Reino de Congo" (1660), p. 90, MS 3533, Biblioteca Nacional de España, Madrid. Cavazzi also noted that Njinga did not practice cannibalism. He wrote, "If the Queen was reluctant to eat human flesh, she did not abstain from drinking human blood." Cavazzi, MSS Araldi, book 2, p. 9.

26 Da Firenze, "Ragguagli del Congo, Succinta Relazione de i tre Regni di Congo, Matamba e Angola" (1711), fols. 88–90.

27 "P. Giovanni Francesco da Roma ai Cardinalli di Propaganda Fide, Rome, Fine Marzo 1648," Africa, Angola, Congo, Documenti, vol. 2 (1646–1653), pp. 92–93, Saccardo Collection.

28 Jadin, *Ancien Congo*, 3:1331.

29 "Carta de Serafino da Cortona aos Cardeais de Propaganda Fide," 5 June 1651, *MMA* 11:43.

30 "Carta de Frei João Francesco de Roma a Propaganda Fide," *MMA* 11:427–428; "Carta de Frei Antonio Romano ao Secretario da Propaganda," *MMA* 11:432–438; "Carta da Rainha Ana Njinga a Propaganda Fide," 15 August 1651, *MMA* 11:70–71. For a translation of Njinga's letter, see Kathryn Joy McKnight and Leo J. Garofalo, *Afro-Latino Voices: Narratives from the Early Modern Ibero-Atlantic World, 1550–1812* (Indianapolis: Hackett, 2009), 45.

31 "Padre Francesco da Roma ai al Cardinali di Propaganda Fide, Roma, Fino Marzo 1648," Congo, Angola, Matamba, Documenti, vol. 2 (1646–1653), pp. 92–93, Saccardo Collection.

32 "Carta de Serafino da Cortona," 22 November 1651, *MMA* 11:113.

33 "Carta de Serafino da Cortona," 22 November 1651, *MMA* 11:113.

34 "Carta de Serafino da Cortona," 22 November 1651, *MMA* 11:113; "Bonaventura de Sorrenta ao Secretaria de Propaganda Fide," 7 May 1652, *MMA* 11:181.

35 "Carta do Padre Serafino da Cortona ao Provincial da Toscana," 15 May 1652, *MMA* 11:191–192.

36 Ibid.

37 "Carta do Padre Jacinto de Vetralla ao Secretário da Propaganda," 30 May 1652, *MMA* 11:195–196.

38 "Antonio da Monteprandone secrétaire de la Propagande," n.d., in Jadin, *Ancien Congo,* 3:1463. Although the report was undated and unsigned, Jadin (p. 1456) notes that it was written after March 1653.

39 "Décisions de la Propagande," 6 May 1653, in Jadin, *Ancien Congo,* 3:1468.

40 Cadornega, *História Geral,* 2:55–57.

41 Cavazzi, *Istorica Descrizione,* book 6, para. 2.

42 Cavazzi, MSS Araldi, book 2, p. 2.

43 Cavazzi, MSS Araldi, book 2, pp. 71–73; Cavazzi, *Istorica Descrizione,* book 6, para. 2.

44 "Carta de Salvador de Sá a el Rei," 6 October 1650, *MMA* 10:571; Cavazzi, *Istorica Descrizione,* book 6, para. 2.

45 Cavazzi, MSS Araldi, book 2, p. 10.

46 Cavazzi, MSS Araldi, book 2, pp. 2–3.

47 Gaeta, *Maravigliosa Conversione,* 70–72.

48 Ibid.

49 "P. Serafino da Cortona a Propaganda Fide," 10 February 1655, Congo, Angola, Matamba, Documenti, vol. 3 (1654–1663), p. 65, Saccardo Collection.

50 "P. Antonio de S. Pedro, Ministro dei Terziari, a un P. di Massangano," Congo, Angola, Matamba, Documenti, vol. 3 (1654–1663), p. 70, Saccardo Collection.

51 "Consulta do Concelho Ultramarino," 13 July 1655, *MMA* 11:497–501.

52 "P. Serafino da Cortona a Padre Provincale de Toscana," 21 November 1656, Congo, Angola, Matamba, Documenti, vol. 3 (1654–1663), p. 62, Saccardo Collection.

53 "Carta do Governo Geral de Angola a el-Rey João 1V," 17 September 1655, *MMA* 11:514.

54 Cavazzi, *Istorica Descrizione,* book 6, para. 2.

55 For the text of this letter, see Cadornega, *História Geral,* 2:500–503; English translation in McKnight and Garofalo, *Afro-Latino Voices,* 45–50.

56 Carta da Camara Municipal ao Rei, Museu de Angola, *Documaentaçao de Angola,* 2:253–262, in Congo Raccolta, 1654–1690, vol. 2, p. 45, Saccardo Collection.

57 Gaeta, *Maravigliosa Conversione,* 80–81; Cavazzi, MSS Araldi, book 2, p. 8, Letter of Governor to Serafim da Cortona, 1 April 1656.

58 Gaeta, *Maravigliosa Conversione,* 84–85.

59 Ibid., 85–86.

60 Ibid.; Saccardo, *Congo e Angola,* 1:511.

61 Gaeta, *Maravigliosa Conversione,* 90–91.

62 Ibid., 93–94.

63 Cavazzi, MSS Araldi, book 2, p. 117; Gaeta, *Maravigliosa Conversione,* 108–111.

64 Gaeta, *Maravigliosa Conversione,* 107–110.

65 For the date of Father Gaeta's arrival, see the editor's note in João António Cavazzi de Montecúccolo, *Descrição Histórica dos Três Reinos do Congo, Matamba e Angola,* trans.

Graciano Maria [Saccardo] de Leguzzano, 2 vols. (Lisbon: Junta de Investigaçoes do Ultramar, 1965), 2:184n27.

66 Gaeta, *Maravigliosa Conversione*, 97–100.

67 Ibid., 101–103, 116.

68 Ibid., 127–132.

69 Ibid., 130–131.

70 Ibid., 233.

71 The signatories of the treaty signed in Matamba included the scribe Francisco Ribeiro Pereira, Njinga, the secretary representing the governor, and seventeen others, including Njinga a Mona, who signed with a cross, Peixoto, the priest Antonio Romano, and Calisto Zelotes; see Saccardo, *Congo e Angola,* 1:514.

72 Gaeta, *Maravigliosa Conversione*, 231–238.

73 Ibid., 106.

74 Saccardo, *Congo e Angola,* 1:512.

75 "Carta do Governor General de Angola a El-Rei D. João IV," 14 October 1656, *MMA* 12:61–63; Gaeta, *Maravigliosa Conversione,* 238.

76 Cavazzi, *Istorica Descrizione,* book 6, para. 16.

77 Ibid., book 6, para. 9; "Carta do Governador Geral a El-Rei D. João IV," 29 July 1656, *MMA* 12:39–41.

78 "Capitulações do Governor de Angola com a Rainha Dona Ana Jinga," 12 October 1656, *MMA* 12:57–60.

79 "Consulta do Ultramarino," 3 October 1656, *MMA* 12:73–75; "Carta Régia ao Governador Geral de Angola," 6 December 1656, *MMA* 12:87–88.

80 Filipe, King of Dongo, to João IV, 8 April 1653, *MMA* 12:286–287.

7. On the Way to the Ancestors

1 Giovanni Antonio Cavazzi da Montecuccolo, *Istorica Descrizione de' tre' regni Congo, Matamba et Angola* (Bologna: Giacomo Monti, 1687), book 6, para. 100.

2 Serafino da Cortona, Relatorio, 9 December 1658, *MMA* 7:195–203.

3 Cavazzi, *Istorica Descrizione,* book 6, para. 14.

4 Ibid.; Antonio da Gaeta, *La Maravigliosa Conversione alla Santa Fede di Cristo della Regina Singa*, ed. Francesco Maria Gioia (Naples, 1669), 176.

5 Cavazzi, *Istorica Descrizione,* book 6, para. 141.

6 Gaeta, *Maravigliosa Conversione,* 174–175; Cavazzi, *Istorica Descrizione,* book 6, para. 86.

7 Cavazzi, *Istorica Descrizione,* book 6, para. 91.

8 Ibid.

9 Cavazzi, MSS Araldi, book 2, p. 10.

10 Cavazzi, *Istorica Descrizione,* book 6 , para. 91.

11 Gaeta, *Maravigliosa Conversione,* 223–238.

12 Ibid.

13 Ibid., 243–246.

14 Ibid., 259.

15 Ibid., 261–263.

16 "Serafino da Cortona to Governor General," 20 March 1657, *MMM* 12:101–103.

17 Ibid.

18 "Relazione sopra la Regina Zinga," Rome, 26 November 1658, Congo, Angola, Matamba, Documenti, vol. 3 (1654–1663), pp. 187–189, Saccardo Collection, Archivio Provinciale dei Cappuccini di Venezia, Venice, Italy (hereafter cited as Saccardo Collection).

19 Cavazzi, *Istorica Descrizione,* book 6, para. 23.

20 "Carta do Padre Serafim de Cortona ao Padre Provincial da Toscana," 10 April 1657, *MMA* 12:108; Cavazzi, *Istorica Descrizione,* book 6, para. 25; Graziano Saccardo, *Congo e Angola: Con la storia dell'antica missione dei cappuccini,* 3 vols. (Venice, 1982–1983), 1:519.

21 "Carta de Frei Antonio Romano ao Superior dos Capuchinos," Matamba, 8 March 1657, *MMA* 12:94–95.

22 "Njinga ao Governo de Angola, Matamba," 12 January 1657, *MMA* 12:92–93.

23 Letter of Commendation from "Ana Jinga" to Manuel Frois Peixoto, 15 January 1657, AHU, Cx. 11, doc. 130.

24 "Relazione sopra la Regina Zinga," Saccardo Collection.

25 "Carta do Governo Geral de Angola a El-Rei D. Afonso VI," 29 August 1657, *MMA* 12:133–134.

26 António de Oliveira de Cadornega, *História Geral das Guerras Angolanas,* ed. José Delgado, 3 vols. (1940–1942; repr. Lisbon: Agência-Geral do Ultramar, 1972), 2:171–173; "Carta da Rainha D. Ana Jinga a Oliveira de Cadornega," 15 June 1660, *MMA* 12:289.

27 "Ginga alla S. Congregazione di Propaganda," Matamba, 15 August 1657, Congo, Angola, Matamba, Documenti, vol. 3 (1654–1663), p. 146, Saccardo Collection; "Carta da Rainha Ana Jinga ao Papa," 8 September 1657, *MMA* 12:138–139; Queen Njinga to the Cardinals of the Propaganda Fide, 8 September 1657, *MMA* 12:140.

28 "Lettera del P. Antonio da Gaeta al P. Serafino da Cortona," Matamba, 20 August 1657, Congo, Angola, Matamba, Documenti, vol. 3 (1654–1663), pp. 86–89, Saccardo Collection.

29 "Carta da Rainha D. Ana Jinga a Frei Serafim da Cortona," 15 August 1657, *MMA* 11:131–132.

30 "Lettera di P. Gaeta alla Serafino da Cortona," Matamba, 8 September 1657, Congo, Angola, Matamba, Documenti, vol. 3 (1654–1663), p. 92, Saccardo Collection.

31 "Lettera del P. Antonio da Gaeta al P. Serafino da Cortona," Matamba, 20 August 1657, Saccardo Collection.

32 Ibid.; Cavazzi, *Istorica Descrizione,* book 6, para. 36. For details of the events of 1658, see Saccardo, *Congo e Angola,* 1:520.

33 "Declaração do Governo de Angola ao concelho e Jinta de Guerra," 9 September 1658, *MMA* 12:173–175.

34 "Consulta do Conselho Ultramarino," 25 January 1659, *MMA* 12:209–211.

35 "Declaração de Guerra ao Rei do Congo," 11 March 1659, *MMA* 12:226.

36 "Carta da Rainha Ana Jinga ao Papa," 8 September 1657, *MMA* 12:138–139.

37 "Consulta do Conselho Ultramarino," 25 January 1659, *MMA* 12:211.

38 "Carta de Frei António Gaeta Romano ao Secretário da Propaganda Fide," 8 September 1858, *MMA* 12:160–163

39 "Carta da Rainha D. Ana Jinga ao Careal D'Este," 2 December 1659, *MMA* 12:279.

40 "Breve do Papa Alexandre VII à Rainha Ana de Sousa Jinga," 19 June 1660, *MMA* 12:290–291.

41 "Carta da Rainha D. Ana Jinga ao Papa Alexandre VII," 25 August 1662, *MMA* 12:402–403.

42 Ibid.

43 "Carta da Rainha D. Ana Jinga a Frei Crisótomo de Génova," 18 March 1663, *MMA* 12:430–431.

44 "Carta da Rainha D. Ana Jinga ao Prefeito da Propaganda," 10 April 1663, *MMA* 12:434–435.

45 "Carta da Rainha D. Ana Jinga a Frei Crisóstomo de Génova," 18 March 1663, *MMA* 12:430–431; "Carta da Rainha D. Ana Jinga ao Prefeito da Propaganda," 10 April 1663, *MMA* 12:434–435.

46 Gaeta, *Maravigliosa Conversione*, 284.

47 Cavazzi, *Istorica Descrizione*, book 6, para. 40.

48 Cavazzi MSS Araldi, book 2, pp. 134–135.

49 Cavazzi, *Istorica Descrizione*, book 6, paras. 52–59.

50 Ibid., book 6, para. 26.

51 Cavazzi, MSS Araldi, book 9, p. 135.

52 Ibid., book 2, p. 7

53 Ibid., book 2, p. 136.

54 Cavazzi, *Istorica Descrizione*, book 6, para. 48.

55 "P. Serafino da Cortona a Propaganda," Rome, November 1659, Congo, Angola, Matamba, Documenti, vol. 3 (1654–1663), p. 222, Saccardo Collection; Cavazzi, *Istorica Descrizione*, book 6, para. 38.

56 Cavazzi, *Istorica Descrizione*, book 6, para. 62.

57 Cavazzi, MSS Araldi, book 2, pp. 1–2, 167–174.

58 Ibid., book 2, pp. 167–174.

59 Cavazzi, *Istorica Descrizione*, book 6, paras. 63–69.

60 Giovanni Antonio Cavazzi da Montecuccolo, "Missione evangelica nel Regno de Congo," volume B, fol. 493. Private collection, Araldi Family, Modena, Italy.

61 Cavazzi, MSS Araldi, book 2, pp. 155–159.

62 Ibid.

63 "Lettera del p. Cavazzi a Propaganda," 12 August 1663, Raccolta L, vol. 2 (1654–1690), p. 165, Saccardo Collection.

64 Cavazzi, *Istorica Descrizione,* book 6, para. 105.

65 "Relazione sopra a Regina Zinga," 26 November 1658, Congo Raccolta L, 1654–1690, vol. 3, pp. 190–191, Saccardo Collection.

66 Cadornega, *História Geral,* 2:171–172.

67 Cavazzi, MSS Araldi, book 2, pp. 5, 22.

68 Cadornega, *História Geral,* 2:171n1.

69 Cavazzi, *Istorica Descrizione,* book 6, para. 96.

70 Ibid., book 6, para. 75.

71 Cavazzi, MSS Araldi, book 2, p. 5.

72 Cavazzi, *Istorica Descrizione,* book 6, para. 79.

73 Ibid., book 6, para. 101.

74 Cavazzi, MSS Araldi, book 2, pp. 18–20.

75 Gaeta, *Maravigliosa Conversione,* 335–337.

76 Cadornega, *História Geral,* 2:157–159; Cavazzi, *Istorica Descrizione,* book 6, paras. 44–46.

77 "Relatorio de Bartholemeu Paes Bulhão," 16 May 1664, AHU, Cx. 8, doc. 8; David Birmingham, *Trade and Conflict in Angola: The Mbundu and Their Neighbours under the Influence of the Portuguese, 1483–1790* (Oxford: Clarendon Press, 1966), 121.

78 Cavazzi, *Istorica Descrizione,* book 6, para. 6.

79 Cavazzi, MSS Araldi, book 11, p. 21.

80 Ibid., book 2, p. 216.

81 Cavazzi, *Istorica Descrizione,* book 6, para. 94.

82 Cavazzi, MSS Araldi, book 2, p. 36.

83 Ibid., book 2, p. 6.

84 Gaeta, *Maravigliosa Conversione,* 336–337.

85 Cavazzi, MSS Araldi, book 2, pp. 150–152.

86 Cavazzi, *Istorica Descrizione,* book 6, para. 59.

87 Cavazzi, MSS Araldi, book 2, p. 3.

88 Gaeta, *Maravigliosa Conversione,* 173–177.

89 Cadornega, *História Geral,* 2:169–170.

90 Cavazzi, MSS Araldi, book 2, p. 22.

91 Cadornega, *História Geral,* 2:223–224.

92 Gaeta, *Maravigliosa Conversione,* 173–177.

93 Cavazzi, MSS Araldi, book 2, pp. 161–164.

94 Ibid., book 2, p. 5.

95 Cavazzi, *Istorica Descrizione,* book 2, para. 120.

96 Ibid., book 2, para. 74.

97 "Lettera del p. Cavazzi a Propaganda," 12 August 1663, Congo Raccolta L 1654–1690, vol. 2, p. 165, Saccardo Collection. At that time, the Portuguese were concerned that Capuchins from Spain might be spies of the Spanish king.

98 Cavazzi, MSS Araldi, book 2, pp. 18–20.

99 Cavazzi, *Istorica Descrizione,* book 6, para. 28.

100 Ibid., book 6, para. 103.

101 Details of Njinga's last days are in Cavazzi, *Istorica Descrizione,* book 6, paras. 107–109. In 2010, I sent Cavazzi's descriptions to Dr. Ana Luiza Gibertoni Cruz, then a fourth-year medical student and my graduate assistant, and Amanda Thornton, then a resident and now a physician specializing in infectious diseases, who provided diagnoses concerning the cause of Njinga's death.

102 Cavazzi, MSS Araldi, book 2, pp. 197–198.

103 Cavazzi, *Istorica Descrizione,* book 6, para. 108.

104 Cavazzi, MSS Araldi, book 2, p. 61; Cavazzi, *Istorica Descrizione,* book 6, para. 111.

105 Cavazzi, *Istorica Descrizione* book 6, paras. 110–111.

106 Cavazzi, MSS Araldi, book 2, pp. 8–9.

107 Cavazzi, *Istorica Descrizione,* book 6, para. 111.

108 Ibid. See also Cavazzi, MSS Araldi, book 2, pp. 200–201.

109 Cavazzi, *Istorica Descrizione,* book 6, para. 111.

110 Cavazzi, MSS Araldi, book 2, pp. 203–204.

111 Cavazzi, *Istorica Descrizione,* book 6, para. 112.

112 Ibid., book 6, para. 113.

113 Ibid., book 6, para. 114.

114 Cavazzi, MSS Araldi, book 2, p. 208.

Epilogue

1 For Cavazzi's published book, see Giovanni Antonio Cavazzi da Montecuccolo, *Istorica Descrizione de' tre' regni Congo, Matamba et Angola* (Bologna: Giacomo Monti, 1687).

2 Cavazzi, Araldi MSS, book 2, pp. 213–214. Thanks so much to Rita Coté, senior lecturer in Italian, Boston University, for translating this poem, as well as other difficult passages from Cavazzi's manuscript. Thanks also to an anonymous scholar of Italian history whom Harvard University Press consulted about the transcription and translation. The names of these notorious women were widespread in the writings of literature that Cavazzi was familiar with. See for example, Agustín de Rojas Villandrando, *El Viaje entretenido* (1604), ed. Manuel Cañete (Madrid, 1901), p. 193.

3 As quoted from Georgina Herrera, *Always Rebellious, Cimarroneando,* bilingual ed. (Chico, CA: Cubanabooks, 2014). The poem first appeared in Georgina Herrera, *Granos de sol e luna* (Havana, 1978).

4 Antonio da Gaeta, *La Maravigliosa Conversione alla Santa Fede di Cristo della Regina Singa,* ed. Francesco Maria Gioia (Naples, 1669).

5 Thanks to Father Dr. Gabriele Bortolami for sharing his unpublished paper "Antonio da Gaeta e la conversione della regina Nzinga Mbandi (1669)" with me.

6 Relazione, Roma, 26 November 1658, fol. 264r, Saccardo Collection, Archivio Provinciale dei Cappuccini di Venezia, Venice, Italy.

7 Gaeta, *Maravigliosa Conversione*, 228.

8 *Njinga, Reine d'angola: La relation d'Antonio Cavazzi de Montecuccolo* (1687). Translated by Xavier de Castro and Alix du Cheyron d'Abzac, preface by Linda Heywood and John Thornton (Paris: Éditions Chandeigne, 2010). See also Catherine Gallouët, "Farouche, touchante, belle, e cannibale: Transmissions et permutations des representations de Njinga, reine d'Angola du 17th au 18th siècle," *Dix-huitieme siècle* 44 (2012): 253–272.

9 For the French translation see, Jean-Baptiste Labat, *Relation historique de L'Ethiopie Occidental: Contenant la description des Royaumes de Congo, Angolle, et Matamba,* traduite de l'Italien du P. Cavazzi, 5 vols. (Paris, 1732). For the German translation see *Historische Beschreibung der in dem untern occidentalischen Mohrenland ligenden drey Königreichen Congo, Matamba, und Angola* (Munich, 1694). A Portuguese translation was not available until 1965.

10 Olfert Dapper, *Naukeurige Beschrijvinge der Afrikaensche Gewesten* (Amsterdam, 1668). A French translation appeared in 1676.

11 See Domingos Gonsalves, *Notícia Memóravel da Vida et Açcoens da Rainha Ginga, Ginga Amena* (Lisbon, 1749); António de Oliveira de Cadornega, *História Geral das Guerras Angolanas,* ed. José Delgado, vol. 2 (1940; repr. Lisbon: Agência-Geral do Ultramar, 1972). A Portuguese translation of Cavazzi's text did not appear until 1965: João António Cavazzi de Montecúccolo, *Descrição Histórica dos Três Reinos do Congo, Matamba e Angola,* trans. Graciano Maria [Saccardo] de Leguzzano, 2 vols. (Lisbon: Junta de Investigaçoes do Ultramar, 1965).

12 For an analysis of the bias in these publications see Gallouët, "Farouche, touchante, belle, e cannibale."

13 Denis Diderot, *Encyclopédie, ou Dictionnaire des sciences, des arts et des métiers* (Paris, 1751).

14 Jean-Louis Castilhon, *Zhinga, Reine d'Angola: Histoire Africaine en Deux Parties* (Paris, 1769), 126–127.

15 See also Emmanuel Sauvage, "Sade et l'exotisme Africain: Images de Noirs," *Études littéraires* 37 (2006): 97–116.

16 Ibid.

17 Marquis de Sade, *Philosophy in the Bedroom* (1795), trans. Richard Seaver and Austryn Wainhouse, digitized and typeset by Supervert 32C Inc., 2002, p. 57.

18 Sauvage, "Sade et l'exotisme Africain."

19 *London Quarterly Review,* vol. 17 (1817), 334–338.

20 G. W. F. Hegel, *Leçons sur la Philosophie de l'Histoire* (Paris, 1998), 78.

21 Duchesse d'Abrantès and Joseph Straszewicz, *Les femmes célèbres de tous les pays: Leurs vies et leurs portraits* (Paris, 1834), 7–25.

22 Ibid., 7–25.

23 *The Britannica Magazine,* vol. 5, no. 57, pp. 50–56; *Royal Ladies Magazine,* vol. 2 (1834), 21–22; *Literary Gazette* (1834), vol. 18.

24 *Almanach de Lembranças Lus-Brasileiro para o anno de 1859* (Lisbon, 1859), 374–376.

25 See, for example, Ralph Delgado, *História de Angola* (Luanda, 1948), 72–73.

26 The traditions about Njinga that circulated among the Mbundus who live in the regions where Njinga was born and that she conquered have yet to be systematically collected and

studied. I arrived at this conclusion from interviews I conducted in Luanda and Malange in 2008 and 2011. The interviews were conducted in Portuguese and in Kimbundu, with the help of a Kimbundu-speaking Angolan interpreter.

27 Agostinho Neto, *Sagrada Esperança*, 11th ed. (Lisbon, 1987), 138–140; República Popular de Angola, *História de Angola* (Ministério da Educação, 1976).

28 República Popular de Angola, *História de Angola*.

29 Manuel Pedro Pacavira, *Nzinga Mbandi* (Luanda, 1975); Pepetela, *A Gloriosa Família* (Alfradige, Portugal: Publicações Dom Quixote, 1997); República de Angola, *Njinga a Mbande e Aimé Césaire: Independência e Universade* (República de Angola, Ministério da Cultura, 2013).

30 Based on interviews with Angolans when I visited Kinaxixe in 2003, 2008, and 2011. The statue is now located at the recently opened Angolan Museum of the Armed Forces in Luanda.

31 Manuel Pedro Pacavira, *Nzinga Mbandi* (Luanda, 1975); Pepetela, *A Gloriosa Família*; República de Angola, *Njinga a Mbande e Aimé Césaire*.

32 Manuel Ricardo Miranda, *Ginga: Rainha de Angola* (Cruz Quebrada, Portugal: Oficina do Livro, 2008).

33 Inocência Mata, ed., *A Rainha Nzinga Mbandi: História, Memória e Mito*, 2nd ed. (Lisbon: Edições Colibri, 2014).

34 https://www.youtube.com/watch?v=m2TVm1GsPFU.

35 See, for example, Rafael Ferreira da Silva, "A mulher na capoeira e a participação no movimento de Resistência ao Sistema racist e patriarchal": www.uneb .brenlacandosexualidades/files/2015/A; Solange Barbosa, "O espírito da Rainha Nzinga Mbandi no Brasil e no Caribe," in Mata, ed., *A Rainha Nzinga Mbandi*, 147–156.

36 Lúis da Câmara Cascudo, *Made in Africa* (Rio de Janeiro, 1965); Roy Glasgow, *Nzinga* (São Paulo: Perspectiva, 1982); http://www.galeriadosamba.com.br/espacoaberto/topico /203340/0/2/0/.

37 Herrera, *Granos de sol e luna*; IONE and Pauline Oliveros, *Njinga, the Queen King: The Return of a Warrior* (DVD, 2010, based on a 1993 play at the Brooklyn Academy of Music); Verna S. Cook and Charlotte K. Brooks, eds., *Distinguished Black Women, 1991–1995*, vol. 3 (Washington, D.C.: Black Women in Sisterhood for Action, 1995); Janie Havemeyer, *Njinga "The Warrior Queen"* (Foster City, CA: Goosebottom Books, 2011).

38 UNESCO, *Njinga Mbandi: Queen of Ndongo and Matamba* (UNESCO, 2015), http://en .unesco.org/womeninafrica/njinga-mbandi/comic.

39 See, for example, her inclusion in Jeroen Duindum, *Dynasties: A Global History of Power, 1300–1800* (Cambridge: Cambridge University Press, 2015).

Acknowledgments

I have been fascinated by famous women in history from childhood, and over the years I have read biographies as well as historical fiction about many women rulers, particularly Elizabeth I of England. I transferred the passion I had for Elizabeth to Njinga once I started teaching early central African history at Howard University in the mid-1980s. Many people supported me over this long journey. This biography could not have been written without the support of colleagues at Howard University and, most important, Boston University, my academic home base for almost thirteen years. Between 2008 and 2015, Boston University provided me with research grants and sabbaticals that allowed me to collect materials for this biography in Angola, Portugal, and Italy. My gratitude goes also to Boston University Center for the Humanities (BUCH) for the publication production award for 2015–2016 that covered the cost of the illustrations and the original maps that exquisitely enhance the book. I have valued the support and encouragement over the years of the various deans in the College of Arts and Sciences at Boston University, and the chairs and fellow faculty members and colleagues in the History Department and in the African American Studies Program.

This book relies on a wide range of archival and published primary sources in Portuguese, Italian, Dutch, and French, and on research conducted in archives and libraries in Angola, Portugal, Italy, France, the Netherlands, England, and Brazil. I have spent the better part of nine years gathering and studying the reports of Portuguese governors that detail the wars they fought against Njinga as well as the diplomatic and economic relations they had with her. I have perused thoroughly the two biographies of Njinga published by contemporaries: Antonio da Gaeta's *La Maravigliosa Conversione alla Santa Fede di Cristo della Regina Singa* (1669) and Giovanni Antonio Cavazzi's *Istorica Descrizione de' tre' regni Congo, Matamba et Angola* (1687). Both missionaries collected many traditions about Njinga's early life from her directly as well as from the elders in her court. I also consulted the unpublished manuscripts of Gaeta's and Cavazzi's biographies and John Thornton's translation of Cavazzi's manuscript, as well as published and unpublished letters and reports that Cavazzi, Gaeta, and other Capuchin missionaries sent to Italy and Portugal. I gleaned other insights into Njinga's leadership style and military stratagem from the records of the Dutch West India Company (collected and translated into French by Louis Jadin) left by the two directors—her future allies—who served in Angola during the height of Njinga's wars against the Portuguese (1641–1648). John Thornton's translation of some of the original Dutch helped me compare the translations with the original documents. Njinga's own views of her military, economic, and diplomatic policies, preserved in the many letters her secretaries wrote on her behalf to the Portuguese, the missionaries, and the pope, provided great insight into the level of political calculation behind her successful dealings with the Portuguese and the missionaries. The published versions of these letters are found in the valuable series *Monumenta Missionaria Africana,* edited by António Brásio. A few of the original letters are available in the holdings of the Portuguese Overseas Archives (AHU) in Lisbon and in archives in Rome. I obtained further insight into Njinga's leadership style and military expertise from reading the many letters sent by Governor Fernão de Sousa to the king of Portugal as well as to his sons during the early years of Njinga's resistance. Beatrix Heintze collected and published these documents in a two-volume collection. Critical for providing a deeper understanding of Njinga's political instincts were the letters sent back to Portugal by the many Portuguese governors who served in Angola during Njinga's time, letters delivered by her ambassadors in her native Kimbundu and translated into Portuguese. The observations of António de Cadornega, the Portuguese soldier who fought in many crucial battles against Njinga and who also corresponded with her when he served in the judiciary in Luanda, proved indispensable. With its many references to Njinga, Cadornega's three-volume history of the Angolan wars offers a true insider's perspective; unlike the colonial governors, Cadornega lived in Angola continuously for more than fifty years, beginning in 1638. I also consulted biographies, books, poems, and articles that appeared in published form in the two centuries following Njinga's death. The published works of early-to-mid-nineteenth-century Portuguese writers eager to claim owner-ship of Njinga through their own reports and revisions also proved essential.

The research could not have been completed without the assistance of the numerous professional staffs at the various libraries and archives where I have worked over the years or who granted me permission to use the illustrations included in the book. I offer my thanks to Arquivo Histórico Ultramarino (Lisbon), Arquivo Histórico Nacional de Angola, the Secret Archives and Library in the Vatican, Archivio Provinciale dei Cappuccini di Venezia (Saccardo Collection, Venice), the Rare Book Division of New York Public Library, Astor, Lenox and Tilden Foundations, Bibliotethèque des Arts Décoratifs, Paris, and the Academia das Ciências in Lisbon. My sincerest thanks to Dr. Vincenzo Negro of Modeno, Italy, who granted me permission to use the six illustrations by Cavazzi from the Araldi manuscript, and to Dr. Cécile Fromont, who allowed me to use the illustration of Njinga with captured missionaries. Thanks also to Aharon de Grassi and Isabelle Lewis for the maps included in the book.

Special thanks go to the Hutchins Center for African and African Amer-ican Research at Harvard University, which allowed me the honor of being a regular Du Bois Fellow during the academic year as well as a summer fellow. The Center's generous financial support enabled me to travel to Angola, Brazil, and Portugal to conduct research on Njinga. I must acknowledge especially Henry Louis Gates Jr., who never doubted that the biography of Njinga had to be done and who always made sure that institutional support was forth-coming to do it. Additionally, the book would not have been completed without the encouragement and support of Executive Director Abby Wolf, Fellows Program Director Krishna Lewis, and all my colleagues and friends at the Hutchins Center. I could not ask for a more stimulating environment in which to conjure up Njinga.

Many thanks are due to the Boston University and Harvard University students who worked as my research assistants and helped translate some of the sources from Italian into English. The translations completed by Miriam Bassi (Boston University, 2007–2008) and Ana Luíza Gibertoni Cruz (M.D., M.P.H. candidate, Harvard School of Public Health, 2009–2010) are particularly appreciated. A special thanks to Luíza Gibertoni, once again, and to Amanda Virginia Heywood Thornton, MD, for the time they put into reading Cavazzi's description of the medical symptoms exhibited by

Njinga in her last days and for reaching similar diagnoses as to the disease that caused Njinga's death.

Thanks so much to Julie Wolf for helping me shape the manuscript into a book that readers from both the academic world and the general public would feel comfortable reading. I could not have completed the manuscript without her expert guidance. Thanks also to Paul Lucas for the advice and suggestions on how to improve the early version of the manuscript. His input allowed me to separate Njinga's life and death from Njinga as a figure of memory, to envision these two aspects of Njinga as rich material. The comments and critiques of the anonymous readers who read the manuscript for Harvard University Press were all greatly appreciated and enriched this book. Finally, I am forever indebted to my editor at Harvard University Press, Kathleen McDermott, for her encouragement, patience, and guidance. From the time she first read the manuscript, Kathleen believed that Njinga's life transcended time and place, and the professional and personal way she handled the entire process has been inspiring.

Lastly, I must thank my family for their unending, unequivocal support and love throughout this project that we have all lived with for the last several years. Just as my daughter Amanda lent her medical expertise to me, my daughter Amara took time from her own busy schedule in London to share emails with me about the manuscript. Tremendous thanks to John, my husband and colleague, and the only specialist in the family on precolonial central African history, for his love, understanding, and unstinting support through these years. The conversations we have had and the research we conducted together on seventeenth-century central Africa allowed me to understand Njinga's place in Angola and the world around her. My greatest hope is that John enjoys reading the life of Njinga that I re-created from the documents he so generously shared with me.

Illustration Credits

Index